ELIZABETHAN DRAMA
AND DRAMATISTS
1583-1603

ELIZABETHAN DRAMA
AND DRAMATISTS
1583–1603

By

ERNEST A. GERRARD

NEW YORK
COOPER SQUARE
PUBLISHERS, INC.
1972

Originally Published, 1928
Published 1971 by Cooper Square Publishers, Inc.
59 Fourth Avenue, New York, N. Y. 10003
International Standard Book No. 0-8154-0407-7
Library of Congress Catalog Card No. 74-184908

Printed in the United States of America

PREFACE

THE present volume is the continuation of, or an outgrowth from, *The Revision of Hamlet and of Romeo and Juliet,* which originally was intended to be Part I of *Elizabethan Drama and Dramatists,* the present volume being Part II. The *Revision* has not as yet been printed.

I began work on *The Revision of Hamlet* in 1914, and finished the two volumes in 1919. Since then I have made a few minor changes in the text, and have added several foot-notes. Otherwise the two volumes remain as finished in 1919.

For obvious reasons it was thought best, for a time, not to publish the manuscript. Finally I decided to present copies to the various members of the Malone Society, many of whom have been working on similar lines, taking it for granted that every one seriously interested in Elizabethan Drama belongs to the Society.

I feel that I have herein presented a mere outline of a vast subject. Nothing is complete, neither the history of companies, actors, theatres, nor plays. The little sketches of individual dramatists are only suggestive, and the assignment of plays to their various authors is but a beginning. I might have allocated the authorship of many more plays, but that was not my object—which was rather to establish recognizable characteristics of individual dramatists.

If this outline has somewhat cleared the tangled path and has opened up new vistas for further research into Elizabethan Drama it will have served its purpose.

The original punctuation of many of the quotations was so misleading that perforce a great number of them have been re-punctuated. For the old punctuation consult the originals or reproductions.

ERNEST A. GERRARD.

June, 1928.

CONTENTS

PART I

PLAYERS, PLAY-HOUSES, AND PLAYER COMPANIES

PART II

ELIZABETHAN DRAMATISTS

PART I

PLAYERS, PLAY-HOUSES,
AND
PLAYER COMPANIES

INTRODUCTORY NOTE

DURING the early part of Queen Elizabeth's reign the theatre as a place of amusement was looked down upon. It had been, and for long years remained, the sport of the aristocracy, on a par with bear-baiting, cock-fighting, and acrobatic exhibitions, to all of which the commoners were admitted as spectators. It is therefore not surprising to find the first London theatres located outside of the city, on the north, in those open fields which were devoted to outdoor sports; nor is it strange that, as bear-baiting, this new amusement was for men only.

The Puritans in London did not approve of the theatre and forced one restriction after another upon the owners of the play-houses. However, those shrewd and stubborn men were not to be beaten. First one, then another, moved across the river, into the county of Surrey, out of the jurisdiction of the London magistrates.

The site chosen for the new adventure was a no-man's-land, responsible to no one but its local magistrate and the Crown. This district was known as the Clink. Here the Puritans had no control, the Lord Mayor of London no authority.

The Clink was a little Monte Carlo where vice and sport ruled supreme, an ancient Montmartre, outside the city gates. It was inhabited chiefly by actors and prostitutes and their dependants, and was frequented by the pleasure-loving males of London. There many of the greatest of English dramas were born, there produced, in this little corner of freedom, by a band of daring unconventional youths, supported by the aristocracy of London. Ladies did not go to the Clink; but many times each year Queen Elizabeth called its inhabitants to her palace. Strange to say the plays produced in this 'cesspool of vice' were more refined, more cleanly, than those of the ensuing period produced in Puritanical London.

I
PLAYER COMPANIES

QUEEN ELIZABETH probably inherited from her father the group of Interlude Players who are last mentioned in the office books of the Treasurer of the Chamber in 1561. The previous year Lord Robert Dudley's company of players and Paules Boys played at Court. Lord Warwick's men appear in the records of 1564; and Lord Rich's players are mentioned together with the Chapel Children in 1568. Lord Admiral Clinton's company appears in 1572–3 as well as Lord Sussex's company.

In 1574–5 a Lord Chamberlain's company first played at Court, whether under Lord Howard or Lord Sussex is unknown. Sussex was then Chamberlain; as Admiral Clinton he was an old man. Lord Howard often acted as his deputy. At other times Howard seems to have deputized for Lord Clinton. For a time both the Sussex and Clinton theatrical companies seem to have looked to Lord Howard as their immediate patron. Howard's men acted as Chamberlain's men in 1575, as Howard's in 1576, and as both Chamberlain's and Howard's in 1577. Thereafter they were called Chamberlain's men until 1583, although they were still under Howard's immediate protection.

Lord Admiral Clinton's company disappears from the Court records with the birth of Lord Warwick's company in 1577. The company seems merely to have changed patrons. The Warwick company last appeared at Court in 1580–1, when another new company, Lord (iv) Derby's, played for the first time, together with 'tumblers' belonging to his son, Lord Strange.

These companies, Leicester's, Chamberlain's (under Howard), Derby's, and Lord Strange's tumblers, continued until 1583, when Sussex died. From then until the death of Admiral Clinton in 1585 Lord Howard and his father-in-law, Lord Hunsdon, had taken turns as acting Lord Chamberlain. Seemingly Howard had been offered his choice of the two positions of Chamberlain or

Admiral. Finally in 1585 he became Admiral and Hunsdon became Chamberlain. During this same period theatrical events are uncertainly recorded. A new Queen's company was formed in 1583 from members of the existing companies. Events become clear again after 1585. There then survived, the Queen's company (under Lord Chamberlain Hunsdon), the Admiral's company (under Lord Howard), Lord Leicester's company, and Lord Strange's men. Lord Derby's and Lord Rich's companies had disappeared.

In 1586 *Lord Leicester's* company, with Will Kempe, went abroad and played at the Danish Court and the Court of Christian, Duke of Saxony. In 1588 Lord Leicester died, and the company broke up. Some of its members reorganized as Lord Pembroke's men, others joined Lord Strange's men.

The *Queen's* company, as the Queen's, the Lord Chamberlain's, or Lord Hunsdon's men, appeared at Court almost every year from 1583 until 1593. (Pipe Rolls.) The last London record mentioning this company is dated 1593 or 1595, when Philip Henslowe loaned money to his nephew to buy a share in the 'Queen's' players when 'they broke and went into the country'. (*Henslowe's Diary*.)[1] The company continued in existence until c. 1599. (See *Sir Clyomon and Sir Clamydes*, printed as a Queen's company play in 1599.)

The *Lord Admiral's* company continued under Lord Howard until 1603, when it became Prince Henry's company. This company was joined by Edward Alleyn, the most celebrated actor of the period, shortly after the death of his former patron Lord Worcester on February 22, 1588. (*History of Dulwich College*.) With Alleyn came other members of the Worcester company, which seems to have been a provincial company. The later history of the Admiral's men is completely recorded in Henslowe's Diary and the Alleyn papers, still preserved at Dulwich College. Lord Howard was at the head of the English navy when the

---

[1] John Towne, one of the Queen's men in 1588, is described as 'one of her majesties plears' in a Nottingham debt-record of July 5, 1597. (Malone Soc. Collections, IV, V.)

Spanish Armada met its fate. His company was the most celebrated of all the acting companies of the period.

When the Queen's company was formed in 1583 it is possible
that Lord (iv) Derby's company was disbanded. It is more likely,
however, that it amalgamated with his son's 'tumblers' into Lord
Strange's company. Some time after the death of Lord Leicester
in 1588, and before 1593, when a partial list of the Admiral's and
Strange's men appears, under the leadership of Alleyn then touring
the provinces, Strange's men were joined by several old Leicester
men. Lord Strange became Earl Derby (v) in September, 1592;
and his men were known as Earl Derby's men until his death
on April 16, 1594. They then became the Lord Chamberlain's
men under Lord Hunsdon.

A second Queen's company. There is considerable evidence
that after the death of Lord Leicester the Queen took at least a
part of his company under her protection. The Court records
for the Christmas season of 1590–1 point to two distinct Queen's
companies. The second Queen's company, if not the original
Leicester company, was most likely the group which appeared
at Court the following year as Lord Pembroke's men.

A new *Sussex* company appeared at Court on January 2, 1592,
and seems to have united with the old Queen's company shortly
after their patron died on December 14, 1593.

A *Pembroke* company seems to have existed as far back as 1575.
The London company of this name is first recorded at Court in
December, 1592–January, 1593. Edward Alleyn in a letter to
Henslowe (September 28, 1593) wrote of the company as the
most important rival to the Admiral's men. As it was possessed
of the greater number of Marlowe's plays, which apparently were
written in part for Lord Leicester's men, it would seem as if it
were a continuation of that company, having been under the
protection of the Queen from 1588 until 1590–1. On October 11,
1597, the Pembroke men joined the Admiral's men at the Rose
theatre. (*Henslowe's Diary.*) The Admiral's men went to the Fortune in 1600. For a time the Pembroke men went on tour, then
returned to the Rose. Lord Pembroke died in January, 1601.

Some of the company then went abroad, and others became members of the Admiral's company.

The Lord Chamberlain's men. The Strange-Derby, 'now Lord Chamberlaines men', played under Lord Chamberlain Hunsdon's name from April 1594 until his death on July 22, 1596. Lord Cobham then became Chamberlain, and the company played under Lord Hunsdon's son. (See *Romeo and Juliet*, 1597.) Cobham died March 5, 1597, and it has been assumed by all historians that the younger Hunsdon then became Chamberlain. This assumption is based on unreliable gossiping letters written by one Rowland Whyte. (See Malone Society, *Remembrancia*.) The 'livery warrant' of Lord Hunsdon is dated May 18, 1599 (Lord Chamberlain's Books, 811, f. 236), which presumably dates his appointment as Chamberlain. This leaves open the period March, 1597– May, 1599. The title-page of an old play furnishes an incumbent for this period. It reads:

THE WEAKEST GOETH TO THE WALL As it hath bene sundry times plaide by the right honorable Earle of Oxenford, Lord great Chamberlaine of England his servants. London. Printed by Thomas Creede for Richard Olive. 1600.

As the only period during which Oxford could have been Chamberlain is this one of 1597–9, and as there is no adequate proof that Hunsdon was finally installed until 1599, it must be assumed that Lord Oxford acted as Chamberlain during this interval.

In 1599, when Hunsdon became Chamberlain, this company was reorganized. Shakespeare, Burbage, and Kempe of the Queen's company joined with Pope, Heminges, and others of the Strange-Chamberlain company and formed the new Chamberlain company under Hunsdon. Other members of these two companies seem to have continued: the Strange-Chamberlain men (Duke, Pallant, Beeston, &c.) as Lord Oxford's men, and the Queen's men (Heywood, Lee, Perkins, and later Kempe) as Lord (vi) Derby's men. (See *Edward IV* by Heywood.) Derby's men appeared at Court under Robert Browne, who had returned from Germany, in 1600 and 1601. They then disappear, their place at Court being taken by Lord Worcester's men. Seemingly they had changed their patron and title.

The Derby-Worcester group was joined in 1602 by Lord Oxford's men. Lord Worcester writes:

> ... the servants of our verey good L. the Earle of Oxford and of me the Earle of Worcester being joined by agrement togeather in on companie (to whom upon noteice of her Maties pleasure at the suit of the Earle of Oxford, tolleracon hath ben thaught meete to be graunted) &c. (*Remembrancia*, March 31, 1602.)

This combination continued as Worcester's men until 1603, when they became Queen Anne's men.

Children companies. An outline of the dramatic companies of the period would not be complete without mention of the Children of the Queen's Revels, the Windsor Chapel Children, and Paules Boys. These choristers were educated not only in music, Latin, Greek, &c., but also in acting and dancing. At first they took part in religious plays only; but by 1569 they began acting secular plays at the Chapel Royal. In later years they were hired out to the actor companies wherever their services were required. This abuse called for reformation, and in 1616 the practice was stopped. Under Queen Elizabeth they regularly enacted plays at Windsor Castle, Paules schoolroom, the Royal Chapel, Blackfriars, and at Court.

Various companies not here mentioned appear and disappear during Queen Elizabeth's reign. Each great lord seems at one time or another to have supported one. Their importance is small, for they could ill afford to buy plays of merit, nor would authors of merit sell their productions to any but the well-established companies.

II

PLAY-HOUSES

THE *Theatre* was built by James Burbage of Lord Leicester's company in 1576–7. The lease for the land was dated April 13, 1576, and ran for twenty-one years. The Theatre stood outside the city walls to the north, in the open fields, near what is now Holywell Lane, Worship Street, E.C.

James Burbage died on February 2, 1597, and was succeeded by his celebrated son Richard, who, with his elder brother Cuthbert, owned the Theatre until the ground lease expired on April 13, 1597, after which the building was torn down and the material used in constructing the Globe theatre in Southwark.

The *Curtain* was built soon after and close to the Theatre, about 1576. It is mentioned in Northbrooke's *Treatise against dicing, &c.*, printed in 1577; in a sermon by John Stockwood, preached at Paul's Cross on August 24, 1578; in Stubbs's *Anatomie of Abuses*, in 1583; in Nash's *Martin's Month's Mind*, printed in 1589. In the records of the lawsuits over the Theatre Dr. C. W. Wallace discovered that from 1585 until 1592 the Curtain belonged to Henry Laneman; and that he and Burbage pooled their profits from the two theatres, sharing half-and-half in the pool.

The Curtain drops out of history in 1592, to reappear in 1596, when it was occupied by the old Strange, ' nowe Chamberlaine ', men until 1599, and by other companies for a number of years afterwards. Evidently it fell into ill repair during the plague of 1592–3 and was vacant until rebuilt in 1596 for the Chamberlain company.

Two taverns, the *Bull* and the *Belsavage*, at which plays were regularly produced are also mentioned by Gosson in his *Schoole of Abuse* in 1578–9.

The *Cross-keys* tavern was used as a theatre as early as 1589, when the Lord Mayor, John Hart, wrote to the Lord Treasurer that the Strange company 'in very Contemptuous manner departing from me wente to the Cross-keys and played that afternoon'.

During the plague of 1593 no plays were allowed in London. In October of 1594 the Lord Chamberlain, who had now become the patron of the old Lord Strange company, wrote to the Lord Mayor asking that his 'nowe companie of players' be allowed 'to playe this winter time within the Cittie at the Crosse Keyes in Gratious street ... where they have been accustomed'. The permission was refused; and thus ends the history of the Cross-keys tavern as a play-house. It was in Grace Street, E.C.

The *Rose*. One set of historians dates the erection of this playhouse in 1587, with extensive repairs in 1592. Another group assigns 1592 as the date of original building. History mentions no Rose theatre before 1592. Indirect proof of its non-existence is contained in Nash's *Martin's Month's Mind* (1589), in which he wrote of the Theatre and the Curtain as the leading houses, whereas the Rose certainly would have been mentioned as the newest and best play-house had it then existed. The list of 'repairs' to be found in Henslowe's Diary is rather too extensive for a house in use but five years. The worst jerry-built houses stand well for a longer period. As it was built for the Strange company, who had acted at the Cross-keys tavern until 1592, the building may be dated from that time. It was situated on the south side of the Thames in Rose Alley, near the end of Southwark bridge, in the Clink. It was last occupied in 1603.

The *Globe* was close to the Rose, the site being at present occupied by a brewery. This theatre was built after 1597 and before 1599, partly from material of the old Theatre. The ground lease was dated February 21, 1599. The Globe remained for many years one of the leading theatres of London. It was burned in 1613 and almost immediately rebuilt.[1]

The *Fortune* was built by Henslowe and Alleyn during 1600, was burned on December 9, 1621, and rebuilt in 1622–3. An

[1] See *Shakespeare and his London Associates*, C. W. Wallace.

account of the catastrophe is to be found in John Chamberlain's letter of December 15, 1621:

> On Sunday night here was a great fire at the Fortune, in Golding lane, the first play-house in this town. It was quite burnt downe in two hours, and all their apparell and play-books lost, whereby these poore companions are quite undone.

This is the saddest bit of English dramatic history, for the loss of a great collection of plays, even better than that of the Globe repertoire, is irreparable.

The Fortune stood near Golden Lane, Cripplegate. The front of the new edifice was still standing in 1811.

These were the only theatres of any real importance in existence during Queen Elizabeth's reign, with the exception of the small semi-private Blackfriars and the Chapel Royal, the latter being the Queen's private theatre.

Blackfriars theatre. The facts concerning Blackfriars theatre were almost entirely discovered by Dr. C. W. Wallace. Blackfriars monastery was originally outside the city walls, hence was not under the control of the Lord Mayor and the city magistrates. The monastery was dissolved in 1538, and about 1547 King Edward VI removed to it from Warwick Inn all the 'tents, furniture, and apparel used in war and hunting, as well as all like material used in Court plays, masks, processions, and revels'.

In 1550 King Edward presented a considerable part of Blackfriars to Sir Thomas Cawarden, who was then Master of the King's Revels. Presumably some part of Blackfriars was even then used for theatrical rehearsals, if not for performances.

In 1571 the office of the Revels and all the theatrical properties were removed to St. John's Jerusalem, where they were stored until c. 1610.

On December 20, 1576, Sir William More (Cawarden's executor) leased a part of the old Priory House to Richard Farrant, Master of the Windsor Chapel Children. The lease ran for twenty-one years. Farrant at once set up his children as a semi-public company of actors. Farrant died on November 30, 1580, and his wife sold the lease to William Hunnis, Master of the Children of the Royal Chapel. In 1583 the Earl of Oxford bought this lease from Hunnis and presented it to John Lyly, theatrical manager of Paules Boys.[1]

Seemingly Paules Boys returned to the vicinity of St. Paul's before 1591, as the editor of *Endimion* (printed in 1591) states:

> Since the Plaies in Paules were dissolved there are certaine Commedies come to my handes by chance, which were presented before Her Majestie at several times by the Children of Paules.

This hints also that Paules Boys were inhibited *c.* 1590. In 1586 the large hall of Blackfriars was leased to the noted fencing-master, Rocho Bonetti, by which time it may have ceased being used as a theatre. (See Feuillerat's *Lyly.*)

On February 4, 1596, James Burbage purchased the Priory House from Sir William More, and even before the expiration of the old lease began remodelling the property into a new playhouse. If Lyly still held the lease this must have been done with his consent. This new Blackfriars was finished late in 1597 and was immediately occupied by the Children of Her Majesties Revels under Harry Evans, in connexion with Nathaniel Gyles, Master of the Chapel Children ('Nathaniel Gyles, Mus.D., son of Thomas Gyles, organist of St. Paul's Cathedral.' See Grove's *Dict. Music*). Harry Evans had been actor manager of Paules Boys under Lyly in 1583.

This arrangement continued until *c.* 1599, when there seems to have been a change in the company. Evans was granted a new lease for twenty-one years; but the Burbages then exacted a bond of £400 as security lest Evans should not be able to 'erect and keepe a companie of Playinge boyes or others to play playes & interludes in the said Play-house in such sort as before tyme had been there used'. Also because 'he was lykelye to be behind with the rent of fortie pounds'.[2] As the company had been very

---

[1] See *The Children of the Chapel*, C. W. Wallace.   [2] *Ibid.*

successful during 1597–9 this hints that the company to be 'erected and kept' by Evans was a new organization.

In his bill of complaint against Kirkman Evans further hints that Blackfriars was unused for a short while before he took the lease in September, 1600, as he refers to it as 'late' in his possession.[1]

[1] See *The Children of the Chapel*, C. W. Wallace.

III

ACTOR COMPANIES AND THEIR PLAY-HOUSES

FROM the evidence available there were from 1576 to 1592 but two public play-houses, the Theatre and the Curtain, though several inns were occasionally used. From 1592 to 1599 there were two play-houses and one inn which were regularly used, the Theatre, the Rose, and the Cross-keys tavern. From 1600 onwards there were four theatres, the Rose, Globe, and Fortune, and the small semi-private theatre, Blackfriars. Yet, during all this period, from 1576 to 1590 there were four or more leading public companies in London—Leicester's, Queen's, Sussex's, Admiral's, and after 1583, Strange's tumblers; and from 1593 to 1599 there were still four or more public companies—Queen's, Admiral's, Pembroke's, and the Strange-Chamberlain's.

Historians have experienced the utmost difficulty in finding homes for all of these companies. Their perplexity has been due to an oversight. They have endeavoured to allot a separate play-house to each company, whereas all the evidence points to joint occupancy. There must have been two companies in each house until 1599, when the Globe was occupied by but one company, which company after 1609 also occupied the small Blackfriars.

William Hunnis made payments to 'James Burbage and his company, servants to the Earl of Leicester' for plays in 1575, 1577, and 1578. Evidently the Leicester company occupied Burbage's Theatre during this period. In their licence (November 28, 1583) they were permitted to play 'at the sygnes of the Bull in Bisshoppesgate streete and at the sygne of the Bell in gratious streete and nowheare else within this cyttye'. This awkward arrangement did not last long. The Theatre was outside the city.

In 1583 the Queen's company was founded. In Fleetwood's report of June, 1584, the following record appears:

> I sent for the Queen's players . . . the chiefest of Her Highnes players advised me to send for the owner of the Theatre who . . . sent me word that he was My Lord of Hunsden's man, &c.

Evidently the Queen's players were in 1584 at the Theatre. There can be no doubt but that the Queen's men and the men of her favourite, Lord Leicester, shared the Theatre so long as both companies were in existence.

John Laneham, who received payments for Court plays acted by the Queen's men in 1589, 1590, and 1591, is definitely placed at the Theatre by Nash in *The Death and Buriall of Martin Marprelate*. Martin is speaking: 'that indeed I had learned in Alehouses and at the Theatre of Lanam and his fellowes.'

The Queen's players were under the direct patronage of her Lord Chamberlain, Hunsdon. It was for this reason that Burbage called himself Lord Hunsdon's man. The company was called indiscriminately the Queen's players, the Chamberlain's company, and Lord Hunsdon's men. In the payments for Court performances in 1585-6 they were paid on December 26 and January 1 as Queen's men, and on January 6 as the servants of the Lord Chamberlain. So again for December 26 and 28, 1593, Burbage (Richard) received payment as a Lord Chamberlain's man, although the company was still the Queen's. This company remained at the Theatre until 1598, when the Burbages tore down the old building.

After the death of Lord Leicester and the break-up of his company the Queen's company shared the Theatre with the Admiral's men (*c.* 1589-92). This company then quarrelled with the Burbages and went to the new Rose under Henslowe's management. (Wallace.)

That part of Lord Leicester's company which found a new patron in Lord Pembroke, or rather a patroness in his wife, Mary Sidney, sister of Philip Sidney, seems to have played at the Curtain until 1592. There is a rhymed verse which connects Marlowe, chief poet of the company, with the Curtain. After 1592 Lord Pembroke's men took the place of the Admiral's men at the Theatre (Wallace), where they remained until it was about to be torn down in 1597, when they joined the Admiral's men at the Rose. (*Henslowe's Diary*.)

When the Queen's company left the Theatre in 1598 they joined the Strange-Chamberlain company at the Curtain. That they were still at the Theatre as late as July 28, 1597, is evident from a letter by the Lord Mayor of that date to the Privy Council in which he requests that plays may be suppressed 'as well at the Theatre, Curtain, and Bankside'.

While the Theatre was shared by the Admiral's and the Queen's men the Curtain must have been occupied by the Pembroke men and Lord Sussex's company until 1592, when the Sussex company played at one of Henslowe's theatres, supposedly Paris Garden, and the Pembroke company went on tour. (*Alleyn Papers*.)

Seemingly the Curtain was not used after the plague of 1592 until 1596. In 1594 the Lord Chamberlain petitioned that his 'nowe' company might play at the Cross-keys tavern. This is strong evidence that the Curtain was then out of commission, also that the Theatre was already occupied by two companies, the Queen's and Lord Pembroke's, otherwise his 'nowe' company could have found room at one or the other of these play-houses.

The Curtain was not in use when the Lord Mayor wrote a letter to the Privy Council on September 13, 1595, but was in use when he again wrote on July 28, 1597. (*Remembrancia*.)

The Rose was built in 1592 and was at once occupied by Lord Strange's men. Young Alleyn of the Admiral's men married the step-daughter of the owner of the Rose on October 22, 1592. When he returned from acting in the provinces after the plague of that year he brought the Admiral's men with him to the Rose. In the meantime the Sussex company had disbanded. This left the Queen's and Pembroke's men at the Theatre and the Strange and Admiral's men at the Rose.

Lord Strange died on April 16, 1594, when his company

found a new patron in the old Lord Chamberlain. The history of the Strange-Chamberlain company thus far is very clear. Evidently it was an entirely different organization from the Burbage-Kempe-Shakespeare organization which was then at the Theatre, but which had at times assumed the title of Chamberlain's men. The Burbage group was in truth the Queen's company, and remained such until after it left the Theatre in 1598.

The Strange-Chamberlain company had never played at the Theatre, nor had the Burbage group aught to do with this company until after 1598.

In 1594 the old Lord Chamberlain explicitly disowned all connexion with the Queen's men, as he wrote 'my nowe' company in the letter to the Lord Mayor wherein he petitions that his men be allowed to resume acting at the Cross-keys. Had his 'nowe' company been the same as the Burbage-Shakespeare group he would not have asked permission for it to play at the 'cross-keys' where 'they have byn accustomed'. The Cross-keys was the original home of the Strange-Chamberlain company, which they left in 1592 for the Rose. The Burbages played at their own play-house, the Theatre, and never, except during the plague, played at any other London house until after 1597.

The Strange-Chamberlain group played at the Rose from 1592 until 1594 except when on tour. During this period, as is well established by many documents, the Burbages were at their own house, the Theatre. (Wallace.) These two companies were distinct and separate and remained so until after the destruction of the Theatre.

The old Lord Chamberlain's petition regarding the Cross-keys tavern was, as Fleay has observed, refused, and his 'nowe' company continued to share the Rose with the Admiral's men. The two companies opened the season at Newington on June 3, 1594, and moved to the Rose on the 15th of the same month, as Henslowe in his diary drew a line between the 13th and the 15th of June, and his receipts immediately changed from shillings to pounds. That the Chamberlain company went with the Admiral's men to the Rose is evident from the continued production of their new play *The Guise* and of their old play *The Jew of Malta.* (*Henslowe's Diary.*)

Incidental proof of the continuance of this company under Henslowe is found in three loans made by Henslowe to divers three of 'my Lord Chamberlenes men'. Two of these loans are undated, but perforce were made after the company assumed its new name in October of 1594. The third loan of three pounds was made to Richard Hoope and is dated January 14, 1595. A fourth member of the Chamberlain company, William Slye, bought a jewel of Henslowe which was paid for in weekly instalments from October 11, 1594, until January 17, 1595. In one of Henslowe's inventories, dated March 13, 1598, there appears, 'Item, Perowes suit which W^m. Sley wore'. Sly was a Chamberlain man.

Both the Admiral and Chamberlain companies remained at the Rose until the end of the summer season in 1596, when the old Lord Chamberlain died, and for a time his son Lord Hunsdon became patron of this company. (John Heminge and George Bryan, 'servantes to the late Lord Chamberlayne and now servants to the Lorde Hunsdon', received payment for a Court play, December 21, 1596.)

Late in 1596 the Hunsdon men went to the Curtain, where they were joined by the Burbage-Kempe-Shakespeare group, the old Queen's company, from the Theatre. This latter group may have once more become 'the Lord Chamberlain's men' under Lord Oxford, who was Chamberlain until 1599. In 1599 Lord Hunsdon became Chamberlain. His company and the Burbage group were then reorganized. Some went to the Globe as Chamberlain's men; others found patrons in Lord Oxford and Lord Derby and played at the Boar's Head.

The fact that the younger Lord Hunsdon did not have anything to do with the Burbages before 1597 is evident in that in 1596, when the Burbages bought the Blackfriars property, Lord George Hunsdon signed the ' petition against the theatre, heere adjoining unto the dwellings of the right honorable the Lord Chamberlaine (Cobham) and the Lord Hunsdon ', dated November, 1596. Had the Burbage company been his own he would not have thus opposed the Burbage endeavour to found a new play-house.

The Admiral's men were alone at the Rose until July, 1597, when the Pembroke company joined them. These two companies shared the Rose until July, 1600, when the Admiral's men went to the new Fortune. The Pembroke men remained at the Rose, having amalgamated with Lord Worcester's men and adopted their patron, until 1603, when they once more joined the Admiral's men at the Fortune.

All of the facts concerning the Rose are to be found in Henslowe's Diary. The interpretation of those facts is the sole point on which commentators can disagree. While all agree as to the dates on which various companies began acting at the Rose, for Henslowe is very explicit on this point, they disagree as to when the various companies ceased their connexions. These dates can be settled only by inference.

While Henslowe never noted when a company ceased acting at one of his theatres he always began a new heading with each change of occupancy. He opened his accounts in 1594 thus: 'In the name of god Amen beginning at Newington my lord Admeralle men & my Lorde Chamberlen men As ffolowethe 1594.' This is the only time he mentions where they began.

When the two companies moved to the Rose on July 15 he merely separated the new accounts from the old by a line. It is to be presumed, therefore, that the continued accounts after July 15 refer to the two companies, otherwise he would have started a new heading, referring to the Admiral's men alone, as he did elsewhere. So also when the Pembroke men joined the Admiral's men on October 11, 1597, he made a note of it; but he never referred to a separation; nor is there a hint that the Admiral's men were ever again in sole occupation of the Rose.

The exact duration of each period of joint occupancy can easily be determined by the number of plays produced. In 1592 (February 19 to June 22, and December 29 to February 1) the Strange company, being alone, produced seven new plays in five months, or one new play each twenty-two days. During the season 1596–7 (October 27 to July 28) the Admiral's men, being alone, produced fourteen new plays, or one for each nineteen days. Seemingly the average production for a single company was one new play each twenty days.

When the Admiral's and Chamberlain's men were together they produced (June 3, 1594, to March 14, 1595) twenty-one new plays, one each fifteen days, this being the summer season; and still later (August 25 to February 27, 1595–6) they brought out thirteen new plays, one each fourteen days; finally (April 12 to July 18, 1596) they produced seven new plays, one each thirteen days. No one company could have produced so many new plays during the same period.

The average production of the Admiral and Pembroke companies during joint occupancy is more difficult to ascertain, as the daily appearance of new plays was then no longer recorded. However, from October, 1597, to August, 1598, Henslowe paid for thirty-six new plays, while from September, 1598, to September, 1599, and October, 1599, to May, 1600, he paid for thirty-two and twenty-five new productions respectively. This makes an average of thirty-four plays per year, which, compared with the fourteen new plays per year produced by the Admiral's men when they were alone (1596–7), leaves little doubt as to the presence of the Pembroke company.

During this same period the Pembroke men toured the provinces. They appeared at Bristol, Leicester, and Dover in 1598, at Bristol, Leicester, York, &c., in 1600.

Henslowe's Diary furnishes further proof of joint occupancy by the Chamberlain's and Admiral's men during the period June 3, 1594, to July 18, 1596. Whole groups of plays then produced disappear from Henslowe's list (after July, 1596) to reappear as Chamberlain plays in after years; while other groups of plays continue to appear in his list as Admiral plays. So also many of the plays produced at the Rose from 1597 to 1600 disappear from Henslowe's repertoire, but reappear in the Pembroke-Worcester repertoire.

The date of the final severance of the Chamberlain connexion with the Rose can be fixed by the disappearance from Henslowe's Diary of such plays as *The Tinker of Totnes*, *Paradox*, and *Troye*. This latter was acted as a new play on July 18, 1596. It drew a full house, yet was never again played at any of Henslowe's theatres. This was the last performance of the Chamberlain company at the Rose.

When playing was resumed at the Rose on October 27 Henslowe marked the absence of the Chamberlain company by beginning a new account, headed:

> In the name of god Amen begynynge one simone & Jewdes daye my lord Admeralles men as foloweth.

Among the plays acted by the Chamberlain's men while at the Rose was *Henry V*, rewritten from the old *Famous Victories of Henry V*, and played for the first time on November 28, 1595. This play was published in 1600 and in 1608 as a Chamberlain play.

Hitherto it has generally been stated that the Queen's company ceased to exist *c.* 1593. This statement arose because Burbage, Shakespeare, and Kempe were wrongly placed in the Strange-Chamberlain company at that date. These men and the Strange-Chamberlain company were then assumed to have moved to Burbage's play-house, the Theatre.

The history of the Pembroke company from 1593 to 1597 has also hitherto been left blank.

From documents recently discovered by Dr. Wallace it is now known that the Queen's company and the Admiral's men shared the old Theatre from *c.* 1589 until 1592, thus proving that joint occupancy was a common practice.

The Strange-Chamberlain company went to the Curtain soon after July, 1596. The elder Burbage died on February 2, 1597, and as his sons were unable to renew the ground lease for the Theatre the Queen's company, forced to find a new home, joined the Chamberlain's men at the Curtain some time after July, 1597. Before his death Burbage had put all his available money into the Blackfriars property, which also carried a mortgage. Thus the Queen's men were without patron, theatre, or financial support. But the company, through Burbage, controlled the material of the old Theatre.

While playing at the Curtain the shareholders of the Queen's company, who once looked upon the Lord Chamberlain as their patron, and the shareholders of the 'nowe' Chamberlain company worked out the details of an amalgamation. Using the materials of the dismantled Theatre as a basis they built with their own funds, saved or borrowed, the new Globe, and there installed themselves under the protection of Lord Chamberlain Hunsdon in 1599. The building was owned by the Burbages. The ground lease was taken by Kempe and Shakespeare of the old Queen's company and Phillips, Pope, and Heminge of the old Strange company. Kempe deserted this combination before the Globe was completed, thus leaving the four to share the ground lease. (Wallace.) His place was afterwards taken by Sly.

The Worcester company were playing at the Boar's Head in March, 1602. Lord Worcester wrote: 'and because we are informed the house called the Bores head is the place they have especially used and do best like of'. (*Remembrancia.*) On August 17 of that year they went under Henslowe's management, probably at the Rose. Before Oxford's men and Derby's men united into the Worcester company one group must have acted at the Boar's Head, the other probably at the Curtain.

Theatrical Companies and their Play-houses.

Leicester, 1574–88. Queen's, 1588–90. Pembroke, 1590–1601.	Theatre, 1576–89. Theatre, 1592–7. Rose, 1597–1601.
Queen's I, 1583–97. Chamberlain's (under Oxford), 1597–9. Split up, 1599.	Theatre, 1583–97. Curtain, 1597–9.
Strange, 1583–92. Derby V, 1592–4. Chamberlain's (Hunsdon I), 1594–6. Hunsdon's, 1596–9. Chamberlain's (Hunsdon II), 1599–1603. King's, 1603.	Cross-keys, 1583–92. Rose, 1592–6. Curtain, 1596–9. Globe, 1599–1613.

Sussex, 1576–94.

Curtain, 1576–92.

Derby VI, 1599–1601. United with Oxford's into Worcester's, 1601–3. Queen Anne's, 1603.

Curtain, 1599–1601. Boar's Head, 1601–2. Rose, 1602–3. Red Bull, 1604.

Admiral's, 1585–1603. Prince Henry's, 1603 on.

Curtain, 1585–9. Theatre, 1589–92. Rose, 1592–1600. Fortune, 1600 on.

IV

THE CHILDREN COMPANIES

WHEN the Children of the Chapel were first used as actors is unknown. In 1569 they acted plays 'on profane subjects in the Chapel Royal'.[1] In 1580 they were performing in Blackfriars. The Windsor Chapel Children had occupied Blackfriars from 1576 to 1580. Paules Boys under Thomas Gyles were performing at St. Paul's School from 1581 to 1583. (*Plays Confuted*, S. Gosson.)

In 1583 the Earl of Oxford presented John Lyly with the lease of Blackfriars. The Earl's Boys under Lyly played at Court New Year's Day at night and Shrove Tuesday at night, both in 1584. While the Court payments specify that on these occasions the plays were presented by the Earl of Oxford's company, Lyly's plays of that year were printed as acted 'by her Majesties children, and the children (or boyes) of Paules'. This suggests that the Earl of Oxford's company of boys, to whom Hunnis gave up Blackfriars in 1583, was a combination of Chapel Children and Paules Boys, or that the Chapel Children acted Lyly's plays at Court, while Paules Boys presented them at Blackfriars.

The Chapel Children and Paules Boys acted at times separately, at times together, from 1583 until 1590, when Paules Boys were inhibited. It would seem therefore that when a number of players were needed both companies were used, when but a few players were needed each company acted independently. Both were under royal patronage. St. Paul's continually trained and supplied men for the Chapel Royal, and the Chapel Royal supplied St. Paul's with at least one Master of Paules Boys, Edward Pierce, in 1600.

The history of the Children companies from 1590 until 1597 is somewhat obscure. Lyly was given a post under the Master

[1] See *The Children of the Chapel stript and whipt.*

of the Revels in connexion with 'tents and toiles' which he held from c. 1583 until 1602 or later. Possibly he followed Mr. Tamworth as head of the 'toiles' department, possibly he was Vice-Master of the Revels under Tilney. Certainly he in some way had control of the royal theatrical properties, as during the Harefield entertainments of 1602 'Mr Lillyes man . . . brought the lotterye boxe to Harefield . . . and received further payment' for 'carriage and tentes from St. Johnes'. (*Edgerton Papers*, August 6, 1602.)

In 1596, when Hunnis arranged with Burbage for the re-establishment of Blackfriars, it was Harry Evans, Lyly's old stage-manager in 1583, who became stage-manager at the new Black-friars; and it must have been through Lyly that this company obtained use of the royal theatrical properties.

The company now set up under Evans and Nathaniel Gyles, son of Thomas Gyles, Master of Paules Boys, was purely an act-ing company. Presumably it was a combination of Paules Boys and Chapel Children, as among them there was Alvery Trussell, a prentice boy belonging to Thomas Gyles. (Wallace.)

This new company lasted until 1599, when Paules Boys sepa-rated from the Gyles-Evans management and resumed acting near St. Paul's. Thomas Gyles must have died about that period, as 'Edward Pearce yealded up his place (in the Chapel Royal) for the Mastership of the children of Poules . . . the 15the August 1600'. (*St. Paul's Records.*)

Under Pierce, Paules Boys acted plays until c. 1608. The Chapel Children were reorganized by Evans and continued until 1608, when the Burbage group took over Blackfriars for the King's company of men. (Wallace.)

It has so often been stated by various historians that the Chil-dren ceased their activities when Blackfriars was first abandoned (1583-6) that it may be interesting to cite some proof to the contrary. It is now known that Lyly presented at Court, dur-ing the years 1582-90, the following Oxford and Paules Boys plays—*Campaspe, Sapho and Phao, Galathea, Endimion, Midas.* Thereafter Lyly presented at Court *The Woman in the Moon.*

Presumably it was acted by the Chapel Children, who played *Summers Last Will and Testament* by Thomas Nash in 1592, and *Dido, Queen of Carthage* by Marlowe and Nash in 1593. The same company must have played Peele's *Old Wives Tale, c.* 1591. There was thus a continuation of Court comedies at least into 1593. The company seems to have rehearsed at St. John's Jerusalem and acted privately at the Chapel Royal.

Direct evidence of the continuity of the Chapel Children, or the Children of Her Majesties Revels, as they were properly called from 1590 until 1599, is to be found in the statement of Robert Keysar in the lawsuit brought by him against the Burbages in 1610.[1] The Chapel Children had been deprived of Blackfriars theatre about 1607 by Burbage. They had been kept by Keysar in the hope that they might be reinstated or else find another theatre. It is to these boys Keysar refers in his sworn statement, which contains the following:

> ... this complainant who all that tyme had a Companye of the moste exparte and skillfull actors within the Realme of England to the number of eighteane or Twentye persons all or most of them trayned up in that service in the raigne of the late Queen Elizabeth for ten yeares togeather, and afterwards preferred unto her Majesties service (i. e. Queen Anne's) to be the children of her Revells by a patent from his moste excellent majestie &c.

Since the Children had been trained ' in the raigne of the late Queen Elizabeth for ten yeares togeather' they must have been in existence and acting from 1593 to 1603, the ten years preceding her death.

After their short stay at Blackfriars (1576–80) the Windsor Chapel Children returned to St. George's Chapel, Windsor, where they continued under Ferrant until his death in 1595. Nathaniel Gyles then became their Master. The Dean and Canons agreed to give Gyles ' an annuity of 81£s, 6sh, 8d ... over and besides all other gifts, rewards, or benevolence that may be given to the choristers for singing of ballads, plays, or the like'. Gyles was to

---

[1] See *Shakespeare and his London Associates,* Wallace.

find them 'sufficient meat, apparel, bedding and lodging at his own costes within the New Commons lately appointed for them'.[1] Evidently these children had been in the habit of acting plays for money before the appointment of Gyles in 1595.

The Children of Her Majesty's Chapel continued at the Royal Chapel under Hunnis until his death on June 6, 1597, three days after which the Children went under the Mastership of Nathaniel Gyles.[2] The continuity of both the Chapel Children and the Windsor Chapel Children is thus well established.

Under Gyles the Chapel Children at once moved into Blackfriars, where they became a semi-public company. Immediately they met with great favour. Evidently they must have been the perfectly trained boys of Her Majesty's Chapel whose repertoire, begun in the days of Edward VI, was added to during each of the years of Queen Elizabeth's reign by the great University dramatists—Lyly, Peele, Marlowe, Nash, &c. It was not a newly organized company.

While every author of the period can be accounted for during the years 1597-9, no disengaged author of importance can be discovered who could have written successful Court plays except Lyly. Dr. Wallace states that an early version of Jonson's *The Case is Altered* was acted at Blackfriars in 1597. The present version of that play was written in 1599. Even were an early version produced in 1597 this one play would not have filled Blackfriars for two years. The plays which proved so popular there were evidently those written for private performance from 1584 to 1597 and then for the first time offered to the general public. Naturally all London flocked to see them.[3]

It is not likely that Queen Elizabeth, who loved the theatre and was parsimonious, should have paid for the upkeep of the Children from 1583 to 1597 and have denied herself the pleasure of their performances. Nor would she have insisted that Lyly should during this period continue to write plays unless they were performed.[4]

[1] See Ashmolean MSS., No. 1125–33, Bodl. Lib.
[2] See Wallace, as above.   [3] See 'Corambis' *Hamlet*.   [4] See Lyly's *Letters*.

V

SHAKESPEARE AND HIS FELLOW ACTORS

ELIZABETHAN actors were usually shareholders in stock companies, which often acquired considerable wealth. To gain an entrance into one of these companies an actor required means as well as ability. Besides shareholders there were hired men, who in turn might save their earnings and buy a share or part share in the company with which they were associated, or in lieu of that in another, though this happened but rarely.

The companies bought plays outright, also costumes, scenery, &c. They usually rented the theatre in which they played, the owner accepting the entire takings of the gallery or some other part of the house in place of a cash payment. When a company broke up, all plays, properties, &c., were divided or sold, after the custom of all joint-stock companies. It will thus be seen that although the companies often changed their patron and title the chief shareholders remained a constant factor.

James Burbage. So far as is known the first document to mention James Burbage was the patent granted to him on May 7, 1594, as leader of Lord Leicester's company. He built the Theatre in 1576, became a Queen's man in 1583, and died in 1597.

After 1583 James Burbage always described himself as Lord Hunsdon's man. This great lord was the Queen's Chamberlain, and as such was the personal representative of the Queen to the company. An interesting sidelight is thrown on his character, as well as information as to his connexion with the Queen's company, in the Fleetwood report of June, 1584. The occasion was one of the periodic attempts by the Puritans to do away with the Curtain and the Theatre.

> I sent for the Queen's players . . . the chiefest of Her Highnes players advised me to send for the owner of the Theatre who was a stubborn fellow and to bind him.

The Queen's men knew the character of their manager.

> I did so; he sent me word that he was my Lord Hunsdon's man, and that he would not come to me, but he would in the morning ride to my Lord ... then I sent the under-sheriff for hym and he brought him to me, and, at his coming, he showted me out very justice; and in the end I shewed hym my Lord his master's hand, and then he was more quiet; but, to die for it, he would not be bound.

The evidence is conclusive. Burbage was the Chamberlain's man, but the company was the Queen's. The Queen's company appeared at Leicester in 1585 as the ' Chamberlain's men '; and in 1593, when they acted at Court during Christmas week; they, though still the Queen's men, were again called the Chamberlain's men.

Richard Burbage. James Burbage had two sons, Richard and Cuthbert. Richard first appears in dramatic history on December 26 and 28, 1593, when with Kempe and Shakespeare he played at Court as the Lord Chamberlain's man, i.e. as a member of the Queen's company. He remained with the Queen's men at his father's play-house until it was torn down in 1597–8. He then, after a short interval at the Curtain, joined the new Chamberlain company in building the Globe theatre in 1599, where he became leading tragedian. His reputation was second only to that of Edward Alleyn.

Cuthbert Burbage was the elder son of James. He managed his father's affairs and became in 1597 chief owner of Blackfriars theatre. He has been confused with the printer Cuthbert Burby, ' son of Edmund Burbie late of Ersley in the county of Bedford, husbandman ', who died in 1607. (See *Stationers' Register.*) Cuthbert Burbage was still living in 1635, having survived his more famous brother.

Will Kempe. Until 1588 Tarleton was the great clown of the Queen's company as Kempe was of Lord Leicester's men. In

1586 Kempe went to Norway and Saxony. In 1588 both Tarleton and Lord Leicester died. When Kempe returned from the Continent he soon took Tarleton's place at the Theatre as a Queen's man. During the plague of 1592 he toured the provinces with Ned Alleyn. *A Knack to Know a Knave* was printed in 1594 as acted by Alleyn's company 'with Kemps applauded merriments of the men of Goteham'. He returned for the Christmas season of 1592–3 and as a member of the Queen's company received the Court payment for Christmas of 1593, together with Burbage and Shakespeare. Kempe remained at the Theatre with the Queen's men until it was torn down, when he went with the company to the Curtain. This is indicated by the presence of his name in the 1599 edition of *Romeo and Juliet*, and again with Cowley's name in the 1600 edition of *Much Ado about Nothing*, both of which plays were printed as Chamberlain plays, the Queen's men having by 1599 amalgamated with the Chamberlain company. However, before the new Chamberlain company moved to the Globe, Kempe sold his share in the new venture to Phillips. He appeared in *Every Man in His Humour* in 1598, but did not appear in *Every Man out of His Humour* in 1599. Both of these were Chamberlain plays by Ben Jonson. During 1599 and 1600 Kempe seems to have done little except perform morris dances. In 1602 he is found in Lord Worcester's company, then consolidated with Pembroke's men. His career after 1602 is uncertain.[1]

William Shakespeare. Innumerable have been the conjectures as to the theatrical career of William Shakespeare. Although hitherto no one has outlined it correctly the evidence is full and convincing. The first mention of him as actor is in connexion with the Court performances of December 26 and 28, 1593. The record of the Treasurer of the Chamber reads—

> To William Kempe, William Shakespeare, and Richard Burbage, servants to the Lord Chamberleyne upon the councils warrent, for

[1] See *Henslowe's Diary.*

twoe severall comedies, or enterludes, shewed by them before her
Majesty in Christmas tyme laste paste on St. Stephens daie [De-
cember 26] and on Innocents day [December 28] in all 20£.
March 15, 1594.

Because the year was sometimes reckoned from March 29
various critics have changed the year of the above Christmas performances to 1594. According to the Pipe Rolls payments it was
the Admiral's company which played at Court on Innocents' Day,
December 28, in 1594. Nor is there mention in the Pipe Rolls
of any company save the Admiral's for that date. Also on December 26, 1594, a company, supposed to be Shakespeare's, played
a version of *The Comedy of Errors* at Gray's Inn. Evidently the
year in which Shakespeare, Burbage, and Kempe played at Court
was that of 1593. As the Queen's men were from the first under
the care of the elder Hunsdon, the Lord Chamberlain, and as they
and the elder Burbage constantly called themselves Hunsdon's
men, there remains no doubt as to Shakespeare having been a
member of the Queen's company in 1593. That he was an influential member of that company is evident. He remained with
the Queen's men until they amalgamated with the 'nowe' Chamberlain company. With this new company he remained until he
retired about 1612. (His earlier history will be found in the chapter devoted to William Shakespeare, reviser.)

Because Shakespeare was a Chamberlain's man after 1598 it has
usually been supposed that he was one of the old Strange-Chamberlain company from 1592 until 1594, when it was called Lord
Derby's company, and during 1594–7, when it was under the
Hunsdons. During the Christmas season of 1593, when Shakespeare, Kempe, and Burbage played at Court, the Strange-Chamberlain company was still under the patronage of Lord Strange,
then Lord Derby, who did not die until April 16, 1594. This dis-
connects Shakespeare from the Strange company at that period,
as he was then the Lord Chamberlain's man of the Queen's company. When, after April 16, 1594, the Lord Chamberlain took
the old Strange company under his patronage he very explicitly
disowned the Queen's company, and (October 8, 1594) distinctly

marked his new connexion by calling the old Strange men ' my nowe companie' of players.[1] The Burbage-Shakespeare group therefore continued as the Queen's company. The confusion as to Shakespeare's career is greatly due to misconception as to the dates and origins of his plays. Wherever a play appeared which in later years was attributed to Shakespeare, there the historians promptly assumed he must have been active. They thus ' discovered' that he acted in every theatre then in existence and wrote for every prominent company.

John Heminge. In the warrant of May 6, 1593, permitting Ned Alleyn to tour the provinces with a combination of Admiral's and other men, appear the names John Heminge, Thomas Pope, Augustine Phillips, George Bryan, and Will Kempe. All these, except Alleyn and Kempe, reappear soon afterwards as Lord Strange's men; and they continue as Strange-Chamberlain men throughout their entire careers. Heminge was evidently the treasurer of the Strange company, as he received the payments for Court performances, with Pope or Bryan from 1596 to 1598, alone in 1599, and with Cowley, originally a Queen's man, in January and February of 1600. The year 1599 marks the official union of the Queen's and the 'nowe' Chamberlain companies. Heminge remained treasurer of the amalgamated companies until he retired in 1623. 1623 was also the year in which Heminge and Condell brought out the Shakespeare Folio. Having in that year given over the management of the company to Lowin and Taylor,[2] these two old actors decided to turn an honest penny by publishing such plays as were still in their possession. To these the printers contributed other plays already published. Ben Jonson was employed to write an introduction; and the entire list was brought out as by William Shakespeare. Heminge and Condell claimed that the production was a labour of love. Had it been such, a more fitting date for its appearance would have been the year of Shakespeare's death. When Lowin and Taylor in their turn retired they also brought out various old manuscript plays.

---

[1] Fleetwood.   [2] See Henry Herbert's Office Book.

However, they were somewhat more honest and candid, for they published them 'for the public use of the ingenious' and 'the private use' of John Lowin and Joseph Taylor. (Malone's *Shakespeare*.)

The histories of actors belonging to companies other than the Queen's company will be found in Greg's edition of *Henslowe's Diary*.

VI

LISTS OF ACTORS FOUND IN THEATRICAL 'PLATTS'

THE main sources of information concerning actors and actor companies are Henslowe's Diary, the payments for Court performances, the licences granted to various companies, and several old play 'platts' or call-boy cards, which give the entrances and exits of characters, often with the actors' names attached.

There have been preserved parts of seven of these platts, all of which are reprinted in volume iii of *Henslowe's Diary* by W.W. Greg. The exact dates of two of them, *Frederick and Basilea* and *Tamar Cam*, both Admiral plays, are well established. Hitherto the dates of the remaining five have not been satisfactorily settled.

The Chamberlain and Queen companies amalgamated at the Curtain in 1597–9. Early in 1599 they moved to the Globe. Many old papers and plays belonging to these companies seem to have been left behind at the Curtain, where they fell into the hands of Lord Worcester's company. Among these papers must have been the platts of the *Seven Deadly Sins*, written by Tarleton for the Queen's company, as is recorded by both Gabriell Harvey and Thomas Nash, and the platt of *Dead Man's Fortune*.

In *Dead Man's Fortune* appear the names Lee and Burbage, both old Queen's men. Lee sold an old play called *The Myller* to the Admiral's men on February 22, 1598,[1] by which time he must have left the Queen's company. He afterwards belonged to Worcester's company.[2] This places this platt either at the Theatre before 1597 or at the Curtain between April, 1597, and February, 1598.

[1] See Henslowe, fol. 44ᵛ.
[2] See Fleay, *Stage* (pp. 191 and 207).

The Seven Deadly Sins contains the names Bryan, Pope, Phillips, Sly, Beeston, and Sinkler, all old Strange-Chamberlain men, and Burbage and Cowley, old Queen's men. Pallant, Beeston, and Duke appear in Worcester's company in 1602, having left the Queen-Chamberlain group before 1599. This platt therefore belongs to the period 1597–9, when the amalgamated companies were at the Curtain.

Shakespeare's name does not appear in either platt; but as he was the play-manager of the company it is quite possible that one or the other of these platts was drawn up and written by him.[1]

The three remaining platts are all of plays belonging to the Admiral's men.

Troylus and Cressida. This platt is not of *Troilus and Cressida*, but is the platt of an old play *Troye*, first played on June 22, 1596, when the boy 'Pigg' (John Pyk) was Alleyn's leading lady. He took the part of Cressida. The same boy 'Pigg' caused a sensation in the role of 'Alice Pierce' in December, 1597, and was with Alleyn on tour in 1593. This old play of *Troye* was expanded (April–May, 1599) into two plays, *Troilus and Cressida* and *Agamemnon*, by Dekker and Chettle. (*Henslowe's Diary.*)

The Battle of Alcazar. This evidently is not a platt of the old play attributed to Peele. It rather seems a continuation of *Muly Mollico*, which was an old Henslowe play, probably built on *Alcazar*, or possibly that play under another name. Jonson states in *Poetaster* that the Moor was cut in two and 'served in' twice. Presumably this was the second serving. The date of this second part cannot be ascertained from Jonson's remark, as only the first part may have appeared at that time. In 1602 Henslowe records various payments for a play called 'felmelanco'. This is likely *Fell-Melanco* (Mollico), the second part of *Muly Mollico*. The platt indicates a fell and gruesome tragedy. It dates 1602.

The Second Part of Fortunes Tennis. The first part of *Fortunes Tennis* was written August–September, 1600, by Thomas Dekker. The above platt seems to refer to a continuation. The

[1] The platt of *The Seven Deadly Sins* seems to be in the handwriting of Antony Munday.

names in the present platt place it after September, 1602, as Tailer and Pav- (Parr) are not found in the platt of *Tamar Cam* in October, 1602.

By consulting these various platts, as well as the lists of actors found in Henslowe's Diary and the Alleyn papers, the changes of personnel in the Admiral's company can be easily followed.

VII

DRAMATISTS AND ACTOR COMPANIES

THE most important source of information concerning the dramatists of the period is Henslowe's Diary, which gives a complete and detailed list of all authors working for him from 1597 to 1603. A second source is the title-pages of such plays as were published during the lifetime of the dramatists concerned, often with a mention of either the theatre or actor company. Still other sources are the Stationers' Register and documents recently discovered by Dr. C. W. Wallace.

From these sources the list below has been compiled. Marlowe, Peele, Greene, Lodge, Kyd, Nash, and the elder Wilson for the most part ceased writing before 1597.

Actor Companies and Dramatists (1597–1603).

Dramatist.	*Henslowe Companies.*	*Unknown and Rival Companies.*	*Chamberlain Company.*
Chapman, Geo.	May, '98–July, '99.	Chapel Children, '99 on.	
Chettle, H.	Feb.,'98–May,1603.		
Day, John	July–Sept., '98. Jan.,1600–May,'03.	Unknown Co., Oct., '98–Jan., 1600.	?
Dekker, T.	Jan.,'98–Sept.,1602.	Paules Boys and *Chapel Children.	
Drayton, M.	Dec., '97–Dec., '98. *'99–1602.	Unknown, *1599–1602.	1599–1602? 1603 on.
Hathway, R.	*April, 1598. 1599–Jan., 1601. All of 1601. *1602–3.	Unknown Co., *1598–1600. *Jan.–Nov., 1602.	?
Haughton, W.	Nov., 1597. Aug., '99–Sept., '02.	Unknown Co., Dec., '97–9.	?
Heywood, T.	Oct., '96–1603.		

* Indicates intermittent labours.

Dramatist.	Henslowe Companies.	Unknown and Rival Companies.	Chamberlain Company.
Jonson, B.	Dec., '97. Jan., '98. Aug.–Sept., '99. Sept., '01. June, '02.	Chapel Children, Aug., '99–Sept., '01.	Aug., '98–Aug., '99. 1602 on.
Lyly, John	— —	Chapel Children, 1597–9. P's. Boys, '99 on.	
Marston, J.	— —	P's. Boys, '99–1602. Ch. Child., '02 on.	
Munday, A.	Dec., '97–Aug., '98 *until 1603.	City Pageants, 1599–1603.	?
Porter, H.	Dec., '96–Mar., '97. Jan., '98–Mar., '99.	Unknown after Mar., 1599.	?
Rankins, W.	Oct.,'98. Jan.–April, 1601.	Unknown, 1599 to 1601.	?
Rowley, S.	Aug., 1597 on.		
Shakespeare,W.	— —	Queen's Co.,1593–8.	1598 on.
Smith, W.	April, 1601–3.		
Wilson, Robert	Mar., '98–Aug., '98. Oct.,'99–Jan.,1600.	Unknown,Aug.,'98– Oct., '99, and Jan., 1600, until death Nov. 20, 1600.	?

* Indicates intermittent labours.

Authorities for the above list.

All those dramatists who worked for Henslowe, with the dates and titles of their compositions, will be found in Henslowe's Diary.

Chapman began writing for the Chapel Children in 1599 and continued with them until they closed down c. 1608. (See Wallace.)

Dekker wrote *Satiromastix* with Marston for Paules Boys in 1601. He wrote a number of plays for the Chapel Children from 1598 onwards. (See printed titles of his plays.)

Heywood wrote one play for Henslowe in October, 1598. He then disappeared, with the Strange-Chamberlain company, from Henslowe's records until 1602, when he returned with Worcester's men. Presumably he was with the younger members of the old Strange company at the Curtain.

Jonson wrote for the Chapel Children from August, 1599, until September, 1601. (See Wallace.) His *Sejanus* was printed as a Chamberlain play in 1603. He was with Henslowe from December, 1597, until August, 1598. (See the *Diary*.) He then went to the Chamberlain company until 1599. (See titles of his plays.)

Lyly wrote under direct patronage of the Queen until *c.* 1599. (See his letters to the Queen and Lord Cecil.) The only company therefore for which he could have written was her company of the Revels, the Chapel Children. Presumably he went to Paules Boys in 1599, when Jonson and Chapman became chief poets to the Chapel Children. That he was with Dekker and Marston in 1599 is evident from Jonson's abuse of him, as Fastidio Brisk, along with the others in *Every Man out of His Humour.*

Marston's early career is unknown. He first appears as one of the chief writers for Paules Boys in 1599. Possibly he wrote for the Chapel Children before that date. He remained with Paules Boys until 1601, when he bought a share in Blackfriars theatre, after which he wrote exclusively for the Chapel Children. (See Wallace.)

Munday's old play *Sir Thomas More* was rewritten for the Chamberlain company *c.* 1597 while he was with the Admiral's men. As the Chamberlain company had the correct manuscript copy of this play, and as no record of it appears in Henslowe's Diary, it must be presumed that it was originally written for the Queen's company. In *The Case is Altered* (Blackfriars, 1599) Jonson calls Munday ' Pageant poet' who writes ' plain ', who keeps ' that old decorum ', and pleases ' the common sort '. He further disparaged him in *Histriomastix*, which contains a sneer at Shakespeare. Apparently Munday wrote for that public company with which Shakespeare was then connected—the Chamberlain, which company Jonson had then newly deserted for the Chapel Children. The company for which Munday was then writing (1599) was also characterized as one which had been travelling and had changed patrons often. This seems to be the same company that is represented in *Poetaster* by 'Historio', who plays to all the 'sinners of the suburbs...on the other side of Tiber' (Thames) at the 'Globe'. In all these plays Jonson drives at the same company; and it was for this company Munday wrote. This seems definitely to connect him with the Chamberlain company after August, 1599. He usually collaborated with Drayton, Hathway, and Wilson.

Shakespeare was with the Burbages, hence at the Theatre with the Queen's company, until 1598. He then became a member of the Chamberlain company. He wrote for the Queen's men until he joined the Chamberlain forces. As author of a Chamberlain play his name first appeared on the title-page of *Love's Labour's Lost*, 'Newly corrected and augmented' by William Shakespeare in 1598. In this same year Meres credited him with a large number of plays, most of which were revisions of either Chamberlain or Queen's company plays of unknown origin. Not one of the Strange-Chamberlain plays published before 1598 bears his name.

VIII

CHAMBERLAIN COMPANY DRAMATISTS
(1597–1603)

HENSLOWE began recording the names of dramatists and titles of plays on November 5, 1597. His record therefore furnishes the earliest continued reliable evidence concerning the authors of the period. Beginning with this same date, and eliminating those employed by Henslowe from the known list of dramatists, there remains a list, with dates, of all those dramatists who could have been employed by the Chamberlain or other companies.

Henslowe's list corresponds closely with the list of dramatists mentioned by Meres in 1598. Presumably the two lists include every important dramatist of the period.

A list of Chamberlain possibilities may be tabulated as follows:

Day. (October, 1598–November, 1599.)

Drayton. (Intermittently 1599 on.)

Hathway. (Intermittently April, 1598–January, 1601; entirely January–November, 1602.)

Haughton. (December, 1597–August, 1599.)

Jonson. (Almost entirely from 1597 to August, 1599, and from June, 1602, on.)

Porter. (After 1599.)

Rankins. Almost entirely October, 1598, to January, 1601.)

Munday. (August, 1598–October, 1599, and intermittently from 1600 on.)

Shakespeare. (1598 on.)

Wilson. (September, 1598–October, 1599.)

Of these men Drayton collaborated with Dekker until January, 1599. Wilson had also assisted him during that period. He worked with Munday and Wilson from 1599 until Wilson's death in 1600, after which he continued with Munday and Hathway, and later with Middleton and Webster. Hathway wrote with Drayton and Munday during 1599 and 1600, but collaborated with Rankins, Haughton, and Smith in 1601, and with Day and Smith in 1602–3. Haughton worked with Day regularly until near the end of 1601, when he began writing with Hathway and Smith.

Had there been but one company for which these men could have written, when they were not with Henslowe, they could with certainty be assigned to that company. However there were, besides the Chamberlain company, the Worcester men, Paules Boys, and the Chapel Children.

Lord Worcester's men came under Henslowe's control in August, 1602. Dramatists working for that company would there-fore presumably reappear in Henslowe's list about that date. Hathway and the new man Smith resumed work for Henslowe in November, 1602. Hathway may therefore be placed, during at least the later part of his absence, with Lord Worcester's men. It was Hathway who brought Rankins to Henslowe in 1601.

Haughton served his apprenticeship with an unknown com-pany from November, 1597, until August, 1599, when he with Day joined Henslowe, writing with Dekker and Chettle. He and Day were probably with the younger men of the old Strange-Chamberlain company, who later became Worcester's men.

The list of actual and probable writers for the Chamberlain men, therefore, may stand as—

Known Chamberlain authors.
    Shakespeare.
    Jonson.
Probable Chamberlain authors.
    Drayton. Hathway. Munday. Wilson.
Possible Chamberlain authors.
    Day. Haughton. Porter. Rankins.

The date on which the Drayton-Hathway-Munday-Wilson group deserted Henslowe (August, 1598) is virtually the date of the union of the Queen-Chamberlain forces. Wilson is sup-posed to have been the son of Wilson, the old Queen's company actor and author. Jonson in his various plays seems to place Munday with the Chamberlain company in 1599. *The First Part of Sir John Oldcastle* was printed in 1600 as by William Shakespeare, although written by this group, which hints that they were then working for his company.

In 1599 Wilson returned to Henslowe; Jonson went to the Chapel Children; Shakespeare, Drayton, Hathway, and Munday remained at the Globe. They may have been assisted by the unknown man Rankins. Hathway seems to have gone to Worcester's company in 1601, when he broke with Drayton and Munday. This leaves Shakespeare, Drayton, and Munday with the Chamberlain company during 1601.

Late in 1601 or early in 1602 Jonson ceased his connexion with the Chapel Children. He did some hack-work for Henslowe in September, 1601, and in June, 1602. About this time he must have rejoined the Chamberlain company, for *Sejanus* was published in 1603 as acted by the Chamberlain company.

In May, 1602, Drayton and Munday wrote one play for Henslowe with Dekker and the new men Middleton and Webster. Both must have returned almost immediately to the Globe, as they wrote nothing further for Henslowe's companies. This leaves Drayton, Jonson, and Shakespeare with the Chamberlain company from 1602 on.

The Chamberlain dramatists may then be catalogued as follows:

Autumn, 1598–9. Drayton, Hathway, Jonson, Munday, Rankins (?), Shakespeare, Wilson.

Autumn, 1599–1600. Drayton, Hathway, Munday, Shakespeare, Rankins (?).

Autumn, 1600–1. Drayton, Munday, Shakespeare, Rankins (?).

Autumn, 1601–2. Jonson, Drayton, Shakespeare, Rankins (?).

IX

THE REPERTOIRE OF THE CHAMBERLAIN COMPANY

IN 1598 Meres credited Shakespeare with almost all the plays which had recently been played by the Chamberlain company. While it is now known that Shakespeare had nothing whatever to do with a number of these plays, the list serves very well as a partial catalogue of the Chamberlain repertoire of that date. Other plays belonging to their repertoire at this period, not mentioned by Meres, were afterwards printed as belonging to the company. Some of these plays had belonged to the old Queen's company, others had belonged to the Strange-Chamberlain company while they were with Henslowe, as is known from his Diary.

The Chamberlain repertoire of 1597–1603 might be reconstructed in part as follows:

Plays originally belonging to the Queen's company, the greater number of which came into the Chamberlain repertoire in 1598:

The Troublesome Raign of King John. Published in 1591. Anon. Reprinted 1611 as by W. Sh.

Locrine. Published 1595 as 'newly set forth, overseen and corrected by W. S.' (Originally by Robert Greene.)

The Honourable History of Friar Bacon and Friar Bungay, by Robert Greene, 1594. (Played by the Strange company in February, 1592, by the Queen's men April, 1594.)

Selimus. Printed 1594. Anon. (Written by Robert Greene.)

The True Tragedy of Richard the Third. Printed 1594. Anon. (Presumably the same as *Buckingham*, played by the Sussex company December 30, 1593.)

The Olde Wives Tale, by G. P., 1595.

The History of Two Valiant Knights, Sir Clyomen . . . and Sir Clamydes. Anon. 1599.

Henry VI, Part I. Published as by William Shakespeare, 1623.

Plays originally belonging to the Strange-Derby-Hunsdon-Chamberlain company, which reappear in the Chamberlain repertoire after 1598:

Henry VI. Played as new, March 3, 1592.

Titus Andronicus. Played as new, January 23, 1594. Published anon. 1594.

Fair Em and the Love of William the Conqueror. Printed 'as acted by Lord Strange's men' in 1623. Referred to in Greene's *Farewell to Folly,* c. 1592. Presumably the same as *William the Conqueror,* an old Sussex play of January, 1594. (Henslowe.)

Edward IV. Printed 1600 as acted by Lord Derby's men. Anon.

Henry V. Played as new, November 28, 1595. Printed anon. 1600 and 1602.

Richard II. Entered S. R. August 29, 1597. Printed 1597, anon. (The first quarto.)

Romeo and Juliet. Anon. 1597. (The first quarto.)

Richard III. Anon. 1597. (The first quarto.)

Henry IV. Anon. 1598. (The first quarto.)

Printed plays, new or revised, which appeared in the Chamberlain repertoire after 1598:

Love's Labour's Lost. Printed 1598 as 'newly corrected and augmented' by William Shakespeare.

The Two Gentlemen of Verona; Comedy of Errors; Love's Labour's Won; Midsummer Night's Dream; Merchant of Venice. (All not printed but ascribed to Shakespeare by Meres in 1598.)

Romeo and Juliet, as ' newly corrected, augmented and amended' by William Shakespeare, 1599.

Richard II, as by William Shakespeare, 1598. (This is the second quarto, a mere reprint of the first quarto, above.)

Richard III, as by William Shakespeare, 1598. (A reprint of the first quarto.)

Much Ado About Nothing was 'staid' in S. R. on August 4, 1600.

As You Like It. (Also 'staid' on the same date.)

Every Man in His Humour, by Ben Jonson, 1598.

Every Man out of His Humour, by Ben Jonson, 1599.

Henry IV, Part I, as 'newly corrected' by William Shakespeare, 1599. (This is the second quarto.)

Henry IV, Part II, as by William Shakespeare, 1600.

A Warning for Faire Women. Anon. 1599. (Probably by Ben Jonson.)

Midsummer Night's Dream, as by William Shakespeare, 1600. (An evident revision of an earlier version.)

The First Part of Sir John Oldcastle, as by William Shakespeare, 1600. (Company not mentioned. An Admiral's company play, new in 1599.)

Thomas Lord Cromwell, by W. S., 1602.

Satiromastix. Played by Paules Boys and by the Chamberlain company. Anon. 1601. (Attributed to Shakespeare in *The Return from Parnassus*, 1600.)

Richard III, as 'newly augmented' by William Shakespeare, 1602. (A reprint of the first quarto.)

The Merry Wives of Windsor, as by William Shakespeare, 1602. (This is the short first quarto.)

The Fall of Sejanus, by Ben Jonson, 1603.

Troilus and Cressida, entered S. R. February, 1603, as a Chamberlain play; printed 1609 as by William Shakespeare.

Hamlet. Anon. 1603. (The short first quarto.)

Hamlet, as 'newly imprinted and enlarged to almost as much againe as it was' by William Shakespeare. (No company mentioned.) 1604.

The London Prodigal, as by William Shakespeare, 1605.

Volpone; or The Fox, by Ben Jonson, 1605.

Richard II, 'with new additions, &c.', by William Shakespeare, 1608.

The Merry Devil of Edmonton. Anon. 1608. Attributed to William Shakespeare in S. R. Sept. 9, 1653, also by King Charles's librarian.

King Lear, as by William Shakespeare, 1608.

The Yorkshire Tragedy, as by William Shakespeare, 1608.

Pericles, Prince of Tyre. Also the Birth and Life of his Daughter Mariana, as by Wm. Shakespeare, 1609.

Mucedorus, as 'amplified with new additions'. Anon. 1610. (Attributed to William Shakespeare by King Charles's librarian. The first quarto was printed anon. in 1598, no company mentioned.

Othello, as by William Shakespeare, 1622.

The Tempest; Macbeth; Twelfth Night; Measure for Measure; Julius Caesar; Timon of Athens; Antony and Cleopatra; Cymbeline; As You Like It; The Winter's Tale; Coriolanus; King Henry VI, Parts I, II, III; King John; The Taming of the Shrew; All's Well that Ends Well. (All these were printed in the 1623 Folio as by William Shakespeare.)

The History of King Stephen was entered in the Stationers' Register in June, 1660, as by William Shakespeare.

Duke Humphrey's Tragedy, a copy of which was once owned by Warburton, was ascribed to William Shakespeare. It was entered S. R. on June 29, 1660.

The Birth of Merlin, printed in 1662 as by William Shakespeare and William Rowley.

While many of these plays were not printed until many years after the Chamberlain company had become the King's men, the greater number presumably belong to the period 1597–1603.

After 1597 all Chamberlain plays, except the first *Hamlet* and some of those by Jonson, were credited to William Shakespeare; also the greater number of these plays were either revisions, 'corrected and augmented' by William Shakespeare, or were originals of unknown origin which were afterwards revised 'by William Shakespeare'.

The wholesale assignment of all Chamberlain plays to Shakespeare was begun by Meres in 1598. It was continued by the printers of the various quartos, by the authors of *The Return from Parnassus*, by the editors of the different folios, and by King Charles's librarian.

All of these 'authorities' made mistakes. Meres included in his list many of the old Strange company plays with which Shake-

speare could have had nothing to do, as he was with the Queen's
company when they were written. The printers published as
Shakespeare's *The First Part of Sir John Oldcastle*, which was
written by Drayton, Hathway, Munday, and Wilson for the
Admiral's men. The authors of *The Return from Parnassus* gave
Satiromastix to Shakespeare because it was played by the Chamberlain company, although it was written by Dekker and Marston
for Paules Boys. The editors of the First Folio gathered together
all the most successful plays available which were then in the
Chamberlain repertoire and, regardless of origin, attributed them
to Shakespeare. And the editors of the succeeding folios, as
King Charles's librarian, simply followed precedent and added
to the Shakespeare list all other Chamberlain plays that could
be discovered.

Since almost all Chamberlain plays were thus indiscriminately
attributed to Shakespeare doubts necessarily arise concerning the
authorship of each and every play bearing his name.[1] Hitherto
doubts have existed as to Shakespeare's share in the 'Apocrypha'
plays; the same doubts must now be entertained as to the authorship of the entire Chamberlain repertoire. Did Shakespeare
in truth write *Othello, The Merry Wives of Windsor*, the 'enlarged' *Hamlet*, or were they merely assigned to him because
they were acted by the Chamberlain company? This opens for
consideration the subject of the Chamberlain repertoire, authors,
and sources.

[1] In 1632 Ed. Blount, who owned the sixteen folio plays which had 'never
been printed' until 1623, sold his share in the 'Shakespeare' Folio to Ed.
Allot. The Folio was then republished. That same year Blount brought out

  'Sixe Court Comedies . . . written by the onely Rare Poet of that time,
  the witie comicall facetiously quicke and unparalelled John Lilly.'

And in his Epistle Dedicatorie he states :

  'Apollo gave him a wreath of his owne Bayes, without snatching. The
  Lyre he played on had no borrowed strings.'

This can only mean that other sets of published plays were written by 'snatchers'
and were revisions of work by other men. Blount, if any one, knew that at
least some of the plays newly reprinted as by Shakespeare were 'snatched'
from others.

X
THE CHAMBERLAIN REPERTOIRE: AUTHORS AND SOURCES

WHEN William Shakespeare joined the Chamberlain forces in 1597–8 there came to him and his collaborators, one of whom was Jonson, several plays belonging originally to the Strange-Chamberlain company. Almost all of these plays were revised during or after 1598. It is therefore only in the additions to these plays that work by Shakespeare, Jonson, and their collaborators may be found.

Among these old plays were *Titus Andronicus*, *Henry V*, *Richard II*, *Richard III*, *Romeo and Juliet*, and *Henry IV*, all of which were published anonymously as Strange-Chamberlain plays before Shakespeare joined that company.

The revised versions of these plays appeared: *Romeo and Juliet* as 'newly corrected, augmented and amended' in 1599, *Henry IV, Part I*, as 'newly corrected' in 1600, *Richard III* as 'newly augmented' in 1602, *Richard II* as 'with new additions' in 1608, *Henry V* in 1623, with many additions, and *Titus Andronicus* in 1623, with an added scene and minor changes.

It is to be noted that not one of the Strange-Chamberlain plays produced or printed before that company was joined by the Queen's men in 1598 was attributed in whole or in part to William Shakespeare, while from 1598 onward Shakespeare was credited with each and every Chamberlain revision.

Of these revised plays *Romeo and Juliet* has been examined in 'The Revision of *Hamlet* and of *Romeo and Juliet*'. The others are noticed in the order of their publication, *Henry IV, Part I*, being treated under *Henry V*.

XI

THE REVISION OF 'RICHARD III'

RICHARD III was first printed in 1597, 'as it hath beene lately acted by the Right honorable the Lord Chamberlaine his servants'. It was reprinted in 1598 as by William Shakespeare, and again in 1602 as 'newly augmented' by William Shakespeare. The additions, however, do not appear in any edition until 1623. It is possible that when Jonson began writing a play on Richard III for Henslowe in June, 1602, additions to the Chamberlain play were made in order to refurbish it because of this new rival.

As Shakespeare and his associates obtained a complete copy of this play from the Old Strange-Chamberlain company the additions will be found to be slight. There are some fifty simple reversals, of which so many are found in the revision of *Romeo and Juliet*. The greater number of changes, however, are ordinary substitutions of one word for another, such as *demand* for *request, act* for *deed, liege* for *lord* and *lord* for *liege, noble* for *valiant, ground* for *field, love* for *zeale, flowted* for *scorned, killd* for *slew, bitter* for *cruel,* &c. By making these unnecessary and often stupid alterations the author hoped to make the old play more his own.

There are few additions. Some of the additions seem to be revised versions of original material which was added after the First Quarto was written; others seem to be additions by the person who wrote the augmentations and changes of the 1623 version. One such appears in a speech by Clarence, Act I, scene iv. The original reads:

> *Clarence.* O Brokenbury I have done those things,
> Which now beare evidence against my soule,
> For Edward's sake; and see how he requites me.
> [*Here he prays silently.*]

The augmenter preferred that the prayer should be made vocal. He therefore provided the following commonplace substitute for the dignity of silence :

> O God! if my deepe prayers cannot appease thee,
> But thou wilt be aveng'd on my misdeeds,
> Yet execute thy wrath in me alone:
> O spare my guiltlesse wife, and my poore children.

Another added passage contains new speeches by Rivers, Buckingham, and Richard. The original reads :

> *Buck.* Me seemeth good that, with some little traine,
> Forthwith from Ludlow the yong Prince be fetcht
> Hither to London, to be crownd our King.

'Some little' here means 'some considerable'. It was misunderstood by the reviser, who undertook to explain the phrase by inserting the following lines:

> *Rivers.* Why with some little Traine, my lord of Buckingham?
> *Buc.* Marrie my lord, lest by a multitude,
> The new-heal'd wound of Malice should break out,
> Which could be so much the more dangerous,
> By how much the estate is greene, and yet ungovern'd
> When every Horse beares his commanding Reine
> And may direct his course as please himselfe,
> As well the feare of harme, as harme apparant,
> In mine opinion, ought to be prevented.

This bears the same signs of confused ideation which were so patent in the revision of *Hamlet*. The addition continues :

> *Rich.* I hope the King made peace with all of us,
> And the compact is firme, and true in me.
> *Riv.* And so in me, and so (I think) in all.
> Yet since it is but greene, it should be put
> To no apparant likelihood of breach,
> Which haply by much company might be urg'd :
> *Hast.* And so say I.

Here the original resumes :

> *Glo.* Then be it so; and go we to determine,
> Whom they shalbe that straight shall post to Ludlow, &c.

The inserted lines are not only needless but are confusing : yet they seem to contain an important, almost a mysterious, cerebration. Had many such additions been made to this play Richard III would have become a mad hunchback as incomprehensible as any of the characters in the enlarged *Hamlet*.

While a few such contorted passages were added to the First Quarto text many an important passage was lost by the augmenter. Evidently he did not possess a copy of any of the various printed editions of this play which had appeared from 1597 onward. Apparently he worked from a manuscript stage copy such as would be in the stock box of the Chamberlain company. Otherwise it is difficult to explain the omission of important passages as well as the disarrangement of parts of the text, and many minor mistakes due to a misreading of the original manuscript.

The oaths to be found in the revised version place it before 1603. It may therefore be assumed that this revision was written shortly before the edition of 1602 appeared with its announcement 'newly augmented'. At this period Jonson was not working for the Chamberlain company. The changes found in the revised text must therefore be laid upon the Drayton group, upon William Shakespeare, or upon the unknown man Rankins.

Since *Richard III* was a Strange-Chamberlain play early in 1597, before this company amalgamated with the Queen's, Shakespeare can have had no share whatsoever in the creation of the original play. If he was the author of the additions as found in the 1623 edition he was in all probability the author of the like additions to *Hamlet* and *Romeo and Juliet*.

XII

THE REVISION OF 'RICHARD II'

THE additions to the First Quarto of *Richard II*, which consist chiefly in the deposing scene, were presumably written before the night of February 7, 1601, when a play in which Richard II was deposed was produced at the Globe theatre at the instigation of the Essex faction. It was written therefore while Jonson was with the Chapel Children. This narrows the probable authors of the additions down to Shakespeare and the Drayton-Hathway-Munday-Smith group.

Various passages among the additions are so exactly in the manner of Drayton that they must have been written by him or by some one working with him at that period who could imitate his work in every particular. A single example will suffice:

> Now marke me how I will undoe myselfe:
> I give this heavy weight from off my head,
> And this unwieldie scepter from my hand,
> The pride of kingly sway from out my heart:

(There is thought rhythm in 'head, hand, heart'.)

> With mine owne teares I wash away my balme,
> With mine owne hands I give away my crowne,
> With mine owne tongue denie my sacred state,
> With mine owne breath release all dutious oathes;
> All pompe and majestie I doe forsweare:
> My manors, rents, revenewes, I forgoe;
> My actes, decrees, and statutes I denie:
> God pardon all othes that are broke to mee,
> God keepe all vowes unbroken made to thee.

(The thought rhythm now changes into end-stopped rhymed verse.)

> Make me, that nothing have, with nothing griev'd,
> And thou with all pleas'd, that hast all atchiev'd.
> Long mayst thou live in Richards seat to sit,
> And soone lie Richard in an earthie pit.

God save king Harry, unking'd Richard sayes,
And send him many yeeres of sunne-shine dayes.
What more remains?
North. No more, but that you reade, &c.

In these few lines are exhibited almost all of Drayton's peculiarities. They are end-stopped, often rhymed, are well measured,
&c. Other speeches by Richard breathe the spirit of piety—
peculiar to Drayton, the ' pious poet '.

A passage similar to the above may be found in Drayton's
Robert of Normandy (second edition) :

So many yeares as he hath worne a crowne,
So many yeares as he hath hopde to rise,
So many yeares upon him did I frowne,
So many yeares he lives without his eyes,
So many yeares in dying ere he dies,
So many yeares shut up in prison strong,
Sorrow doth make the shortest time seem long.

As Drayton must have been working for the Chamberlain
company when the additions to *Richard II* were made, and as
none of his collaborators would probably have dared to imitate
his work so closely, it may safely be concluded that he was the
author chiefly responsible for the additions to this play.[1]

Shakespeare did not write the First Quarto of *Richard II*, published in 1597 as a Strange-Chamberlain play, nor did he write
Drayton's additions. Presumably therefore he had no hand whatsoever in this drama. None of the additions seem to have been
made by the unknown muddle-minded author who rewrote *Hamlet, Richard III*, and *Romeo and Juliet*. The additions to this
play are logical and are well and concisely expressed.

[1] It is held by some commentators that this deposing scene was a part of the
original play, but was omitted from the earlier Quarto lest it should offend the
Queen. The probabilities are that there was a deposing scene in the original,
that it was suppressed for a time, and was rewritten and enlarged when the
play was presented before Merrick and the Essex faction in 1601.

XIII

THE REVISION OF 'HENRY IV' AND 'HENRY V'

THE three plays dealing with Henry V are so intimately bound together that they may be treated as one. *Henry IV*, *Parts I* and *II*, originally existed in the form of a single play, which has been preserved in somewhat garbled form in what is known as the 'Deryng manuscript' history of Henry IV. This manuscript play contains the story of Henry V as told in *Henry IV*, *Part I*, together with that part of *Henry IV*, *Part II*, which deals with the death of Henry IV and the coronation of Henry V. The greater part of the present version of *Henry IV*, *Part II*, consists of material added to this old manuscript version.

This original play, the Deryng manuscript, is a consistent whole, as it begins the story when Prince Hal was a roistering young man in disgrace with his father, and shows his change due to the serious internal disturbances caused by Lord Percy and Northumberland, his reconciliation with his father, and his determination, when crowned, to put aside youthful follies and become England's great leader, the Henry V of the play bearing that title.

That the two parts of *Henry IV* were worked up from the Deryng manuscript is evident, not only in the scene wherein Falstaffe quarrels with the Hostess, but in the slavish manner in which the confused arrangement of the scenes of the Deryng manuscript is followed in *Henry IV*, *Parts I* and *II*.

In the Falstaffe-Hostess scene, as it appears in *Henry IV*, *Part II*, the Hostess, with two officers, Fang and Snare, are on the stage: to them enters Falstaffe, who exclaims:

How now? Whose Mare's dead? What's the matter?

Fang. Sir John, I arrest you, at the suit of Mist. Quickly.

Falst. Away Varlets, draw Bardolfe: cut me off the Villaines head: throw the Queane in the channell.

Thus far Dame Quickly has not spoken in the presence of Falstaffe. Why then does he threaten to throw her into the 'channell' (the canal)? This is made clear only in the Deryng manuscript. In that version there is no Fang. The officers remain 'below'. Sir John and Hostess Quickly enter, and the following ensues:

> *Fals.* But thinge; thou wilt not lay a pewter pestle on my shoulders; saie?
>
> *Hostess.* I am undone by thy goeing. Thow art an infinitive thinge upon my score. Thou owest me a hundreth markes almost. And I have borne, and I have borne, and I have borne; fub'd off, and fub'd off, and fub'd off, from this daie to that daie, that it is a shame to be thought on. Unless a woman should be made an asse and a beast to beare every knaves wrong . . .

Falstaffe can no longer suffer her caterwauling and breaks in upon her with:

> Peace kitten; or you shall now in the channell.

Thus Falstaffe's remark is made clear, also the cause of it.

In the Deryng manuscript several scenes were inadvertently shifted from the first part of what became *Henry IV, Part I*, to the latter part of what became *Henry IV, Part II*. One such is the scene wherein the King inquires after Prince Hal and learns that he is 'with Poynes & others his continual followers' at a tavern, upon which the King declares that Hal can but bring the kingdom into evil ways. This scene should come before Hal proved himself worthy and received the commendation of his father, after the battle in which he killed Harry Hotspur. So also the King's first apoplectic stroke, inadvertently joined to the second stroke which causes his death, should come early in the story, for it is during this first stroke that Hal enters and, thinking the King his father is dead, takes away the crown. His father, recovering from the first stroke, reproves Hal for wishing his death. Hal answers this reproof on the field of battle, where, having saved his father's life, he exclaims:

> O God, they did me too much injury
> That ever said I harkened to your death.
> If it weare so: I might have lett alone
> The insulting hand of Dowglas, &c.

It was the first interview between Hal and his father which first caused Hal to change his course of life. In it he states:

> If I doe faine:
> O lett me in my present wildness die:
> And never live to shew the incredulous world
> The noble change that I have purposed.

Surely this should be immediately before he sets forth to battle against his father's enemies, and not after he had conquered, after he had already become a changed man.

When the King has a second stroke and is about to die he has a second interview with Hal, with the changed Hal. It should open with the words:

> Come hither, Harry, and sitt thou by my bed,
> And heare (I think) the very latest counsille
> That ever I shall breathe, &c.

These two interviews, both following apoplectic strokes, were unfortunately linked together in the Deryng manuscript and were so used in *Henry IV, Part II*.

As originally written *Henry IV* must have consisted of but one action dealing with Hal's wildness, his reformation, his father's death, and his assumption of the crown. It was a perfect, logical play, artistically and dramatically arranged. As divided into the two parts, *Henry IV, Parts I* and *II*, it has become two imperfect plays: Part I ending inconclusively with the overthrow of the rebels under Percy, Part II resuming with a new rebellion in which Hal has no part, and ending with his coronation. The second part seems to have been written partly to exploit Falstaffe, but chiefly to exalt 'Lord Westmerland'.

In the two parts of this revision very little new material is to be found in Part I. The scene between the carriers, Gadshill, and the Chamberlain in the tavern yard is new. It is entirely irrelevant and mediocre. The scene of the robbery is so thoroughly entangled that it cannot be unravelled without the aid of the Deryng manuscript. The actions of Hal, Poines, Falstaffe, Harvey, Peto, Bardolph, and Rossile are often puzzling in the enlarged version, as the authors thereof were never clear as to the interrelations of the members of this group and at times substituted one for another, dragging in also Gadshill from the old play *The Famous Victories of Henry V*.

The added idea as to how Bardolph, Falstaffe, &c. caused themselves to appear smeared with blood also came from *The Famous Victories*, where Dericke gained credit for valour as follows:

> I would take a straw, and thrust it into my nose,
> And make my nose bleed, and then I would into the field;
> And when the Captaine saw me, he would say,
> 'Peace, a bloody soldier', and bid me stand aside.

About the time this play was enlarged low Welsh comedy was in vogue. The presence of Glendower in the original version gave opportunity for an addition in which Glendower speaks, and ' the lady ', his daughter, sings, Welsh.

A third addition is one in which Hal and the now omnipresent ' Westmerland ' are made to desert their forces somewhere about the Severn in Gloucestershire in order to bandy words with Falstaffe near Coventry.

The greater additions to the original play necessarily appear in the second part of the revision. To make over what was once the resolution of a play into an entire drama necessitated much new material. This was obtained, first by renewing the rebellion, which is carried on by Northumberland and the Archbishop opposed by Prince John and 'Westmerland', second by exploiting Falstaffe. Falstaffe is given a Page, is made to encounter the Lord Chief Justice of the old *Famous Victories*, Pistol and Doll Teresheet of the old *Chronicle History of Henry V*, and Justice Shallow of *The Merry Wives of Windsor*. To these were added a younger Justice Shallow (Cousin Justice Silence), also a servant to Justice Shallow (Davy), and a series of recruits, Rafe, Mouldy, Simon Shadow, Thomas Wart, Francis Feeble, and Peter Bull-calfe, as well as two sergeants, Phang and Snare.

It has been observed by various commentators that in this second part of *Henry IV* Falstaffe loses quality save in the quarrel scene with Dame Quickly, already mentioned, which was part of the original play. The reason is evident in that all the other scenes are but parts of the padding with which Part II was enlarged.

In the epilogue to Part II the revisers announce that they will continue the story 'with Sir John in it and make you merry with faire Katherine of France'. As the authors of the revised version of *Henry IV* thus lay claim to the revised version of *Henry V* it may be well to examine that play before attempting to discover their identity.

'HENRY V'

The first-mentioned play on this subject was *The Famous Victories of Henry the Fifth*, licensed on May 14, 1594, to Thomas Creede and published by him in 1598 'as it was plaide by the Queenes Majesties Players'. There is evidence that Tarleton acted the Clown in this play as early as 1585; and it is supposedly to this play that Nash refers in *Pierce Pennilesse* in 1592. It was acted at one of Henslowe's theatres on May 14, 1592, when he received for his share but one shilling.

The next play on the same subject is mentioned by Henslowe in the entry: 'The 28 of Novembr, 1595, n.e. R at Harey the V. III£. 6 sh.' This was evidently a Strange-Chamberlain play. It was acted at the Rose until July 15, 1596, when the company went to the Curtain. This was either the Deryng manuscript or the play printed in 1600 by Creede for Thomas Millington and John Busby as *The Chronicle History of Henry the Fifth* 'as it hath bene sundry times playd by the Right honorable the Lord Chamberlaine his servants', authorship not mentioned.

In the meanwhile the enlarged version of *Henry V* had been written. It was entered for publication on August 15, 1600, by Thomas Pavyer as *The Historye of Henry the Fifth* and was 'staid' together with *As You Like It*, *Every Man in His Humour*, and the much older play *Much Ado About Nothing*, from which latter the printing restriction was immediately withdrawn. Creede and Millington were able to print the old *Chronicle History*, although it dealt with the same subject, only because it was an old play and not the version which had been 'staid'. That the enlarged *Henry V* was entered in the Stationers' Register is evident in that Blount and Jaggard in 1623 classed it among those plays 'formerly entered to other men', the other man in this case being Pavyer.

In the year 1623 the enlarged version appeared in the Shakespeare Folio. That this enlargement was made early in 1599 is shown in that the Chorus to Act v mentions Lord Essex's imminent or recent departure to Ireland : ' Were now the General of our gracious Empresse, as in good time he may, from Ireland comming.' Essex departed in April, 1599, and returned in September of the same year.

Although a comparison of corresponding portions of any passage of these two versions of *Henry V* should convince any one that the earlier text was the first written, there are still critics who hold that the text of 1597 is a distortion of the text of 1599. It therefore seems necessary to point out that the earlier text is not distorted, but is a fairly correct transcript of a very fine drama, such as could be produced by no one except a great dramatist. It is not as literary as the longer version, but as a stage play for production on a stage it is superior to the later text.

This point can easily be settled by comparing the two versions of the episode containing the celebrated ' Crispin day ' speech. The First Quarto reads :

> *Enter King.*
>
> *Warwick.* O would we had but ten thousand men
> Now, at this instant, that doth not worke in England.
>   *King.* Whose that, that wishes so, my cousin Warwick ?
> Gods will, I would not loose the honour
> One man would share from me, not for my kingdome.
> No faith, my cousin, wish not one man more.
> Rather proclaime it presently through our camp
> That he that hath no stomacke to this feast
> Let him depart, his passport shall be drawn,
> And crownes for convey put into his purse.
> We would not die in that man's company
> That fears his fellowship to dye with us.
> This day is called the day of Crispin ;
> He that out-lives this day, and comes safe home,
> Shall stand a-tipto when this day is named,

And rowse him at the name of Crispin:
He that outlives this day, and sees old age,
Shall yearly on the vigill feast his friends,
And say, to morrow is S(aint) Crispin's day:
Then shall we in their flowing bowles
Be newly remembred: Harry the King,
Bedford and Exeter, Clarence and Gloster,
Warwicke and Yorke, (*and Salisbury*),
Familiar in their mouths as household wordes.
This story shall the good man tell his son,
And from this day unto the general doome
But we, in it, shall be remembred;
We few, we happy few, we bond of brothers, &c.

The enlarged version reads:

> *Enter Gloster, Bedford, Exeter, Erpingham with all his Hoast.
> Salisbury and Westmerland.*

To stage 'the hoast' of Erpingham must have been difficult.
'Westmerland' does not appear in the Quarto version, but in the
enlarged version is ever and again substituted for the fire-eater
Warwick. The obstreperous 'Westmerland' is given the word
when the King enters.

> *Westmerland.* O that we now had here
> But one ten thousand of those men in England,
> That doe no worke today.
> *King.* What's he that wishes so?
> My cousin Westmerland. No, my faire cousin.

> [*Here follows an addition.*]

> If we are markt to dye, we are enow
> To doe our countrey losse; and if to live,
> The fewer men, the greater share of honour.

> [*The ensuing line is from the original.*]

> Gods will, I pray thee wish not one man more.

> [*Another insertion follows.*]

> By Jove, I am not covetous for Gold,
> Nor care I who doth feed upon my cost:
> It yernes me not, if men my Garments weare;
> Such outward things dwell not in my desires.
> But if it be a sinne to covet Honor,
> I am the most offending Soule alive.

[*A return to the original.*]
No faith, my Couze, wish not a man from England:
Gods peace, I would not loose so great an Honor,
As one man more methinkes would share from me,
For the best hope I have. O, doe not wish one more.

The additions are redundant. The original is again followed.

Rather proclaime it (Westmerland) through my Hoast,
That he which hath no stomack to this fight
Let him depart, his Passport shall be made,
And crownes . . ., &c.

Though somewhat altered this version follows the original until:

Then shall our names,
Familiar in his mouth as household words,
Harry the King, Bedford and Exeter,
Warwick and Talbot, Salisbury and Gloucester,
Be in their flowing cups freshly remembred.

Here the reviser forgot his 'Westmerland' and reverted to the original 'Warwick,' with whom he coupled 'Talbot' in place of Yorke. Talbot is not elsewhere mentioned in the entire play.

These few changes and mistakes demonstrate not only that the Folio *Henry V* was augmented from the earlier Quarto version, but that it was revised by the same author who truckled to Lord 'Westmerland' in the two-part version of *Henry IV*.

The dates of these three revisions, dealing with the history of Henry V, can be ascertained to a nicety. Late in 1598 Meres mentions one *Henry IV*. The second *Henry IV* must therefore have been written very late in 1598, and *Henry V* early in 1599. During this period Ben Jonson and Shakespeare were chief playwrights to the Chamberlain company. To one or the other, or both, these revisions may therefore be assigned. From internal evidence alone the greater number of additions to *Henry IV*, *Part II*, and to *Henry V* may be attributed to Jonson. The attempts at humour in *Every Man in His Humour* closely parallel the additions to *Henry IV*, *Part II*. The names of Jonson's characters during his 'humorous' period—Downright, Wellbred, Roger Formal, and Justice Clement (an old merry magistrate)—

correspond in construction and intention with Mouldie, Shadow, Bullcalfe, Phang, Snare, and Justice Silence, characters which appear only in the additions to *Henry IV, Part II.*

The following is a monologue from *Every Man in His Humour* by Cob the water-carrier:

> *Cob.* What, Tib, shew this up to the Captaine. Oh, an' my house were the Brazen-head now! faith it would e'en speak 'Mo fools yet'. You should ha' some now would take this Mr. Matthew to be a gentleman, at the least, his father was an honest man, a worshipful fishmonger, and so forth; and now does he creep, and wriggle into acquaintance with all the brave gallants about town such as my guest is: O, my guest is a fine man, and they flout him invincibly. . . . And here's the jest he is in love with my masters sister, Mrs. Bridget, and calls her mistress: and there he will sit you a whole afternoon sometimes, reading o' these same abominable, vile (a pox on em, I cannot abide them!) rascally verses, Poyetry, Poyetry; and speaking of interludes; 'twill make a man burst to hear him. And the wenches, they do so geer, and ti-hi him . . . well, should they do so much to me, I'd forswear them all, by the foot of Pharaoh. There's an oath! . . . By St. George, the foot of Pharaoh, the body of me, as I am a gentleman and a soldier: such dainty oaths! &c.

Compare this 'patter' with the speech by Falstaffe addressed to his Page:

> *John.* Men of all sorts take a pride to gird at me: the braine of this foolish compounded clay-man is not able to invent anything that intends to laughter, more then I invent, or is invented on me. I am not only witty in my selfe, but the cause that wit is in other men. I do here walk before thee, [*his Page*] like a sow that hath overwhelm'd all her litter but one. If the Prince put thee into my service for any other reason then to sett me off . . . the juvenall, the Prince your master, whose chin is not yet fledge, I will sooner have a beard grow in the palme of my hand, then he shal get one off his cheek, and yet he will not sticke to say his face is a face royal, God may finish it when he will, tis not a haire amisse yet, he may keepe it still at a face royall, for a barber shall never earne sixpence out of it, &c.

Both of these extracts are 'patter'; neither contains a hint of true comedy. Both are truly Jonsonian.

Jonson's verse is usually plain prose stuffed full of classical allusions and cast in the form of blank verse. In it, though always pompous, he usually treads a measure even heavier than when he is labouring to be nimble witted in prose 'patter'. Dekker called him a treader of mortar. As well as being laboured his verse lacks the leaven of imagination.

Unfortunately in Jonson's published works there is nothing written between 1597 and 1600 which deals with history or war. However, the prologue to *Henry IV, Part II* by Rumour may be compared with the prologue to *Poetaster* by Envy:

> *Envy*. Light, I salute thee, but with wounded nerves,
> Wishing thy golden Spleandour pitchy darkness.
> What's here! the arraignement? I; this, this is it,
> That our sunk eyes have wak'd for all this while:
> Here will be subject for my snakes and me.
> Cling to my neck and wrists, my loving wormes,
> And cast you round in soft and amorous folds,
> Till I do bid uncurl; then break your knots,
> Shoot out yourselves at length, as your forc'd stings
> Would hide themselves within his malic'd sides
> To whom I shall apply you. Stay! the shine
> Of this assembly here offends my sight; &c.

He then addressed the audience:

> Wonder not, if I stare; these fifteen weeks
> (So long as since the plot was but an embrion)
> Have I, with burning lights mix'd vigilant thoughts
> In expectation of this hated play.

The first portion is a fair example of Jonson's figurative prose; the latter portion is plain prose which should never have been cast into verse form. The ensuing example is from *Henry IV, Part II*:

> *Rumour*. Open your eares; for which of you will stop
> The vent of hearing, when lowd Rumor speaks?
> I, from the orient to the drooping west
> (Making the wind my paste-horse) still unfold
> The acts commenced on this ball of earth.
> Upon my tongues continuall slanders ride,
> The which in every language I pronounce,
> Stuffing the eares of men with false reports, &c.

This again is prose in verse form. It is all so intellectual, so obvious, so Jonsonian.

Internal evidence of this sort is seldom satisfying. However, in the present case there is as well external evidence of Jonson's connexion with the Prince Hal series. In Dekker's *Satiromastix* one of Jonson's followers (Asinius Bubo) magnifies Jonson with 'Answere, as God judge me, Ningle; for thy wit thou mayest answer any Justice of peace in England I warrant'. And Ningle Jonson replies, 'What you prettie Diminitive roague, we must have false fiers to amase these spangle babies, these heires of Mr. Justice Shallow'. Thus Dekker hints of Jonson's share in *Henry IV, Part II.*

More direct evidence is given by Jonson himself in *Every Man out of His Humour* (1599), where Fastidius Brisk, speaking of Sogliardo, a raw youth from the country, says, ' This is a kinsman to Justice Silence'. For Jonson thus gratuitously to drag into one of his plays a statement that one of his characters is closely related to a character in another play rather proclaims that the second character was also one of his creations, for Jonson never went out of his way to praise the work of another dramatist. The reference, be it noted, is to Silence, not to Shallow, whom Jonson did not create.[1]

While much of the three *Henry V* plays must be assigned to Jonson there are evident signs of revision, such as the great number of reversed and patched lines in *Henry V*, which must rather be attributed to the person who rewrote *Romeo and Juliet*, *Hamlet*, &c. They are in the same manner. It is impossible to believe that Jonson resorted to such niggling, especially if the straightforward additions to *The Spanish Tragedy* are of his making. These many minor changes presumably belong to Shakespeare.

---

[1] Lord Westmorland was the leader of the Papist rebels who were intriguing against England during the later part of Queen Elizabeth's reign. After the rebellion of 1569 he made his escape to France and died on the Continent in November, 1601. The author of the ' Westmerland' additions was therefore an ardent Papist. Such in 1598-9 was Ben Jonson, who became a convert to the Roman Church while in prison in 1597, after having killed Gabriel Spenser.

The Welsh Additions.

There are three stages evident in the Welsh additions to the *Henry IV–V* plays. In *Henry IV*, *Part I*, no Welsh or Welsh-English lines appear. However, there are stage directions such as 'The Lady speaks in Welsh'. In *Henry IV*, *Part II*, not even this slight attempt to foist into the series a bit of popular Welsh comedy was attempted. In *Henry V* not only were Flewellen's original lines greatly developed, but new episodes were added in order to exploit his peculiarities. In these a third hand is evident.[1]

In *Satiromastix* Captain Tucca, speaking to Horace (Jonson), remarks: 'and Demetrius (Dekker) shall write a scene or two in one of thy strong garlicke comedies: and thou shalt take the guilt of conscience for't, and sweare tis thine owne, lad, tis thine owne.' This seems to refer to the leek-eating scene in *Henry V*. Low comedy in dialect was one of the specialties for which the 'play dresser' Dekker was in constant demand.

[1] It is the second part of *Henry IV* which is so 'rich in references to the Stratford district', where Shakespeare and Jonson were wont to 'gather humours'.

XIV

FURTHER PLAYS REVISED FOR THE CHAMBERLAIN COMPANY

BESIDE the plays which originally belonged to the Strange-Chamberlain company, and which were revised by William Shakespeare and his co-workers, there is a considerable number of plays, the sources of some of which are unknown, which also were revised for that company. Among these those of which the original and a revised version still exist are:

Henry VI, Part II. Printed as *The Contention between . . . Lancaster and Yorke, &c.* Anon. 1594; revised version printed as by William Shakespeare in 1623.

Henry VI, Part III. Printed as *The True Tragedy of Richard Duke of Yorke.* Anon. 1595; revised version as by William Shakespeare, 1623.

Mucedorus. Printed anon. 1598; revised version anon. 1610.

Sir John Oldcastle. Anon. 1600; revised version as by William Shakespeare also in 1600.

The Merry Wives of Windsor. Printed as by William Shakespeare in 1602; revised version also as by William Shakespeare in 1623.

Hamlet. Printed anon. in 1603; revised version as by William Shakespeare in 1604.

King Lear. Printed as by William Shakespeare in 1608; revised version ditto in 1623.

Troilus and Cressida. Printed as by William Shakespeare in 1609; revised version ditto in 1623.

Othello. Printed as by William Shakespeare in 1622; revised version ditto in 1623.

King John. Printed as *The Troublesome Raign of King John.* Anon. in 1591; revised version as by William Shakespeare in 1623.

Further plays were revised for the Chamberlain company, such as *Love's Labour's Lost* and *A Midsommer night's Dreame.* Of these the originals have never been discovered. *Hamlet* and *Romeo and Juliet* have been considered at length in 'The Revision of *Hamlet* and of *Romeo and Juliet*'. Some of the remaining plays will be examined in the order of publication.

XV

REVISION OF 'HENRY VI', PARTS II AND III

ALTHOUGH the Folio versions of these plays were not printed until many years after the shorter Quarto editions had appeared, a careful comparison of the texts of the rival versions at once establishes the fact that stage copies of the Folio versions existed before the Quartos were written, and that these stage copies were used by the author of the Quarto versions.

In order to make this point clear corresponding passages from the different versions follow. The lines are reciprocally numbered.

Folio edition of *Henry VI, Part II*. (Suffolk's last interview with the Queen, page 136 of the Folio.)

1   *Queen.* Fye Coward woman, and soft harted wretch,
2 Hast thou not spirit to curse thine enemy?
3   *Suf.* A plague upon them : wherefore should I cursse them?
4 Would curses kill, as doth the Mandrakes grone,
5 I would invent as bitter searching termes,
6 As curst, as harsh, and horrible to heare ;
7 Deliver'd strongly through my fixed teeth,
8 With full as many signes of deadly hate,
9 As leane-fac'd envy in her loathsome cave.
10 My tongue should stumble in mine earnest words, &c.
11   *Qu.* Enough sweet Suffolke, thou torment'st thy selfe,
12 And these dread curses like the Sunne 'gainst glasse,
13 Or like an over-charged Gun, recoile,
14 And turnes the force of them upon thy selfe.
15   *Suf.* You bad me ban, and will you bid me leave?
16 Now by the ground that I am banish'd from,
17 Well could I curse away a Winters night,
18 Though standing naked on a Mountaine top,

19 Where byting cold would never let grasse grow,
20 And thinke it but a minute spent in sport.
21   *Qu.* Oh, let me intreat thee cease, give me thy hand,
22 That I may dew it with my mournfull teares:
23 Nor let the raine of heaven wet this place,
24 To wash away my wofull Monuments.
25 Oh, could this kisse be printed in thy hand,
26 That thou might'st thinke upon these by the Seale,
27 Through whom a thousand sighes are breath'd for thee.
28 So get thee gone, that I may know my greefe,
29 'Tis but surmiz'd, whiles thou art standing by,
30 As one that surfets, thinking on a want:
31 I will repeale thee, or be well assur'd,
32 Adventure to be banished my selfe: &c.

[*Lord Vaux enters, announces the Cardinal's death, and departs.*]

33   *Qu.* Aye me! What is this World? What newes are these?
34 But wherefore greeve I at an houres poore losse,
35 Omitting Suffolkes exile, my soules Treasure?
36 Why onely Suffolke mourne I not for thee?
37 And with the Southerne clouds, contend in teares?
38 Theirs for the earths encrease, mine for my sorrowes.
39 Now get thee hence, the King thou know'st is coming.
40 If thou be found by me, thou art but dead.
41   *Suf.* If I depart from thee, I cannot live,
42 And in thy sight to dye, what were it else,
43 But like a pleasant slumber in thy lap?
44 Heere could I breath my soule into the ayre,
45 As milde and gentle as the Cradle-babe,
46 Dying with mothers dugge between it's lips.
47 Where from thy sight, I should be raging mad,
48 And cry out for thee to close up mine eyes:
49 To have thee with thy lippes to stop my mouth,
50 So should'st thou eyther turne my flying soule,
51 Or I should breathe it so into thy body,

52   And then it liv'd in sweete Elizium.
53   To dye by thee, were but to dye in jest,
54   From thee to dye, were torture more then death :
55   Oh let me stay, befall what may befall.
56   *Queen.* Away : Though parting be a fretful corosive,
57   It is applyed to a deathfull wound.
58   To France sweet Suffolke : Let me heare from thee :
59   For wheresoere thou art in this worlds Globe,
60   Ile have an *Iris* that shall finde thee out.
61   *Suf.* I go.
62   *Qu.* And take my heart with thee.
63   *Suf.* A Iewel lockt into the wofulst Caske,
64   That ever did containe a thing of worth,
65   Even as a splitted Barke, so sunder we :
66   This way fall I to death.
67   *Qu.* This way for me.   *Exeunt.*

The Quarto version of *Henry VI, Part II,* printed as *The First Part of the Contention,* &c. Pages 40 and 41 of the 1594 edition.

1–2   *Q.* Fie womanish man, canst thou not curse thy enemies ?
3   *Suf.* A plague upon them, wherefore should I curse them ?
4   Could curses kill as do the Mandrakes groanes,
5   I would invent as many bitter termes
6
7   Delivered strongly through my fixed teeth,
8   With twice so many signes of deadly hate,
9   As leave fast envy in her loathsome cave,
10   My toong should stumble in mine earnest words, &c.
11   *Qu.* Inough sweete Suffolke, thou torments thy selfe.

15   *Suff.* You bad me ban, and will you bid me sease ?
16   Now by this ground that I am banisht from,
17   Well could I curse away a winters night,
18   And standing naked on a mountaine top,
19   Where byting cold would never let grasse grow,
20   And thinke it but a minute spent in sport.

21–58 *Queene*. No more. Sweete Suffolke hie thee hence to France
59 Or live where thou wilt within this worldes globe,
60 Ile have an Irish that shall finde thee out,
31 And long thou shalt not staie, but ile have thee repelde,
31–32 Or venture to be banished my selfe.

25 Oh let this kisse be printed in thy hand,
26 That when thou seest it, thou maist thinke on me.

28 Away, I say, that I may feel my griefe,
29 For it is nothing whilst thou standest here.

[*Lord Vaux enters and announces the death of the Cardinal, and departs.*]

33 *Qu*. Oh what is worldly pompe, all men must die,
34 And woe am I for Bewfords heavie ende,
34–35 But why mourne I for him, whilst thou art here?
58–39 Sweete Suffolke hie thee hence to France,
39–40 For if the King do come, thou sure must die.
41–42 *Suff*. And if I go I cannot live: but here, to die,
42–43 What were it else, but like a pleasant slumber
43 In thy lap?
44 Here could I, could I, breath my soule into the aire,
45 As milde and gentle as the new borne babe,
46 That dies with mothers dugge betweene his lips,
47 Where from thy sight I should be raging madde,
48 And call for thee to close mine eyes,
51–49–50 Or with thy lips to stop my dying soule,
51 That I might breathe it so into thy bodie,
52 And then it liv'd in sweete Elyzam,
53 By thee to die, were but to die in jeast,
54 From thee to die, were torment more then death,
55 O let me staie, befall, what may befall.
* *Qu*. O mightst thou staie with safetie of thy life,
* Then shouldst thou staie, but heavens deny it,
* And therefore go, but hope ere long to be repelde.
61 *Suff*. I goe.

62   *Qu.* And take my heart with thee.
            She kisses him.

63   *Suff.* A jewell lockt into the woefulst caske,
64   That ever yet containde a thing of woorth,
65   Thus like a splitted barke so sunder we.
66   This way fall I to deathe.   *Exet Suffolke.*
67   *Queene.* This way for me.   *Exet Queene.*

Were there any doubt as to the priority of these two versions
the single passage wherein Suffolke likened himselfe to a cradle-
babe crying out in order that its mother (the Queen) should
with her lips stop his mouth, thus either turning his 'flying
soule' from its contemplated journey, or while being kissed
breathing his soul into his mother's body, should settle all doubts.
The reviser of this passage, having lost one complete line (50)
and therewith the idea that the 'flying' soul should be turned,
perforce changed 'flying' into 'dying' in order to make some
kind of sense. The original of this passage is perfectly clear in
that the mother, placing her lips to the child's mouth, should
either recall the 'flying' soul or allow it to be breathed into
her body. The revision is not clear, for there is no mention of
the child's mouth, nor any explanation of how the mother with
her lips might stop a 'dying' soul. Evidently the 'dying soule'
of the Quarto is a garbled revision of the 'flying soule' idea of
the Folio.

There is a simple reversal in line 53. This is but one of many
dozen to be found in the entire play. The passage, lines 58–60,
has been transferred from its proper place at the end of the scene,
as in the Folio. For where should a farewell passage appear but
at the end of an episode? It is placed, most stupidly, after line 20,
evidently to replace the lost passage, lines 21–4, which began
with an entreaty by the Queen. As this insertion connected better
with lines 31–2 of the original text it was advanced. Thus the
passage 25–9 became the conclusion of the Queen's speech.

The line 58, 'To France sweet Suffolke', was again used at
line 39, when the Queen suggests that Suffolke must leave her

lest the King should come. So also the idea that she would have him recalled (line 31) was by the reviser used at both lines 31 and 61, where it, with the assistance of three new lines, filled the space voided when lines 58-60 were transferred.

From passage 25-9 a line and a half were lost, so that instead of the Queen's wish that the kiss printed in his hand were a seal which each time he looked upon it would remind him of her tears breathed through with a thousand sighs, the reviser's Queen merely wishes to place the kiss in his hand, that when he sees it, the kiss, he may think of her. Similar misplaced passages occur throughout the entire play.

Line 1 of the Quarto version is a combination of parts of lines 1 and 2 of the original. So also lines 34 and 35 were combined into one line. From lines 39-40 a new line resulted, which consists of the end of the first line and the beginning of the second. This same process gave rise to the line 'With thy lips to stop my dying soule'. Such lines, formed from parts of two original lines, are very common in the Quarto revision. A great number of half-lines were entirely lost.

In the above Quarto passages there are grammatical errors in lines 11 and 65. Similar mistakes occur throughout the entire revision, especially the use of a singular verb with a plural subject.

The use of the word 'Exet' instead of 'Exit' displays the author's ignorance of Latin, which is evident in his abuse of every Latin word and every classical allusion throughout the entire play. 'Exet' is consistently used in place of 'Exit' and 'Exeunt', 'Ceres' is written as 'Cearies', 'Ditis' as 'Dytas', 'Cocytus' as 'Sosetus', and the Italian 'Bonna terra mala gens' of the original becomes 'bona, terra' only.

Despite these signs of illiterate origin this old version of *Henry VI, Part II* has usually been attributed to Robert Greene, who was M.A. of both Oxford and Cambridge!

'HENRY VI', PART III

The third part of *Henry VI* continues the history of the Lancastrian wars. That the Quarto version of this play was rewritten from a stage copy of the Folio version is evident in that the same method was pursued as in the revision of Part II. A comparison of the Folio and Quarto versions of such a scene as that wherein King Edward has his first interview with Lady Grey, Richard and Clarence being present, will at once disclose that the Quarto was rewritten from the Folio version.

In the Folio version of this scene Richard and Clarence hear all that passes between the King and the Lady until after she has told how many children she has. The King then requests his brothers to go aside. From this point on Richard and Clarence pass remarks on the actions of the King and Lady Grey, but obviously no longer overhear their conversation.

In the Quarto the various parts of this episode have been shifted, so that parts which originally came before the King's request for privacy appear after he has voiced his request. The result is that Richard and Clarence are made to hear many remarks made by the King and Lady Grey after they have been requested to withdraw. This blunder came about through the fact that in the original the King's request stood between two parts, both of which treat of how the widow may regain her lands. The reviser joined these two 'land' passages together, followed them by Richard's remark, also concerning lands, and placed the entire group after the King's request. It is evident that the King's observation, 'Twere pittie they [her children] should lose their father's lands', should precede his desire for a private interview with the Lady wherein he discloses how those lands may be obtained. And Richard's aside, 'then Ile warrant you all your lands', &c., necessarily should come before he was sent out of the range of their conversation.

That this Part III was rewritten by the same person who rewrote Part II is evident in that the same method was pursued throughout. Direct evidence of this may be gathered by comparing the original, the revised version, and the secondary source of the revision of Richard's account of the death of Warwicke's brother Montague. The original, p. 155 in the Folio, reads :

> *Rich.* Ah Warwicke, why hast ÿ withdrawn thyselfe ?
> Thy brother's blood the thirsty earth hath drunk,
> Broach'd with the steely point of Cliffords Launce :
> And in the very pangs of death, he cryde,
> Like to a dismall clangor heard from farre,
> Warwicke revenge; Brother, revenge my death,
> So underneath the belly of their steeds,
> That stain'd their fetlocks in his smoaking blood,
> The noble Gentleman gave up the ghost.

The Quarto revision reads :

> *Rich.* Ah Warwike, why haste thou with drawne thyselfe ?
> Thy noble father in the thickest thronges,
> Cride still for Warwike his thrise valiant son,
> Untill with thousand swords he was beset,
> And manie wounds made in his aged brest,
> And as he tottring sate upon his steede,
> He waft his hand to me and cride aloud :
> Richard, commend me to my valiant sonne,
> And still he cride Warwike revenge my death
> And with those words he tumbled off his horse,
> And so the noble Salsbury gave up the ghost.

The first and last lines as well as a general underneath-a-horse idea came from the Folio original. Old Salisbury, Warwick's father, whom the reviser confused with Montague, Warwick's brother, does not figure in this play. Presumably his fighting days were over when he was last seen at the end of *Henry VI, Part II.* It was, however, from Salisbury's last appearance in Part II that the reviser borrowed material wherewith to concoct the above garbled story. It was Richard who reported concerning Salisbury at that time. The reviser's version of that recital reads :

> *Rich.* My lord, I saw him in the thickest throng,
> Charging his Lance with his old weary armes,
> And thrise I saw him, beaten from his horse,

And thrise this hand did set him up againe,
And still he fought with courage gainst his foes
The boldest spirited man that ere mine eyes beheld.

The Folio original reads:

Three times today I holpe him to his horse,
Three times bestrid him, &c.

The reviser of the present *Henry VI, Part III*, meeting once again with a person who was under horses' feet, jumped to the conclusion that it was again old Salisbury. Perchance he thought Salisbury went through life tumbling from horses, while Richard followed ever after trying to set Humpty Dumpty up again.

While the reviser of Part III makes all the usual mistakes to be found in the revision of Part II, his education has advanced sufficiently to enable him to write 'Exit' and 'Exeunt'. He has also acquired the words 'Omnes' and 'Solus'.

Hitherto it has been held that the longer Folio versions of these two *Henry VI* plays were enlarged from the Quarto versions. It is possible that a brilliant playwright could take a poor play and rewrite it into a good one; but no one not possessed of a jigsaw-puzzle mind could have carefully fitted into old plays such as these the hundreds of odd words, half-lines, lines, and passages found only in the Folio editions. No man of genius ever could or ever will waste his energies rewriting a play in this manner. Such work is for literary hacks of such calibre as he who enlarged *Hamlet*. On the other hand, any half-intelligent hanger-on of the theatre could easily patch together incorrect versions similar to the Quarto editions of these plays, provided he had even an incomplete copy of the original of the Folio versions.

HISTORY OF 'HENRY VI', PARTS II AND III

Having established the priority of the stage versions of the Folio texts of the two *Henry VI* plays, it is now possible to trace their history and ownership.

Three actors' names appear in the text of the third part of *Henry VI*: Sinklo, Spencer, and Humphrey (Jeffes); and a single actor's name, Holland (John), appears in Part II. Holland's name occurs again in the platt of *Seven Deadly Sins*, acted by the combined Queen's-Chamberlain's forces while they were at the Curtain. He must have belonged to either the one or the other of these companies when he acted in *Henry VI, Part II*.

Sinklo, who played in Part III, also played in *Seven Deadly Sins*. These two actors presumably belonged to the same company, which company must have included as well the two Jeffes and Spencer.

The two Jeffes and Spencer both figure in Henslowe's Diary. Henslowe first mentions them on October 11, 1597:

> A Juste acownt of all suche money as I have layd out for my lord Admeralles players bygynyng the xi of October whose names ar as foloweth: borne. gabrell. shaw. Jonnes. dowten. Jube. towne. singer. & the ij geffes.

Spencer is herein referred to by his Christian name (Gabrell) only, and both Spencer and the two Jeffes were then shareholders in the Admiral's company. This account dates from before the Admiral's men were joined by Lord Pembroke's men on the 21st of the same month. While Spencer and the Jeffes were shareholders in 1597 they seem to have had a slightly different standing from that of the other members of the company, as they evidently had a special claim on the gallery receipts. The company started to buy out their gallery rights on the 21st of January, 1598, but relinquished the idea on the 4th of March; and the two Jeffes and Spencer continued receiving their gallery takings until the end of the season in July. Spencer was then killed by Ben Jonson in September; and thereafter the Jeffes became regular members of the company.

Evidently these men came to the Admiral's company before October 11, 1597, under special conditions. It would seem that they had originally been members of the Strange-Chamberlain company together with Sinklo and Holland, and had joined the Admiral's men in October, 1596, when the Strange-Chamberlain forces deserted Henslowe's Rose for the Curtain. This suggests that the two *Henry VI* plays originally belonged to the Strange-Chamberlain company while they were still at the Rose. If so, some record of them should appear in Henslowe's Diary.

The third part of *Henry VI* must have been written shortly before Greene wrote his *Groatsworth of Wit* in October, 1592, in which he accuses Shakespeare of having stolen this play. Henslowe records, on March 3, 1592, a new play entitled *Harey VI*. Of the three parts of the present series it is only the third part which could appropriately be called simply *Harey VI*. The short Quarto version was printed in 1595 as a Pembroke play. Obviously *Henry VI, Part III* was a Strange-Chamberlain play, acted for the first time on March 3, 1592, appropriated almost immediately for the Pembroke company by some one, whom Greene supposed was Shakespeare, and acted before October, 1592, by that company in the garbled form printed in the 1595 Quarto.

Incidentally this positively places William Shakespeare with the Pembroke company in 1592. Greene was then writing for the Henslowe forces. The revision may or may not have been by Shakespeare; nevertheless the fact that it was written for the Pembroke company by one of their members, whom Greene supposed was Shakespeare, places him in that company.

Since the third part of *Henry VI* was a Strange company play, its earlier companion must also have belonged to that company, and it also should appear in Henslowe's Diary if it were played while the Strange men were at his theatre. The first performance of this play could not have been recorded in the diary, as the record does not begin until February 19, 1592. However, on November 28, 1594, Henslowe records the revival of a play which in his peculiar manner he spells 'Warlamchester'. This evidently was intended for 'War Lancester', which wars constitute the subject-matter of the second part of *Henry VI*.

These two plays did not remain in the Chamberlain repertoire after the company left Henslowe. Not only does Meres fail to mention them in 1598, but Jonson in the prologue to *Every Man in His Humour*, played by the Chamberlain company in 1598, speaks scathingly of them, which he would never have done had they then belonged to the company with which he was for the time connected. These plays, therefore, went either to the Admiral's men with Spencer and the Jeffes, or to Lord Worcester's company with Beeston, Duke, and Pallant.

As the correct versions of *Henry VI, Parts II* and *III*, belonged to the Strange-Chamberlain company until 1596 and to some rival company thereafter, Shakespeare could have had no connexion with these plays beyond, as Greene accuses, rewriting them into the garbled Quarto versions of 1594 and 1595 for the Pembroke company, which versions were ascribed to him by the publishers when they were reprinted in 1619.

There is no record of *Henry VI, Part I*, in Henslowe's Diary. This seems to have belonged to another company, possibly the Queen's, the two later plays being entirely independent of Part I.

XVI

THE REVISION OF 'THE MERRY WIVES OF WINDSOR'

THE first known version of this play is the Quarto edition of
1602, the title-page of which reads :

> A most pleasaunt and excellent conceited comedie, of Syr John
> Falstaffe and the merie Wives of Windsor. Entermixed with sun-
> drie variable and pleasing humors, of Syr Hugh the Welch knight,
> Justice Shallow, and his wise cousin M. Slender. With the swag-
> gering vaine of Ancient Pistole, and Corporall Nym. By William
> Shakespeare. As it hath bene divers times Acted by the right
> Honorable My Lord Chamberlaines servants. Both before her
> Majestie, and elsewhere, &c.

This version was reprinted in 1619.

There are at least two deceptive statements in this title-page.
This Quarto version was not the one played before her Majesty,
as it does not contain the material found in the Folio version,
which evidently was written for the Court performance. Nor
does this version contain the new material dealing with Shallow
and Slender, which appears only in the Folio edition. However,
the above title discloses the fact that the Folio version was written
before this 1602 Quarto was published.

The Folio version was printed in 1623 and again independently
as a Quarto in 1630. Both of these editions were based on an
earlier Quarto or manuscript. This is evident in that in the 1630
Quarto scenes iv and v of Act III both bear the heading ' Scoena
Quarta '. These two scenes as printed are in wrong order, as the
second ' Scoena Quarta ' should precede the first. Hence they
must have been copied from an earlier play or manuscript similarly
numbered in which these scenes were accidentally misplaced.
In the Folio they are also in wrong order, although the later
scene has been headed ' Quinta '.

These two scenes appear in correct sequence in the short

Quarto of 1602, therefore it cannot be closely related to either of these later editions.

While the larger, Folio, version of this play was written shortly before 1602, an earlier version, it is now agreed by all critics, must have existed about 1593. This is established by the reference to the German cozener who came to Court, a 'cosen garmoble'. The German cousin in question was Count Mumplegart, who was at Windsor in 1592. The play on Mumple-gart in 'gar-moble' is evident. This hit at Mumplegart does not appear in the later versions.

Fleay suggested that this early version appears in Henslowe's Diary as *The Jealous Comedy*, performed by Lord Strange's men as new on January 5, 1593. It was acted but once. Henslowe's takings show that there was a good house. Yet the play was never revived. If this were the original of *The Merry Wives of Windsor* it may have been suppressed because of the reference to the noble count.

Among the plays adapted for the German stage from English originals *The Adultress*, containing the plot of *The Merry Wives*, was brought out in 1594 by Duke Julius of Brunswick (see Cohn). As Falstaffe does not appear in this German version it may be assumed that this early comedy (*The Jealous Comedy* (?)) was rewritten, incorporating Falstaffe at some later period. The Falstaffe business is not a necessary part of Ford's jealousy, and rather interferes with the story of the rivalry between the Doctor, the Parson, and Fenton for the hand of Anne Page. Therefore it may be assumed that some time prior to the appearance of the 1602 Quarto *The Jealous Comedy* was rewritten into a version, now lost, which combined the old elements of the *Jealous Comedy* with the new matter centred about Falstaffe.

From internal evidence it is clear that the first Quarto version of 1602 and the Folio version of 1623 are not closely related. Each lacks elements found in the other. The Quarto especially lacks all hint of the greater number of speeches belonging to Shallow and Slender; while the Folio lacks a number of important and necessary lines found only in the Quarto.

A comparison of these two versions forces the conclusion that the First Quarto is a garbled, stolen revision of a lost original; while the Folio version is an enlarged revision of an incomplete copy of the same lost original. The material contained in the lost original may be largely reconstituted by taking from the Folio all material also found in the Quarto, though in garbled form, and adding thereto all material found only in the Quarto.

All material found only in the Folio, of which no hint appears in the Quarto, presumably was added to the lost original when it was rewritten for the Chamberlain company, c. 1602. These additions differ considerably from the remaining parts of the play both in style and feeling. They seem to be of a later date. These include the greater number of the speeches falsely announced by the editor of the Quarto as ' Sundrie Variable and pleasing humors of Syr Hugh the Welch knight, Justice Shallow, and his wise cousin M. Slender', as well as many additions to the parts of Page, Ford, and their wives. The remaining characters, Falstaffe, Pistol, Bardolfe, Nym, the Host, Nurse Quickly, and the Doctor, remain virtually as in the lost original. Falstaffe, however, is given a Page, the same Page who first appears in *Henry VI, Part II.*

The First Quarto was printed as ' by William Shakespeare '. This may have been a false statement. However, in the 1619 reprint appear the words ' written by W. Shakespeare '. There are many peculiarities found in this first version which are identical with those of the First Quartos of *Henry VI, Parts I* and *II.* Illiterate spelling abounds; and wherever the author is not following the original manuscript he often drops into grammatical errors, such as—

> I rather take them to be paltry lying knaves,
> Such as rather speakes of envie,
> Then of any certaine they have
> Of anything. And for the knight, perhaps
> He hath spoke merrily, as the fashion of fat men are. &c.
>   *Ford and the Host talkes.*

But more characteristic than these mistakes through ignorance are the reversals and transpositions, which are all in the

manner of the earlier plays. Parts of dialogue between Anne
Page and Slender which belong in the latter part of the play
appear inserted into their conversation in the first scene of Act I.
Anne Page's parts are on the whole sadly confused. This possibly was due to the fact that it was always difficult for a reporter to follow girl parts, which were spoken by boys. The
same was noted in the case of Ofelia and Lady Grey.

A comparison of the Folio and the Quarto versions of Falstaffe's recital of his adventure in the buck-basket will serve to
demonstrate that the method of revision here is the same as in
Henry VI, Parts II and *III*. The original seems to have been
closely followed in the Folio version, which reads (p. 53):

> *Ford.* A Buck-basket?
>
> *Fal.* Yes: a Buck-basket: ram'd mee in with foule Shirts
> and Smockes, Socks, foule Stockings, greasie Napkins, that
> (Master *Broome*) there was the rankest compound of villanous
> smell, that ever offended nostrill.
>
> *Ford.* And how long lay you there?
>
> *Fal.* Nay, you shall heare (Master *Broome*) what I have
> sufferd, to bring this woman to evill, for your good: Being
> thus cram'd in the Basket, a couple of *Fords* knaves, his Hindes,
> were cald forth by their Mistris, to carry mee in the name of
> foule Cloathes to *Datchet-lane*: they tooke me on their shoulders:
> met the jealous knave their Master in the doore; who ask'd
> them once or twice what they had in their Basket? I quak'd
> for feare least the Lunatique Knave would have search'd it: but
> Fate (ordaining he should be a Cuckold) held his hand: well,
> on went hee, for a search, and away went I for foule Cloathes: But
> marke the sequell (Master *Broome*) I suffered the pangs of three
> severall deaths: First, an intollerable fright, to be detected with
> a jealious rotten Bell-weather: Next to be compass'd like a good
> Bilbo in the circumference of a Pecke hilt to point, heele to
> head. And then to be stopt in like a strong distillation with
> Stinking Cloathes, that fretted in their owne grease: thinke of
> that, a man of my Kidney; thinke of that, that am as subject

to heate as butter; a man of continuall dissolution, and thaw: it was a miracle to scape suffocation. And in the height of this Bath, when I was more then halfe stew'd in grease (like a Dutch-dish) to be throwne into the Thames, and coold, glowing-hot, in that serge like a Horse-shoo; thinke of that; hissing hot: thinke of that (Master *Broome*).

The Quarto revision reads:

1   *Ford.* A buck basket!
2   *Fal.* By the Lord a buck basket, rammed me in
3   with foule shirts, stokins, greasie napkins,
4   that M. *Brooke*, there was a compound of the most
5   villanous smel, that ever offended nostrill.
6   Ile tell you M. *Brooke*, by the Lord for your sake
7   I suffered three egregious deaths: First to be
8   crammed like a good bilbo, in the circomference
9   of a pack, Hilt to point, heele to head: and then to
10   be stewed in my owne grease like a Dutch dish:
11   A man of my kidney; by the Lord it was marvell I
12   escaped suffication; and in the heat of all this
13   to be throwne into Thames like a horshoo hot:
14   Maister *Brooke*, thinke of that hissing heate, Maister
15   *Brooke*.

Three minor points disclose that this Quarto is a revision. These are: the change of 'pecke' to 'pack' (line 9), a peck basket being the obvious idea; the change of 'height' to 'heat' (line 12); and the change of 'hot' in 'thinke of that; hissing hot:' to 'heate' (line 14), 'thinke of that hissing heate'. This last mistake was due to a misconception of both the punctuation and the grammar of the original.

The long-omitted passage was lost because the reviser brought together the two 'suffered' passages of the original. This method was used in the revision of *Hamlet*, *Romeo and Juliet*, and the *Henry VI* plays.

The Folio Falstaffe states that he suffered three several deaths. He then details them under 'first', 'next', and 'and then', all referring to statements which he had made in the passage which does not appear in the Quarto. The author of the Quarto also mentions three deaths. The first one he lost. He therefore begins with the second, which he entitles 'first'; omits the second; and ends with the third 'and then'. In this revision Brooke is never told how Falstaffe was conveyed from under his nose to the Thames; yet later in the play Brooke is made to have a knowledge of this lost passage.

The two original lines 'fretted in their own grease' and 'stew'd in grease (like a Dutch-dish)' were combined into one— 'and then to be stewed in my owne grease like a Dutch dish'. Although stewed in grease, Falstaffe was stewed in the grease of the clothes, not in his 'owne' grease.

From the evidence it appears: that both the Folio and Quarto versions of *The Merry Wives of Windsor* are revisions based on a third version now lost; that the First Quarto was written by the reviser of *Henry VI, Parts II* and *III*; that at least the Folio revision belonged to the Chamberlain company; that one or the other of the three versions may have been written by William Shakespeare.

The additions to *Titus Andronicus, Troilus and Cressida, Mucidorus, King Lear, Othello*, and *Sir Thomas More* are relatively unimportant, and may be omitted from present consideration.

XVII

WILLIAM SHAKESPEARE (REVISER)

WILLIAM SHAKESPEARE'S activities as a reviser may most conveniently be divided into three periods: I, when he was with my Lord Pembroke's men (c. 1589-93); II, when with the Queen's company (1593-7); III, when with ' my Lord Chamberlaine's men ' (1598-1607).

During the Pembroke period he associated with Kyd, presumably with Drayton, possibly with Marlowe. Five plays have been preserved in the form in which they were acted by this company: *The Taming of a Shrew*, *Arden of Faversham*, *Edward II*, *Titus Andronicus*, and *The True Tragedy of Richard Duke of York*, *&c*. All of these plays have at one time or another been attributed to Shakespeare. To this list should be added *The Contention*, *&c.*, Part I (*Duke Humphrey's Tragedy*), which must have been a Pembroke play although it was not printed as belonging to that company. As *Duke Humphrey's Tragedy* it was attributed to Shakespeare in Warburton's list of plays. Shakespeare's share in the first four of these plays must remain problematical; however, his revision of *Henry VI*, *Parts II* and *III*, into the two Pembroke tragedies will serve as examples of his work during this first period.

It was during this period that Greene wrote of Shakespeare as ' an upstart . . . beautified with our fethers, that . . . supposes he is as well able to bombast out a blank verse as the best of you ; . . . an absolute Johannes factotum '. Chettle mentioned his civil demeanour, his excellence in ' the qualitie he professes ' (acting), ' his uprightness of dealing, which argues his honesty ', and finally his ' facetious grace in writing '.

From these observations it is evident that as early as 1592 Shakespeare had made a name as an actor, and that he was concerned in the company's finances. Therefore he must have been one of the company's most influential shareholders. To these activities he now added that of reviser. Had he revised the repertoire of his own company Greene could not have complained; but when his revision consisted in garbling into caricature the property of rival companies, the creations of professional dramatists, complaint was more than justified.

As a shareholder in the Pembroke company it was Shakespeare's business to obtain plays as cheaply as possible. Legally there was no property in plays. Therefore if Shakespeare could obtain dramas of merit from rival companies by the simple process of appropriation and revision he and his company benefited financially. Conversely this process of obtaining plays deprived the professional dramatist of possible remuneration. This was the chief cause of Greene's complaint. To a contest of this sort there is but one outcome: to whom the shekels accrue comes victory. Greene, Marlowe, Peele, and Nash all died in poverty, while Shakespeare was laying the foundation of a fortune.

When Shakespeare came to London, at what date he turned actor, is unknown; however, it seems evident that he began work as a reviser about 1591. The two *Henry VI* plays must have been among his first revisions. His additions and revisions as found in these two plays are precisely such as might be expected from an unlettered actor. His mistakes in grammar and spelling have been noted in the comments on these two plays in the chapter 'The Revision of *Henry VI, Parts II* and *III*', also his lack of Latin and his ignorance of ancient mythology. These are all negative qualities.

Among positive qualities may be noted a dogged persistence which enabled him to rework these plays from the mutilated versions which came into his hands into a semblance of presentable revisions. It is true that he twisted and reshaped various passages into awkward caricatures of the originals. Yet this did not prevent him from pursuing his task to the end. Perhaps his lack of learning assisted him in his task; for only an ignorant workman could for long have produced such botchery.

Of the first part of Eleanor's last speech to her husband, Duke

Humphrey, Shakespeare must have possessed some such broken version as:

1   Ah Gloster, teach me to forget my selfe:
2   For whilst I thinke I am thy married Wife,
3   And thou a Prince, Protector of this land;
4   . . . . thus be led . . .
5   Mayl'd up in shame, with Papers on my back,
6   . . . .
7   . . . .
8   The ruthlesse Flint doth cut my tender feet,
9   And when I start, the envious people laugh,
10   And bid me be advised how I treade.
11   Ah Humfrey, can I beare this . . . .
12, 13, 14, 15.
16   Sometime Ile say, I am Duke Humfreyes Wife,
17   And he a Prince, and Ruler of the Land:
18   Yet so he rul'd, and such a Prince he was,
19   As he stood by, whilest I, his forlorne Duchesse,
20   Was made . . and a . . . ing stock
21   To every idle Rascall follower.

This much of the original he used; presumably it was as much of it as he possessed. Faced with such a passage the ordinary literary craftsman would have recast the entire speech into new form, keeping only the general ideas intact. Not so Shakespeare. He preserved each patch of this speech; he fitted the pieces together, supplying only such thread and additional material as seemed necessary to unite all into one piece. That the joins were a bit obvious and that his finished product became a patchwork concerned him not at all. Shakespeare's revision reads:

1   Ah Gloster teach me to forget my selfe
2   For whilst I thinke I am thy wedded wife,
a   Then thought of this, doth kill my woefull heart.
8   The ruthlesse flints do cut my tender feete,
9   And when I start the cruell people laugh,
10   And bids me be advised how I tread,
b   And thus with burning Taper in my hand
5   Malde up in shame with papers on my backe,
11   Ah Gloster, can I endure this and live.
16   Sometime ile say I am Duke Humphreys wife,

3–16 And he a Prince, Protector of the Land,
18   But so he rulde, and such a Prince he was,
19   As he stood by, whilst I his forlorne Duches
20   Was led with shame, and made a laughing stocke,
21   To every idle rascald follower.

Line 3 of the original being so like line 1, they were combined in this revision. The new line 'a' was inserted to connect lines 2 and 8 of the original. This left line 5 suspended. It was inserted after line 10. Line 'b', built on the hint contained in 'thus' of the original, was then inserted to piece-in the patch.

Originally this passage read:

5   Mayl'd up in shame, with papers on my back,
6   And followed by a Rabble, that rejoyce
7   To see my teares, and heare my deepe-set groanes.

Having lost lines 6 and 7 Shakespeare left line 5 incomplete, resuming with line 11. It may be supposed he intended this suspension to indicate an emotional lacuna. There is a grammatical error in his line 10; and there are several peculiar spellings. This patch is of a piece with the whole of the first and second parts of the *Contention* plays. Though patchwork it is conscientiously pieced together and has a certain rhythmic grace.

In the first speech by Queen Margaret in the second part of *The Contention* (Shakespeare's revision of *Henry VI, Part III*) there are two peculiar lapses. The speech opens:

Queen. What patience can there?   Ah timerous man.

Evidently 'be' was omitted after 'there'. The second lapse occurs in the last line of a later passage of the same speech:

The Northern Lords that have forsworne thy colours
Will follow mine if once they see them spred,
And spred they shall unto thy deep disgrace.

These lapses may have been due to Shakespeare's rhythmic habitude. Both occur at the caesura.

Actors, especially those in stock companies who daily learn new parts, do not as a rule memorize entire passages as such, but, as parrots, memorize a mere succession of words. To accomplish this successfully the words are divided into speech groups, or phrases. The ordinary line of blank verse is normally composed of two of these speech groups divided at the caesura.

While by the scholarly dramatist the caesura is often negligently overlooked by the actor it is often over-emphasized. To the one it is an accident; to the other a necessity. That any one trained as an actor should, when writing blank verse, over-emphasize the caesura is therefore but natural. That Shakespeare did so is disclosed, not only in that he twice omitted an unemphasized 'be' which occurred at the caesura in Queen Margaret's speech, but also in the marked way in which he made use of it in the lines below, all of which appear only in his revision of the *Henry VI* plays.

From *The Contention*, Part I:

Stand up you simple men, / and give God praise,
For you did take in hand / you know not what,
And go in peace / obedient to your King,
And live as subjects, / and you shall not want,
Whilst Henry lives, / and weares the English crowne.

Here sir John, / take this scrole of paper here,
Wherein is writ / the questions you shall aske,
And I will stand / upon this Tower here,
And here the spirit, / what it saies to you,
And to my questions, / write the answeres downe.

Proud Traitor, / I arest thee on high treason,
Against thy soveraigne Lord. / Yeeld thee false Yorke,
For here I sweare, / thou shalt into the tower,
For these proud words / which thou hast given the King.

From *The Contention*, Part II:

Come noble Summerset, / lets take horse,
And cause retrait / be sounded through the campe,
That all our friends / that yet remaine alive,
Maie be awarn'd / and save themselves by flight.

I will not stande aloofe / and bid you fight,
But with my sword / presse in the thickest thronges,
And single Edward / from his strongest guard,
And hand to hand / enforce him for to yeeld,
Or leave my bodie / as witnesse of my thoughts.

Verse which thus often comes to a stop in the middle as well as at the end of each line soon degenerates into doggerel or into prose. If the stops are at regular intervals it becomes singsong doggerel; if they are at irregular intervals it becomes prose. An example of pure doggerel singsong is:

> If our King Henry / had shooke hands with death,
> Duke Humphrey then / would looke to be our King:
> And it may be / by pollicie he workes,
> To bring to passe / the thing which now we doubt.

So also:

> The foxe barkes not when he would steale the Lambe,
> But if we take him ere he do the deed,
> We should not question if that he should live.

An example of doggerel (*a*) followed by prose (*b*) follows:

(*a*) And do thou take in hand to crosse the seas,
> With troupes of Armed men to quell the pride
> Of those ambitious Irish that rebell.
> Well madame sith your grace is so content; &c.

(*b*) Let me have some bands of chosen soldiers,
> And Yorke shall trie his fortune against those kernes.

In the first part of *The Contention* this jog-trot verse is used almost exclusively for all Shakespeare's additions. In the second part, while the greater portion of the new material is in like doggerel, a different style of verse appears towards the end of the play. Possibly Shakespeare, pressed for time, allowed these passages to escape him before they had been cast into rhythmic form. Possibly the printer was at fault. An example of non-doggerel lines:

> *Edw.* Brothers of Clarence, and of Glocester,
> What thinke you of our marriage with the ladie Gray?
> *Cla.* My lord, we thinke as Warwike and Lewes
> That are so slacke in judgement, that theile take
> No offence at this suddaine marriage.
> *Edw.* Suppose they doe, they are but Lewes and
> Warwike, and I am your king and Warwikes
> And will be obaied.

A somewhat similar passage was incorrectly printed in seven lines. When printed in six lines it becomes true to form:

King. Thus from the prison to this princelie seat,
By Gods great mercies am I brought / again,
Clarence and Warwike / doe you keepe the crowne,
And governe and protect / my realme in peace,
And I will spend / the remnant of my daies,
To sinnes rebuke / and my Creators praise.

Blank verse is composed of ten strands of warp which bind together the word-coloured woof of a story. If the shuttle of the woof threads through the ten strands of the warp with mathematical regularity the warp serves only to bind the woof into a bolt of material, the pattern being regular but meaningless. However, does the shuttle thread through the warp with designed irregularity, patterns full of meaning can be obtained. Blank verse with its ten-strand woof may therefore be rhythmically colourless, as in the examples of doggerel cited above, or it may be full of rhythmic colour and design.

At its worst the unchanging regularity of doggerel forces into the woof of the story unnecessary material which it were stronger without. Nash complained of Kyd and the Pembroke authors because they ' bodge up a blanke verse with iffs and ands '. While in his patching of these *Henry VI* plays Shakespeare did not use many ' iffs ' he did unmistakably ' bodge up ' his doggerel with innumerable ' ands '.

The device most commonly resorted to by writers of doggerel is the use of unnecessary individual words. Those having a larger culture ' bodge ' with adjectives and adverbs; the less lettered members of the craft make use of conjunctions, prepositions, and a great variety of small-fry words with which to fill gaps in the rhythmic pattern. Those used most frequently by Shakespeare in these two *Contention* plays are—*and, and to, if and, but, hence, thence, here, now, there, then, where, as, for, before, as for, for to, for why, for that,* &c.

While in these two plays Shakespeare's rhythm never rises above the simplest form of jog-trot doggerel, while he lacked the ability to weave rhythm through rhythm in the intricate manner of Marlowe, Greene, or Peele, it must not be overlooked that his doggerel, as doggerel, usually runs smoothly. Although the simple rhythm is ceaselessly reiterated it seldom becomes disagreeable. Since Shakespeare used the same doggerel throughout both plays it may be presumed that in it he had found a medium suitable to his immediate need and development.

Of true dramatic ability Shakespeare at this period possessed little. In the first part of *The Contention* he followed the original closely, except in the Jack Cade scenes, the passage wherein Warwick laments the loss of Anjou and Maine, the passage wherein the Queen boxes the ears of Lady Eleanor, and the final battle episode.

Shakespeare overlooked the fact that Duke Humfrey went out of the council chamber because he was angered by the false accusations brought against him and returned only when he had mastered his anger. Realizing nevertheless that the Duke must have been absent when the Queen boxed his wife's ears, Shakespeare caused the Duke to depart and return for no reason save that he needs must be absent while the ladies quarrelled. This entire episode he fitted in after the episode dealing with Peter and his master, the armourer.

The last scene but one of this play is located in London. In it the house of York bids defiance to the King and the Lancastrians and challenges them to the combat. The final scene is the field of battle. Originally the episodes of this battle were arranged as follows : (*a*) Warwick enters seeking Clifford ; (*b*) to him Yorke ; (*c*) to them Clifford. (*d*) Exit Warwick. Clifford and Yorke fight. Clifford is slain. Exit Yorke. (*e*) Enter Young Clifford and exit with the body of his father. (*f*) Enter Richard and Somerset. They fight. Somerset is slain. (*g*) Enter King, Queen, &c. ; (*h*) to them Young Clifford. All fly the field. (*i*) Enter the house of Yorke triumphant. Curtain.

In his revision Shakespeare transferred the later part of the London scene to the battle-field and opened the battle scene with the challenge. In the original of this challenge scene Richard spoke the last line. That may have been the reason that Shakespeare opened the battle with the fight between Richard and Somerset (*f*). This he followed by the Warwick-Yorke-Clifford episodes (*a*, *b*, *c*, *d*) and the entrance of Young Clifford (*e*). Here he correctly registered ' *Enter Richard* '; however, as he had already used the Richard-Somerset episode, he now made Richard enter to Young Clifford. Here his lack of dramatic insight betrayed him, for Richard, Richard the most intrepid dare-devil of the entire ' War of the Roses ' series, was made to hesitate while Young Clifford ' lies downe his father ' from off his back. They fight, and Shakespeare ends the episode with ' and Richard flies away againe ', while Young Clifford screams after him :

> Out crooktbacke villaine, get thee from my sight,
> But I will after thee, and once againe
> When I have borne my father to his tent,
> Ile try my fortune better with thee yet.
> > *Exet yoong Clifford with his father.*

In the original version Richard's final victory over Somerset is designedly made the crowning achievement of the house of York, after which the King and his followers flee in dismay. Shakespeare crowns the achievements of the house of York by this cowardly scuttle of their boldest warrior. This worried him not a whit. In his next episode he exhibits the King in full flight for London, where he has not friends to aid him, as in the original, but where he may—

> Sommon a Parlament with speede,
> To stop the fury of these dyre events.

Needless to remark there are no indications of character-work in Shakespeare's added lines. His treatment of Richard is sufficient testimony of his entire lack of any true conception of character or of the ability to differentiate one character from another. His people all speak the same language, all mouth the same free-flowing doggerel.

In the second part of *The Contention* the most noticeable blunder in construction is to be found in the series of episodes immediately after Warwick's return from France, King Henry being then in the Tower and Edward on the throne. Originally the series was arranged as follows: (*a*) Edward and his army are camped near York. Warwick and his army, having arrived from France, seize Edward, send him to the Archbishop of York as a prisoner, and march away towards London to re-establish Henry. (*b*) London. Lady Grey and Rivers hear of Edward's defeat. (*c*) Near York. Richard and Hastings rescue Edward, and all fly to Flanders. (*d*) London. Henry is re-enthroned. News arrives of Edward's escape. (*e*) Before York. Edward and Richard with an army arrive from Flanders. The mayor opens the gates to them. Edward is crowned King at York. (*f*) London. Henry and Warwick hear that Edward is marching from York. All, save Henry, depart to muster troops. Edward arrives in London and dethrones Henry. (*g*) Coventry. The armies of Edward and Warwick meet and join battle.

Shakespeare changed the sequence of these episodes into *a, c, b, e, d, f, g,* thus making Richard rescue Edward before Lady Grey had heard of his capture, and making Edward return from Flanders before Henry had even heard of his escape. Shakespeare thus makes Edward go to Flanders, raise an army, and return in less time than a messenger could travel from York to London. Also, since his Warwick did not arrive in London and re-establish Henry until after his Edward had returned from Flanders, his Edward makes the double journey in less time than it took Warwick to march from York to London, although he had started on the journey in episode *a*.

Shakespeare made these mistakes in following his customary practice of joining like to like. He linked together the two York episodes (*a* and *c*), then later linked together the two London episodes (*d* and *f*). He was so intent on smoothly uniting the minor patches of this play that he did not notice that he had misplaced large parts, thus playing havoc with the time element and destroying the continuity of the story.

Shakespeare's Second Period.

The only work assigned to Shakespeare while he was with the Queen's men is his revision of an old play by Greene entitled *Locrine*, printed in 1595 'as newly corrected by W.S.' As Shakespeare had already rewritten several of Greene's plays, as the 'newly corrected' *Locrine* contains many a passage borrowed from Greene's *Selimus*, an old Queen's company play, and as *Locrine* also must have belonged to this company, it is evident that the ' W. S.' who ' newly corrected ' this play for that company was William Shakespeare, who with Kempe and Burbage belonged to the Queen's company from 1593 until 1598.

Although the original of *Locrine* has not been preserved there are many distinct signs of revision in the extant text, which revisions can with considerable assurance be assigned to Shakespeare. The greater part of Greene's share in this play is in verse form. Shakespeare's lines disclose themselves often in that they either break into the original verse form or are cast in the unrhymed doggerel of the *Contention* plays.

From Greene's *Selimus* Shakespeare borrowed six of the following lines:

> Were they as mighty and as fell of force
> As those old earth-bred brethren, which once
> Heap'd hill on hill to scale the starry sky,
> When Briareus, arm'd with a hundreth hands,
> Flung forth a hundreth mountains at great Jove;
> And when the monstrous giant Monichus
> Hurled Mount Olympus at great Mars his targe,
> And darted cedars at Minerva's shield.

These he inserted into a passage also treating of the might of an enemy :

> *Hum.* How bravely this yoong Brittain, Albanact,
> Darteth abroad the thunderbolts of warre,
> Beating downe millions with his furious moode,
> And in his glorie triumphs over all.
> [*Here the connecting link.*]
> Moving the massie squadrants of the ground;

[*Here the borrowed passage.*]
Heape hills on hills, to scale the starrie skie
As when Briareus, armed with an hundreth hands,
Floong forth an hundreth mountains at great Jove,
And when the monstrous giant Monichus
Hurld mount Olympus at great Mars his targe,
And shot huge caedars at Minervas shield.

Presumably Shakespeare·had a correct copy of *Selimus* in the
company strong-box, yet he must have trusted to his memory,
otherwise he could not have made so many mistakes in six short
lines. There is one grammatical error; and several peculiar spellings may be noticed. There is also the high-sounding connecting
link, ' Moving the massie squadrants of the ground ', which line
no one seems able to interpret.

Besides such evident adaptations from *Selimus* there are to be
found many lines in *Locrine* which either exploit or reduplicate
an idea already expressed. Such are the two lines beginning with
' and ' in the following:

You ugly sprites that in Cocitus mourne,
And gnash your teeth / with dolorous laments,
You fearful dogs that in black Lœthe howle,
And scare the ghoasts / with your wide open throats:
You ugly ghoasts that, flying from those dogs,
Do plunge your selves in Puryflegiton, &c.

Both ' and ' lines are divided at the caesura; both are gra-
tuitous exuberances. There are numbers of such throughout
Locrine. Almost always they break into the regular verse
form.

Although his doggerel had improved, Shakespeare had not as
yet outgrown his love of the caesura, nor had his penchant for
joining like to like diminished. This later trait is well exemplified in his use of a considerable passage which originally appeared
in *Selimus*.

In both *Locrine* and *Selimus* a leading character is forced into
the wilderness by his enemies. In *Selimus* when Corcut nears

starvation he chances upon the clown Bullithrumble, who, having fled from his termagant wife to the foot-hills, is about to enjoy a meal when the starving Corcut accosts him, exclaiming, ' Give some meat ', &c. The clown succours him and then takes him into his service. In *Locrine*, as originally written, Humber, King of the Scythians, also wanders in the desert, starving. Into this starving scene Shakespeare, joining like to like, introduced the clown, dinner, scolding wife, &c., from *Selimus*, to the utter un-doing of the original scene.

It is not difficult to discover Greene's original intent despite Shakespeare's additions. Humber with his Scythians, having in-vaded England, defeats the English under Albanact, who is slain. His brother, Locrine, gathering an army, meets and defeats Humber. Humber becomes a fugitive. He curses his gods, longing for ' some desart wildernesse '. In the midst of his ravings the ghost of Albanact appears to him, swearing revenge. Humber bids the ghost defiance. From this there ensues one of the most awe-inspiring tragedies in all English drama. Humber came to conquer England, to put the people to the sword. What punish-ment were fit for such a king ? Greene's answer is, hunger and thirst shall pursue him, and his enemy's ghost shall exult over him even unto death.

A stage presentation of slow starvation calls for several epi-sodes. Humber spends seven years in the wilderness, a fugitive ; yet Shakespeare, joining like to like, presents the three original episodes which unfolded this tragedy of slow starvation almost simultaneously. The first and second episodes he placed in one scene, dividing them only by the introduction of the clown from *Selimus*; and the second and third episodes he separated by only a short monologue by Locrine. As presented on the stage by Shakespeare Humber's long suffering thus becomes a thing of exceeding short duration.

The folly of introducing the clown is evident. Humber dared not disclose himself: discovery means death. If he could thus meet with the clown, who was only a short distance from his home and tilled fields, food could have been obtained. Yet he repeatedly states there is 'not a root, no fruite, no beast, no bird' available. In truth the tragic element consisted greatly in the fact that he could not and did not during the seven long years meet with a human or civilized being save the tormenting ghost of Albanact. The introduction of this clown at once reduces high tragedy to farce. Since Will Kempe, chief comedian to the Queen's company, habitually elaborated his lines the comic passages, rewritten for the clown, may have been reconstructed by him rather than by Shakespeare. As printed in *Locrine* they are among the most vulgar to be found in all Elizabethan literature.

While some of the clown's 'patter' may have been due to Kempe, the connecting links of these starving episodes must be Shakespeare's own. When Humber discovers the clown the following ensues:

> *Humber.* O Jupiter, hast thou sent Mercury,
> In clownish shape to minister some foode?
> Some meate! some meate! some meate!
> *Strumbo* (the clown). O, alasse, sir, ye are deceived.
> I am not Mercury; I am Strumbo.
> *Humber.* Give me som meat, villain; give me som meat,
> Or gainst this rock Ile dash thy cursed braines,
> And rent thy bowels with my bloodie hands.
> Give me some meat, villaine; give me some meat!
> *Strumbo.* By the faith of my bodie, good fellow, I had rather give an whole oxe then that thou shouldst serve me in that sort. Dash out my braines? O horrible! terrible! I thinke I have a quarry of stones in my pocket.

A peculiarly long stage-direction follows:

> *Let him make as though hee would give him some and as he putteth out his hand, enter the ghoast of Albanact, and strike him on the hand; and so Strumbo runnes out, Humber following him.*

This is rough farce. It is followed by a bit of the original in which the ghost does appear, not to strike the hand of the clown who was originally in another play, but to exult over Humber,

who faints from lack of food, also to drive home the moral of
Humber's downfall :

> *Ghost.* Loe, here the gift of fell ambition,
> Of usurpation and of trecherie!
> Loe, here the harmes that wait upon all those
> That do intrude themselves in other's lands,
> Which are not under their dominion.

This is not farce, nor had Humber run off the stage after the
clown before these lines were spoken.

The reconstruction of this entire scene is carried out in the
illogical manner of the *Henry VI* revisions. Shakespeare still
lacked dramatic insight.

Despite the despoiling of *Selimus* in order to spoil *Locrine*
Shakespeare has clearly made progress since 1592. He dares to
insert into *Locrine* material not only from *Selimus* but as evidently
from other sources. His verse is smoother ; and he has discovered
the fascination of full-sounding though obscure lines, such as—
'Moving the massie squadrants of the ground' and 'And scare
the earth with my condemning voice '.

Shakespeare's Third Period.

Shakespeare's third period, while he was with the Chamberlain company, dates from *c.* 1597 to *c.* 1608. His first work for
this company seems to have been the revision of *Romeo and
Juliet.* As has been shown, he could have had no connexion
whatsoever with the First Quarto of this play, which was printed
as acted by Lord Hunsdon's company at the Curtain, while
Shakespeare was still a Queen's company man at the Theatre.
The Second Quarto appeared in 1599 as ' Newly corrected, augmented, and amended '. Shakespeare's name does not appear
on the title-page, but the play was assigned to him by Meres late
in 1598, and by Weever in 1599. There can be no hesitancy
therefore in attributing this second ' corrected ' copy to William
Shakespeare.

There are many lines in each copy which do not appear in the other. However, the greater part of the First Quarto reappears in the Second in duplicated or augmented form. Seemingly Shakespeare did not possess a complete copy of *Romeo and Juliet*. Of that portion which fell into his hands he used one half of the lines without change; the other half he 'corrected and amended'. Besides correcting and amending the original version he augmented the text to such an extent that one-fourth of his version is 'new'. That he has made further progress as a reviser is evident both in his amendments and in his augmentations.

Shakespeare's budding love for grandiloquent, though often obscure, verse was noticed in his revision of *Locrine*. In *Romeo and Juliet* he develops this new inclination and makes further general progress. His verse flows with greater freedom and sonorousness. The caesura ceases to exert so much influence. The first example of his new methods appears in the two four-line additions to the first speech by Prince Eskales :

Prince. Rebellious subjects, enemies to peace,
[*Here the first four-line addition.*]
Prophaners of this neighbor-stayned steele,
Will they not heare ? what ho, you men, you beasts !
That quench the fire of your pernicious rage,
With purple fountaines issuing from your veines :
[*Here two lines of the original.*]
On paine of torture from those bloudie hands,
Throw your mistempered weapons to the ground
[*Here another added line.*]
And heare the sentence of your moved Prince :
[*Here three lines of the original.*]
Three civill brawles bred of an ayrie word,
By thee old Capulet and Montague,
Have thrice disturbd the quiet of our streets,
[*Here the second four-line addition.*]
And made Veronas auncient citizens
Cast by their grave beseeming ornaments,
To wield old partizans, in hands as old,
Cancred with peace, to part your cancred hate.

That the caesura still retained some of its old influence is evident in the next insertion. Benvolio is describing his fight with Tybalt:

[*From the original.*]

Ben. Here were the servants of your adversarie,
And yours, close fighting ere I did approach,

[*Here the addition.*]

I drew to part them, in the instant came
The fierie Tybalt, with his sword preparde,
Which as he breathd defiance to my eares,
He swoong about his head; and cut the windes,
Who nothing hurt withall, hist him in scorne:
While we were enterchaunging thrusts and blowes,
Came more and more, and fought on part and part,
Till the Prince came, who parted either part.

Paronomastic lines are a new development. There are several in the additions to this play.

The next considerable addition furnishes a good example of Shakespeare's reputed 'facetious grace', because of which he was called 'honey-tongued'. Montague is discoursing on Romeo's moodiness:

Mounta. Many a morning hath he there bin seene,
With teares augmenting the fresh morning's deawe,
Adding to cloudes, more clowdes with his deepe sighes,
But all so soone, as the alcheering Sunne,
Should in the farthest East begin to draw,
The shadie curtaines from Auroras bed.
Away from light steales home my heavie sonne,
And private in his chamber pennes himselfe,
Shuts up his windowes, locks faire daylight out,
And makes himselfe an artificiall night:

'Sunne' and 'Sonne' is the second play upon words, Shakespeare's latest discovery. The metaphors in this passage, as has been previously noted, are somewhat mixed, yet the addition is full of 'facetious grace'.

Of lines in which the order of words has been changed this

play contains some hundred and twenty specimens. This habit seemed to be growing on Shakespeare. Examples:

> Q 1. And I am nothing slacke to slow his haste.
> Q 2. And I am nothing slow to slacke his haste.
> Q 1. So, I am sure, you will, that you love me.
> Q 2. So will ye, I am sure, that you love me.
> Q 1. If she be well, then nothing can be ill.
>   Then nothing can be ill for she is well.
> Q 2. For nothing can be ill if she be well.
>   Then she is well and nothing can be ill.

Shakespeare turned this last into caricature. However, he made it his own.

As Shakespeare possessed a fairly complete copy of the original play he preserved the correct sequence of the episodes. His habit of joining like to like could therefore manifest itself only in minor details. During his stage career he had picked up innumerable lines which readily lent themselves to quotation and adaptation. The 'augmented' parts of *Romeo and Juliet* are chiefly composed of such bits, suggested by something in the original text, at times the one suggesting another, that still another, until an entire series was formed. An example of such reduplicating of metaphors occurs in Lady Capulet's praise of Paris to Juliet. The original reads:

> *Nurce.* Nay he is a flower, in faith a very flower.
> *Lady Capulet.* Well, Juliet, how like you of Paris' love?

This, slightly altered, was augmented with:

> *Old Lady.* This night you shall behold him at our feast,
>
> [*This line was derived from Benvolio's suggestion that Romeo shall see Rosaline at the feast. The 'Old Lady' continues.*]
>
> Reade ore the volume of young Paris face,
> And find delight, writ there with bewties pen,
>
> [*This suggested another.*]
>
> Examine every married liniament
> And see how one another lends content:

[*This another.*]
And what obscurde in this faire volume lies,
Finde written in the margeant of his eyes,
[*This another.*]
This precious booke of love, this unbound lover,
To bewtifie him, onely lacks a cover.
[*This suggested a fish-sea comparison.*]
The fish lives in the sea, and 'tis much pride
For faire without the faire, within to hide.
[*This suggested.*]
That booke in manies eyes doth share the glorie
That in gold claspes lockes in the golden storie:

Thus wandering from one metaphor to another Shakespeare has journeyed a long way from the original idea: that Juliet was to look at the face of Paris and to like him if his beauty pleased her.

The line ' O serpents heart hid with a flowering face ' also suggested comparisons:

Did ever dragon keepe so faire a cave ?
Bewtiful tirant, fiend angelicall :
Ravenous dove-feathered raven, wolvish ravening lamb,
Despised substance of divinest showe :
Just opposite to what thou justly seemst,
A dimme Saint, an honourable villaine :
O nature what hadst thou to do in hell
When thou didst bower the spirit of a fiend,
In mortall paradise of such sweete flesh ?

Here follows, slightly altered from the original, the line which suggested the above-quoted bound-book series :

Was ever booke containing such vile matter
So fairely bound ?
[*This suggested another.*]
                    ô that deceit should dwell
In such a gorgious Pallace.

It will be noticed that in the excitement the ' wolvish-lamb ' parallel went wrong. It should have been a lamblike wolf. When thus duplicating metaphors Shakespeare almost always wrecked the initial conception.

A strange insertion appears in Romeo's lament that he must leave Juliet. The original reads:

> More courtship lives
> In carrion flyes, than Romeo: they may seaze
> On the white wonder of faire Juliet's skinne,
> And steale immortall kisses from her lips;
> But Romeo may not, he is banished.
> Flies may doo this, but I from this must flye.

Into this Shakespeare endeavoured to insert an idea suggested by 'immortal kisses from her lips'. His version reads:

> More courtship lives
> In carrion flies, then Romeo: they may seaze
> On the white wonder of deare Juliet's hand,
> And steale immortall blessing from her lips,
> [*Here the insertion.*]
> Who even in pure and vestall modestie
> Still blush, as thinking their owne kisses sin.
> [*Here he returns to the original, though shifting the words about to make them his own.*]
> This may flyes do, when I from this must flie, &c.

'Pure and vestall modestie' was well remembered. Unfortunately, although it has 'facetious grace', it fails to fit into the text.

Other tag-ends such as:

> Some griefe shews much of love;
> But much of griefe shews still some want of wit.

were fitted in more cleverly. Yet the fact that Shakespeare attempted to place such an idea as 'pure and vestall modestie' in the very heart of a complete paragraph shows an ingenuous boldness as well as an inability to inhibit inopportune associations.

The disastrous disintegration of the characters caused by Shakespeare's corrections and additions has been treated in 'The Revision of *Hamlet* and of *Romeo and Juliet*'. He still lacked any true realization of character, of character interaction, and presumably of plot when he revised this play in the year 1597–8.

The next set of Chamberlain plays with which Shakespeare can be connected is the *Henry V* series, which were written during the years 1598 and 1599. While Jonson seems to have made the greater number of the more important additions to these three plays Shakespeare presumably had a share in the minor changes.

A correct copy of the original play upon which *Henry IV*, *Parts I* and *II*, was founded has not been discovered, the nearest approach being 'the Deryng manuscript'. The fact that this manuscript seems to have been penned by the same person who penned the body of Shakespeare's will, for the handwriting is almost identical, also points to Shakespeare's connexion with these plays. Whether or no Shakespeare wrote both documents himself or had them penned for him by some scribe, they are closely related to one another and to Shakespeare.

Lacking a correct copy of the original *Henry IV*, little can be judged as to Shakespeare's share in the greater part of *Henry IV*, *Parts I* and *II*. However, the additions to Part I contain little, if any, trace of Jonson, hence they may with some confidence be attributed to Shakespeare. The ensuing passages closely reemble the additions to *Romeo and Juliet*:

(1)   *Mor.* I understand thy kisses, and thou mine,
And that's a feeling disputation:
But I will never be a truant love,
Till I have learnd thy language, for thy tongue
Makes Welsh as sweet as ditties highly pend,
Sung by a faire queene in a summers bowre,
With ravishing division to her lute.

(2)   *Glen.* She bids you on the wanton rushes lay you downe,
And rest your gentle head upon her lap,
And she will sing the song that pleaseth you,
And on your eyelids crowne the god of sleepe,
Charming your bloud with pleasing heavinesse
Making such difference betwixt wake and sleepe,
As is the difference betwixt day and night,
The houre before the heavenly harnest teeme
Begins his golden progresse in the east.

Here is a series of more or less bastard similes, each one suggesting or suggested by another. At times the grammatical construction falls to pieces. This is certainly not in Jonson's vein.

The second part of *Henry IV* is so overwhelmingly Jonsonian that it is useless endeavouring to separate from it elements which may or may not be Shakespearian.

In the revised version of *Henry V* the large additions have the Jonsonian ring, but the reversed lines, of which there are more than a hundred, and the minor revisions, together with many interlinear lines and phrases, are so unlike Jonson and so like those corrections and augmentations with which the established Shakespearian revisions are interlarded that they must be ascribed to Jonson's co-worker. Jonson wrote additions to various plays; but so far as is known the great egotist never condescended to ' correct' or 'amend' the work of a rival dramatist.

A fair example of revision as carried out in *Henry V* is that of the short scene after the French rout. The First Quarto reads:

> *Enter the foure French lords.*
>
> *Gebon.* O diabello.
> *Con.* Mor du ma vie.
> [*The spelling is phonetic to assist the players.*]
> *Orle.* O what a day is this!
> *Bur.* O jour du honte.[1] All is gone; all is lost.
> *Con.* We are enow yet living in the field,
> To smother up the English,
> If any order might be thought upon.
> *Bur.* A plague o' order. Once more to the field;
> And he that will not follow *Burbon* now,
> Let him go home, and with his cap in hand,
> Like a base leno hold the chamber doore,
> Whilst by a base slave no gentler than my dog,
> His fairest daughter is contamuracke.
> *Con.* Disorder that hath spoild us, right us now.
> Come. We in heaps will offer up our lives
> Unto these English, or else die with fame.
> Come, come along; lets dye with honor,
> Our shame doth last too long.
>
> [1] This was misprinted ' dei haute '.

Shakespeare's revision reads (Folio, p. 88):

> *Con.* O diable.
> *Orl.* O signeur le jour et perdia, toute et perdie.
> *Dol.* Mor Dieu ma vie, all is confounded all,
> Reproach, and everlasting shame
> Sits mocking in our Plumes.
> O meschante Fortune, do not runne away.
> *Con.* Why all our rankes are broke.
> *Dol.* O perdurable shame, let's stab our selves :
> Be these the wretches that we plaid at dice for?
> *Orl.* Is this the King we sent too, for his ransome?
> *Bur.* Shame, and eternall shame, nothing but shame,
> Let us dye in once more backe againe,
> And he that will not follow *Burbon* now,
> Let him go hence, and . . . &c.
> *Con.* Disorder that hath spoyl'd us, friend us now,
> Let us on heapes go offer up our lives.
> *Orl.* We are enow yet living in the Field,
> To smother up the English in our throngs,
> If any order might be thought upon.
> *Bur.* The divell take Order now, Ile to the throng;
> Let life be short, else shame will be too long.

'Mor du ma vie' was turned into 'Mor **Dieu** ma vie'. The passage 'Come. We in heapes will offer up our lives', which became 'Let us on heapes go offer up our lives', must have been badly written in the original manuscript, as it was first printed 'Come we in heapes, we'll offer up our lives', hence Shakespeare's probable confusion. This passage with 'heapes' was in the revision joined to the similar passage containing 'smother', to which was added 'in our throngs'.

The entire episode as revised, with its 'perdurable shame', its suggestion of suicide in the manner of old Roman tragedy, its final hint that Burbon hastens out to find instantaneous death, has become highly rhetorical. It is less logical, but more theatrical.

The added line, 'Be these the wretches that we plaid at dice for?' was borrowed from the old play *The Famous Victories of Henry the Fifth*, a Queen's company play, in which there is an

entire episode in which the French do 'play at dice' for the
persons and belongings of the English. There is nothing similar
in the First Quarto of *Henry V* save the remark by Orleans,
'Well, who will go with me to hazard for a hundred English
prisoners?' to which the Constable answers sagely, 'You must
to hazard yourselfe before you have them'. This is but one of
the many ideas which were borrowed from the old play which
belonged to Shakespeare's old company. Evidently these odd
bits of 'business' remained in his memory.

Of all revisions the most successful that has ever been written
is without doubt the enlarged version of *Hamlet*, the last important revision with which Shakespeare can be definitely connected.
This revision, made in 1603, has been considered at length in
'The Revision of *Hamlet* and of *Romeo and Juliet*'; yet its chief
characteristics may be summarized in this chapter in order to
complete the outline of Shakespeare's development. In it appear
all the peculiarities already noted in connexion with the earlier
plays. While reversed words in single lines are not as numerous
as in *Romeo and Juliet*, passages which have been rearranged
are even more common. This denotes a greater daring, a bolder
attempt at larger invention. The habit of padding passages by
means of added quasi-quotations remains. These quotations fit
more aptly into the body of the work than was the case in his
earlier plays. They have also become more exuberantly sonorous. The habit of joining like to like has not only continued
from his earliest plays through the entire series, but has now
become so dominating that it has played havoc, not only with
individual speeches such as the monologues, but has torn asunder
the ordered arrangement of the original 'Corambis' *Hamlet* and
brought about a patchy reconstruction entirely lacking in unity
of design. The patches and insertions have incidentally rendered the characters so unbalanced that they all seem mad.

Hamlet marks the climax of Shakespeare's development. It
is his master work. Yet in it he still lacks all understanding of
true dramatic construction, of dramatic unity. Like a jobbing

mason he still patches bit to bit. Doing so he still distorts the
original characters, rendering them incomprehensible beings
whose actions are never logically conceived nor executed, whose
interrelations are rendered slipshod and haphazard. Shakespeare
seems to have understood character and character interaction
even less than he understood the building of an episode and the
interrelations of the various episodes which, properly arranged,
constitute a play.

Wherein then lay the cause of Shakespeare's popularity, for
popular he assuredly was? This must be sought in that quality
because of which he first found favour, his 'facetious grace in
writing', in conjunction with his love of high-sounding, mouth-
filling words and his inveterate habit of adding like to like.
A combination of these qualities will be found in the following
from his *Hamlet*:

> Most holy and religious feare it is
> To keepe those many many bodies safe
> That live and feede upon your Majestie.
> [*A reduplication of the idea follows.*]
> The single and peculiar life is bound
> With all the strength and armour of the mind
> To keepe it selfe from noyance, but much more
> That spirit, upon whose weale depends and rests
> The lives of many,
> [*A further quasi-quotation follows.*]
>   the cesse of Majestie
> Dies not alone; but like a gulfe doth draw
> What's neere it, with it,
> [*This was then reduplicated.*]
>   or it is a massie wheele
> Fixed on the somnet of the highest mount,
> To whose hough spokes, tenne thousand lesser things
> Are morteist and adjoynd, which when it falls,
> Each small annexment petty consequence
> Attends the boystrous raine,
> [*The anti-climax follows.*]
>   never alone
> Did the King sigh, but with a generall grone.

The air was full of these ideas from the time of the Essex rebellion until the death of Queen Elizabeth. The passage beginning ' The cesse of Majestie dies not alone ' resounds hypnotically, for it has a happy smoothness together with high-sounding words. Such strained metaphors almost always lack lucidity. As ' cesse ' means end or death, this line contains in itself a reduplication. A ' massie wheel' on the ' highest mount' with ' hough spokes' is truly Shakespearian in its sententious turgidity.

It was some time before Shakespeare became master of flamboyant rhetoric; but once he discovered its fascination he used it with a free hand, seldom worrying as to what the teratology meant so long as it was startling and fitted into his rhythmic pattern.

Rhythmic repetition of undigested thought clothed thus in startling phrases tends towards the hypnotic. That Shakespeare aimed at hypnotism cannot be asserted; he simply used such skill as he possessed to the best of his ability, the accidental result of which brought him fame and fortune.

The above seems to be the true measure of William Shakespeare, reviser. That his revisions pleased is evident from the long popularity of his enlarged *Hamlet*, his enlarged *Romeo and Juliet*, his enlarged *Henry V* and *Richard III*. In order to gain success through rhythm and teratology he necessarily must have been interested almost alone in sound and the effect sound produced upon his hearers. Had he been interested in ideas he could not have sacrificed sense to sound so nonchalantly.

To carry on work in this peculiar manner it was necessary that Shakespeare should have his mind stored with an infinite number of usable aphorisms. These he had gathered in the course of his long career as an actor from contemporary poets and essayists. It was also necessary that he should have command of a long list of plays which were so nearly perfect in plot and character work that the distortion due to his revision should not entirely render them ludicrous. His one recorded failure in this respect was *Pericles, Prince of Tyre*, for which his contemporaries censured him : ' But Shakespeare the Plebian Driller, was founder'd in 's *Pericles*.' Shakespeare was fortunate because, as a shareholder in first one company, then in others, he had access to a large repertoire which for many years furnished him with well-constructed old and new plays into which, to the delight of his audience, he inserted sonorous overcharged metaphors. When he had redecorated the entire repertoire of the Chamberlain company, when dramatists led by Jonson began publishing their own productions, his task was ended and he retired to Stratford.

It may now be interesting to compare this new Shakespeare with William Shakespeare the dramatist as depicted by his contemporaries. First, Greene's angry outburst:

> There is an upstart Crow, beautified with our feathers, that with his Tygers heart wrapt in a Players hide, supposes he is as well able to bumbast out a blank verse as the best of you: and being an absolute Johannes fac totem, is in his owne conceit the onely Shake-scene in a countrie. O that I might intreate your wits [*Marlowe, Peele, and Nash*] to be imployed in more profitable courses [*than play-writing*] & let these Apes imitate your past excellence, and never more acquaint them with your ádmired inventions.

Although severe, this certainly fits Shakespeare the reviser. Chettle follows:

> The other, whome at that time [*when printing the above by Greene*] I did not so much spare, as since I wish I had . . . because my selfe have seene his demeanor no lesse civill, than he excellent in the qualitie he professes [*acting*]: Besides, divers of worship have reported his uprightnes of dealing, which argues his honesty, and his facetious grace in writing, that approves his art.

This also applies to Shakespeare the reviser.

Ben Jonson's contributions were subject to humours. The first was written when he was angry with his rival:

On Poet-Ape.

Poor Poet-ape, that would be thought our chief,
Whose works are e'en the frippery of wit,
From brokage is become so bold a thief
As we, the robb'd, leave rage, and pity it.

[*This was written after the Henry V plays, in which Jonson had a share, had been printed as by William Shakespeare. ' Brokage' refers to Shakespeare's activities as play-broker, or buyer, for the Chamberlain company.*]

At first he made low shifts, would pick and glean,
Buy the reversion of old plays; now grown
To a little wealth, and credit in the scene,
He takes up all, makes each man's wit his own.
And, told of this, he slights it. Tut, such crimes
The sluggish gaping auditor devours;
He marks not whose 'twas first: And after-time
May judge it to be his, as well as ours.

[*This exactly applies to Shakespeare the reviser, as does the ending, which is addressed to Shakespeare direct.*]

Fool! As if half eyes will not know a fleece
From locks of wool, or shreds from the whole piece!

Could language more clearly state that Shakespeare's work consisted solely in patches borrowed from all and added to plays already written by other men. That this epigram was on Shakespeare no one who has studied the period can doubt. A poet-ape was an actor. Shakespeare was the only actor at that period who was also a dramatist and a theatrical manager. In later years Heywood followed closely in his footsteps as actor, manager, and reviser.

After Shakespeare's death Jonson was employed by Heminge and Condell to write the introduction to the Folio edition of the Globe repertoire. William Basse had already written an ' Elegie' on Shakespeare's death. Jonson would not let himself be outdone by any one, so whereas Basse wrote:

Renowned Spenser, lie a thought more nigh
To learned Chaucer; and rare Beaumont lie
A little nearer Spenser, to make room
For Shakespeare in your three-fold, four-fold tomb.

Jonson thundered:
                    Soule of the Age!
The applause! delight! the wonder of our Stage!
My Shakespeare, rise; I will not lodge thee by

Chaucer, or Spenser, or bid Beaumont lye
A little further, to make thee a roome:
Thou art a Moniment, without a tombe. . . .

Having thus in rivalry lashed his Pegasus into a gallop he continued in Rodomonte's vein:

I should commit thee surely with thy peeres,
And tell, how farre thou didst our Lily out-shine,
Or sporting Kid, or Marlowes mighty line.
And though thou hadst small Latine, and lesse Greeke,
[*Here Pegasus must have stumbled.*]
. . . Looke how the fathers face
Lives in his issue, even so, the race
Of Shakespeare's minde, and manners brightly shines
In his well torned and true-filed lines: &c.

Three years later Jonson ridiculed Shakespeare's *Julius Caesar*
in *The Staple of News*, thus showing that he did not really believe quite all he wrote in the Folio eulogy.

Jonson's final opinion is to be found in his *Timber*:

De Shakespeare nostrat. Augustus in Hat.

I remember the players have often mentioned it as an honour
to Shakespeare, that in his writing (whatsoever he penned) he
never blotted out a line. My answer hath been, Would he had
blotted out a thousand. Which they thought a malevolent speech.
I had not told posterity this, but for their ignorance, who chose
that circumstance to commend their friend by, wherein he most
faulted; and to justify mine own candor: for I loved the man, and
do honour his memory, on this side idolatry, as much as any.
[*The players evidently idolized him.*] He was (indeed) honest, and
of an open and free nature; had an excellent phantasy, brave
notions, and gentle expressions; wherein he flowed with that
facility, that sometimes it was necessary he should be stopped:
Sufflaminandus erat, as Augustus said of Haterius. His wit was
in his own power, would the rule of it had been so too. Many
times he fell into those things could not escape laughter: as
when he said in the person of Caesar, one speaking to him,
'Caesar thou dost me wrong'. He replies, 'Caesar did never
wrong, but with just cause', and such like; which were ridiculous.
But he redeemed his vices with his virtues. There was ever more
in him to be praised than to be pardoned.

Evidently Jonson, when his anger and love had somewhat cooled, looked back upon Shakespeare as a most likeable companion, though anything but a great dramatist. Those who take other men's ideas and present them in pretentious language, be they poets, preachers, or politicians, are usually 'open free natures' who are popular among their fellows who have 'brave notions'; also they usually, in their revisions, flow with that facility that sometimes they should be 'stopped'; and as often they make blunders which cannot 'escape laughter'. Jonson's evidence, be it bitter or laudatory, all coincides with what has been deduced concerning Shakespeare the reviser, who wrote 'true-filed' lines and had an 'open free' nature and 'brave notions' and evinced an inability to inhibit inopportune parallelisms.

Mr. Aubrey (1625–1700), one of the most careful and exact of biographical historians, collected whatever he could find concerning Shakespeare. His statements read:

William Shakespeare's father was a butcher [*fact*], and I have been told heretofore by some of the neighbors, that when he was a boy, he exercised his father's trade [*village gossip*]; but when he killed a calfe, he would do it in a high style, and make a speech [*village gossip founded on Shakespeare's love of high-sounding language*]. This William, being inclined naturally to poetry and acting came to London, I guesse, about 18 [*a guess*], and was an actor at one of the playhouses, and did act exceeding well [*fact*]. Now Ben Jonson was never a good actor, but an excellent instructor [*fact*]. He [*Shakespeare*] began early to make essays in dramatic poetry [*fact*], which at that time was very lowe [*personal opinion*], and his plays took well [*fact*]. He was a handsome well shaped man; verie good company, and a very ready, and pleasant, and smooth wit [*facts*]. The humor of the constable in Midsummer-nights Dreame [*a mistake for 'Much Ado about Nothing'*] he happened to take at Crendon in Bucks. (I think it was Midsummer night that he happened to be there); which is the road from London to Stratford; and there was living that constable about 1642, when I came first to Oxon. Mr. Jos Howe is of the parish and knew him [*one of Howe's tales*]. Ben Jonson and he did gather humours [*anecdotes*] of men wherever they came [*fact*]. One time as he was at the taverne at Stratford, Mr. Combes, an old usurer, was to be buryed; he makes then this extemporary epitaph upon him:

Ten in the hundred the Devill allowes,
But Combes will have twelve, he sweares and he vowes:
If any one aske who lives in this tomb,
Hoh! quoth the Devill, 'tis my John o' Combe.

[*A village tale probably based on fact.*] He was wont to go to his native country once a yeare [*fact*]. I think I have been told that he left near 300£ to a sister [*fact, except it was to a daughter*]. He understood latin pretty well; for he had been in his younger yeares a school-master in the country. [*This last was in answer to Jonson's criticism of small Latin and less Greek, and is a probable fact.*]

While Aubrey thus furnishes a true and fairly complete outline of Shakespeare the man, he gives but one hint of Shakespeare the author. This is contained in the 'extemporary' epitaph on his friend Combes, which characteristically is a revision. Several earlier versions of this witticism exist, but the following seems to have served as a basis for Shakespeare's enlarged or augmented edition:

Ten in the hundred lies under this stone,
And a hundred to ten to the devil he's gone.
1608.

Shakespeare the man as disclosed by Jonson and Aubrey, and Shakespeare the reviser as disclosed by his additions and amendments, seem to be one and the same person. From the foregoing examination of his work as a reviser it is evident that to plan a play, elaborate its plot, and develop its characters was beyond the powers of William Shakespeare, reviser. Who then wrote the plays which he patched, which so indiscriminately have been attributed to him? In the *Poet-Ape* Jonson states that Shakespeare took up plays from 'all'. Presumably, then, the various plays of the Globe repertoire must be redistributed among 'all' the playwrights of the period.

PART II
ELIZABETHAN DRAMATISTS

INTRODUCTORY NOTE

HAVING shown in the first part of this volume that William Shakespeare could not have been the original author of the plays found in the Globe repertoire, possible authors must be found to take his place. In the short studies of dramatists following, an endeavour is made to ascertain as nearly as possible from his known work each author's peculiar characteristics. This accomplished, some of the many Elizabethan plays have been assigned to their apparent authors. In assigning these plays many can with certainty be put down to their real authors on reliable external evidence alone.[1] Others must be assigned on internal evidence only. In each case the distinction is drawn between registered fact and speculation. Plays allocated on registered fact permit of no discussion. Those assigned on internal evidence alone may be mistakenly allocated. The author does not pretend to be unfailingly correct in these later assignments, especially considering that almost every play of the period, as it appears in print to-day, was originally the work of several hands, which work was often reshaped by still other hands. However, each workman has usually left his mark on each play touched by him. The discovery of the mark of each important workman is an interesting pursuit, and the search among the plays for these marks, whereby to establish authorship, is quite as interesting. It is to be hoped that further marks will be discovered, leading to identification of workmanship on other plays.

[1] Henslowe's Diary is reliable evidence. Publishers' announcements, the assignments by Meres, the editors of the Folio (Shakespeare's), and other contemporary publishers cannot be accepted as altogether satisfactory evidence.

I

JOHN LYLY

(COURT COMEDY)

COMEDY based on smart repartee has always appealed to the intellectual side of the English mind. It especially appeals to youths and maidens, and it is most enjoyable when confined to their irresponsible ingenuousness. Among grown people it becomes tedious. England has produced a long series of such Attic dramatists; but the first and most original of them all was John Lyly.

John Lyly, son of Peter Lyly, prebendary and registrar at Canterbury, grandson of William Lyly the grammarian, was born about the year 1553. Wood states: 'John Lylie or Lylly a Kentish man born, became a student in Magd. coll. in the beginning of 1569, aged 16, or thereabouts.' He received his B.A. in 1573, his M.A. in 1575. In 1578 his *Euphues: the Anatomy of Wyt* appeared, to be followed by a long series of pamphlets, masques, and Court comedies.

While at Oxford Lyly was fathered by Lord Burleigh, High Treasurer of England; and soon after returning to London he became secretary to Lord Burleigh's son-in-law, the Earl of Oxford. For his services the Earl of Oxford bought and presented to Lyly in 1583 the lease of Blackfriars theatre and several adjoining tenements; and in 1584 he gave him 'the Manor House, Bentfeylde, Burye Lodge, lands, &c., situate near Burye'. (Feuillerat.)

About 1588 Lyly was appointed to a post in connexion with the Revels Office, with a half-promise of the Mastership on the death of Edward Tylney. He may have succeeded Edward Buggyn as Clerk-controller, or he may have been Master of the department of Toiles in succession to Mr. Tamworth.

About 1590 Lyly must have been writing for the Queen's
company as well as for Paules Boys, for whom he wrote from
1583 to 1590, as Gabriel Harvey wrote of him: 'He hath not
played the Vicemaster of Paules and the Foolmaster of the
Theatre for naughts . . . sometime the fiddlestick of Oxford, now
the very bable of London.' Harvey also discloses that Lyly was
still writing for the Theatre in 1593. (See NASH.)

After the inhibition of Paules Boys in 1590 Lyly devised a
number of entertainments given by various noblemen to Queen
Elizabeth. On November 17, 1590, he planned and carried out
a pageant at the Tiltyard when Sir Henry Lea yielded his place
as Master of 'Her Highnesse Armorie' to George, Earl of Cumber-
land. On May 10, 1591, he carried out the entertainment given
by Sir Robert Cecil, Lord Burleigh's second son, to the Queen
at Theobalds. George Peele collaborated in this entertainment.
In mid-August, 1591, Lord Montecute entertained the Queen at
Cowdray, when Lyly again provided several days' amusement.
The Queen then went to Chichester, Petworth, Portsmouth, &c.,
and arrived at Elvetham on the 23rd of August, where the Earl
of Hertford with Lyly's assistance provided four days' entertainment.

During the ensuing year, 1592, there were similar entertainments at Quarrendon in mid-August (Sir Henry Lea), at Bisham
late in August (Lord Russel), at Sudeley in mid-September (Lord
Chandos), and at Rycote in early October (Sir William Norris).
For these outdoor masques, plays, and entertainments, which
usually lasted three days, Lyly devised picturesque settings and
wrote many of the speeches and songs. Of like entertainments,
after the plague years of 1592-3, no records have been found
except that of Lord Keeper Egerton's entertainment in July–
August of 1602, and the plays by Marlowe and Nash.

That Lyly continued writing for the Queen's entertainment
is nevertheless evident from his letter to her written in 1597:

I was entertayned your Majesties Servant; by your owne gratious
favour: strangthened with conditions, that, I should ayme all my
courses att the Revells; (I dare not saye, with a promise, butt a

hopeffull Item, of the Reversion) ffor the which this tenn yeares, I have attended . . . vouchsaffe in your never erringe Judgement some plancke, or rafter; to waffe mee into a countrye where, in my sadd and setled devotion; I maye in every corner of a thatcht cottage wryte prayers in stead of playes.

On December 22, 1597, Lyly further wrote to Lord Robert Cecil:

I will cast my wittes in a new mould, and turn the water source by a contrary sluce, for I find it folly that on[e] foot being in the grave, I shuld have the other on the stage.

He was therefore writing plays as well as entertainments in 1597.

In a later letter to Lord Cecil, dated February 27, 1600, Lyly wrote: 'If hapely it be moved after 13 yeres service for ye Revells,' &c., and again he wrote to the Queen on about the same date:

Tyme cannot worke my peticions nor my peticions the tyme. After many yeares servyce [if] it pleased your Majestie to except against Tents and Toyles (I wish for Tents I might put in Tene-ments, soe would I bee eased of some Toyles) some lands, some goodes, fynes of forfeytures, that should ffall by the just ffall of the most ffalce traytors, that seeinge nothinge will come by the Revells I may praye uppon the Rebells;)

In a letter to Lord Cecil of February 4, 1602, Lyly wrote: 'My wife delivered my petition to the Queen who accepted it graciously,' &c.

Edward Blount, who published six of Lyly's plays in 1638, states that: 'I have dig'd up the Grave of a Rare and Excellent Poet whom Queen Elizabeth then heard, Graced, and Rewarded.' It may be supposed from this that Lyly's petition was favourably answered.

John Lyly married Beatrice Browne at St. Clement Danes, London, on November 22, 1583. (Feuillerat.) On the death of Queen Elizabeth he was granted seven yards of mourning for himself and four yards for his servants. He sat as a member of the seventh Parliament in 1588–9 for Wiltshire, as a member of the eighth in 1592–3 for Aylesbury, of the ninth in 1597 for Appleby, and of the tenth in 1601 for Aylesbury. Lyly was thus intimately connected with Court and Parliament from the day he left Oxford until his death in 1606.

With his position at Court and his keen wit Lyly at once assumed the role of Court jester. He often mentions himself as such ; certainly he took to himself all the privileges of one. He alone, among all the writers of the age, dared condemn the vices of those in power, the sting of his censure being ever hidden under his gay mockery.

Jonson caricatured Lyly in *Every Man out of His Humour* (1599) as Fastidious Brisk : 'a neat spruce affected courtier, one that wears clothes well.' Nash recorded that he was small of stature and a smoker.

Lyly's dramatic career divides itself into two parts—that before and that after the inhibition of Paules Boys in 1590. To his first period belong *Campaspe* (1589), a short historical allegorical comedy, *Sapho and Phao, Endimion,* and *Midas,* allegorical Court comedies, *Gallathea* and *Loves Metamorphosis,* pastoral comedies which resemble masques, and *Mother Bombie,* a realistic comedy. These were all in prose, with songs and dances interspersed. To the second period belong *The Woman in the Moon,* a poetical pastoral written in blank verse, and various later plays.

In his early Court comedies various elements were certain to make their appearance. Played as they were by children they inclined towards farce, fantasy, and song. Children cannot act tragedy, nor can they simulate deep emotion. Being produced before a cultured aristocracy his plays tended to become allegorical, the allusions being usually to those within the Court circle. By making the best possible use of his material Lyly produced light comedies, which by their artistic grace, brilliant dialogue, songs, and dances pleased the generality, and by the added zest of their half-hidden allusions flattered and piqued the Court.

The restrictions put on Lyly in the creation of these comedies were many and onerous. Never could he for a moment doff
his cap and bells, but must always seem a fool, however serious
his strictures or deep his philosophical discourses.

These, his early plays, might well be called the serio-comedies
of the Court jester. They are touched in lightly. The people,
while differentiated in manners, speak the same idiom. There
is a lack of chiaroscuro. The plots are thin. These are faults
common to all Court comedies, especially when performed by
children or amateurs.

Because, in these early plays, Lyly kept to his role he has
met with little but condemnation from scholastics. 'The showy
and superficial was always the first consideration with Lyly;
wit before learning, speech before thought,' &c. He who writes
such a criticism of Lyly is deluded, for there is always an idea
beneath the froth of his banter which shapes the play into an
intellectual unity, a true organism.

A drama cannot be made of the facetious talk of ingenuous
youths, nor can a play, despite many modern attempts, be made
of studied cleverness. Herein Lyly proved himself a consummate
artist, while his imitators have merely exposed their short-
coming.

Many people never realize the difference between a creator
and an imitator. A creator produces a work which expresses
his soul, even as a bramble produces a rose. There is a certain
unity about his work, for it is an expression, an inner mood,
thought, or feeling, eventually crystallizing in tangible form. This
movement from the centre outward, this unity of origin, is ever
felt in the work of all true creators.

The imitator begins and ends with externals. There is no ex-
pansion, no growth, but a gathering together of petals which,
more or less firmly glued together, are presented as a perfect
flower. It is a strange commentary on the intellect of the average
human being that it more often prefers the imitation to the real
creation. Genius dies in poverty; the imitator survives in flattered luxury.

There has been no writer in England more imitated than John Lyly. It is therefore necessary, if any proper idea of his worth is to be gained, that the soul underlying the manifestation be discovered. The outward characteristics of his work are so marked, that the real author and creator of those peculiarities may be overlooked.

When Lyly wrote his first great work, *Euphues*, Queen Elizabeth was a maiden lady of forty-four or forty-five. She was just entering the sentimental age so common to unmarried ladies who have passed the normal marriage period and have entered the second sexless one: she remained in this sentimental state for a number of years. One of the most noticeable characteristics of this period is an abnormal intellectual curiosity as to love and all pertaining to Cupid's court. Lyly's early work thus found fertile soil. Favoured by the great Queen, euphuism at once became the fashion, almost the only concern of the moment.

But beneath the flippant discussion of *affaires du cœur* there remained the soul of a great artist. Something there was in his plays which touched the heart and imagination of the English race and held it firmly for many years, something his imitators lacked, something which can be felt to-day despite the artificial style, the grotesque, untrue intellectual similes, something besides the sentimentality of a maiden lady of forty-five, something other than the sexless intellectuality of a boy of twenty-three.

Under Queen Elizabeth the days of chivalry came to an end. Tournaments, jousts, courts of love, were continued as pastimes; but the institutions were fast becoming obsolete. Gunpowder, cannon, fired by an unknown hand, killing an unknown foe, suddenly ended the days of individual combat, of knighthood. The pistol brought into being the desperado lacking a sense of honour, a moral code. During this period commercial England sprang into existence. Men of business became rich and powerful, and here again there was a weakening of the chivalric code.

In all of Lyly's prose works, in all of his tales, there is at

the end of every one, howsoever light the banter, howsoever
filled with roses the pleasing pathway, howsoever inconsequent
the travellers, a finger pointing the way of honour. His motto
might have been: *Knight-errantry passes; honour abides.* And,
as a true Englishman, the more he was in earnest the more
capricious and volatile he seemed in his writings.

Of Lyly's early plays examples have been preserved which
cover the period from 1580 to 1590. These probably appeared
in the following order: *Campaspe, Sapho and Phao, Gallathea,
Endimion, Midas,* and *Mother Bombie.*

In these plays, written chiefly around love-stories, Lyly developed certain types and evolved a new variety of smart-talk
comedy. Gradually he progressed from a slight plot which served
as a framework for much intellectual matter to a complex plot
full of intrigue. In the earlier plays the framework was but slightly
related to the incidental matter; in the later plays both are interdependent. These later plays thus become perfect examples of
intriguing comedy.

It is a characteristic of intriguing drama, where the interest is
chiefly centred in plot and counterplot, that the characters should
be types rather than individuals; and this is true of all of Lyly's
early comedies. His courtiers, ladies, precocious pages, &c., tend
to have a certain similarity. Each is varied; yet each remains
a type rather than an individual. This was necessitated also
partly because of the use to which they were put when they
were exploiting the incidental matter, such as songs, dances, smart
talk of the foibles and problems of the day, allegories, &c.

It was not because Lyly could not create individuals that he
used types in these plays, but because in plays of intrigue types
are the better medium. When Lyly changed to lyrical plays, such
as *The Woman in the Moon,* he began to create real characters,
such as Gunophilus and Pandora.

Lyly was too artistic to descend to didactic drama. Sermons
and morals abound in these plays; but they are cleverly presented rather as the incisive comments of a Court jester than as
the sorrowful censures of a woe-ye-worldlings puritan.

Lyly's artistic sense also prevented him from concocting comedies of pure plot and counterplot, for almost all of the grace and beauty of these plays is contained in the incidental matter. At first this material, which to Lyly must have been more important than his plot, was introduced on the slightest pretext. Later he so managed his plots that all incidental matter became an integral part of the comedy.

The prose of these plays is concise, condensed. Gradually Lyly developed this instrument until he achieved with it the utmost possible in prose comedy. Then he began to search for a new medium. For he found that while prose will serve for all intellectual expression it is a poor instrument through which to express feeling and emotion. Although he discovered and used parallel words and phrases in his prose even to excess he began to long for a freer use of rhythm and sound. The following examples show how far he carried parallelism in prose before he sought a more perfect medium.

From *Midas*.

1. *Eristus*. To have gold and not love (which cannot be purchast by gold) is to be a slave to gold.

Martius. To possesse mountains of gold, and a mistresse more precious then gold, and not commande the world, is to make Mydas new prentise to a mint, and Jorneman to a woman.

Mellicrites. To enjoy a faire ladie in love, and wante faire gold to give: to have thousands of people to fight, and no peny to paye—wil make ones mistresse wilde, and his soldiers tame.

2. *Midas*. O my Lords, when I call to minde my cruelties in Lycaonia, my usurping in Getulia, my oppression in Sola: then do I finde neither mercies in my conquests, nor colour for my warres, nor measure in my taxes. I have written my lawes in blood, and made my Gods of golde; I have caused the mothers wombes to be their childrens tombes, cradles to swimme in blood like boates, and the temples of the Gods a stewes for strumpets. . . . Have not I entised the subjects of my neighbor Princes to destroy their natural Kings? like moths that eate the cloth in which they were bred, like vipers that gnawe the bowels of which they were borne, and like wormes that consume the wood in which they were ingendred?

From *Endimion.*

Flowers in theyr buds are nothing worth till they be blowne, nor blossoms accounted till they be ripe fruite: and shal we then say they be changeable, for that they growe from seedes to leaves, from leaves to buds, from buds to theyr perfection? Then, why be not twigs that become trees, children that become men, and Mornings that grow to Evenings, termed wavering, for that they continue not at one stay? Aye, but Cynthia, being in her fulnes decayeth, as not delighting in her greatest beautie, or withering when she should be most honoured. When Mallice cannot object anything, Folly will, making that a vice, which is the greatest virtue. . . . Tell mee Eumenides, what is he that having a Mistris of ripe yeeres and infinite vertues, great honors, and unspeakable beauty, but woulde wish that shee might grow tender againe? getting youth by yeeres, and never decaying beauty by time, whose fayre face, neyther the Summers blaze can scorch, nor Winters blast chappe, nor the numbring yeeres breede altering of colours. Such is my sweete Cynthia, whom Tyme cannot touch, because she is divine, nor will offend because she is delicate.

This method of arranging words so as to make patterns was in common use during the Middle Ages. It was practised by medieval preachers; and the art was taught by almost all grammarians. Lyly absorbed it from his father, his grandfather, and their associates. Its ornate detailed pattern corresponds to the lacework tracery of Renaissance architecture.

Lyly's whimsical dialogue did not continue in this euphuistic vein. The youth grew to manhood, married, had children, entered Parliament. Though he never ceased trifling there appeared less of raillery and more of censure in his work, less of Touchstone and more of melancholy Jacques. His strictures on the frivolous feminism of his day became more severe, his songs less light-hearted.

Intellectual drama is through its very nature reduced to plot and counterplot as a medium. The Latin authors used it because of their delight in intrigue; Lyly used it as a means of expressing ideas of truth, justice, moral conduct, and chivalry.

In 1589 a sect called Martinists made themselves so obnoxious to the bishops, that Lyly and Nash turned on them in pamphlets and plays. One or more of these lampoons was staged, privately by the Paules Boys, publicly by the Queen's company at the Theatre. For staging these plays Paules Boys were inhibited in 1590.

The Woman in the Moon, which marks the beginning of Lyly's second period, is the first of his acknowledged plays that was not acted by Paules Boys. It was written after they were inhibited. Therefore it must have been written for the Chapel Children. This is a woman's play centring in Pandora, epitome of womanhood, who is subjected to the influences of the various planets. She is exhibited as melancholy, sullen, self-willed, tongue-tied, tearful; as ambitious, disdainful; as jealous, vixenish; as gentle, kind, loving, liberal, chaste, &c. The other characters, somewhat subject to the same influences, are also more fully developed than are those in the plays written for Paules Boys. The clown Gunophilus carries all the comedy, being thus the first of a long line of true comedians.

This play is the first play in which blank verse as well as prose was used by Lyly. While he may be said to have invented prose comedy, and had consistently used it in his earlier plays, he now turned to blank verse as a better medium for poetical and allegorical expression. Prose he relegated to realism as found in *Mother Bombie*.

The Woman in the Moon is poetic in conception as well as in execution. As a lyric it must be placed near, if not above, *The Tragedie of Dido* of Marlowe and Nash. In *Mother Bombie* Lyly fixed for ever the style of realistic prose comedy. In *The Woman in the Moon* he is found experimenting with the new medium of blank verse. The fusing of these elements gave rise to the new medium, poetical comedy, to such plays as *Twelfth Night* and *As You Like It*.

Examples of blank verse:

[When Pandora is under the influence of Luna, Stesias and Gunophilus being present.]

Ste. Now I perceive that she is lunaticke:
What may I do to bring her to her wits?

Gun. Speake, gentle maister, and intreat her fayre.
Ste. Pandora, my love Pandora!
Pan. Ile not be fayre; why call you me your love?
Love is a little boy; so am not I!
Ste. I will allure her with fayre promises;
And when I have her in my leavie bower,
Pray to our water Nimphes and Silvane gods,
To cure her of this piteous lunacye.
Pan. Give me a running streame in both my hands,
A blew kings fisher, and a pible stone,
And Ile catch butter-flies upon the sand,
And thou Gunophilus shalt clippe their wings.

What rare filigree, all dainty charm, containing the essence and witchery of woman!

(Under Venus, answering the protestations of Iphicles,
        Pandora says:)
He that would do all this, must love me well;
And why should he love me and I not him?
Wilt thou for my sake goe into yon grove,
And we will sing unto the wilde birdes notes,
And be as pleasant as the Western winde,
That kisses flowers and wantons with their leaves.

(When Pandora is mad the clown Gunophilus says of her:)
I was nere in love with her till now. O absolute Pandora! because folish; for folly is womens perfection. To talke idely, to loke wildly, to laugh at every breath and play with a feather, is that would make a Stoyke in love, yea, thou thyselfe. Gravity in woman is like to a gray beard upon the breaching boies chinne, which a good Schoolmaister would cause to be clipt, and the wise husband to be avoyded.

The Woman in the Moon is one of the most fascinating music dramas that has ever been written. Unfortunately it is little known and has not been staged since the days of Queen Elizabeth.

Solyman and Perseda, entered in the Stationers' Register in 1592, was founded on the first story in a collection called *Printemps d'Iver,* by Jacques Yver, which was published in 1572, and was translated into English in 1578 by Henry Wotton.

This play is a romantic mock-heroic tragedy of blood. It is full of similes from natural history, of antitheses, play upon words, classical allusions, balanced sentences, alliterations, &c., all in the manner of Lyly. The drama is brought about and the characters are controlled by Love, Fortune, and Death, even as the action is caused, and Pandora is ruled, by the Gods in *The Woman in the Moon*.

Solyman and Perseda has been attributed to both Kyd and Peele; but it lacks the distinctive marks of either and has almost all of those qualities which are common to Lyly's known work. In it he relates a tale of murder and blood; but despite serious situations he carries the whole through as mock-tragedy. The verse runs smoothly, the horrors are treated in a spirit of jest. Piston, the light comedian, is one of Lyly's clowns. The play ends with the murder of all concerned. Even Solyman, the last survivor, is poisoned, so that the play may finish after the fashion of all tragedies of blood. An epilogue contains one of Lyly's usual compliments to Queen Elizabeth. There is nothing in the play which Lyly might not have written, and there is much which could have come from no other author.

Greene essayed heroic tragedy in blank verse with little success. In this mock-tragedy of gory romance Lyly produced one of the most popular plays of the period. Solyman, or Zolziman as he was often called, remained a favourite character for many years. Lyly's familiar use of alliteration will be found in the following:

> And when my soule from body shall depart,
> Trouble me not, but let it passe in peace,
> And in your silence let your love be showne.
> And now pale death sits on my parting soule.
> And now, to end our difference at last,
> In this last act note but the deedes of Death.
> Their loves and fortunes ended with their lives, &c.

There are many examples of his nature similes, such as:

> Amongst those worthies will Erastus troupe,
> Though like a gnat amongst a hive of Bees.

Put Lambe-like mildnes to your Lyons strength.

Heele justle like a jade.

He will jet as if it were a goose on a greene.

The one's a Lyon almost brought to death,
Whose skin will countervaile the hunter's toile;
The other is a Waspe with threatening sting,
Whose hunny is not worth the taking up.

No one but Lyly the *farceur* would have allowed one of his knights to boast:

> As I remember, there happened a sore drought in some part of Belgia, that the jucie grasse was seared with the Sunne-God's element: I held it pollicie to put the men children of that climate to the sword, that the mothers teares might releeve the pearched earth. The men died, the women wept, and the grasse grew; else had my Frizeland horse perished, whose losse would have more grieved me than the ruine of that whole country.

Another like example is:

> Upon a time in Ireland I fought on horseback . . . insomuch that my steed began to faint. I, conjecturing the cause to be want of water, in which place there was no such element, dismounted; . . . and, all on foote, like an Herculian offspring, endured some three or foure howers combat, in which process my body distilled such dewy showers of swet that from the warlike wrinckles of my front my palfrey coold his thirst.

Solyman and Perseda dates c. 1591, being contemporary with Peele's *Olde Wives' Tale*. Like that comedy it ridiculed improbable romantic histories and impossible tragedies of revenge. Through it Lyly helped to laugh the old style plays out of favour.

The Woman in the Moon is the last play which is usually catalogued as belonging to Lyly. That he continued writing for the stage is evident from his letters to Queen Elizabeth and Sir Robert Cecil, in both of which he mentions the fact that his dramatic activities had not ceased.

Several of Lyly's Paules Boys' plays were publicly acted by the
Queen's company, at least one in conjunction with them. When
the Boys were inhibited in 1590 he may have turned for a short
time to the Queen's company. If so, it could have been for a
short time only. From 1593, when Marlowe died, to 1596 Lyly,
Peele, and Nash must have furnished the greater number of Court
plays; and from 1596, when Peele died, to 1599 Lyly was the
only important author who could have been writing for ' Her
Majesties Children '. All other known authors can be accounted
for during this period. It is evident, therefore, that the great
favour which the Children attained at Blackfriars from 1596 to
1599 was due in chief to Lyly.

Such of his plays as were written for Blackfriars were composed under new and, to Lyly, novel conditions. The favourite
and distinguished Court jester was here rudely divorced from his
environment. How did he survive the change from the refined
Court of Queen Elizabeth to the popular, though select, audience
at Blackfriars? The severe plague of 1592–3 brought in its wake
a great humanitarian movement. What effect did this have on
Lyly's work?

For Lyly to change his nature was impossible. A fastidious
artist he remained, and a jester always. However, he was forced
to find new subjects and new methods for his comedies. He could
no longer indulge in allegorical allusions to individual members
of his audience. Satire, censure, or praise must now be of characters such as were known to his general audience. His plots must
become human.

The line of Lyly's new development was indicated in *Mother
Bombie* and *The Woman in the Moon*. While neither of these
conforms to the newly imposed conditions, both are full of sugges-
tions. In the one he had developed intrigue in prose; in the
other he had discovered lyricism in blank verse. His new need
was to combine these two into humanitarian comedy.

Blank verse, which soon developed into free rhythm in the
hands of Peele, while eminently suited to serious emotional work,
is a poor medium for comedy, especially if it contains a farcical

element. Prose, on the other hand, does not lend itself to lyricism and emotion. Between these two Lyly sought and found a new medium in rhymed free rhythm, which exactly fitted his new need, his temperament and genius.

Early in his career Lyly had discovered the technical secret that rhyme lends to verse a feeling of artificiality, at times of farce. This he exploited in many of his early songs:

Hey downe a downe did Dian sing,
   amongst her Virgins sitting:
Then love there is no vainer thing,
   for maidens most unfitting,
And so think I, with a downe downe derrie, &c.

Often these songs were divided up among several as conversation, as in the *Three Fidlers* song:

All 3. The Bride this night can catch no cold,
   No cold; the Bridegroome 's yong, not old;
   Like Ivie he her fast does hold,
1 Fid. And clips her,
2 Fid.   And lips her,
3 Fid.   And flips her too.
All 3. Then let them alone, they know what they do.
1 Fid. At laugh and lie down, if they play,
2 Fid. What asse against the sport can bray?
3 Fid. Such tick-tacke has held many a day,
1 Fid. And longer,
2 Fid.   And stronger,
3 Fid.   It still holds too.
All 3. Then let them alone, they know what they do.
   This night,   in delight
   Does thump away sorrow.
   Of billing   take your filling,
   So good morrow, good morrow.

This method Lyly now developed to its utmost. And it is a strange fact that, with the exception of Dekker, he was the only dramatist of the age who realized and made conscious use of this peculiarity of rhyme.

Rhymed free rhythm, as a medium for the expression of farce and persiflage, marks all of Lyly's later work. It was daring indeed to hark back to discredited end rhymes, but Lyly was always original in his experiments. The ancient rhymed couplets of well-measured blank verse were serious and stilted. Lyly's sprightly internally and externally rhymed free rhythm was a new creation, born of his peculiar and whimsical spirit, the poetical outcome of euphuistic parallelism. With it he could still make patterns, but with greater freedom and better results.

During the period 1589–97 almost all plays were published anonymously. There is also very little extant evidence from which clues of identity can be obtained. It is therefore necessary to search for some internal evidence which may serve as a guide to the authorship of each play. Collaboration and revision had already begun. Nash wrote plays with Lyly in 1589, with Marlowe in 1591–2, with Greene before 1593. Shakespeare had revised plays by Greene, Peele, and Nash before 1593.

Almost all of the Elizabethan dramatists have some marked peculiarity by which their work can be recognized. But when it is known that two or more worked on any one play the question remains, Did they collaborate or did one revise the work of the other? In the case of Nash and Lyly, who were fast friends, collaboration is presumed.

Much Ado about Nothing was published as a Lord Chamberlain play ' written by William Shakespeare ' in 1600. That it was played by the Queen's company before 1597 is disclosed by the accidental printing in the text of the names ' Kempe ' and ' Cowley ', who were Queen's men from 1592 to 1598, and who acted the parts of Dogberry and Verges. It is certainly a Nash-Lyly production belonging to *c.* 1592. After having written the anti-Martinist plays of 1589–90 these two continued their collaboration.

Much Ado about Nothing begins with Lylian prose and carries on with a mixture of prose, blank verse, and rhymed free rhythm. The greater part of the comedy seems to have been

written by Lyly ; yet here and there are to be found bits of
genuine Nash, such as the following by Beatrice :

> If the Prince be too important, tell him there is measure in
> everything, and so daunce out the answer, for here me Hero,
> wooing, wedding, and repenting, is as a Scotch jigge, a measure,
> and a cinquepace : the first suite is hot and hasty like a Scotch
> jigge (and full as fantasticall) the wedding manerly modest, (as a
> measure) full of state and aunchentry, and then comes repentance,
> and with his bad legs falls into the cinquepace faster and faster,
> till he sincke into his grave. (See NASH.)

Lyly's rhythmical development is more advanced in this play
than in *The Woman in the Moon*. The same smooth though
piquant rhythm is found in Ursula's lines :

> The pleasantst angling is to see the fish
> Cut with her golden ores the silver streame,
> And greedily devoure the treacherous baite :
> So angle we for Beatrice, who even now
> Is couched in the wood-bine coverture.

It is also found in the following of Beatrice :

> But Nature never framde a womans hart
> Of prowder stuffe then that of Beatrice :
> Disdaine and scorne ride sparkling in her eies,
> Misprising what they looke on, and her wit
> Valewes itselfe so highly, that to her
> All matter els seemes weake.

This is the rhythm of *The Woman in the Moon*. Evidently it
is not by Nash, whose rhythm was always rugged and uneven.

Much Ado yields the first hint of Lyly's later use of rhyme ;
witness the following by Beatrice :

> What fire is in mine eares ? can this be true ?
> Stand I condemn'd for pride and scorne so much ?
> Contempt, farewell, and maiden pride, adew ;
> No glory lives behind the backe of such.
> And Benedicke, love on, I will requite thee,
> Taming my wild heart to thy loving hand :
> If thou dost love, my kindnesse shall incite thee
> To bind our loves up in a holy band.
> For others say thou dost deserve, and I
> Beleeve it better then reportingly.

Much Ado about Nothing is seldom staged. It is so clever and is keyed so high that it necessitates a quick-witted, cultured audience and an appreciative theatrical manager, a man of taste and insight, for which combination it still waits, yielding place meanwhile to Sheridan's less brilliant though somewhat similar comedies. The extant edition seems to contain additions by Jonson and Shakespeare.

Love's Labour's Lost, printed as Shakespeare's in 1598, contains the broken-vow idea of *Gallathea*. It is filled with Lyly's prose banter; the serious poetry is in his vein; and many, if not all, of the characters are Lylian.

This play contains much rhymed free verse, which is used for repartee, quibbling, and inconsequential jesting. Berowne introduces the frolic in rhyme and continues in it:

> *Longavill.* You swore to that Berowne, and to the rest.
> *Ber.* By yea and nay sir, then I swore in jest.
> What is the end of study, let me know?
> *Fer.* Why that to know which else we should not know. &c.

> *Ber.* Come on then, I will sweare to studie so,
> To know the thing I am forbid to know:
> As thus, to study where I well may dine,
> When I too fast expressely am forbid;
> Or studie where to meet some mistresse fine,
> When mistresses from common sense are hid.
> Or having sworne too hard a keeping oath,
> Studie to breake it, and not breake my troth.
> If studies gaine be thus, and this be so,
> Studie knowes that which yet it doth not know.
> Sweare me to this, and I will nee're say no.

Eventually all the characters join in the rhymed merriment. Rosaline and the King, both disguised, converse:

> *King.* The musicke playes, vouchsafe some motion to it.
> *Rose.* Our eares vouchsafe it.
> *King.*   But your legges should doe it.
> *Rose.* Since you are strangers, and come here by chance,
> Wee'll not be nice, take hands, we will not dance.

King. Why take you hands then?
Rose.   Onelie to part friends;
Curtsie sweet-hearts, and so the measure ends.
King. More measure of this measure, be not nice.
Rose. We can afford no more, at such a price.
King. Prise yourselves: what buyes your companie?
Rose. Your absence onelie.
King.   That can never be, &c.

While each artificial situation is thus rendered in rhymed free-verse the serious passages are unrhymed, the which is convincing evidence that the author used rhyme consciously as an art medium for the expression of persiflage and fantasy.

This play is so like Lyly's early work that it is impossible to believe any one but he could have written it; if not by Lyly it certainly was written by a courtier having an exactly similar mind. Lyly and Peele were the only dramatists of the period who were regularly connected with the Court circle. This play must belong to one or the other, not likely to Peele, almost certainly to Lyly.

Many lines of this quaint comedy were disfigured by Shakespeare or his associates in the revision of 1598, various characters were confused, and a few inferior passages were added.

The Two Gentlemen of Verona, founded on Montemayor's *Diana*, was attributed to Shakespeare in 1598 by Meres. There is but one edition, that of 1623.

In this comedy rhyme is occasionally used, as in *Love's Labour's Lost* (p. 21):

Julia. What thinkst thou of the faire sir Eglamoure?
Lucette. As of a Knight, well-spoken, neat, and fine;
But were I you he never should be mine.
Ju. What think'st thou of the rich Mercatio?
Lu. Well of his wealth; but of himselfe, so, so.
Ju. What think'st thou of the gentle Protheus?
Lu. Lord, Lord: to see what folly raignes in us!
Ju. How now? what meanes this passion at his name?
Lu. Pardon deare Madame, 'tis a passing shame,
That I (unworthy body as I am)
Should censure thus on lovely gentlemen, &c.

The serious parts of this comedy are not rhymed; witness
Julia over the torn letter:

Oh hatefull hands, to teare such loving words;
Injurious Waspes, to feede on such sweet hony
And kill the Bees, that yeelde it, with your stings;
Ile kisse each severall paper, for amends.
. . . .
Loe, here in one line is his name twice writ.
' Poore forlorne Protheus, passionate Protheus:
To the sweet Julia:' that Ile teare away:
And yet I will not, sith so prettily
He couples it, to his complaining Names;
Thus will I fold them, one upon another;
Now kisse, embrace, contend, doe what you will, &c.

Much of the prose is in Lyly's vein; and the clown Launce is
akin to Gunophilus, and Speed is akin to Licio in *Midas*.

The original version of this comedy must have been by Lyly,
assisted in all probability by Nash. Unfortunately no early edition
has been preserved.

The Comedy of Errors, mentioned by Meres in 1598 as by
Shakespeare, and first printed in 1623, also contains all of Lyly's
familiar mannerisms. The prose, the rhymed farcical passages,
the unrhymed verse, the characters, and the subject-matter are
Lylian. Seemingly he wrote this play alone. How much it was
revised cannot be determined.[1]

A Midsommer Nights Dreame, credited to Shakespeare in 1598,
was twice printed in 1600. The greater part of this play must
be assigned to Peele; yet there are touches which hint strongly
of collaboration by Lyly. It contains various additions, probably
by Jonson. In places the characters have been confused in the
revision.

Rhymes are sometimes used in this play in order to gain an
added feeling of fancifulness, especially in the scenes between
the four lovers. These parts are presumably by Lyly. Rhyme
was also used by Peele, but without this same idea of its bizarre
effect. The donkey's ears, the fairies, both good and bad, the

[1] Paules Boys acted a comedy of 'Errors' on New Year's Day at night, 1577.

enchanting and restoring drugs had all been used by Lyly in plays before 1590.

Many lines found in *A Midsommer Nights Dreame* must have been written by some one who was present at the celebrated Kenilworth festivities of 1575, which were carried out chiefly by the Master of the Children of the Chapel Royal, William Hunnis, who designed many of the pageants and wrote much of the poetry and music. Very early in his career Lyly was connected with the Revels Office. Thomas Benger was Master of the Revels in 1575, and in 1578 Sir Edmund Tilney succeeded him. Seemingly at that time the post was applied for by Lyly, who was eventually given one under Tilney, together with the Vice-Mastership of Paules Boys. He was then ' reinjoined to give his attention to Her Majesties Revels ', with the suggestion that he might eventually be appointed Master.

Exactly when Lyly began his connexion with the Revels Office is thus left in doubt. He took his M.A. at Oxford in 1573, and then entered the service of his patron, Lord Burleigh. He was certainly at Kenilworth during the summer of 1575, either professionally connected with the office of the Revels or under the patronage of Lord Burleigh.

Whether Peele was also at Kenilworth cannot be ascertained; nevertheless he was closely associated with Hunnis throughout his entire career, and must have had the festivities described in detail to him by Hunnis and Lyly. In 1575 Shakespeare was a boy of eleven at Stratford-on-Avon.

Hunnis in one of his letters to the Queen complained of the meagre pay which the Chapel Children received, which he stated was 6*d.* per day. And in *A Midsommer Nights Dreame*, when mourning the supposed loss of Bottom, a fellow actor remarks:

O sweete bully Bottome: thus hath he lost sixepence a day, during his life; &c. And the Duke had not given him sixpence a day for playing Piramus, Ile be hang'd, &c.

This somewhat definitely places this play to the credit of the Chapel Children, as otherwise the sixpence joke would have been without point.

As the Chapel Children were more or less affiliated with the Queen's company from 1583 to 1596, in all likelihood the greater number of Court plays were enacted by 'Her Majesties Children', assisted by the Queen's company of grown actors. As a member of the Queen's company Shakespeare was able to obtain copies of a number of these plays; others he obtained from Evans when Lyly deserted Blackfriars and Evans for Paules Boys in 1599. Such of these old Chapel Children plays as he could obtain Shakespeare rewrote for the Queen-Chamberlain company, and they were then printed as ' revised by William Shakespeare '.

Twelfe Night, or, What you will, was played Twelfth-Day night (January 6), 1599, or earlier, as Morley published the song 'O Mistress mine, where are you roaming' in his *Consort Lessons* that same year. Morley was writing for the Chapel Children at the time. That the play was written for the Chapel Children by Lyly is evident. No other person then living could have written it. That the song appeared originally in the play is also plain. The words are by Lyly; and it is inconceivable that he would use one of his old songs in a new play, especially such a play as *Twelfe Night.* In *Every Man out of His Humour,* first acted in 1599 at the Globe, Ben Jonson ridicules *Twelfe Night* (iii. vi). This proves that it belonged to a rival company.

It was in 1597 that Lyly petitioned the Queen for a subsidy. Unfortunately for Lyly, but fortunately for the world at large, he was forced to continue his dramatic labours, otherwise he might never have written this his masterwork. All his powers had now reached their utmost development; his wit and philosophy had ripened and mellowed. His thoughts flowed easily and his pen recorded them with grace and facility. His sense of character had broadened. Andrew Ague-cheeke and Toby Belch, though related to his earlier clowns, are much more human, more real. Malvolio is a richer study than those of his earlier gulls. So also Viola has lost much of the pertness of his earlier heroines, but has gained a sweeter feminism.

Lyly's method in this play is the same as in all his later work.

End rhymes are used to denote inconsequentiality, and are dropped in the more serious passages. The rhyme is smoother; but it is usually end-stopped, seldom arriving at free rhythm. The plot, although purely intellectual, is one of his best.

The Wisdom of Doctor Dodypoll was played in 1599 by Paules Boys. Seemingly this was an old play rewritten when Paules Boys resumed acting. The greater part of the play is in Lyly's manner. The part of the French Doctor (Doctor Dodypoll) contains many a Dekkerian touch. Presumably the play was an old Lylian comedy redone by Dekker in 1599. The entire plot, especially the various love episodes, the madness of Prince Alberdure, the philosophy and euphuism, are Lylian. The word Dodypoll was in common use in 1593. (See Alleyn's letter to his wife in the *Henslowe Papers*.)

Compare the following song with Lyly's known songs:
> What thing is love?
> For sure I am it is a thing.
> It is a pricke; it is a thing.
> It is a prittie prittie thing [sting?].
> It is a fire; it is a coale,
> Whose flame creeps in at every hoale.
> And as my wits do best devise
> Loves dwelling is in Ladies eyes.

Compare the mad lines of Alberdure with those of Pandora. Alberdure mistakes a peasant for his love Hyanthe:
> Weepe not Hyanthe; Ile weep for thee:
> Lend me thy eyes. No, villaine, thou art he
> That in the top of Ervines hill
> Daunst with the Moone, & eate up all the starres,
> Which made thee like Hyanthe shine so faire.
> But villaine I will rip them out of thee.
>
> [*His mood changes.*]
> O this way, by the glimmering of the Sunne,
> And the legeritie of her sweet feete,
> She scowted on; and I will follow her.
> I see her like a golden spangle sit
> Upon the curled branche of yonder tree.
> Sit still, Hyanthe, I will flee to thee.

The scene between Lucilla and the Enchanter is purely Lylian.
A part of it reads:

> *Lucilla.* I had a lover, I thinke. But who it was,
> Or where, or how long since, aye me, I know not:
> Yet beat my timerous thoughts on such a thing.
> I feel a passionate heate, but find no flame;
> Thinke, what I know not, nor know what I thinke.
> *Enchanter.* Hast thou forgot me then? I am thy love,
> Whom sweetly thou wert wont to entertaine,
> With lookes, with vowes of love, with amorous kisses.
> Lookst thou so strange. Doost thou not know me yet?
> *Lucilla.* Sure I should know you.
> *Enchanter.* Why, love, doubt you that?
> Twas I that lead you through the painted meades
> Where the light fairies daunst upon the flowers,
> Hanging on every leafe an orient pearle,
> Which, strooke together with the silken winde,
> Of their loose mantels made a silver chime.
> Twas I that, winding my shrill bugle horne,
> Made a guilt pallace breake out of the hill,
> Filled suddenly with troopes of knights & dames
> Who daunst and reveld whilste we sweetly slept
> Upon a bed of Roses wrapt all in goulde.
> Doost thou not know me yet?
> *Lucilla.* Yes, now I know you.
> *Enchanter.* Come then confirm thy knowledge with a kiss.
> *Lucilla.* Nay stay! You are not he. How strange is this!

Were it not for the evident signs of revision this play might
be dated 1599. Since it is a revision it probably was originally
written *c.* 1592. The 'orient pearle' simile reappears in *A Midsommer Nights Dreame*:

> I must go seeke some dew drops heere,
> And hang a pearle in every cowslips eare.

Lyly's mad lovers derive from *Orlando Innamorata*; they gave
rise to Ophelia.

Other comedies in which Lyly had a hand can be discovered
by those who search. His touch remained subtle and fastidious
to the end. Though he habitually wore the cap and bells his

finger pointed to each moral blemish in Court and common-
wealth, and indicated the path of correct chivalric conduct. His
maidens remained insouciant, enticing ladies-in-waiting to Her
Majesty the Queen. That he was still a force in 1600 is proved
by Ben Jonson's caricature.

Lyly was a genuine artist, a courtier, a scholar, witty, original,
the greatest of King's fools, the first creator of allegorical Court
comedy, of modern prose comedy, of comedy in mingled rhymed
and unrhymed verse, the first Englishman to write intellectual
plays of plot and counterplot.

II

JOHN LYLY, THE CHAPEL CHILDREN, AND PAULES BOYS

WHEN Paules Boys were inhibited in 1590 Lyly and his assistant Harry Evans became associated with the Children of 'Her Majesties Revels'. Seemingly this was a reorganization of the Chapel Children and Paules Boys into one new company, that of ' Her Majesties Revels ', which acted plays by Lyly, Peele, Marlowe, and Nash, privately at the Chapel Royal and at the houses of great lords on festive occasions. In 1596 this company was given permission to act in public. They arranged through Evans for the reoccupation of Blackfriars theatre, where they opened late in 1597. (Wallace.) Assuredly they were under the direction of Lyly. Peele was then dead, and Lyly is the only known author who could have supplied this theatre with Court plays.

During 1597–9, Evans being leaseholder, Lyly there presented to the general public a large number of plays which had hitherto been played privately during the years 1583–96, as well as new plays written chiefly by Lyly during 1596–9. These plays were at once successful, and the new Blackfriars became the most popular theatre of the moment.

In 1599 permission to resume acting was granted to Paules Boys. The Children of 'Her Majesties Revels' then split up again into their original parts of Paules Boys and Chapel Children. Lyly went with Paules Boys to a theatre 'neere St. Paul's church', where he was assisted by at least Dekker and Marston, and later by other writers. The Chapel Children under Evans remained at Blackfriars. Evans found new authors in Chapman and Jonson, who wrote for him until 1602, when Jonson was supplanted by Marston, who bought a one-sixth share in the Blackfriars lease. (Wallace.)

Part of the repertoire of the Revels company went with Lyly
to Paules Boys and part remained in the hands of Evans. Evans
evidently sold some of his plays, such as *A Midsommer Nights
Dreame*, in 1599 when he was pressed for ready money. Other
plays, such as *The Tempest* and *Pericles*, he held until Blackfriars was taken over by Burbage, Shakespeare, and company
c. 1607.

Paules Boys were bought out *c.* 1607 by the Burbages and
Rosseter, their master, Pierce, receiving £20 per annum for
cessation. What became of the Paules Boys' plays at that date is
unknown. Possibly they were sold to Shakespeare and Burbage
or to Rosseter at Whitefriars; possibly some were lost when
St. Paul's library was burned in 1666. It is to be presumed that
Evans sold his 'goodes, playebookes, properties for playes and
other like thinges' of which he had a list in 1611 to Burbage
and Shakespeare, as was charged by Robert Keysar when he sued
them in 1610. (See the *Keysar-Burbage Lawsuit*, Wallace.)

It was thus through Evans that various plays written for the
Revels Children by Lyly and Peele, as well as later Lyly plays,
came into the hands of Shakespeare to be revised and published
as his own.

III

CHRISTOPHER MARLOWE

(HEROIC BLANK VERSE AND FREE RHYTHM)

CHRISTOPHER MARLOWE was born at Canterbury on February 26, 1564; and was educated at King's School, Canterbury, and Benet Hall, Cambridge, taking his B.A. in 1583, his M.A. in 1587. In 1588 his *Tamburlaine* appeared. From then until his death he busied himself chiefly writing plays, his minor energies being given to disquisitions on philosophy and religion.

Much ink has been wasted over, and many a moral drawn from, Marlowe's ' atheism ' and his ' sad end '. Fortunately there remain fragments of an article written by Marlowe which contains an outline of his religious opinions (Harleian MS. 6848). From this it is evident that his views are almost identical with those of Emerson. Were he alive to-day he would be ranked as a Unitarian. That he was deeply and sincerely religious this document proves conclusively. But to be a Unitarian in the year 1592 was to be considered an atheist.

Marlowe passed his youth in Canterbury, which was then the very heart of religious conservatism. He was a child of the new awakening, and as such revolted against the outworn forms and exalted the forgotten soul of all religion. This was his crime. ' The Nature divine is single, communicable to no creature, comprehensible of no create understanding, explicable with no speech.' God to him was 'Everlasting, Invisible, incommutable, incomprehensible, immortal, living and true', &c.

Among the writers of the Elizabethan age Marlowe had the greatest mind. He was the most original thinker, the boldest inventor; and of all he most thoroughly voiced the spirit of the Renaissance.

> Nature, that fram'd us of foure elements,
> Warring within our breasts for regiment,
> Doth teach us all to have aspyring minds:
> Our soules . . . . . .
> Still climing after knowledge infinite,
> . . . .
> Wils us to weare our selves and never rest,
> Untill we reach the ripest fruit of all, &c.

Thus Marlowe declares himself in *Tamburlaine*. Not to be great was, to Marlowe, not to be.

Marlowe's first accredited interlude had for its theme 'Tamburlaine the Great. Who, from a Scythian Shepherd . . . became a most puissant and mightye Monarque. And . . . was termed, The Scourge of God.' His next interlude was Faustus, supremest of philosophers; then followed Barrabbas, supremest of Machiavellians, in *The Jew of Malta*.

As a fitting medium for his supermen Marlowe, with sure instinct, adopted blank verse. Blank verse of a sort had been used in *Gorboduc*, but he made of it a new medium. There can be no doubt but that this medium is eminently suited for heroics, and for heroics only. It is epical; its power and impetus are such that, if used for anything but the sublime or terrible, it overwhelms its subject and becomes bombastic, farcical.

Tamburlaine created a furor. In a day it remade dramatic history. All that had gone before seemed lifeless. It opened a new horizonless world; but it was a world inhabited only by gigantic heroes.

Whether or no Marlowe was the first to perceive the limitations of his new medium will ever remain an unsolved point. Certain it is that all his contemporaries, save Kyd, began soon to revile 'the swelling bombast of a bragging blank verse'. Born in 1588 it was dead by 1592. That Marlowe was not satisfied with his new medium is disclosed in this very interlude which made blank verse famous:

> If all the pens that ever poets held
> Had fed the feeling of their maister's thoughts,
> And every sweetnes that inspir'd their harts,

Their minds, and muses on admyred theames :
If all the heavenly quintessence they still
From their immortall flowers of poesy,
Wherein as in a myrrour we perceive
The highest reaches of a humaine wit ;
If these had made one poems period
And all combin'd in beauties worthinesse,
Yet should ther hover in their restlesse heads
One thought, one grace, one woonder at the least,
Which into words no vertue can digest :

As well as being a great thinker Marlowe was a master emotionalist. But in order to capture the inner spirit which vivifies every intense expression some more perfect medium than the grandiloquent march of blank verse must be discovered. This Euripides found and Marlowe refound in free rhythm. Blank verse is intellectual; free rhythm is of the soul. In its most perfect form it follows all the delicate modulations of each high-keyed emotion.

The difference between the two is best expressed in terms of music. Blank verse is a 2/4 rhythm, beginning on an unaccented note and ending on an accented one, there being always five accents or bars in each phrase or measure, thus : two one, two one, two one, two one, two one. The unaccented beat consists at odd times of two eight notes, either or both of which can be replaced by a rest in the first, third, or fourth bar. This same rhythm continues throughout the entire composition.

Free rhythm is the use of each and every rhythm found in music ; the phrase may be long or short ; there may be rests wherever desired, and suspensions, rhythms within rhythms, or double rhythms. Rhythms are marked by natural speech accents, by alliteration on accented or unaccented notes, by rhymes, by rests, by phrase division through punctuation marks, and by division into printed lines.

No race is more imbued with rhythmic feeling than the English. Among a dozen London street urchins dancing to a barrel-organ some two or three will always be found improvising rhythms. Yet the poets and musicians of England are almost without exception rhythmically sterile. This is partly due to intellectuals who, knowing nothing of music, write of free rhythm as if it were a bastard blank verse. They call it ' run over blank verse '. It resembles blank verse as little as a landscape resembles a chequer-board.

Here and there in *Tamburlaine* Marlowe strives after a freer rhythm. In *The Tragedie of Dido* his measured blank verse continually breaks up into new ever-changing rhythmic figures. His work then resembles that of those Italian painters who against architectural designs traced harmonious figures replete with flowing lines, which seem the more delicate because of the stern background.

Nash, Greene, Peele, and Lyly were all using free rhythm in 1593; and its use was continued by Chettle, Dekker, Tourneur, and finally by Fletcher and Webster. The rhythmic skill of these great artists varied as much as that of the musicians of the same period, Byrde, Morley, Weekes, Wilbye, &c. Unfortunately Marlowe was killed when he had almost perfected this new medium, otherwise he would have produced masterpieces overflowing with an infinitude of variant rhythms, stern as in the blank verse of *Tamburlaine*, dainty as in the free rhythm of *The Tragedie of Dido*.

The value of free rhythm lies in its adaptability; every passion, each least mood, can be fitted with a rhythm which becomes the soul of the poesy, binding the words into a more intensive organism.

Free rhythm must not be confounded with *vers libre* introduced from France. *Vers libre* is usually highly coloured prose cut into short lines in imitation of poetry. In the hands of a great rhythmist it at times becomes true free rhythm; in the hands of a prosaic intellectualist it degenerates into affected bombast. Free rhythm is usually printed in lines of four, five, or six accents to the line. Strictness of form facilitates the use of rests. Contrary to all strictly measured verse the accents are never forced, but fall on such words as are stressed in normal speech.

The history of Tamburlaine was continued in a second part.

This was followed by *Doctor Faustus*. These plays firmly established Marlowe as the leading playwright of the Leicester-
Pembroke company. Among his followers were Kyd and the
beginner Shakespeare. Of this entire group Nash in the preface
to Greene's *Menaphon* (1588-9) wrote:

> I am not ignorant how eloquent our gowned age is growen of
> late; so that everie moechanicall mate abhorres the english he was
> borne too, and plucks with a solemne periphrasis, his *ut vales* from
> the inkhorne; which I impute not so much to the perfection of
> the arts, as to the servile imitation of vain-glorious tragoedians,
> who contend, not so seriouslie to excell in action, as to embowell
> the clowdes in a speach of comparison; thinking themselves more
> than initiated in poets immortalitie if they but once get Boreas
> by the beard, and the heavenlie bull by the deaw-lap.

The early plays of Marlowe and the Pembroke group lack
action, and are filled with ' comparisons '. 'Boreas by the beard '
refers to the stolen Pembroke play *The Taming of A Shrew*,
originally a Strange company play probably written by Greene.
(See also Appendix to DEKKER.)
    Nash continues:

> But herein I cannot so fully bequeath them to follie as their
> idiote art-masters, that intrude themselves to our eares as the
> alcumists of eloquence, who (mounted on the stage of arrogance)
> think to outbrave better pens with the swelling bumbast of a
> bragging blanke verse.

This hit was directed chiefly at Marlowe's *Tamburlaine*.
    In this same introduction Nash returns to the charge, and
berates Kyd directly as the author of an early *Hamlet* and other
tragedies of blood. Thus he connects Marlowe with Kyd, and
both with the Pembroke company.
    In these early plays Marlowe remained true to interlude form
—a series of episodes strung together to make a story. Each
episode he treats almost as if it were an individual lyric. Where-
ever possible he gives to each of these lyrics as gorgeous a stage
setting as his theatre could contrive. It was as much through

scenic display as through the overwhelming power of the verse and ideas that *Tamburlaine* caused its commotion.

Shortly after Marlowe's death, June 1, 1593, Kyd wrote a letter to Sir John Puckering, a portion of which reads:

> Amongst those waste and idle papers . . . were founde some fragments of a disputation . . . shufled with some [papers] of myne, unknown to me, by some occasion of our wrytinge in one chamber twoe yeares since. . . . My first acquaintance with this Marlowe rose upon his bearing name to serve my lord.

This points to collaboration of Marlowe and Kyd during 1591-2. Certainly one of the plays which they wrote together was *Titus Andronicus*, which contains some of Marlowe's finest touches mixed with Kyd's well-known handiwork. A second play was *The Jew of Malta*. The company for which they wrote together was evidently the Pembroke, not the Sussex company, as has sometimes been stated. Sussex was dead when Kyd wrote the above letter, and could no longer have been Kyd's lord; nor is there any record of Kyd's having written for the Sussex company, while he and Marlowe both wrote for the Pembroke company. (See also KYD.)

The Jew of Malta, written *c.* 1591, was not published until 1633. During the forty-odd years of its theatrical life it must have suffered considerable change; however, many a passage of unadulterated Marlowe remains.

While the greater part of this play must be assigned to Kyd, all the refined passages, which raise it out of the commonplace, bear Marlowe's touch. Originally Barrabas the Jew urged on from one crime to another in Kyd's usual manner. To Marlowe such a development seemed inartistic. How did he remedy this? Incidentally by touches of superb poetry, which enrich and in a manner ennoble Barrabas; but more thoroughly through the use of that unique figure Ithamore.

Ithamore, a worthless slave, first appears on sale in the market-place. There Barrabas, who needs such a tool, buys him as a bargain. Solemnly the new master instructs his slave,

'be thou void of these affections: compassion, love, vain hope,
and heartless fear'. Ithamore speaks and reveals himself—'O
brave master! I worship your nose for this.' Barrabas then demands—'how hast thou spent thy time?' The grotesque animal
replies:

> Faith, Master, in setting Christian villages on fire, chaining of
> Eunuches, binding gally-slaves. One time I was an hostler in an
> Inne, and in the night time secretly would I steale to travellers
> chambers, and there cut their throats. Once at Jerusalem, where
> the pilgrims kneel'd, I strowed powder on the marble stones, and
> therewithall their knees would ranckle, so that I have laugh'd a-good
> to see the cripples goe limping home to Christendome on stilts.

This slave furnishes much of the comic relief of the tragedy.
To such an irresponsible crimes are but merry pranks. And since
it is in this spirit that he carries out the heinous devices of his
master he robs them of the greater part of their awfulness. When
he shares a crime his joy in achievement makes all seem incongruous, lacking reality. Without him *The Jew of Malta* would
have been insupportable. Shylock meanly attempts a personal
injury; Barrabas commits wholesale murder, yet is less revolting.
This is entirely due to Ithamore. While he is the tool of Barrabas,
he is also the foil.

When this soulless gargoyle makes love all turns to comedy;
and when he cozens his master of gold the comedy borders on
farce. Ithamore's inamorata is the courtesan Bellamira.

> *The Courtesan.* Now, gentle Ithimore, lye in my lap.
> Where are my maids? Provide a running banquet;
> Send to the merchant; bid him bring me silkes.
> Shall Ithimore my love go in such rags?
> *The Slave.* And bid the jeweller come hither too.
> *The Courtesan.* I have no husband; Sweet, I'le marry thee.
> *The Slave.* Content: but we will leave this paltry land,
> And saile from hence to Greece, to lovely Greece!
> I'le be thy Jason, thou my golden fleece!
> Where painted carpets o're the meads are hurl'd,
> And Bacchus vineyards ore-spread the world;
> Where woods and forrests goe in goodly greene,
> I'le be Adonis, thou shalt be Loves Queene;

The meads, the orchards, and the primrose lanes,
Instead of sedge and reed, beare sugar canes :
Thou in those groves, by Dis above,
Shalt live with me and be my love!

Ithamore not only robs this tragedy of blood of its horror, but turns its very ugliness into grotesque Gothic comedy. His like is not to be found in all Elizabethan literature. Would Marlowe had created such another Gargantuan fool as a foil to Faustus, as a clown to Tamburlaine. The idealistic seriousness, the lyricism, of Gothic architecture necessitates such grotesque relief.

For more than forty years *The Jew of Malta* held its audience. It then served as a basis for new plays. Judiciously revived it would again prove popular.

The Tragedie of Dido Queen of Carthage was printed in 1594 as by Marlowe and Nash. It belongs among the interludes played by the Chapel Children before the Queen and Court, and was designed for musical accompaniment, which was probably furnished by William Byrde, who was then a Queen's chapeller.

It has been suggested that this was an early work by Marlowe left incomplete and finished by Nash. It is so perfect a thing, and the parts of the two authors are so intimately fused, that it must have been well on the way towards completion while both were living. The work of Nash is more mature than in his *Summers Last Will*, and the work of Marlowe is purely lyrical, quite free of his earlier heroic strain. Its date is surely 1592. It contains many of Marlowe's most exquisite lines, lines moulding themselves to the emotion they would express.

The emotional passages breathe the fire of Marlowe; the connecting links seem to have been supplied by Nash. Many a Nash-like expression occurs in the narration of the fall of Troy by Aeneas. But it is Marlowe who supplies Dido's interjections and comments, as well as the ensuing episode between Venus and Cupid. Marlowe apparently selected for himself Dido, Venus, Cupid, Anna, and Iarbus, leaving the Troyans for the most part to Nash[1].

[1] Several episodes in this play are wrongly placed.

The Cupid scenes are especially delightful and show Marlowe in a new light. Whereas he once stormed through blaring horns and rattling drums, he now makes use of flutes and muted strings. There is a loss of strength, but a commensurate gain in lyricism, lyricism touched with the new humanism.

Venus plans to substitute Cupid for Ascanius, the small son of Aeneas:

> *Venus.* [*to Ascanius*] Faire child stay thou with Didos wait-
> ingmaide,
> Ile give thee sugar-almonds, sweete conserves,
> A silver girdle, and a golden purse,
> And this yong Prince shall be thy playfellow.
> *Ascanius.* [*to Cupid*] Are you Queene Didos son?
> *Cupid.* [*deceiving him*] I, and my mother gave me this fine
> bow.
> *Ascanius.* Shall I have such a quiver and a bow?
> *Venus.* Such bow, such quiver, and such golden shafts,
> Will Dido give to sweete Ascanius:
> For Didos sake I take thee in my armes,
> And sticke these spangled feathers in thy hat;
> Eate comfites in mine armes; and I will sing.

Unfortunately the songs of almost all the Court plays were not inserted in the play-house manuscripts. The world is there-fore the poorer by the loss of what must have been some of Lyly's and Marlowe's best verse.

The ensuing eighteen lines must be assigned to Nash. Marlowe resumes after the exit of Cupid:

> *Venus.* [*to Ascanius*] Sleepe my sweete nephew in these cool-
> ing shades,
> Free from the murmure of these running streames,
> The crye of beasts, the ratling of the windes,
> Or whisking of these leaves, all shall be still, &c.

The comic element is supplied by Anna, Dido's sister, who is enamoured of Iarbus and insists on pursuing him, to his disgust, for he loves Dido. Anna finds him sacrificing to Jove, dream-ing of Dido. He exclaims to the intruder:

> O leave me, leave me to my silent thoughts, &c.

Anna. [*refusing to go*] I will not leave Iarbus whom I love,
In this delight of dying pensivenes :
Away with Dido, Anna be thy song,
Anna, that doth admire thee more than heaven.
  Iarbus. I may [not], nor will list to such loathsome chaunge,
That intercepts the course of my desire :
Servants, come fetch these emptie vessels (here),
For I will flye from these alluring eyes,
That doe pursue my peace where ere it goes.
  [*They gather up the sacrificial vessels and depart.*]
  Anna. [*endeavouring to detain him*] Iarbus stay, Loving Iarbus
    stay,
For I have honey to present thee with :
Hard-hearted, wilt not deigne to heare me speake !
Ile follow thee with outcryes nere the lesse,
And strewe thy walkes with my discheveld haire.

Another bit of comedy is provided by the old Nurse, who
becomes amorous each moment she takes disguised Cupid in her
arms, and sensible each time he deserts her.

  Cupid. [*artfully*] Nurse, I am weary ; will you carry me ?
  Nurse. Aye, so you'll dwell with me, and call me mother.
  Cupid. So you'll love me, I care not if I do.
  Nurse. [*the boy in her arms*] That I might see this boy a man !
How prettily he laughs ! Go, ye wag !
You'll be a twigger when you come to age.
    [*Becoming amorous*]
Say Dido what she will, I am not old ;
I'll be no more a widow. I am young.
I'll have a husband, or else a lover.
  Cupid. [*deserting her*] A husband ! And no teeth !
  Nurse. [*sobered*] O, what mean I to have such foolish
    thoughts ?
Foolish is love, a toy.
    [*Taking Cupid in her arms, inflamed*]
                  O sacred love !
If there be any heaven in earth, 'tis love !
  Cupid. (*deserting her*) Especially in women of your years.
    Blush,
Blush for shame ! Why shouldst thou think of love ?
A grave, and not a lover, fits thy age.

[*Having reproved her he again caresses her.*]

Nurse. A grave! Why, I may live a hundred years;
Fourscore is but a girl's age : Love is sweet . . .

[*Cupid moves away and the ecstasy passes.*]

My veins are wither'd, and my sinews dry;
Why do I think of love, now I should die?
Cupid. Come, Nurse.
Nurse. [*catching him up, amorously*] Well, if he come a-wooing,
    he shall speed;
O, how unwise was I to say him nay.[1]

This little episode is touched in subtly. It is a model of all
that is best in lyrical comedy.

When a great lyricist would depict strong emotion or deep
passion he must sacrifice beauty to power. Had Marlowe lived a
few years longer and shared in the humanistic movement of the
next few years he certainly would have sacrificed some of his
lyricism in order the better to depict the depths of emotion.
Dido was written to be acted by children. It was designed to
be a thing of grace, a symphony, rather than a tragedy. Therefore Dido's emotion never breaks the bonds of lyricism. Yet
within those bonds it is carried as far as is possible.

Fearing lest Aeneas should sail away, Dido ordered the oars,
sails, and tackling of his ships to be brought to her palace. Of
the oars she remarks:

Is this the wood that grew in Carthage plaines,
And would be toyling in the watrie billowes
To rob their mistresse of her Troian guest?
O cursed tree, hadst thou but wit or sense,
To measure how I prize Aeneas love,
Thou wouldst have leapt from out the sailers hands, . . .
And yet I blame thee not. Thou art but wood. &c.

When Aeneas comes to say farewell he turns his face away,
and Dido reproves him:

Dido. Why look'st thou toward the sea? The time hath been
When Dido's beauty chain'd thine eyes to her.

[1] The spelling and punctuation of this little episode has been modernized.

[*She waits. He is silent.*]
Am I less fair than when thou saw'st me first?
O, then Æneas, 'tis for grief of thee.
[*She pleads with him.*]
Say thou wilt stay in Carthage, with thy Queen,
And Dido's beauty will return again.
[*He remains silent.*]
Æneas, say; how canst thou take thy leave?
[*He kisses her.*]
Wilt thou kiss Dido? O, thy lips have sworn
To stay with Dido.
[*He takes her hand.*]
                     Canst thou take her hand?
Thy hand and mine have plighted mutual faith, &c.

After Aeneas has gone Dido sends Anna after him.

    Dido. (*to Anna*) Once didst thou go, and he came back again;
Now bring him back, and thou shalt be a queen;
And I will live a private life with him.
.   .   .   .
Request him gently, Anna, to return:
I crave but this: he stay a tide or two,
That I may learn to bear it patiently.
If he depart thus suddenly, I die.[1]

While the Aeneas of Nash remains more or less the old-fashioned lay figure, Marlowe's complex *Dido* stands out clearly, eminently human, pathetic, the first of a long series of adorable Elizabethan creations. It must not be forgotten that Dido, though created after Lyly's Pandora, appeared several years before such simple characters as Juliet, Portia, and Rosalind. Thus Marlowe once more proves himself an innovator.

As a study of two similar and yet dissimilar poets *Dido* is most interesting. The smooth lyrical flow is Marlowe's, the startlingly expressive words and metaphors are by Nash. Marlowe always painted largely with a free arm; Nash used brisk touches surcharged with meaning. Marlowe's *Faustus* sings of Helen:

    Oh thou art fairer than the evening air
    Clad in the beauty of a thousand stars;

        [1] Spelling and punctuation modernized.

Brighter art thou than flaming Jupiter,
When he appeared to haplesse Semele:
More lovely than the monarch of the sky
In wanton Arethusa's azured arms: &c.

He had that large free English mind which runs to exuberance, untrammelled, vehement, elemental—emotional Gargantuism—but withal an intense feeling for rhythm and assonance. This latter quality Nash lacked; rhythm never led him a longer journey. Free of its spell, his mind concentrated into sudden words and phrases ideas which Marlowe would have expanded into bars of music. In *Dido* there are lines by Nash which have been made smooth-flowing by Marlowe, and passages by Marlowe which have been vivified by Nash.

This little interlude of *Dido* is perhaps the most charming of all the music dramas played by the Children of her chapel before Her Majesty Queen Elizabeth.

Some critics have assigned to Marlowe the old play *The Taming of A Shrew*, acted by the Strange company on June 11, 1594, and printed that year in a very garbled form, 'as it was sundrie times acted by the Right honorable the Earle of Pembrook his servants'. (For a discussion of this play see Appendix to DEKKER.)

The True Tragedy of Richard Duke of York, another Pembroke play, is often assigned to Marlowe and Greene. There is no reason to believe that Marlowe and Greene ever worked together. This play has been considered under 'The Revision of *Henry VI*, Part *II*'.

The Massacre at Paris, with the death of the Duke of Guise, was printed for Edward White (no date), 'as it was plaide by the right honorable the Lord High Admirall his servants', 'written by Christopher Marlowe'. Henslowe records the first performance of a play called *The Tragedy of the Guyes* on January 30, 1593. Bishop Tanner mentions an elegy by Nash wherein the tragedy of *The Duke of Guise* is put down to Marlowe. If Marlowe wrote the 1593 Guise play which was then newly acted by the Admiral's company it would have been his latest production. There is more of Marlowe's later work in the extant version of *The Massacre at Paris*. However, there are lines in it which resemble his earlier work; and in *England's Parnassus* there is a two-line quotation under his name, a revised version of which appears in the *Massacre*. The extant *Massacre* is a Huguenot play, written against the Duke of Guise by a staunch Protestant. The deduction follows that the new tragedy of 1593 was a revision of a still earlier play which had been written by Marlowe. (See also DRAYTON.)

Edward II. This tragedy has been usually ascribed to Marlowe. By some it is regarded as 'the summit of his art'. Even a superficial examination of the metre should have convinced the most amateur of critics that it is not the work of the originator of blank verse. Imagine the powerful artist who created blank verse in *Tamburlaine*, who put an end to the 'jugging veine of rhyming mother wits', who wrote such perfect free rhythm as is found in *Dido*, returning in his most mature period to the measured verse and the rhymed couplets so profusely used in this play! Often the rhymes of those couplets are legitimate, but as often they are bastard. Marlowe was never guilty of such work. Nor is there the least sign of his forceful imagination in this play where all is 'purity and pretiousnesse'.

Past generations of critics have usually worked after a very simple formula. Whenever passable blank verse was found they placed it to the credit of either Marlowe or Shakespeare. If it dated before 1593 they assigned it to the former, if after that date to the latter. Thus *Edward II* became Marlowe's production. There is not a vestige of reliable external evidence in favour of such an assumption; and the internal evidence is all against it. (See also DRAYTON.)

Machiavel, revived by the Strange company in Mar.–April, 1591; *Mahomet*, revived by the Admiral's men in August, 1594; and *Phaeton*, rewritten by Dekker in 1598, were possibly Marlowe plays.

Marlowe's career thus divides itself into a first period, before 1590, when he wrote plays centred each about one forceful individual; a second period, when he wrote historical interludes; and, finally, *The Tragedie of Dido* suggests that he had just entered a third period of lyrical idealism. His intellectual power, his emotional depth, his singing verse, point to such a consummation. His earlier plays are true interludes; his later ones were beginning to assume dramatic form. Assuredly in time he would have written powerful music dramas after the manner of Euripides.

Marlowe lived but thirty years. His contemporaries worshipped him as a fellow craftsman, and loved him as an individual. Nevertheless various puritan critics have 'discovered' in statements by Greene evidence of contempt, and a covering up of most damnifying evidence in remarks by Chettle. The facts are as follows: On his death-bed Greene wrote a last exhortation addressed 'To those Gentlemen, his Quondam acquaintance, that spend their wits in making Plays'. Therein he wrote:

> Wonder not, (for with thee [*Marlowe*] wil I first begin) thou famous gracer of Tragedies, that Greene, who hath said with thee, like the foole in his heart, There is no God, should now give glorie to his greatnesse: ... Why should thy excellent wit, his gift, be so blinded, that thou shouldst give no glory to the giver? Is it pestilent Machivilian pollicie that thou hast studied? &c.

Here follows a tirade against Machiavellianism. He then admonishes Nash, 'With thee I joyne young Juvenall, that byting Satyrist, that lastlie with mee together writ a comedie. Sweete boy,' &c. Finally he warns Peele, 'And thou no lesse deserving then the other two, in some things rarer, in nothing inferior,' &c. These were all friendly admonitions. He then becomes specific and warns them that they will be 'Base minded men al three of you, if by my miserie ye be not warned'; and here follows the bone of his contention: 'for unto none of you (like me) sought those burres to cleave: those Puppets (I meane) that speake from our mouths, those Anticks [i.e. actors] garnisht in our colours.' After further remarks on actors he turns on various imitators. First he castigates Shakespeare. Evidently he went

on, in a passage cut out by Chettle before the copy was sent to
the printer, to warn his friends against other imitators, for after
treating of Shakespeare he continues:

> O that I might intreate your rare wits to be imployed in more
> profitable courses: & let these apes imitate your past excellence,
> and never more acquaint them with your admired inventions . . .
> for it is pittie men of such rare wits should be subject to such
> rude groomes.

'These apes', 'them', and 'groomes' must refer to several
imitators. Hence not to Shakespeare alone. The identity of at
least one of these imitators can be established from a further
passage:

> But now returne 1 to you three, [i. e. Marlowe, Nash, and
> Peele] knowing my miserie is to you no news: and let me
> heartily intreate you to bee warned by my harmes. Delight not
> (as I have done) in irreligious oaths. . . . Despise drunkenness. . . .
> Flie lust. . . .

Here again he comes to his true theme:

> Abhorre those Epicures, whose loose life hath made religion
> lothsome to your eares: and when they sooth you with tearmes
> of Maistership, remember Robert Greene, whome they have often
> so flattered, perishes now for want of comfort. Remember, gentle-
> men, your lives are like so many lighted Tapers, that are with care
> delivered to all of you to maintaine: &c.
>
> > Desirous that you should live,
> > though himselfe be dying.
> >   Robert Greene.

This letter bespeaks utmost admiration for his three friends,
utmost concern that they should live pure and devout lives, and
above all that they should abominate actors and imitators.

Chettle states that Greene's pamphlet was by 'one or two'
playmakers taken 'offensively'. Shakespeare was one. Marlowe's
detractors have jumped to the conclusion that Marlowe was the
other. It is evident, however, that the other was not Marlowe,
but one of those 'apes' or 'Epicures' who 'sooth with tearmes of
Maistership'.

Chettle further states, ' With neither of them that take offence was I acquainted, and with one of them [not Shakespeare, but the other] I care not if I never be '. That Chettle and Marlowe were intimate friends will be shown. Hence ' the one ' could not have been Marlowe. Of this ' one ' Chettle further wrote :

> For the first, whose learning I reverence, and at the perusing of Greene's Booke, stroke out what then in conscience I thought he in some displeasure writ : or had it beene true, yet to publish it, was intollerable : him I would wish to use me no worse than I deserve.

Greene's address to Marlowe shows no signs of displeasure, but of anxious concern for his welfare. Who then was this ' ape ', ' Epicure ', imitator, associate of Shakespeare ?

As has been shown in Part I of the present volume, at the time Greene wrote this pamphlet Shakespeare was writing for Lord Pembroke's men in association with Kyd. Marlowe was Kyd's art-master, as may be discovered from the introduction to Greene's *Menaphon*. The following year Kyd was put upon the rack for atheism and, for his evil life, was disowned by his parents. Can there be any doubt but that the second person who objected to Greene's remarks concerning imitators, &c., with whom Chettle was not acquainted, and cared not if he never were, was this same degenerate Kyd ?

That Chettle and Marlowe were close friends is evident from Dekker's statement in his *Newes from Hell*. The scene is Elysium, the time shortly after Chettle's death.

> Whilst Marlow, Greene, and Peele had got under the shades of a large vine, laughing to see Nash (that was but newly come to their colledge,) still haunted with the sharpe and satyricall spirit that followed him heere upon earth. . . . He [Nash] had no sooner spoken this, but in comes Chettle sweating and blowing, by reason of his fatnes ; to welcome whom, because hee was of olde acquaintance, all rose up, and fell presentlie on their knees, to drink a health to all lovers of Hellicon.

It is also evident from Gabriel Harvey's slander (1593) that Nash ' shamefully and odiously misuseth every friend . . . Greene,

Marlowe, Chettle, and whom not'. Also from Nash's rejoinder in *Have with you to Saffron Walden*, 1596: 'Further ... I never abusd Marloe, Greene, Chettle in my life, nor anie of my frends that usde me like a frend.'

Heywood in his edition of *The Jew of Malta* wrote of Marlowe and Alleyn in 1633:

> We know not how our play may pass the stage, but by the best of poets in that age the Jew of Malta had being and was made; and by the best of actors played.

Among all the great writers of the period not one save ' Judas ' Kyd can be found who did not reverence ' kindly Kit Marlowe ', ' the man that hath been dear to us '.

During the greater part of his career Marlowe wrote for Lord Pembroke's men. There is a ballad extant which connects him with the Curtain, hence with that company : ' He hath a player been upon the Curtain stage,' &c. Eventually almost all of his plays came into the hands of Alleyn of the Admiral's company. The greater number of them appear in Henslowe's Diary. It is therefore possible that shortly before his death he began writing for the Admiral's men.

NOTE.—Since writing the above the mystery of Marlowe's death has been solved by J. Leslie Hotson. (See *The Death of Christopher Marlowe*, 1925.)

IV

THOMAS KYD

(REVENGE TRAGEDIES)

THOMAS KYD, son of Francis Kyd, scrivener, was born in the autumn of 1558. He was entered at the Merchant Taylors' School on October 26, 1565. Spencer was a contemporary at this school, as he entered *c.* 1561 and did not leave until 1569. How long Kyd remained is not known. He did not go to either University, which accounts for his defective knowledge of Latin, French, Italian, and general history.

After leaving school Kyd seemingly was apprenticed to his father. Nash, in the introduction to *Menaphon*, hints at such a career.

It is a common practise now a daies amongst a sort of shifting companions, that runne through every arte and thrive by none, to leave the trade of *Noverint*, whereto they were borne, and busie themselves with the indevors of Art, that could scarcelie latinise their necke-verse if they should have neede; yet English *Seneca* read by candle light yeeldes manie good sentences, as *Bloud is a begger*, and so foorth; and, if you intreate him faire in a frostie morning, he will affoord you whole *Hamlets*, I should say hand-fulls of tragicall speaches. . . . *Seneca* let bloud line by line and page by page at length must needes die to our stage: which makes his famisht followers to imitate the Kidde in *Æsop*, who, enamored with the Foxes newfangles, forsooke all hopes of life to leape into a new occupation, and these men, renowncing all possibilities of credit or estimation, to intermeddle with Italian translations: wherein how poorelie they have plodded . . . let all indifferent Gentlemen that have travailed in that tongue discerne by their twopenie pamphlets: and no mervaile though their home-born mediocritie be such in this matter, for what can be hoped of those that thrust *Elisium* into hell, and have not learned, so long as they have lived in the spheares, the just measure of the Horizon without an hexameter. Sufficeth them to bodge up a blanke verse with ifs and ands, and other while for recreation after their candle stuffe, having starched their beardes most curiouslie, to make a peripateticall path into the inner parts of the Citie, and spend two or three howers in turning over French *Doudie*, &c.

The 'trade of Noverint' was that of a scrivener.

From the comments of Nash it would seem that Kyd had taken up the career of dramatist shortly before 1588. His *Householder's Philosophie*, translated from the Italian of Torquato Tasso, was published in 1588. This was probably the last of his early translations.

Kyd's *Hamlet* dates about this same year, 1588, as it was newly staged when Nash wrote of it in 1589, as also was *The Spanish Tragedy*. *Soliman and Perseda*, which various critics ascribe to Kyd, must have been written *c.* 1590, as it as well as Lyly's *Endimion* is caricatured in Peele's *Olde Wives' Tale*.

In his letter to Lord Puckering, written in midsummer, 1593, Kyd states that he and Marlowe wrote 'in one chamber two years synce' (1591). What influence Marlowe may have had upon Kyd cannot be fully determined. That the commonplace soul of Kyd could not keep pace with the soaring idealism of Marlowe is obvious. Their friendship soon ended, and almost immediately afterwards came Kyd's downfall. In the summer of 1592 he hurriedly wrote the sensational tract 'The Murder of John Brewen', an evident pot-boiler. And on May 12, 1593, he was arrested and thrown into Bridewell prison on a charge of seditious libel.

Whether or not Kyd was one of those who had 'set uppon the wal of the Dutch churchyard' 'divers lewd and mutinous libells', one of which 'doth exceed the rest in lewdnes', or whether he was, as he professed, innocent of that charge, he was nevertheless seized upon. The warrant gave the commissioners wide powers:

> And after you shal have examined the persons, if you shal finde them dulie to be suspected, and they shal refuse to confesse the truth, you shal by aucthoritie hereof put them to the Torture in Bridewell, and by th'extremetie thereof, to be used at such times

and as often as you shal think fit, draw them to discover their knowledge concerning the said libells, &c.

This order was dated May 11, 1593. Kyd was arrested the following day, being strongly suspected. That he was tortured is clear from the Puckering letter; and although it would seem that nothing was found to convict him of mutinous libels against the Dutch, papers were found at his lodgings which hinted at the more damnable crime of atheism.

How long Kyd was imprisoned and tortured is not recorded. Some time after Marlowe's death on June 1, Kyd wrote his letter ' To the R. honorable Sr John Puckering Knight Lord Keeper of the great seale of Englande ' denying everything, Marlowe's friendship included, and begging the said lord's intervention in his behalf. Puckering turned a deaf ear.

Kyd was now a broken man. He once more tried his hand at translation, and in 1594 brought out anonymously his *Cornelia*, translated from Garnier's *Cornelie*. The dedication to the ' Countesse of Sussex' begins: 'Having no leysure (most noble Lady) but such as evermore is travel'd with th'affliction of the minde, then which the world affords no greater misery,' &c. The dedication did not regain him the lady's favour; and in despair and misery Kyd gave up the fight some time before the end of the year.

Even in death Kyd's own parents did not forgive him his sins, as on December 30 (Christmas-tide), 1594, Francis and Anna Kyd renounced all rights of administration of his goods.

This is the bare outline of the life of Kyd. There is a portion of the introduction to Chettle's *Kind-heartes Dreame* which hitherto seemed somewhat incomprehensible. Referring to the two among 'divers playmakers' by whom Greene's *Groatsworth of Wit* ' is offensively taken', he remarks, 'With neither of them that take offence was I acquainted, and with one of them I care not if I never be: the other,' &c. This ' other ' has been correct'.y identified as Shakespeare; but the ' one of them ' whom he did not care to know has been wrongfully supposed to be Marlowe. It certainly was Shakespeare's associate Thomas Kyd. (See also MARLOWE.) It is worthy of note that in 1592, before Kyd was publicly disgraced, the kindly Chettle puts on record his wish never to know the man.

Greene evidently refers to Kyd in 'let these apes [Shakespeare, Kyd, &c.] imitate your past excellence, and never more acquaint them with your admired inventions'. A second reference seems more directly aimed at Kyd: 'Abhorre those Epicures, whose loose life hath made religion lothsome to your eares: and when they sooth you with tearmes of Maistership, remember Robert Greene, whome they have often so flattered, perishes now for want of comfort.' The relationship of the master Marlowe and the sycophant Kyd, of the 'curiously starched beard', is evident.

In order to understand the feeling against Kyd and Shakespeare it must be recalled that English secular drama was born in the Universities and was fostered and developed solely by University men. Lyly made of it a felicitous vehicle for the refinement of the English tongue. Greene carried on this tradition. To Nash the development of the English language was almost a religion, and the play-house a temple wherein all glorious deeds of history were enacted for the elevation of the populace. Peele put his most profound and tender thoughts into his secular and ecclesiastical dramas; and Marlowe infused with supreme inspiration every play he touched. Into the sacred precincts of these refined enthusiasts two illiterate time-servers thrust themselves. Naturally both were despised, Kyd for the very things in which he took most pride, his self-acquired knowledge and stately blank verse which was carefully filled to measure with 'ifs' and 'ands'.

Notwithstanding the contempt of the University men Kyd's plays became at once very popular, and, despite the continued abuse of each succeeding group of playwrights, continued to be so for over thirty years.

Hamlet in its first form was Kyd's. Not only does Nash credit him therewith, but there are still extant lines and passages in the 'Corambis' *Hamlet* which could have come only from his pen. In the play within the play the parts of the Duke and Duchesse are but slightly remodelled Kyd.

Duchesse. O speake no more, for then I am accurst,
None weds the second, but she kils the first:
A second time I kill my Lord that's dead,
When second husband kisses me in bed.
    Duke. I doe beleeve you sweete, what now you speake,
But what we doe determine oft we breake,
For our demises stil are overthrowne,
Our thoughts are ours, their end's none of our owne; &c.

So again part of Hamlet's description of his father's portrait:

An eye, at which his foes did tremble at,
A front wherein all virtues are set downe
For to adorne a king, and guild his crowne, &c.

Part of Hamlet's address to the Ghost has much of Kyd in it:

But say why thy canonizd bones hearsed in death
Have burst their cerements: why thy Sepulcher,
In which wee saw thee quietly interr'd,
Hath burst his ponderous and marble Jawes,
To cast thee up againe: &c.

There are many more such lines, which are full of strained effort, of an attempt at Herculean mightiness, which are quite at variance with the easy humanism of the greater part of the 'Corambis' *Hamlet.*

The Spanish Tragedy was first staged *c.* 1587, and was played intermittently for thirty years. It was rewritten in 1597, and again by Jonson in 1601. It was without doubt the most popular melodrama of the age.

This is the one drama which all authorities assign to Kyd. In it his characteristics and peculiarities are strongly marked. The first and most noticeable trait, differentiating Kyd's work from all others, is a tremendous physical energy. His verse fills the mouth to overflowing and urges on in a stormy current; each line is full to the utmost brink; and all strains onward with the continuity of a devastating flood.

After Horatio is hanged old Hieronimo enters in his night-shirt, and exclaims:

What outcries pluck me from my naked bed,
And chill my throbbing hart with trembling feare,

Which never danger yet could daunt before?
Who calls Hieronimo? Speak! Heere I am.
I did not slumber; therefore 'twas no dreame.
No, no; it was some woman cride for helpe;
And heere within this garden did she crie;
And in this garden must I rescue her, &c.

Finally he discovers the hanging body of his son, Horatio:

Alas, it is Horatio, my sweet sonne.
O no, but he that whilome was my sonne.
O was it thou that call'dst me from my bed?
O speak, if any sparke of life remaine.
I am thy father. Who hath slaine my sonne?
What savadge monster, not of humane kinde,
Hath heere beene glutted with thy harmeles blood,
And left thy bloudie corpes dishonoured heere,
For me amidst these darke and deathful shades,
To drowne thee with an ocean of my teares? &c.

Here again appears the uneasy physical force, unruly, spasmodic, unable to find a moment's calm or peace.

The plot also urges on from one catastrophe to another, until the finale—the murder of all concerned. No other ending is possible for such plays.

There is little room for character analyses, no time for subtle emotion in such drama; yet the people are boldly splashed in, full-blooded, great, beefy, vehement, exactly such as are found in many of the paintings of Rubens.

That such dynamic drama should find favour in the Elizabethan age was natural. To a succeeding generation these blood-choked people seemed coarse, their seething energy fatiguing.

It has been usual to regard Kyd as a mere follower and imitator of Marlowe. In truth he was the elder brother; and although he modified his verse from end rhymes to blank verse it was in conformity with the dramatic evolution of the period, not in imitation of Marlowe. While in his later work he strove after the lyricism of Marlowe his earlier work was too individualistic to be that of an imitator, too strong to be that of aught but an original creator.

In 1590 or 1591, when Kyd and Marlowe occupied the same chambers, they collaborated in writing at least two plays which bear the impress of both, *The Jew of Malta* and *Titus Andronicus*. *The Jew of Malta* was played by the Strange company on February 26, 1592, and thence fortnightly until the end of the season. The receipts during this period were so large that it must have been a new play late in 1591, about the time when Kyd and Marlowe were collaborating. Heywood in the prologue to the only extant edition attributes the play to Marlowe, whose lines are both numerous and unmistakable. The plan and the greater portion of the play are, however, Kyd's. The restless tension of his straining cannot be mistaken:

> But rather let the brightsome heavens be dim,
> And natures beauty choake with stifeling clouds,
> Then my faire Abigal should frowne on me.

This is beyond doubt Kyd's, as is the following:

> *Barrabas.* O unhappy day!
> False, credulous, inconstant Abigall!
> But let 'em go: and, Ithimore, from hence
> Ne're shall she grieve me more with her disgrace;
> Ne're shall she live to inherit aught of mine,
> Be blest of me, nor come within my gates,
> But perish underneath my bitter curse,
> Like Cain by Adam for his brother's death. . . .
> Ithimore, intreat not for her, I am mov'd,
> And she is hatefull to my soule and me:
> And least thou yeeld to this that I intreat,
> I cannot thinke but that thou hat'st my life. &c.

Kyd was still 'bodging up' a blank verse with ' ands ', if not with ' ifs '. Note the breathless effort in the following by Ferneze:

> Bashaw, in briefe, shalt have no tribute here,
> Nor shall the heathens live upon our spoyle:
> First will we race the city wals our selves,
> Lay waste the Iland, hew the Temples downe,
> And shipping of our goods to Sicily,
> Open an entrance for the wastfull sea,
> Whose billowes beating the resistlesse bankes,
> Shall overflow it with their refluence.

This passage contains various lyrical attempts. Association with Marlowe opened the eyes of Kyd to the fact that there is something infinitely finer than the measured march of five feet in a blank verse.

Heywood wrote a prologue and an epilogue to this play and supplied the only known version with many stupid asides. The original version, entered Stationers' Register in 1594, must have been a stronger and better drama than the garbled version now available. From 1591 to 1594 it was, from a box-office point of view, the best of known plays.

Titus Andronicus was first played by 'the Earle of Sussex his men' as a new play on January 23, 1594. This was while the Henslowe companies were on tour because of the plague. It was entered in S. R. on February 6, 1594, and printed that same year, as acted by Derby's (i.e. Strange's), Pembroke's, and Sussex's men. As the Earl of Derby died April 16, the date of publication must have been between February 6 and April 16.

From the evidence it would seem that *Titus Andronicus* was originally a Pembroke play. Having been bought from that company, along with *Hamlet*, *Faustus*, and other plays, by Henslowe, it was loaned to the Sussex company on January 23. It was then sent to Alleyn and the Strange men, who acted it in the provinces.

After their return to London the Strange men, now entitled 'my Lord Chamberlaines men', acted *Titus* twice at Newington, on June 5 and 12. This was immediately after the death of Marlowe and the imprisonment of Kyd. Although *Titus* had been, and evidently once more became, popular, on these two occasions it played to almost empty houses, because it was known to be a Kyd play. Kyd's *Hamlet* shared the same fate.

So far as is known *Titus* was not revived by the Chamberlain company until c. 1597, when it was rewritten and enlarged by Shakespeare, to whom it was credited by Meres in 1598. Shakespeare's version was lost, all save one scene, which appears in the Folio, being inserted into what is virtually a reprint of the original Quarto.

Kyd's *Titus Andronicus* was written shortly before the beginning of the plague of 1593, which delayed its appearance until
1594. It was written therefore either while Marlowe and Kyd
were collaborating or shortly afterwards. It belongs chiefly to
Kyd; but this is a new Kyd, much changed by his association
with the master of lyrical verse. In this play there is line after
line almost, though never quite, as good as Marlowe's own.
Lavinia pleads for her life:

Tis true, the raven doth not hatch a larke,
Yet have I heard—Oh could I find it now!—
The lion, moved with pitty, did indure
To have his princely pawes parde all away.
Some say that ravens foster forlorne children,
The whilst their owne birds famish in their nests:
Oh be to me, though thy hard hart say no,
Nothing so kinde but something pittiful.

When Aron entraps the sons of Titus into a pit Quintus speaks
to his fallen brother:

What art thou fallen? What subtile hole is this,
Whose mouth is covered with rude growing briers,
Upon whose leaves are drops of new-shed blood,
As fresh as morning's dew distilled on flowers,
A very fatall place it seemes to me.
Speake brother! Hast thou hurt thee with the fall?

Then follows a true Kyd reply by Martius:

O brother, with the dismal'st object,
That ever eye with sight made hart lament.

Martius describes the dead Bassianus, found in the pit:

Upon his bloody finger he doth weare
A precious ring, that lightens all the hole:
Which like a taper in some monument,
Doth shine upon the dead man's earthly cheekes,
And shewes the ragged intrailes of this pit:
So pale did shine the moone on Piramus
When he by night lay bath'd in maiden blood.
O brother helpe me with thy fainting hand—
If fear hath made thee faint, as mee it hath—

Out of this fell devouring receptacle,
As hatefull as Ocitus' mistie mouth.

This comes very near being in Marlowe's vein; yet it remains Kyd's, having all his peculiarities except the 'ifs' and 'ands', which, however, are replaced by 'ohs'.

At times Kyd returns to his 'ands' in this play, as when Titus speaks to Tamora:

The dam will wake, and if she winde you once,
Shee's with the lyon deepely still in league,
And lulls him whilst she playeth on her back.
And when he sleepes will she do what she list.
You are a young huntsman Marcus, let it alone,
And come, I will goe get a leafe of brasse,
And with a gad of steele will write these words,
And lay it by: the angry northerne winde
Will blow these sands like Sibels leaves abroad,
And where's your lesson then; boy what say you?

Kyd's irritating turbulence continues throughout this entire drama. No other author of the period was possessed of this same spirit.

Marlowe's share in this play, if any, must have been slight indeed. A line here and there seems too perfect to have come from another hand. Were it not for these stray jewels scattered amongst the meaner stones any part might be denied him. The evidence rather favours the supposition that he merely added a few words and rare lines.

In all Kyd's work a peculiar use of adjectives marks his style. Beginning as a translator he resorted to the use of redundant qualifying adjectives wherewith to fill out his lines. This is a vice common to almost all translators who attempt to reproduce the measure as well as the meaning of the original. Ifs, ands, ohs, fors, &c., are used for the same purpose. Of this vice Kyd never succeeded in entirely curing himself. Association with Marlowe tended to make him realize the value of adjectives when used to add a quality to the noun they accompany, but he slipped from grace easily. In his later translations, as *Cornelia*, he returned to a constant use of the redundant adjective.

Cornelia was undertaken as a pot-boiling stopgap. In it Kyd returns to his earlier manner. Once more he uses end rhymes in order to reproduce as closely as possible the feeling of the original.

The following is a part of a scene between Cicero and Cornelia:

> *Cic.* O, but men beare misfortunes with more ease,
> The more indifferently that they fall;
> And nothing more (in uprores) men can please
> Then when they see their woes not worst of all.
> *Cor.* Our friendes misfortune doth increase our owne.
> *Cic.* But ours of others will not be acknowne.
> *Cor.* Yet one man's sorrow will another tutch.
> *Cic.* I, when himselfe will entertaine none such.
> *Cor.* Anothers teares draw teares fro forth our eyes.
> *Cic.* And choyce of streames the greatest River dryes.
> *Cor.* When sand within a whirl-poole lyes unwet,
> My teares shall dry, and I my griefe forget.
> *Cic.* What boote your teares, or what availes your sorrow . . . .

Compare the ensuing speech with the King's remarks on death to Hamlet, as found in the 'Corambis' *Hamlet*, p. 7:

> Nought is immortall underneath the sunne;
> All things are subject to Death's tiranny:
> Both Clownes and Kings one self-same course must run,
> And what-soever lives is sure to die.
> Then wherefore mourne you for your husband's death,
> Sith, being a man, he was ordain'd to die?

Arden of Faversham, a Pembroke play, was printed in 1592 for Edward White, for whom *Titus Andronicus* was also printed in 1594. This play, though somewhat more realistic in theme and treatment than *Titus Andronicus*, belongs to the same school of oratorical bombast. Kyd's hand seems evident throughout, not only in the subject-matter, but in such passages as:

> Me thinks I see them with their bolstred haire
> Staring and grinning in thy gentle face,
> And in their ruthles hands their dagers drawne,
> Insulting ore thee with a peck of oathes,
> Whilest thou submissive, pleading for releefe,
> Art mangled by their irefull instruments.

Black night hath hid the pleasurs of ye day,
And sheting darknesse overhangs the earth
And with the black folde of her clowdy robe
Obscures us from the eiesight of the worlde,
In which swete silence such as we triumph.
The layzie minuts linger on their time,
Loth to give due audit to the howre,
Til in the watch our purpose be complete
And Arden sent to everlasting night.

If not written by Kyd this play of infidelity and murder was certainly composed by some one belonging to the Marlowe-Kyd school.

Soliman and Persida has been ascribed to Kyd chiefly because the same story was used by him in the play within the play of *The Spanish Tragedy*. While there is much which resembles Kyd's work in this play it lacks the strained nervousness of his other work. Instead of being ferociously intense it is filled with a spirit of mockery, as if the Tragic muse had her tongue in her cheek. The horrors are not real, the roaring is feigned. The lines are not filled out with redundant adjectives, and, although there are some 'ands', there are few 'ifs'. It rather seems to be a caricature of the old 'tragedy of blood' such as Kyd wrote. (See LYLY.)

The First Part of Jeronimo has also been attributed to Kyd, although later critics are prone to believe that he had no part in it. There is no sign of his handiwork in the entire play. Presumably there was once a second part which may have served as a basis for Kyd's *Spanish Tragedy*. The workmanship of this old play greatly resembles that of Greene.

Kyd was the most unfortunate of all the celebrated Elizabethan dramatists. He began his career in competition with University men who wrote for a cultured aristocracy, and ended it before the rise of the self-educated playwrights, who catered for a less discerning democracy. Had he been the associate and rival of Jonson, Heywood, and Shakespeare, all self-educated men, he would have been their natural leader; had he catered for the multitude he would have become their idol; for he had greater talents than Ben Jonson, whom in many ways he resembled, greater than his pupil Shakespeare, who also 'bodged up' blank verse with grandiloquent rhetoric. Having arrived before the world was ready for sanguinary melodrama, he tried at times to imitate, at times to rival, men of culture and genius. This brought him much derision and ended in his downfall. Endowed with an unlimited energy which at his best he transmitted into his work, he became, despite his piecemeal education, despite the disdain of his more learned rivals, one of the most popular dramatists of his age. The boisterous paroxysms of his play-people caught his audience and carried it, heedless of 'ifs' and 'ands' and redundant adjectives, through murder after murder, until revenge was meted out to each recreant. He never realized wherein lay his strength, and died disgraced, almost a failure, having never completely expressed himself.

V

GEORGE PEELE

(MUSIC DRAMA)

GEORGE PEELE, 'having studied nine years', took his
M.A. at Christ Church, Oxford, in 1579, when twenty-one
years of age. He remained at Oxford some time afterwards, working on plays with Dr. Gager, gaining in the meantime national
reputation as a poet. He came to London c. 1582, about which
time he produced his first Court play. While at Oxford he
married. His wife died before 1583, leaving him more or less
independent, as in his deposition at Oxford (March 29, 1583)
he mentions 'land which had descended to him in the right of
his wife'.

In 1587 Nash wrote of him in his *Address to the Gentlemen
Students of both Universities*, 'I dare commend him unto all that
know him as the chief supporter of pleasance now living'; and
later Greene, comparing him with Marlowe, wrote, 'in some
things rarer, in nothing inferior'. Greater praise from better
authorities no one could receive.

All the leading characteristics of Peele's work are to be found
in his first Court play, *The Arraignment of Paris* (c. 1583), which
was acted by the Children of the Chapel Royal. It discloses his
intimate knowledge of Greek mythology and of English folk-
lore. He had translated one of the *Iphigenia* plays by Euripides
several years previously. It hints at his love of quaint English
characters and their songs. It displays his delight in pageantry,
his ability to use serious verse on occasion, his skill as a song-
writer, and his experiments in blank verse, which were superior
to anything of the kind until Marlowe startled the world with
his irresistible resonance. With all of which it also introduces
for the first time an author who could make his characters live.
However abstract an allegorical figure, it became alive in Peele's

imagination, and assumed some kind of human form in his plays.

With pageantry, poetry, and characterization Peele combined music (not his own but that of William Byrde), and eventually dancing, thus uniting all the possible elements of drama into one consistent whole.

Marlowe's *Tamburlaine* appeared *c.* 1587. How much of his blank verse was influenced by Peele's, and how much of Peele's was influenced by Marlowe's, is a matter of conjecture. That they created the new rhythmical medium between them is certain. They were close friends. Peele wrote of Marlowe after his death,

> Marley, the muses darling for thy verse
> Fit to write passions for the souls below,
> If any wretched souls in passion speak.

Peele followed in the footsteps of Euripides and the Greeks; Marlowe in those of Virgil and the Latins. From Euripides Peele caught the charm of infinitely varying rhythm; from Virgil Marlowe caught the force and power of measured heroic verse. The welding of Greek grace and Latin vigour in Elizabethan free rhythm was the work of these two master artists.

Some time between 1583 and 1588 Peele wrote the only one of his ecclesiastical dramas which has as yet been discovered, *The Love of David and Fair Bethsabe*. Some critics have put this down as Peele's greatest work; others have called it 'stuff'. Certainly it is the greatest ecclesiastical drama written in modern times. Almost one hundred years later Racine, most profound of French dramatists, wrote a similar drama in almost exactly corresponding circumstances. But Racine's *Esther*, also built on Greek lines, is a weak and empty play compared with that of Peele.

King David is also a music drama. It is full of pageantry and choruses; but its rhythm is not in Peele's happiest vein, for this is a solemn play; even the blank verse partakes of religious gravity and never once is allowed the freedom of movement displayed in *The Arraignment of Paris*, written several years previously. This play has depth of thought and feeling as well as moral intensity. It expresses, not the illiterate raving of a fanatical puritan, but the deep moral emotion of a great and cultured thinker. Seconded by the lofty music of Byrde it must have created a feeling of religious awe such as nothing since produced has been able to duplicate. Beside it the music dramas of Haydn and Handel resemble ecclesiastical light opera.

Marlowe's powerful cadences made a sudden end of the old stilted blank verse with its insufferable end rhymes. But Marlowe was not alone in his war against conventions. In *The Olde Wives' Tale* Peele as adroitly, but with more charm and grace, belittled the old formulas. Greene inveighed against ' Hobbinall ' Harvey in bitter pamphlets; Peele laughed him out of court with the ' sulphurous huff-snuff ' of Huanebango.

This *Olde Wives' Tale* is a joyous caricature, similar to, but much better than, Fielding's *Tom Thumb*. Whilst of the slightest texture it nevertheless shows Peele in his later development. With its innumerable local hits this little skit must have created great merriment when it was first produced. Despite its age and topical characters its fun is still fresh. Although the critics have usually looked upon it as a serious production it is caricature from beginning to end, and only as such can be understood or appreciated. It must date *c.* 1591, as it ridicules *Endimion, Soliman and Perseda*, and *Orlando Furioso*.

In *The Olde Wives' Tale* Peele's characteristics are again manifest: his vast fund of folk-lore, his ability to visualize the haunting figures of a nation's imagination, his lilting doggerel verses (peculiarly his own), his clowns, his pageantry, and his keen feeling for music which permeates all. Therein he also displays to the full his love of odd names. No poet ever invented similar names, for they have a learned character despite their whimsicality. Could Gabriel Harvey be better caricatured than as Huanebango? Other names are Calypha, Thelia, Lampriscus, Corebus, Berechythia, Dionora, Pargopolineo, Buste, Wiggen, Gusteceridis, &c.

In the list of play platts, Part I, occurs, as a Queen's company play, *Dead Man's Fortune*. This was written before 1597, and the names alone proclaim it as a platt of one of Peele's plays.

Who but he could have invented Urganda, Alcione, Tesephoun, Asspida, Euphrodore, &c.? The plot as indicated in this platt is that of a music drama; and it contains all of the Peele concomitants, Panteloun and Pesscode, three antic fairies, a number of pseudo-Greek characters who furnish the serious plot, a king, lords, executioners, &c.; and all are blended into a musical interlude with an evidently happy ending.

Among the music dramas of the Globe repertoire there are several which present all the unmistakable characteristics of Peele. He who examines Peele's work with any understanding cannot for a moment doubt that he was the originator of *A Midsommer Nights Dreame*. There is the Greek setting, a whole list of Peele names, Greek and English. For is not Clutch the blacksmith in *The Olde Wives' Tale* own brother to Snug the joiner and Snout the tinker? Are not Theseus, Egeus, and Hermia cousins to the groups found in *The Olde Wives' Tale* and in *Dead Man's Fortune*? Are not Oberon and Titania and Peaseblossom of the same family as Pesscode? Are not these lilting verses by the same hand?

> Be not afraid of every stranger;
> Start not aside at every danger;
> Things that seem are not the same;
> Blow a blast at every flame;
> For when one flame of fire goes out,
> Then come your wishes well about.
>
> Be thou as thou wast wont to be;
> See as thou wast wont to see;
> Dian's buds, or Cupid's flower,
> Hath such force and blessed power.

Is not the sense of music which permeates both the same? Is not the great intellect beneath all, the playfulness, aye, the very soul of each the same?

A Midsommer Nights Dreame was written by Peele and Lyly for the Children of the Queen's Chapel. The music for it must have been composed by William Byrde. The fairies were the Children of the Chapel, all boys with well-trained voices; and doubtless many of the lines now put down as speeches were

either chanted or sung. Although Lyly wrote songs for, and used
incidental music in, many of his plays a musical atmosphere such
as envelops the greater part of this play was beyond his powers.
(See also LYLY.)

A great love of things Greek runs through these plays. *The
Arraignment of Paris* is Greek ; *King David* has a Greek chorus ;
and, although the characters remain Biblical, Prologus calls on
Jove and Adonai. *Dead Man's Fortune* and *A Midsommer
Nights Dreame* are both Graeco-English.

Those critics who establish the authorship of individual plays
by the discovery of a few chance words or a single phrase appearing in different works might ascribe *The Winter's Tale* to Peele
on the strength of 'a merry winter's tale would drive away
the time trimly' and ' to drive away the time with an old wives
winter's tale' which appear in *The Olde Wives' Tale.* But the
soul of a great man can be traced more surely by noting its own
peculiar mode of expression, by divining the thoughts and feelings such a soul should possess and must give birth to. Un-
doubtedly Peele wrote *The Winter's Tale*, but the proof does not
lie in accidental evidence.

The Winter's Tale abounds in Peele names, Archidamus, Poli-
xenes, Mamillius, Autolicus, Florizell, Perdita, Mopsa. Again he
uses the Graeco-English assemblage; and again the songs have
the lilt so distinguishingly Peele-like in character. His fondness
for folk-lore is once more evident, together with his love of quaint
lower-class English character. All is wrapped in a literary atmosphere, learned, yet whimsical ; and, although less a music drama
than *A Midsommer Nights Dreame*, a feeling of music underlies
the whole, knitting and binding it into a great harmony. It was
founded on Greene's *Pandosto* (1588). *A Winter's Night's Pastime*
was entered in the Stationers' Register on May 22, 1594. In *Dido,
Queen of Carthage* the following lines seem also to refer to *The
Winter's Tale*:

> Who would not undergoe all kinds of toyle
> To be well storied with such a Winter's Tale?

Seemingly *The Winter's Tale* was written in 1592 or 1593.

George Peele was Court poet during his entire London career. From the age of twenty-three until his death he was a Court favourite, singing at times of the great Queen 'Eliza', at times describing the royal tournaments. Recall the deep gravity of his *King David*, recall his great learning and his whimsicality, and find these elements, together with courtliness and all the elements found in his other works, in the greatest of his plays, the most profound musical interlude of his age, *The Tempest*.

There is scant need to labour all the proof that Peele wrote *The Tempest*; names (Prospero, Miranda, Ariel, Caliban), verses, comedy, characters, are all Peele's. But more than these minor things the persistent undercurrent of music which permeates every word, every speech, which is in the air, the wind, the sea, almost in the earth, the comprehensive orchestration of the whole is Peele's. Ariel sings:

> Where the bee sucks, there suck I,
> In a cowslips bell I lie,
> There I couch when owles doe crie, &c.

Caliban sings drunkenly:

> No more dams Ile make for fish,
> Nor fetch in firing, at requiring,
> Nor scrape trenchering, nor wash dish,
> Ban' ban'; cacal' ban
> Has a new master; get a new man.

This play furnishes many an example of Peele's matchless use of free rhythm. Note the dragging effect of Ferdinand's lines in:

> There be some sports are painfull, & their labour
> Delight in them sets off: Some kinds of basenesse
> Are nobly undergone; and most poore matters
> Point to rich ends: This my meane taske
> Would be as heavy to me as odious, but

Note the change of rhythmic feeling when he now speaks of Miranda:

> but
> The mistris which I serve quickens what's dead
> And makes my labours pleasures.

The Tempest marks the consummation of Peele's genius. In it he has gathered to the utmost his extensive culture. It is his soul's voice. Nothing finer, nothing more completely expressing the whole of a man's being, was ever written. It throbs and vibrates as a great instrument voicing in supreme artistic form the thought and feeling of its creator. His earnest philosophy, his courtly associations, his humorous gaiety are there, enveloped in music, orchestrated into a great symphony. Rarely is it given to man to express himself so thoroughly.

One can but wonder if Byrde, master musician of the age though he was, wrote music worthy of this great interlude; and one wonders what sweet-voiced boy from the Queen's Chapel played and sang the part of that most spiritual of fairies, Ariel.

In all probability this was Peele's swan-song. In 1597 he died.

The Tempest was revived *c.* 1613 with music by Robert Johnson, a Court lutist, and a number of additions by William Shakespeare. Commentators have dated *The Tempest* 1606, 1608, 1613. The oaths to be found in it place the original writing of it definitely before 1603. Peele probably finished it *c.* 1595.

After the death of Marlowe in 1593 Peele was the sole writer of interludes who used strict free rhythm. Dekker and Chettle used free rhythm of a sort; but they never consistently kept to the form of blank verse. Nash and Lyly never felt free rhythm keenly, and seldom availed themselves of its varied cadences. Marlowe, Greene, and Peele were the sole Elizabethans who used it with ease; and all plays which contain much of it can be attributed to one of these three. Of them Peele had the greatest facility, both Marlowe and Greene having died before the medium was perfected.

After the death of Peele the use of true free rhythm was discontinued for many years, so that all Elizabethan plays containing it can be dated before the end of 1597. Jonson and the rest wrote, not free rhythm, but blank verse.

Peele's Historical Plays.

Peele's activities were not confined to music drama. He wrote various pageants, some of them with Lyly, a considerable amount of verse, and at least a few historical interludes.

'The famous chronicle of King Edward the first, surnamed Longshanks, with his return from the Holy Land. Also the Life of Lleuellen Rebel in Wales. Lastly, the sinking of Queen Elenor, who sunk at Charing Crosse, and rose again at Potter's hith, now named Queen hith', printed in 1593 as by George Peele, seems to be a garbled combination of several of Peele's plays mixed with extraneous matter.

Anthony à Wood, writing of Peele's plays, states:

> Those I have seen are only these following:
> The Famous chronicle of K. Ed. I,⎫
> surnamed Ed. Longshankes.   ⎬Lond. 1593. qu.
> Life of Llewellen of Wales.   ⎭
> The Sinking of Q. Eleanor at Charing-Cross, and of her rising again at Potters-Hith, now named Queen-Hith. London. 1593. Qu. This and a ballad of the same subject, are now usually sold by ballad-singers or ballad-mongers.

There can be no doubt but that Wood refers to three distinct and separate plays.

Henslowe records a new play on Edward I called *Longshanks*, on August 29, 1595, which belonged to Alleyn; and in November he records a second play called *The Welshman*, presumably the life of Llewellen of Wales. *Longshanks* was either rewritten in 1595 or else it was a popular old favourite of Alleyn's before he joined the Admiral's men. *The Welshman* was an old play revived for but one performance. It netted Henslowe 7 shillings, whereas *Longshanks* continued to net him 30, 32, 14, and 30 shillings, showing that these plays were not one and the same as the extant version of *Edward I*.

A quotation, found in *Edward I*, appears in *England's Parnassus* (1600), where it is assigned to Peele; and two passages reappear in his *Polyhymnia* (1590). One of the plays in this medley, printed as *Edward I*, was originally an Oxford play, as is shown by the manner in which the founding of Balliol College is introduced. As Peele finally severed his connexion with Oxford in 1583 this portion of *Edward I* must have been taken from one of his earliest plays.

The Arraignment of Paris was written in 1582. In it Peele had already discovered blank verse, at times using run-over lines. Parts of *Edward I*, which praise rather than asperse Queen Elinor, display a more facile use of the medium. These parts, though corrupt, may safely be attributed to Peele, and belong to some play on Edward I and Queen Elinor, written after 1583, possibly *Longshanks*. The weaker lines, wherein Queen Elinor is defamed, were added to Peele's work by some rabid protestant. Peele's hand is evident in the passage wherein King Edward orders the burial of Joan of Acon and Queen Elinor:

> You peeres of England, see in royall pompe,
> These breathles bodies be entombed straight,
> With traild colours, cover'd all with blacke,
> Let Spanish steedes, as swift as fleeting winde,
> Convey the princes to their funerall:
> Before them let a hundred mourners ride;
> In everie town of their enforste aboade,
> Reare up a crosse in token of their worth,
> Whereon fair Elinor's picture shall be plac'd.
> Arriv'd at London, neare our palace-bounds,
> Interre my lovely Elinor, late deceas'd,
> And, in remembrance of her royalty,
> Erect a rich and stately carvèd crosse,
> Whereon her stature shall with glory shine,
> And henceforth see you call it Charing-crosse;
> For why the chariest and choisest queen,
> That ever did delight my royal eyes,
> There dwells in darkness whilst I die in griefe.[1]

This versification greatly resembles that of *The Arraignment of Paris*, except that it is not rhymed. The thought is noble, the language direct and forceful.

About 1599 Ben Jonson rewrote an old play into the extant version of *Histrio-Mastix*. It has been suggested by Mr. Richard

---

[1] This has been slightly corrected.

Simpson that the original of this play was written by Peele (1589–92). In this suggestion he is probably correct, as the older parts of this play correspond closely with the early work of Peele. Despite Jonson's revision it still contains a few of Peele's favourite names, such as Mavortius, Philarchus, Hiletus, Chrisoganus, Landulpho, &c. There are also various names among the comedy characters which may have been Peele's—Incle, Belch, Gut, Gulch, Clowt. Jonson probably found this play in the repertoire of the Children of Her Majesty's Revels in 1599 and rewrote it in order once more to revile 'posthaste' Munday, dramatist and ballad-maker.

'*The Battle of Alcazar* in Barbarie . . . with the death of Captaine Stukeley, as it was sundrie times plaid by the Lord High Admiral his servants' (1594). Two quotations from this play appear in *England's Parnassus*, one attributed to Peele, the other to Dekker. It was written by Greene and revised (?) by Dekker, but contained parts of an earlier Stukeley play probably written by Peele. This early play has never come to light. (See GREENE.)

The First and Second Parts of the Troublesome Raigne of John King of England, published anonymously in 1591, as 'sundry times acted by the Queen's Majesties Players', were written chiefly by Antony Munday. *King John*, printed in the Shakespeare Folio, was in turn condensed from the two parts of *The Troublesome Raigne, c.* 1597, and mentioned by Meres in 1598.

Whereas King John was the centre of interest in the older plays, the Bastard has become the picaresque hero of the condensed version. This bespeaks Nash, as does the following quotation:

> Now for the bare-pickt bone of Majesty
> Doth dogged Warre bristle his angry crest,
> And snarleth in the gentle eyes of Peace;
> Now powers from home and discontents at home
> Meet in one line; and vast Confusion waites,
> As doth a raven on a sicke-falne beast,
> The iminent decay of wrested pompe.

That Nash had a hand in this revision seems evident; yet there are lines which betray a second origin. Bits of free rhythm appear which cannot have come from his pen. One such is Arthur's pathetic speech before he leaps from the wall to death:

> The Wall is high; and yet I will leape downe.
> Good ground be pittifull, and hurt me not:
> [*He hesitates.*]
> There's few or none do know me. If they did
> This ship-boyes semblance hath disguised me quite.
> [*He looks down.*]
> I am afraide; and yet Ile venture it.
> If I get downe, and do not breake my limbes,
> Ile finde a thousand shifts to get away;
> [*Courageously.*]
> As good to dye and go; as dye, and stay.

Another piteous passage is that wherein Arthur begs Hubert for his eyes:

> Hubert, the utterance of a brace of tongues
> Must needes want pleading for a paire of eyes:
> Let me not hold my tongue. Let me not, Hubert.
> Or, Hubert, if you will, cut out my tongue,
> So I may keepe mine eyes. O spare mine eyes!
> Though to no use, but still to looke on you.
> Loe, by my troth, the instrument is cold,
> And would not harme me.
> Hubert.   I can heate it, boy.
> Art. No, in good sooth, the fire is dead with grief, &c.

Both of these passages seem to have been 'revised' by Shakespeare. The opening lines of the latter should read:

> Hubert, the pleading for a paire of eyes
> Must needes th'utterance of a brace of tongues.

During the Elizabethan period there were three men who could write thus pathetically; and whenever sympathetic lines are found they may be accredited to one of these three. They were Greene, Peele, and Dekker. Nash and Peele were both writing for the Chapel Children, 1590–3; it is possible therefore that Peele assisted Nash in writing this play.

Sir Clyomon and Sir Clamydes, once attributed to Peele, is no longer foisted upon him. It belongs to the period before the discovery of blank verse.

Another play which has been attributed to Peele is *The Wisdom of Doctor Dodypoll*, entered in S.R. October 7, 1600, and printed that year 'as it hath bene Sundrie times acted by the Children of Powles'. The Children resumed playing in 1599. Peele died three years earlier, and so far as is known never was in any way connected with Paules Boys. (See LYLY.)

Pericles. On May 20, 1608, Edward Blount entered in S.R. his copy of a book called *The booke of Pericles Prince of Tyre.* Seemingly he did not print this book, nor is there anything on record to show that he assigned it to another publisher. The extant play of *Pericles* was printed in 1609 by Henry Gossen as:

> The Late and much admired Play called Pericles Prince of Tyre with the true Relation of the whole Historie, &c. As also the no lesse strange and worthy accidents in the Birth and Life of his Daughter Mariana. As it hath been divers and sundry times acted by his Majesties servants at the Globe on Bankside by William Shakespeare.

This version was reprinted without date by Pavier, in 1611 by Pavier, in 1619 for Pavier, in 1630 for Bird, in 1635 for R. Cotes, and in the Third Folio in 1664.

Before this play was printed George Wilkins in 1608 brought out his novel 'The Painfull Adventures of Pericles Prince of Tyre Being the true Historie of the Play of Pericles, as it was lately presented by the worthy and ancient Poet John Gower. At London. Printed by T. P. (Pavier) for Nat: Butter, 1608'.

In this novel Wilkins entreats his readers to 'receive this Historie in the same manner as it was ... by the Kings Majesties Players excellently presented'. This, however, contains a false suggestion as the novel was not written from the play. The novel was written first.

While the novel was written before the play it was nevertheless based in part on a play, or on two plays, as well as on *The Patterne of Painefull Adventures*, &c., 'gathered into English by Laurence Twine', printed 1576, and reprinted in 1607. (In this novel, as in all the old versions of the same tale, the hero is called Apollonius, not Pericles.)

From the above facts it would seem that in 1607/8 Wilkins found an old play called *Pericles Prince of Tyre*, he obtained a copy of Twine's novel, and probably still another old play on Mariana, and from these concocted his 'historie'. He then sold the old play to Blount, and the novel to Pavier and Butter. He then worked the material into a new play, possibly with the assistance of Shakespeare, and sold it to the King's Players. In 1605 he wrote a pamphlet on a 'bloodie Murther of Master Coverly a Yorkshire gentleman . . . comitted upon his two children', which he sold to V. Simms and Nathaniel Butter, and then worked it up into *A Yorkshire Tragedy*, which he sold to 'the Kings Majesties Players'.

That 'Shakespeare's' *Pericles* was written chiefly by Wilkins is amply demonstrated by several writers. But they have failed to note that, although the Wilkins-Shakespeare play is based on Wilkins's novel, his novel is based on an anterior play.

Parts of this old play can be gathered from the Wilkins-Shakespeare play, and parts from Wilkins's novel. In it the hero's name was first changed from Apollonius to Pericles. This was probably done because the author wished to avoid associating his hero with the Apollonius legend. This old play treated of the life of Pericles from the time he went to Antioch until his marriage with Thaysa, Princess of Pentapolis. Thus far Wilkins in his novel was evidently following a drama. Many of his lines still retain the rhythm of the original blank verse. He then began following Twine's novel closely until Mariana is discovered in Mitylene, when he again deserted Twine and seems to have followed a second play. The first play was based on Gower, but the second seems to have been based on Twine; however, there is much material in this later part of Wilkins's novel which does not appear in Twine.

From Wilkins's novel it seems that the old play on Pericles was designed as a music drama, in celebration of a wedding. The last act contained songs and music by Pericles (off stage); and it had a charming scene wherein the King, awakened by the music, received a letter from Thaysa, full of euphuism, telling him she would wed with none but Pericles. As recast in Wilkins's novel the King then decides in favour of Pericles. Pericles enters to him and is shown the letter, and is charged with being a traitor ' that thus disguis'd art stolen into my court with the witchcraft of thy actions to bewitch the yeelding spirit of my tender child '. Pericles replies with heat and the King decides to refer the matter to Thaysa, who then enters. Pericles questions her : ' If ever he by motion or by letters, by amorous glances or by any meanes that lovers use to compasse their desseignes,' &c. And the forward maiden answers: ' Suppose he had. Who darst take offence thereat?' The King assumes anger: ' How, minion, is this a fit match for you? A stragling Theseus borne we know not where, one that has neither bloud nor merite for thee to hope for,' &c. Thaysa defends her choice and ends her plea entreating the King ' to remember that she was in love, the power of which love was not to be confined by the power of his will '. This strife continues until the jolly King takes a hand of each as if to lead them to prison, then ' clapt them hand in hand ', and they kissed; and about then the old play must have ended.

This must have been a Court comedy, probably by Peele.

VI

ELIZABETHAN MUSIC DRAMA

ELIZABETHAN music drama has never seriously occupied the attention of the various historians who have written so copiously of English drama; yet it is a subject which should appeal strongly to the inherent instincts of the Anglo-Saxon race. There have been times when intellectual drama has failed to interest; but there has never been a period when music drama has lost its hold. Be the drama and music never so poor the English soul still craves for the combination, ecclesiastical as well as secular.

In its beginnings Elizabethan music drama was ecclesiastical; and the chief source of its origin was the Queen's Chapel. When it began is uncertain; but it was in being under the celebrated *Thomas Tallis* (1515–85), who passed the greater part of his life as a Queen's chapeler.

In 1575 *Tallis*, with William Byrde, received a royal patent conferring on them a monopoly of musical publication. After the death of Tallis Byrde retained this patent under his own name until *c.* 1597.

William Byrde (1545–1623), a pupil of Tallis, was the most famous musician of Queen Elizabeth's reign. A Queen's chapeler, he composed for the Chapel Children until 1597, when he gave up his printing patent and for many years dissociated himself from the Children and ecclesiastical music.

Another celebrated musician of the era was *Thomas Campion* (1540–1623). A physician by profession, he was also a poet of some merit, wrote songs and masques, and published the first known English treatise on counterpoint. With what theatrical company he was connected is unknown.

Thomas Morley (1557–1602), a pupil of Byrde, was until 1592 one of Paules Boys. He then became a Queen's chapeler until 1602. In 1597, when Byrde left the Queen's service, Morley took his place and was granted the patent for musical publication. He also wrote a treatise on composition, and published many of his songs and madrigals.

William Hunnis. From 1580 until 1583 the Chapel Children were located at Blackfriars theatre under the Mastership of William Hunnis (*c.* 1530–97). Although Hunnis had, in his younger days, written many interludes and much music for the Children, he ceased writing in 1583 and confined himself to the general direction of the company. William Byrde became his chief musical composer, George Peele his playwright. His last play, *A Game of Cards*, produced on December 26, 1582, synchronizes with the advent of Peele.

The Earle of Oxford's company. In the summer of 1583 the Earl of Oxford purchased the lease of Blackfriars theatre, together with several tenements adjoining, and presented all of them to John Lyly, who was his poet in chief. The company acted at Blackfriars until 1584, when they amalgamated with Paules Boys.

Paules Boys had gained considerable reputation before 1581 under the direction of Sebastian Westcott. When he died on December 26 of that year he was succeeded by Thomas Gyles. Gyles assisted in combining Paules Boys with the Earl of Oxford's Boys; and the two companies acted at Blackfriars until 1584, when Gyles, Lyly, and Harry Evans, the Earl of Oxford's man, transferred the company to an unknown theatre near St. Paul's, where they continued until they were inhibited in 1590. Harry Evans was afterwards connected with the Children of Her Majesty's Revels, for whom he leased the remodelled Blackfriars from the Burbages in 1597.

The Chapel Children. Under this title were grouped the choristers, boys and men, who sang in Her Majesty's Chapel, the members of the Chapel orchestra, the various instructors of the Children, the Master, Vice-Master, and various musical composers. As there seems to have been no provision for composers as such, they were assigned some instrument and were rated as members of the orchestra. Plays were acted almost exclusively by the Children.

Hunnis bought the lease of Blackfriars in 1580, and held it until 1583, when it was sold to the Earl of Oxford. Presumably the Children acted at the Chapel Royal from that date until 1597, when they returned to Blackfriars. From 1590 until 1599 they were usually called 'The Children of Her Majestie's Revels'.

Under Hunnis and Byrde the Chapel Children had attained considerable efficiency, so that when Peele joined them as Court playwright in 1583 he found to hand a perfect instrument for the expression of music drama.

Peele's interest in music drama began at Oxford in the study of the plays of Euripides. From them he learned free rhythm, the use of orchestra and chorus. With rhythm he there experimented in his historical plays; but it was not until he came to London that he could experiment with a complete orchestra, chorus, and set of actors. While such an instrument as the Chapel Children was a necessity to Peele, he was quite as necessary to that instrument. Together they developed Elizabethan music drama.

While Peele and Byrde seem to have enjoyed a monopoly of play-writing and musical composition for the Chapel Children until 1590, after that date Nash, Greene, Marlowe, and Lyly shared honours with Peele, and Morley assisted Byrde. The Chapel Children thus came to be served by all the greatest poets of the period. Music drama had by then become the most favoured of the arts.

Greene died in 1592; Marlowe was killed in 1593; Nash soon found his true bent in other lines; Peele and Lyly were left to carry music drama to perfection. At times they collaborated; at times they worked separately. Peele died in 1597; and even as secular music drama had been greatly created and brought to perfection by him, so after his death it withered and passed away.

After Peele's death Lyly and Morley carried on at Blackfriars until 1599, when Lyly revived Paules Boys, and Chapman, Jonson, and Marston wrote for the Children. However, few of the plays written after 1597 can be classed as music dramas.

Although the career of music drama was short, and centred chiefly in the activities of George Peele, it must stand as the most brilliant episode in English drama. The plays were written entirely by University men, outsiders being excluded; they were witnessed by the most select and cultivated audience to be found in England, the mob having no share therein. The Royal Chapel was the Covent Garden of Queen Elizabeth's reign; but the plays of Peele, Marlowe, Greene, Nash, and Lyly were infinitely superior to the libretti of any succeeding era, and the music of Hunnis, Byrde, and Morley was more akin to the matter than that of any later composers.

Peele based his dramas on those of Euripides; but he re-modelled the Greek usage to suit English needs. He combined music, speech, pantomime, dancing, and scenic effects into a satisfying unity, such a unity as Wagner dreamed of but never accomplished.

VII

ROBERT GREENE

(ROMANTIC INTERLUDES)

ROBERT GREENE was born in Norwich in 1560. He entered Cambridge, St. John's College, in 1575. After a year or more he deserted college for a period of foreign travel, returning to Cambridge about 1580. He took his M.A. in 1583. After writing novels for several years he went to Oxford, then the mother of dramatists, and there took his second M.A. in 1588.

The early part of Greene's career was thus devoted to study and the writing of novels. In 1588, when his *Pandosto* appeared, he was the most popular literary man in England. In 1589 *Menaphon* marked the climax and almost the end of his novel-writing.

It must have been about 1588, when Greene returned to London, that he became friends with Marlowe and began his career as a dramatist. From his confessions it would appear that the actors sought him out and begged him to write for them. Be that as it may he suddenly became the most prolific and popular of playwrights, and so continued until his death on September 3, 1592, when he was but thirty-two years old.

Greene's life in the Bohemian world is well known from his own confessions. His degradation, his sad end, are held up as warnings to all youths. There are always men like Greene in every Bohemia, naturally open-hearted, unsuspicious, really conventional. When thrown into Bohemia, where all is unconventional, where daring spirits like Marlowe preach soul freedom and live and love unrestricted, these men always meet with tragedy.

It is easy for unconventional people to live in Bohemia, and easy for conventional beings to live with Puritans; but the

Puritan in Bohemia or the Bohemian among Puritans meets with disaster. The dominant mind of Marlowe urged Greene into every sort of excess; but each outburst of freedom was severely paid for; on the morrow there was no joy in his Puritan soul, but misery only, which misery in turn urged him to new excesses.

It has been the habit of Puritan scholastics of all ages to belittle the work of Greene because of his life. This was begun almost before he was dead by Ben Jonson. However, to state the truth, Greene's art was formed and a great part of his work was done before he entered Bohemia; and his work continued to the end on the very lines of his earlier successes. Whatsoever he made of his life it did not affect his art.

Another thing for which Greene has been much condemned was his attack on Shakespeare as ' an upstart crow '. That the attack was justified and contained nothing but the truth there can be no doubt.

Beginning in 1583, while still at Cambridge, Greene turned out during the ensuing seven years somewhat more than two novels each year. The earlier ones were much tinged with euphuism; but gradually as he found himself they assumed more and more the form of romantic love stories, always with a strong moral trend. The people are those usually found in romantic stories: kings, princesses, shepherds, sailors, soldiers, fools; and the country where all the strange events take place is the usual land of romance, a far-away kingdom.

In order to succeed as a writer of romance an author must have something in his being which appeals directly to his reader, otherwise any one might write such tales. That which made Greene so popular is his unending grace and charm, the which he instils into all his characters, his songs, his scenery. His great facility added even more gracefulness; his prose flows like a hesitant stream through flower-strewn wood and ' plaisance ', reflecting an unending mosaic of fresh colour. His novels resemble the romantic paintings of Ghirlandajo and the early Italian Renaissance painters, which combine pure colour with utmost grace in design.

From Greene's novel *Menaphon*, 1589 :

Menaphon . . . walking solitarie downe to the shore, to see if any of his ewes and lambes were straggled downe to the strond to brouse on sea ivie, whereof they take speciall delight to feede; he found his flockes grazing upon the Promontorie Mountaines hardlie: whereon resting himselfe on a hill that over-peered the great Mediterraneum, noting how Phoebus fetched his Lavaltos on the purple plaines of Neptunus, as if he had meant to have courted Thetis in the royaltie of his roabes: The Dolphines (the sweete conceipters of Musicke) fetcht their carreers on the calmed waves, as if Arion had touched the stringes of his silver sounding instrument: the Mermaides thrusting their heades from the bosome of Amphitrite, sate on the mounting bankes of Neptune, drying their waterie tresses in the Sunne beames: &c.

Weepe not my wanton! Smile upon my knee!
When thou art olde, there's griefe inough for thee!

With this lullaby the babie fell a sleepe, and Sephestia laying it upon the greene grasse covered it with a mantle, and then leaning her head on her hand, and her elbow on her lap, she fell a fresh to poure foorth abundaunce of plaintes, which Lamedon the old man espying, although in his face appeared the mappe of discontent, and everie wrinckle was a catalogue of woes, yet to cheere up Sephestia, shrowding his inward sorrow with an outward smile, he began to comfort her in his manner, &c.

Greene's other prose works were 'Conny-catching pamphlets', a series of pictures of low life evincing a close study of the inhabitants of the Clink, 'Civic and patriotic pamphlets' glorifying England, and 'repentances' in which Puritan Greene laments the excesses of Bohemian Greene.

Greene was not insincere in his repentances. He was no hypocrite; he was simply a Puritan, who loved the beautiful and fine things of life, an artist, a scholar, a refined gentleman, who unfortunately strayed into Bohemia, and there became confused, losing all sense of life's values. The Puritans disliked him for his free life and the denizens of the Clink disdained his Puritanism. He died miserably alone, neglected of all.

In the year of Greene's death Chettle described him as 'a man of indifferent yeares, of face amible, of body well proportioned, his attire after the habite of a schollerlike Gentleman, onely his haire was somewhat long '. Nash adds—'a jolly long red peake [beard] he cherished continually without cutting ', and ' a jolly fellow he was '. Also: ' He might have writ another " Galataeo " of manners, for his manners everie time I came in his companie.'

When Greene began writing plays the prevailing medium was the rhymed couplet. To this medium he took kindly, as is proved by his constant use of it in his songs and earlier plays. While Peele sought inspiration from the Greeks, and Marlowe from the Latins, Greene followed in the footsteps of the Renaissance Italians. Many of the speeches in his earlier plays are cast in stanza form; their rhythm is that of a series of closely connected melodies.

> *Locrine.* Accursèd starres, dam'd and accursèd starres,
> To abreviate my noble father's life!
> Hard-harted Gods, and too [too] envious fates,
> Thus to cut off my father's fatall thread!
> Brutus, that was a glorie to us all,
> Brutus, that was a terror to his foes,
> Alasse, too soone, by Demagorgon's knife,
> The martiall Brutus is bereft of life!

This greatly resembles an Italian small-song. The ensuing speech is less regular, but is nevertheless in verse form, and is full of music.

> No sad complaints may move just Aeacus;
> No dreadfull threats can feare judge Rhodomanth.
> Wert thou as strong as mightie Hercules,
> That tamde the hugie monsters of the world,
> Plaidst thou as sweet, on the sweet-sounding lute,
> As did the spouse of faire Euridise,
> That did enchant the waters with his noise,
> And made stones, birds, and beasts to lead a dance,
> Constraind the hillie trees to follow him,
> Thou couldst not move the judge of Erebus,
> Nor move compassion in grimme Plutos heart;
> For fatall Mors expecteth all the world,
> And every man must tread the way of death. &c.

The same characteristics will be found in the following, by the Ghost:

> I, traiterous Humber, thou shalt find it so.
> Yea, to thy cost thou shalt the same behold,
> With anguish, sorrow, and with sad laments.
> The grassie plaines, that now do please thine eies,
> Shall ere the night be coloured all with blood:
> The shadie groves, which now enclose thy campe,
> And yield sweet savours to thy damnèd corps,
> Shall ere the night be figured all with blood:
> The profounde streame, that passeth by thy tents,
> And with his moisture serveth all thy campe,
> Shall ere the night converted be to blood;
> Yea, with the blood of those thy stragling boyes;
> For now revenge shall ease my lingring griefe,
> And now revenge shall glut my longing soule.

As in *Richard III* he here makes effective use of the refrain.

Another more striking example of the use of refrain is Guendoline's complaint, which ends:

> What said I? Falsehood? I, that filthie crime;
> For Locrine hath forsaken Guendoline.
> Behold the heavens do waile for Guendoline.
> The shining sunne doth blush for Guendoline.
> The liquid aire doth weep for Guendoline.
> The verie ground doth grone for Guendoline.
> I, they are milder than the Brittaine King,
> For he rejecteth lucklesse Guendoline.

This resembles Orlando's verse to Rosalind in *As You Like It*.

Locrine, printed in 1595 as 'newly set foorth, overseene and corrected, by W. S.', was registered on July 20, 1594, and printed by Thomas Creede, who also brought out *James IV*, *A Looking-glass for London*, *The Famous Victories of Henry V*, *Alphonsus*, and *The Tragical Raigne of Selimus*.

Greene's peculiarities are to be found in every episode of *Locrine*. There is his unchecked lyrical play, beautiful but diffuse, his prolix use of adjectives, which add colour if not always meaning, his great love of nature, his romantic situations and names, his classical allusions, &c. The date of its creation is uncertain, but the fact that it was revised by Shakespeare before 1594, and the general style of the whole, point to the period 1588.

The story of Locrine was told in verse by Greene's friend, Thomas Lodge. It is possible, therefore, that Lodge assisted Greene in writing this play as well as *A Looking-glass for London*. The names Elstred, Sabrine, and Guendolen as they appear in Lodge's *Complaint* are presumably correct, and were corrupted by Shakespeare into Estrild, Sabren, and Guendoline.

Greene's budding ability as a dramatist may be judged from the death-scene between Locrine and Elstred:

> *Locrine.* Farewell, faire Elstred, beautie's paragon,
> Fram'd in the front of forlorne miseries!
> Ner shall mine eyes behold thy sunshine eyes,
> But when we meet in the Elysian fields;
> Thither I go before with hastened pace.
> Farewell, vain world, and thy inticing snares!
> Farewell, foule sinne, and thy inticing pleasures!
> And welcome, death, the end of mortal smart,
> Welcome to Locrine's overburthened heart!
> [*He kills himself.*]
>
> *Elstred.* Break, heart, with sobs and greevous suspirs!
> Streame forth, you teares, from forth my watry eyes;
> Help me to mourne for warlike Locrine's death!
> Powre downe your teares, you watry regions,
> For mightie Locrine is bereft of life!
> O fickle fortune! O unstable world!
> What else are all things that this globe containes,
> But a confused chaos of mishaps,
> Wherein, as in a glasse, we plainly see
> That all our life is but as a Tragedie?
> Since mightie Kings are subject to mishap—
> I, mightie Kings are subject to mishap!—
> Since martiall Locrine is bereft of life,
> Shall Elstred live, then, after Locrine's death?
> Shall love of life barre her from Locrine's sword?
> O no, this sword, that hath bereft his life,
> Shall now deprive me of my fleeting soule:

Strengthen these hands, O mightie Jupiter,
That I may end my woefull miserie.
Locrine, I come; Locrine, I follow thee!
    [*She kills herself.*]

The Battle of Alcazar, printed in 1594 by Edward Allde for Richard Bankworth 'as it was sundrie times plaid by the Lord high Admirall his servants', is a later play, and has been assigned to Peele. If *Locrine* were written by Greene so also was *Alcazar*. Compare the ensuing quotations—

From *Locrine*:

> You ugly sprites that in Cocitus mourne,
> And gnash your teeth with dolorous laments:
> You fearfull dogs that in black Laethe howle,
> And scare the ghoasts with your wide open throats:
> You ugly ghoasts that, flying from these dogs,
> Do plunge your selves in Puryflegiton:
> Come, all of you, and with your shriking notes
> Accompanie the Brittaines conquering hoast.
> Come, fierce Erinnis, horrible with snakes;
> Come, ugly Furies, armèd with your whippes;
> You threefold judges of black Tartarus,
> And all the armie of you hellish fiends,
> With new found torments rack proud Locrine's bones!

'Fiery Phlegethon' was misprinted as 'Puryflegiton'. 'Phlegethon' appears also in *The Battle of Alcazar* and in Greene's *Orlando Furioso*.

From *Alcazar*:

> You bastards of the Night and Erebus,
> Fiends, furies, hags that fight with steel,
> Range through this army with your iron whips,
> Drive forward to this deed this Christian crew,
> And let me triumph in the tragedy . . .
> . . . .
> Ride, Nemesis, ride in thy fiery cart,
> Descend and take to thy tormenting hell
> The mangled body of that traitor-king.
> Rack'd let him be on proud Ixion's wheele,
> Pin'd let him be with Tantalus' endless thirst,
> Prey let him be to Tityus' greedy bird,

Wearied with Sisyphus' immortal toil;
And lastly for revenge, for deep revenge,
Whereof thou goddess and deviser art,
Damn'd let him be, damn'd and condemn'd to bear
All torments, tortures, plagues and pains of hell.

Alcazar is more forceful than the earlier play; but it makes the same use of adjectives, classical allusions, situations, names, stanza form, and refrain. It is not in the least like anything ever written by Peele.

The problem of assigning various historical plays to Marlowe, Peele, and Greene—Nash, Chettle, Drayton, and Munday having been overlooked—has greatly harassed the commentators. They usually agree that all such plays containing good blank verse belong, those before 1593 to Marlowe, and those after 1593 to Shakespeare. The remainder are given to Peele and Greene.

To separate Peele's work from Greene's was for them a more difficult problem, which usually resolved itself into a hunt for reappearing words and phrases. *Edward I* was assigned to Peele because it contains a passage which reappears in his *Polyhymnia* and a quotation assigned to him in *England's Parnassus*. This is a fairly safe method.

Two quotations from *The Battle of Alcazar* also appear in *England's Parnassus*; the one is attributed to Peele, the other to Dekker. And further passages from *Alcazar* appear in *Tom Stukeley*, a much later play. The probability is that both *Alcazar* and *Tom Stukeley* were based upon and borrowed from an early Peele or Marlowe play which is mentioned by Peele in his *Farewell to Drake*, written in 1589.

To assign plays on such scant evidence is a doubtful method. But the most indefensible one is that of Fleay, who puts down to Peele all historical plays in which the phrase 'sandy plain' can be found, his contention being that no one but Peele ever wrote of such plains and that Peele wrote of none but sandy ones. (For Greene's Historical Plays see GREENE and NASH.)

The Tragedy of Selimus, sometime Emperour of the Turkes, was first printed in 1594, as a Queen's company play, by Thomas

Creede. It is one of Greene's earliest dramas, abounding in rhyme and in speeches cast in verse form. A few critics have attributed it to Marlowe.

Into this play Greene crowds many current Machiavellian speculations. Before embarking on his career of crime Selimus arms his ' heart with irreligion ' :

> Amongst us men, there is some difference
> Of actions, term'd by us ' good ' or ' ill ' :
> As he that doth his father recompense,
> Differs from him that doth his father kill.
> And yet I think, think others what they will,
> That parricides, when death hath given them rest,
> Shall have as good a part as [have] the best :
> And that's . . . just nothing : for, as I suppose,
> In Death's void kingdom reigns eternal Night,
> Secure of evil, and secure of foes,
> Where nothing doth the wicked man affright,
> No more than him that dies in doing right.
> Then since in death nothing shall to us fall,
> Here while I live, Ile have a snatch at all,
> And that can never, never be attain'd,
> Unless old Bajazet do die the death, &c.

In this play Greene had not as yet discovered the power of the refrain. He had nevertheless begun experimenting :

> *Bajazet.* Happily dealt the forward fates with thee,
> Good Alemshae, for thou didst die in field
> And so preventedst this sad spectacle ;
> Pitiful spectacle of sad dreeriment !
> Pitiful spectacle of dismal death !
> But I have liv'd to see . . ., &c.

Strict verse form is preserved in a speech by Bajazet :

> Ah, Aga, Bajazet fain would speak to thee,
> But sudden sorrow eateth up my words.
> Bajazet, Aga, fain would weep for thee,
> But cruel sorrow drieth up my tears.
> Bajazet, Aga, fain would die for thee,
> But grief hath weakened my poor agèd hands.

How can he speak, whose tongue sorrow hath tied?
How can he mourn, that cannot shed a tear?
How shall he live, that full of misery
Calleth for Death, which will not let him die?

In 1588 Marlowe's *Tamburlaine* appeared, written in such majestic blank verse that it was at once acclaimed as the ideal medium through which to express the heroic deeds of a vigorous age. It crushed the old-fashioned rhymed couplet and for a time ruled supreme.

That this pompous verse did not agree with Greene's genius is evinced by the comparative failure of his *Alphonsus, King of Arragon*. Greene disliked the new medium, as did Peele, Nash, and Lyly; Kyd alone adopted it. The others stormed against it as 'the swelling bombast of a bragging blank verse', as verses which 'jet upon the stage in tragical buskins, every word filling the mouth like the farburden of Bo-bell'. However, they soon killed the braggart with ridicule. Greene assisted with his clever satire, *Orlando Furioso*. In this play he attains at times to Euripidean free rhythm, which soon proved itself so adaptable that all who could made use of it.

> *Orlando.* I fynd hir drift phappes the modest pledg
> of my content hath with a privy thought
> and sweet disguise restrayned her fancy thus
> shadowing Orlando under Medors name
> fyne drift, faire nymphe, orlando hopes no lesse
>
> *Orlando.* Clyme up the clowdes to Galaxsia straight
> and tell Apollo, that orlando sitts
> making of verses for Angelica
> yf he denye to send me downe the shirt
> that Deianyra sent to Hercules
> to make me brave, upon my wedding day
> Ile up the Alpes, and post to Meroe the
> watry lakishe hill, and pull the harpe
> from out the ministrills handes, and pawne
> it straight to lovely Proserpine, that she
> may fetch me fayre Angelica
> vilayne will he not send me it

Greene has been accused of selling this play to two companies, the Queen's company being one. Certainly he wrote additions to this play for Edward Alleyn. How Alleyn came by the original version is not known. As he was an honest man it must be presumed that he obtained it in an honourable manner. For Greene to write additions to his own play was also legitimate. However, the fact that the Strange company produced a play also produced by the Queen's company was sufficient to cause his detractors to charge Greene with double-dealing. Presumably this was the last play Greene wrote for the Queen's company. His later work went to Alleyn and Lord Strange's men.[1]

Exactly when Greene fell under the spell of Nash is uncertain; but it must have been c. 1590. While in his earlier plays Greene uses perfectly simple language, in *Friar Bacon and Friar Bungay* occasional new Nash-like expressions appear:

'Mine eyes pleaded with tears, my face held pity and content at once.' 'In frigates . . . shalt thou wanton on the waves, and draw the dolphins to thy lovely eyes, to dance lavoltas in the purple streams.' 'Banish thou fancy, and embrace revenge, and in one tomb knit both our carcasses.'

Nash instilled into Greene a keener observation and a more condensed style, so that what he lost in facility he gained in richness. As the drama is more condensed than the novel this condensation perfected his form. In his novels Greene painted many a scene, and in his plays he still revelled in scenic effects. Even his histories are embellished with an unending series of settings designed mainly to appeal to the eye.

Despite the enormous success of his histories those plays do not exhibit Greene at his best. The consummation of his genius is exhibited in comedies such as *As You Like It*, which in all probability was the one 'lastlie writ' with Nash.

[1] Only slight portions of this play exist as written by Greene. These are preserved at Dulwich. The entire play as printed in the Quarto was rewritten : see *Two Elizabethan Stage Abridgements*, by W. W. Greg, Malone Society, 1923. This revision is so like the revision of *Locrine* that it may safely be attributed to William Shakespeare during his second period. If this be correct then the two versions are accounted for. Shakespeare sold his revision to the Queen's company, while Greene sold the original play to Alleyn.

As You Like It was based on *Rosalynde, Euphues Golden Legacie* by Greene's friend Thomas Lodge, which was printed in 1590. It is a romance in the Italian manner common to so many of Greene's plays and novels. In it he revelled in highly coloured romance, and the play, even as it appears in the 'Shakespeare' Folio, is infused with Greene's joyous outdoor spirit. Although much of this play was afterwards rewritten, many of the songs, the colouring, the settings, the rich insouciant romanticism, are Greene's. Many of the serious parts are by Nash, and much of the euphuistic dialogue is by or in imitation of Lyly; but the planning and body of this interlude were by Greene. Celia and Audrey could have been created by no one but the 'Homer of Women', as Nash called him. Orlando is in this play no longer 'furioso', but inamorato. He again finds the name of his sweetheart decorating his woodland retreat.

In *As You Like It* Greene returns to the land of his early romances. The people are once more shepherds, kings, queens, lords, and ladies; but now they have become more real, more sympathetic, nor less lovable. The charm of his tales is infused into this interlude. It unfolds with grace and felicity; for now Greene has mastered his dramatic medium. His speeches vary from verse form, with occasional end rhymes, to faultless free rhythm. It is still Italianate, still brave in its colour and distinct in its slight formalism, distinguishing marks which differentiate it from the work of Peele. The refrain has also been mastered and is now used almost unconsciously, adding a new charm of its own.

Example of verse form:

> *Orlando.* If ever you have look'd on better dayes:
> If ever beene where bels have knoll'd to Church:
> If ever sate at any good mans feast:
> If ever from your eye-lids wip'd a teare,
> And know what 'tis to pittie, and be pittied:
> Let gentlenesse my strong enforcement be,
> In the which hope, I blush, and hide my sword.
> *Duke.* True is it that we have seene better dayes,

And have with holy bell been knowld to Church,
And sat at good mens feasts, and wip'd our eies
Of drops, that sacred pity hath engendred :
And therefore sit you downe in gentlenesse, &c.

Example of refrain :

From the east to westerne Inde,
   no jewel is like Rosalinde,
Hir worth being mounted on the winde,
   through all the world beares Rosalinde.
All the pictures fairest Linde,
   are but blacke to Rosalinde :
Let no face bee kept in mind,
   but the faire of Rosalinde, &c.

Here and there a few Shakespearian additions and corrections must be discounted, otherwise this 'lastlie writ comedie' stands as Greene's most finished monument. Nash called Greene master of all 'in the plotting of plays'. Had he written 'interludes' he would have hit nearer the mark. As an interlude *As You Like It* is wellnigh perfect.

The simple sweetness of all of Greene's romantic work is well displayed in *As You Like It*, also his love of scenic display ; and, as in almost all of his discovered work, some figure sits pathetically a-mourning. The reference to Marlowe in this play would seem to be a later insertion. (See also NASH.)

It has been usually stated that Greene wrote entirely for the Queen's company. That this is false is evident from the fact that *Henry VI, Parts II* and *III*, were Strange company plays, that the additions to *Orlando* were written for Alleyn, and that several of his plays belonged to the Strange company.

In his *Apologie for Pierce Peniless*, edition of 1593, Nash wrote that Greene was 'chiefe agent of the companie, for whom he writ more than four others'. Although Nash does not mention the name of the company it could not have been the Queen's. Presumably it was Lord Strange's company. Although Greene began with the Queen's company he went to the Strange company about 1589 and wrote for them until his death in 1593. (For Greene's Historical Plays see GREENE and NASH.)

VIII

THOMAS NASH

(PICARESQUE MELODRAMA)

THOMAS NASH, son of William Nash, ' minester ' of Lowestoft, was born in November, 1567. He matriculated in October, 1582 (aged 15), ' as a sizar of St. John's college', Cambridge; and became ' a Scholar on the lady Margaret's foundation ' in 1584. He remained at Cambridge ' seven yere together, lacking a quarter ' until 1589, when he went to London.

The first literary work published in his name is his Introduction to Greene's *Menaphon* (1589), which shows him as the friend of Greene, the admirer of Peele, the scoffer at Marlowe's bombastic vein, and the scourge of the Pembroke dramatists. At the beginning of his career he was thus connected with the dramatists then writing for the Queen's company.

This same year, 1589, he produced his *Anatomie of Absurditie*, an ' embrion of my youth '. This pamphlet had probably been written while he was still at Cambridge.

The year 1589 brought Nash into close touch with Lyly. Both were employed to write, first pamphlets, then plays, against the Martinists. So far as is known these anti-Martinist plays were his first dramatic productions. The controversy led to the suppression of Paules Boys in 1590, when Nash must have turned to other work. His Epistle before Sir Philip Sidney's *Astrophel and Stella*, printed in 1591, with its elaborate compliment to Lady Pembroke, Sidney's sister, indicates that he hoped to find in her a patroness. In this he probably was disappointed, as in *Pierce Penilesse* (1592) he indicates that he was still unattached.

While Nash associated with Lyly in writing the anti-Martinist tracts and plays he saw little of Greene. In *Foure Letters Confuted* (1593) he wrote:

A thousand there be that have more reason to speak in his behalfe than I, who, since I first knew him [Greene] about town, have beene two yeares together and not seene him.

Their collaboration in play-writing must therefore have begun in 1591 and continued until Greene's death in 1592. During this period they wrote together at least one comedy (see GREENE) and various other plays. (See NASH AND GREENE.)

Some time before he was joined by Nash in 1591 Greene had deserted the Queen's company for Lord Strange's men. He had also begun a quarrel with Gabriel Harvey, which was continued by Nash in Greene's defence until 1596.

By 1593 Nash had become definitely attached to the family of the Lord Chamberlain, Henry Carey, first Baron Hunsdon. During that year he dedicated his *Christ's Teares over Jerusalem* to the Lord Chamberlain's daughter-in-law:

> To the most Honored, and Vertuous Beautified Ladie, The Ladie Elizabeth Carey: Wife to the thrice magnanimous, and noble descended Knight, Sir George Carey, knight Marshall, &c.

Exactly when Nash became George Carey's retainer cannot be determined; however, in *The Terrors of the Night* (1594), which is dedicated to 'Mistres Elizabeth Carey', sole daughter to Sir George Carey, he wrote of his patron:

> Whatsoever minutes intermission I have of calmed content, or least respite to call my wits together, principall and immediate proceedeth from him. Through him my tender wainscot studie doore is delivered from much assault and battrie: through him I looke into, and am looked on in the world: from whence otherwise I were a wretched banished exile. . . . Much more may I acknowledge all redundant prostrate vassailage to the royall descended Familie of the Carey's: but for whom, my spirit long ere this had expyred, and my pen serv'd as a puniard to gall my owne heart.

In *Have with you to Saffron Walden* (1596) Nash states: 'Till the Impression of this Book, I have got nothing by Printing these three yeres.' And in his *Foure Letters Confuted* (1593) he wrote:

> For the order of my life, it is as civil as a civil [Seville] orenge: I lurke in no corners, but converse in a house of credit, as well

governed as any Colledge, where there bee more rare qualified
men, and selected good schollers than in any Noblemans house
that I knowe in England. If I . . . were a base shifting companion, it stoode not with my Lords honour to keepe me, &c.

In 1592 he wrote that he would have corrected the proof of
Pierce Penilesse ' had not feare of infection detained me with my
lord in the country'. His connexion with the Careys began in
1592–3 and continued into 1596. As he lived with them he
moved in the Court circle during this period.

When Lord Strange died on April 16, 1594, Henry Carey,
the Lord Chamberlain, took over the Strange company of actors,
which then became ' my Lord Chamberlain's company'. Presumably it was greatly due to Nash that this company came under
the patronage of his benefactor. This placed Nash in a most
favourable position, and, if he were not already the company's
chief playwright, he then became their ruling genius.

Nash had collaborated in writing plays with Lyly in 1589–90,
with Greene during 1591–2. In 1593 he wrote with Marlowe.
Dame Fortune deprived him of two of these friends about the time
the Careys took him into their favour. In 1593 he formed
a close friendship with Chettle, who in *Kind-hartes Dreame*
defended Nash against the attacks of Shakespeare and Kyd;
and in 1596 in *Have with you to Saffron Walden* Nash turns to
Chettle for further assistance. There, answering a charge by
the infamous Gabriel Harvey that he abused his friends, Nash
wrote :

> Further than further bee it knowne (since I had one further
> before) I never abusd Marloe, Greene, Chettle in my life, nor
> anie of my frends that usde me like a frend : which both Marloe
> and Greene (if they were alive) under their hands would testifie,
> even as Harry Chettle hath in a short note here.

While Chettle defended Nash, Nash assisted Chettle by
favouring the printing-house of Danter, Chettle, and Hoskins
with the greater number of his pamphlets. In 1596 Nash wrote
of the company familiarly as ' our printing house ', and from a

statement in *Have with you to Saffron Walden* he seems to have then resided at, possibly above, the printing-house:

> My Printers Wife too, hee [i.e. Harvey] hath had a twitch at in two or three places about the midst of his booke . . . talkes of her 'moody tung', and 'that she wil teach the storme winde to scolde English'; but let him looke to himselfe, for though in all the time I have lyne in her House, and as long as I have knowen her, I never saw anie such thing by her.

Thus Nash and Chettle were in daily, almost hourly, communication, be the 'Printers Wife' the wife of Chettle or of Danter.

This close friendship had far-reaching consequences, for it must have been through the influence of Nash that Chettle took up the writing of plays. Greene and Marlowe being dead, Nash as chief playwright to 'my Lord Chamberlain's men' sought a new collaborator, one who could take the place of Greene in 'plotting plays'. Such a one he found in his friend 'Harry' Chettle. That these two should collaborate was most natural, especially after they discovered that Chettle could plot plays. For a play-plotter was exactly what Nash most needed; and that Chettle could perform that task his extant work amply demonstrates.

When the Plague descended on London in 1592 Nash went with his patron on a journey through Kent as a member of the Queen's household. In the autumn, while at Croydon, the Queen was entertained by a pageant play called *Summers Last Will and Testament*. This is the only play which hitherto has been attributed to Nash. Evidently it was a hurried production written more or less for the amusement of children.

On returning to town Nash, probably at the instigation of 'Kind-heart' Chettle, as hinted by Harvey in his *Pierces Supererogation*, having tried his best to make friends with the intractable Gabriel in *Christ's Tears*, settled down to writing plays such as *Dido, Queen of Carthage*, written in collaboration with Marlowe, and occasional verse for his friends and patrons.

These three years, from 1593 to 1596, were those in which

Fortune smiled. Disaster soon followed. Harvey continued his attacks, but Nash, secure and happy in the circle of the Lord Chamberlain, did not reply until 1596, when, wearied by Harvey's boasting that he had silenced Nash, he brought out *Have with you to Saffron Walden*. Possibly he lost his patron this same year, as the Lord Chamberlain died on July 22, 1596, and his son Lord Hunsdon had little time to devote to his retainers. The Chamberlain company moved to the Curtain theatre. Seemingly Nash went with them. Certainly he had severed his connexion with the Rose theatre before midsummer in 1597, when the Admiral's men took one of his incomplete skits and produced it as the *Ile of Dogs*.

In *Lenten Stuffe* Nash states:

> I having begun but the induction and first act of it, the other foure acts without my consent, or the least guesse of my drift or scope, by the players were supplied, which bred both their trouble and mine to.

This implies that he had severed his connexion with the Admiral's men and the Rose; otherwise he would have been asked to complete the play.

The *Ile of Dogs* scandal forced Nash into banishment. He slipped out of London, probably by water, and went to Great Yarmouth, where he wrote in 1599:

> My case is no smothred secret, and with light cost of rough cast rhetoricke it may be tollerabely playstered over, if under the pardon and priviledge of incensed higher powers it were lawfully indulgenst me freely to advocate my owne astrology. Sufficeth what they in their grave wisedomes shall proscribe, I in no sorte will seeke to acquite, nor presumptuously attempte to dispute against the equity of their judgementes, but humble and prostrate, appeale to their mercies.

Nash stopped in Yarmouth six weeks:

> At greate Yarmouth in Norfolke, I arived in the latter ende of Autumne . . . for six weekes first and last under that predominant constellation of *Aquarius* or *Joves Nectar* filler, tooke I up my repose, and there mette with such kind entertainment and benigne hospitality, &c.

While making his head-quarters at Yarmouth he amused himself by taking excursions up and down the coast:

> One becke more to the balies of the cinque portes, whome I
> were a ruder Barbarian then *Smill* the Prince of *Crinis & Nagayans*,
> if in this action I should forget (having had good cheare at their
> tables more then once or twice whiles I loytred in this paragon-
> lesse fish town), &c.

To the north Nash wandered at least as far as Edinburgh, as is evident from the line, 'This language or parley have I usurpt from some of the deftest lads in all Edenborough towne', found in the following:

> The Scotish Jockies or Redshanks . . . upholde and make good
> the same. Their clacke or gabbling to this purport: 'How in
> diebus illis, when Robert de Breaux their gud king sent his deare
> heart to the haly land, for reason he caud not gang thider him-
> selfe . . . they had the staple or fruits of the herring in their road
> or channell, till a foule ill feud arose amongst his sectaries and
> servitors, and there was mickle tule, and a blacke warld, and a
> deale of whinyards drawne about him, and many sacklesse wights
> and praty barnes run through the tender weambs, and fra thence
> ne farry taile of a herring in thilke sound they caud gripe.' This
> language or parley have I usurpt from some of the deftest lads in
> all Edenborough towne, which it will be no impeachment for the
> wisest to turne loose for a trueth, without any diffident wrastling
> with it . . . and if any further bolstring or backing be required,
> it is evident by the confession of the sixe hundred Scotish witches
> executed in Scotland at Bartelmewtide was twelve-moneth, that
> in Yarmouth road they were all together . . . when the great floud
> was, & there stood [stirred] up such ternados & furicanos of
> tempests, in envey (as I collect); that the staple of the red her-
> ring from them was translated to Yarmouth, as will be spoke of
> there whiles any winds or stormes & tempests chase & puffe in
> the lower region.

Eventually Nash went into 'the country', where he wrote *Lenten Stuffe*:

> Of my note-books and all books else here in the country I am
> bereaved, whereby I might enamell and hatch over this device
> more artificially and masterly, and attire it in his true orient
> varnish and tincture.

Nash died, presumably in the country, some time after writing the above in 1599, some time before his friend Chettle passed away, certainly before 1606, where or when has not as yet been discovered.

Almost all of Nash's characteristics can be discovered in his prose. He was a poor poet, although he was passionately fond of poetry, and was greatly influenced by Lyly, Greene, Marlowe, and Peele. His dictum on Peele is well known. Of Marlowe he wrote, in 1599: 'Leander and Hero of whom divine Musaeus sung and a diviner muse than he, Kit Marlowe.' He mentions 'immortal Sidney' and 'heavenly Spenser'. He loved poetry because it was the poets who 'have cleansed our language from barbarism, and made the vulgar sort here in London, to aspire to a richer purity of speach than is communicated with the comminalty of any nation under heaven'. This evinces wherein lay his real regard for the poets. Not for their rhythmic or emotional abilities—for lyricism seems to have been lacking in his nature —but because of their ability to create and use miraculous words, to express noble and refined ideas by means of full-fraught words and expressions.

> 'I account of Poetrie, as of a more hidden & divine kinde of Philosophy, enwrapped in blinde Fables and darke Stories, wherein the principles of more excellent Arts and morall precepts of manners . . . are contained.' 'In Poems the thinges that are most profitable are shrouded under the Fables that are most obscure.' 'I trust . . . there is no man so distrustful to doubt that deeper divinitie is included in Poets inventions.'

Nash seems to have regarded poetry as a symbolical presentation of philosophy, history, religion, and morals. It was poetic because it was presented symbolically. While poetry is great in proportion to the intensity of its concentration into symbolism, without rhythm such condensed symbolism remains prose.

Nash, who so exalted the idea and its symbolic presentation that he overlooked rhythm, nevertheless understood true poetry better than those other extremists to whom poetry consists in rhythm alone. Of his shortcomings as a rhythmist Nash wrote :

> Indeede, to say the truth, my stile is somewhat heavie-gated, and cannot daunce, trip, and goe so lively, with 'Oh my love, ah my love; all my love's gone'. . . . Onely [however] I can keepe pace with Gravesend barge, and care not if [provided] I have water enough to lande my 'ship of fooles' with the Tearme (the tyde 1 should say). . . . Some, to goe the lighter away, will take in their fraught of spangled feathers . . . and then beare out their sayles as proudly, as if they were balisted with Bul-beife.

Certainly Nash believed in being fraught with something of real worth.

The above was written in 1591. In 1599 he wrote:

> Let me speake to you about my huge woords. . . . Know it is my true vaine to be *tragicus Orator*, and of all stiles I most affect & strive to imitate *Arentines*, not caring for this demure soft *mediocre genus*, this is like water and wine mixt togither; but give me pure wine of it self, & that begets good bloud, and heates the brain thorowly : . . . I had as lieve have no sunne, as have it shine faintly, no fire as a smothering fire of small coales, no cloathes rather then weare linsey wolsey.

Throughout his career Nash strove to present large thoughts in forceful language. His unending desire to beautify and enrich the English language, his unfailing use of the perfectly fitting word, stand out as his most prevailing traits. They stamp everything he wrote. Nor was he always satisfied with one word, but often gave one substitute after another. So great was his wealth that he seemed to scatter words about for the mere joy of seeing them scintillate, words full of expression which live and breathe. For this he was abused and misunderstood. In his own defence he wrote :

> 'No winde that blows strong, but is boystrous, no speech or wordes of any power or force to confute or persuade but must bee swelling and boystrous.' 'Our English tongue of all languages most swarmeth with the single money of monosyllables . . . halfe-pence, three-farthings and two-pences. Therefore what did me I, but . . . had them to the compounders immediately, and exchanged them foure into one, and others into more.'

While Nash changed his small coin into large pieces of pure gold he hated bombast, high-sounding words without meaning, and even censured his friend Marlowe for using them. He scorns the ' tragedians' who ' embowell the clowdes in a speech of comparison; thinking themselves more than initiated in poets immortality, if they but once get Boreas by the beard and the heavenlie bull by the deaw-lap'.

It is to be doubted if any author has so loved words and has so embellished the English language as Thomas Nash. In *Pierce Penilesse* he wrote of gluttons:

> ' Stall-fed cormorants to damnation.' ' Let but our English belly-gods punish their pursie bodies with this strict penaunce.' ' It is not for nothing that other countreyes . . . call us burstenbellyed gluttons; for we make our greedy paunches powdering tubs of beef,' &c.

Examples of rough rhythm:

Of dogs in *Summers Last Will*:

> Nay; they are wise, as Homer witnesseth,
> Who, talking of Ulisses comming home,
> Saith, all his houshold but Argus his Dogge,
> Had quite forgot him; I, his deepe insight,
> Nor Pallas Art in altering his shape,
> Nor his base weeds, nor absence twenty yeares,
> Could go beyond, or any way delude.
> That Dogges Phisicians are, thus I inferre:
> They are ne're sicke, but they know their disease,
> And find out meanes to ease them of their griefe;
> Speciall good Surgions to cure dangerous wounds;

Another characteristic passage is:

> Smooth-tounged Orators, the fourth in place,
> Lawyers, our common-wealth intitles them,
> Meere swash-bucklers, and ruffianly mates,
> That will for twelve pence make a doughtie fray,
> Set men for strawes together by the eares.
> Skie-measuring Mathematicians:
> Golde-breathing Alcumists also we have,

Both which are subtill-willed humorists,
That get their meales by telling miracles,
Which they have seen in travailing the skies.

This is cast in the form of blank verse of a sort, but it is some-what 'heavie-gated'.

While Nash failed to appreciate assonance and rhythm, his auditory impressions being inadequately reproduced, he was most sensitive to visual impressions, which he registered in picturesque imagery. Examples:

> 'Nothing of that castle save tatered ragged walls nowe re-maines, framed foure square, and overgrowne with briars and bushes.' (*Lenten Stuffe.*)

> 'The weather was colde, and good fires hee kept, (as fishermen, what hardnesse soever they endure at sea, they will make all smoake, but they will make amendes for it, when they come to land) and what with his fiering and smoking, or smokie firing, in that narrow lobby,—his herrings, which were as white as whales bone when hee hung them up, nowe lookt as red as a lobster.' (*Lenten Stuffe.*)

> 'To this feast Juliana addresses herselfe like an Angell: in a littour of greene needleworke, wrought like an arbor and open on everie side, was she borne by foure men, hidden under cloth rough plushed and woven like eglantine and woodbine. At the foure corners it was topt with foure round christall cages of Nightin-gales. For footemen, on either side of her went foure virgins clad in lawne, with lutes in their hands, playing. . . . Before them went foure score bead women she maintained in greene gownes, scattering strowing hearbs and floures. After her followed the blinde, the halt and the lame, sumptuously apparailed like Lords: and thus past she on to Saint Peters.' (*Jack Wilton.*)

> 'In the marrow of your bones snakes shall breede. Your mome-like christall countenaunces shall be netted over, and (masker-like) cawle-visarded, with crawling venomous wormes. Your orient teeth, Toades shall steale into their heads for pearle; of the jelly of your decayed eyes shall they engender their young. In theyr hollowe Caves (theyr transplendent juice so pollutinately employd) shelly snayles shall keepe house.' 'O what is beauty more then a wind-blowne bladder', &c. (*Christ's Teares.*)

Nash had a peculiar predilection for old folk-rhymes. When no authentic folk-rhyme could be found to serve his purpose he invented one for the occasion. Such are:

> ' Fye, fye, of honesty fye!
> Solstitium is an asse, perdy.'

> ' Sol, sol ; ut, re, mi, fa, sol,
> Come to church, while the bell toll.'

> ' Orion, Urion, Arion,
> My Lord thou must looke upon.'

> ' Harvest, by West, and by North,
> And by South and South-east,
> Shewe thy selfe like a beast.'

> ' Sicke, sicke, and very sicke,
> And sicke, and for the time ;
> For Harvest your Master is abusde
> Without reason or rime.'

> ' O tis a precious apothegmaticall Pedant who will finde matter inough to dilate a whole daye on the first invention of
> " Fy, fa, fum,
> I smell the bloud of an English-man ".'

The brain of Nash was so active that fresh ideas continually sought expression before the original idea was completely recorded. This gave rise to a succession of modifying clauses and parenthetic statements which make him at times difficult to follow, especially when, as sometimes happens, he fails to return to the original thought. This habit grew upon him and will be found most exaggerated in *Lenten Stuffe*:

> Downe shee ranne in her loose night-gowne, and her haire about her eares (even as *Semiramis* ranne out with her lie-pot in her hand, and her blacke dangling tresses about her shoulders, with the ivory combe ensnarled in them, when she heard that *Babilon* was taken) and thought to have kist his dead corse alive againe, but as on his blue jellied sturgeon lips she was about to clappe one of those warme plaisters, boystrous woolpacks of ridged tides came rowling in, and raught him from her, (with a minde belike to carrie him backe to *Abidos*).

Plays by Nash.

In his *Groatsworth of Wit* (1592) Greene mentioned Nash as 'Young Juvenall, that byting satyrist, that lastlie with me together writ a comedie'. Nash had then for a time ceased his connexion with Lyly and had joined forces with Greene. From the wording of Greene's statement it seems that they had written other plays together beside 'a comedie'. That they did so is confirmed in a statement by Nash in *Saffron Walden*. At this period Greene was writing for Lord Strange's men; Nash was in the country with Her Majesty and the Children of her Revels. Therefore such of their plays as survived would in all likelihood eventually reappear in the repertoire of the Strange-Chamberlain company.

As You Like It, built upon the tale *Rosalynde* by Lodge, was in all probability the 'comedie' in question. Audrey, Touchstone, and Jaques are new additions to the tale. Touchstone and Jaques are possibly studies of Lyly's character as observed by Nash. The Jaques speeches are especially full of keen word-pictures such as Nash alone could create. The 'seven ages' in its verse form is an exact counterpart of the 'eight kinds of drunkenesse' to be found in *Pierce Penilesse* and the 'three measures' of *Much Ado About Nothing*; and Rosalinde is remade from Lodge's romantic heroine into a picaresque adventuress, sister to Prince Hal.

The 'eight kinds of drunkenesse' of *Pierce Penilesse* reads:

> Nor have we two kinds of drunkards onely,
> But eight kinds. The first is ape drunke;
> And he leapes and sings,
> And daunceth for the heavens:
> The second is lion drunk, and he
> Flings the pots about the house,
> Calls his hostesse whore, breaks
> The glass windows with his dagger,
> And is apt to quarrel with any man
> That speaks to him: The third is
> Swine drunk; heavie lumpish and sleepie,
> And cries for a little more drinke,
> And a few more clothes:

The fourth is sheep drunke;
Wise in his owne conceit, when he
Cannot bring forth the right word:
The fifth is maudlin drunke;
When a fellow will weep for kindnes
In the midst of his ale, and kiss you,
Saying, ' By God, Captain, I love thee ', &c.

The 'seven ages' of *As You Like It* reads:

At first the infant,
Mewling, and puking in the nurses armes;
Then, the whining schoole-boy with his satchell
And shining morning face, creeping like snaile
Unwillingly to schoole. And then the lover,
Sighing like furnace, with a wofull ballad
Made to his mistresse eye-brow. Then, a soldier,
Full of strange oaths, and bearded like the pard,
Ielous in honor, sodaine, and quicke in quarrell,
Seeking the bubble reputation
Even in the canons mouth. And then, the Justice
In faire round belly, with good capon lin'd, &c.

Who can doubt that these two passages are of like origin ? The 'three measures' passage from *Much Ado About Nothing* is quoted under LYLY.

In another passage Jaques states: ' Invest me in my motley; give me leave to speak my mind, and I will through and through cleanse the foul body of the infected world—if they will patiently receive my medicine.' This is exactly what Nash himself undertook in his prose essays.

As Chettle's ' Babulo ' Jaques is a philosopher and, although crabbed, a humorist. He is not constructed with the all-round solidity of a Babulo, yet he is an unforgettable figure. He contributes something to the story, yet his lines are almost all incidental.

As You Like It marks the beginning of the change of poetical Nash into picaresque Nash, follower of Rabelais. This play was written during the transition stage and contains elements of both periods. A mention of Marlowe in this play has caused the commentators to place it some five years after his death:

Dead shepherd, now I find thy saw of might,
He never loved that lov'd not at first sight.

At least the one word 'dead' must have been inserted after Marlowe's death. It may have read 'dear' in the first version, or the entire passage may have been inserted shortly after Marlowe's death in 1593, certainly before 1598.

Summers Last Will and Testament was written while Nash was still under the influence of Lyly and Greene. It was privately acted before the Queen at the Archbishop's palace in Croydon (1592) and was printed in 1600.

This play is full of words and phrases such as Nash always used. It betrays his inability to handle rhythm. The lines are full of meaning, but they seldom flow smoothly. This is especially true of the various doggerel verses. As Nash grew older his poetic enthusiasm diminished, his lines became more rugged, but more and more filled with meaning.

Summers Last Will is an indoor pageant in celebration of the harvest festival, designed merely to while away an idle hour. It was written hurriedly, to be acted once and cast aside and forgotten. It is similar to some of Lyly's 'honorable entertainments', but contains somewhat more of Greene's realistic comedy.

This is probably the only Elizabethan play written entirely around the harvest festival. In this respect it resembles the religious dramas of Greece and the mysteries of the Druids. Its plan is simple: Summer, now at death's door, summons the seasons to report on their year's activities.

First comes Spring 'with his trayne, overlayd with suites of greene mosse . . . singing'. After the song and some conversation he goes out and returns with 'the Hobby horse & the morris daunce, who daunce about'. Then he brings in ' 3 clownes, & 3 maids, singing this song, dauncing'. Solstitium next appears 'like an aged Hermit, carrying a payre of ballances, with an houre-glasse in either of them; one houre-glasse white, the other blacke: he is brought in by a number of Shepherds, playing upon Recorders'. Sol enters 'verie richly attir'de, with a noyse of Musicians before him'. Orion appears 'like a hunter, with a horne about his necke, all his men after the same sort hallowing and blowing their hornes'. Harvest comes ' with a sythe on his neck, & all his reapers with siccles, and a great blacke bowle with a posset in it, borne before him: they come in singing'. Bacchus is first seen ' riding upon an Asse, trapt in Ivie, himselfe drest in Vine leaves, and a garland of grapes on his head; his companions having all Jacks in their hands, and Ivie garlands on their heads: they come in singing'. So this pageant play continues. Each character reports and is praised or blamed; each defends himself. Finally Summer, about to die, makes his ' last will and testament', from which the play derives its title:

This is the last stroke my toungs clock must strike,
My last will, which I will that you performe.
My crowne I have disposde already of.
Item, I give my withered flowers and herbes,
Unto dead corses, for to decke them with.
My shady walkes to great mens servitors,
Who in their masters shadowes walke secure.
My pleasant open ayre, and fragrant smels,
To Croyden and the grounds abutting round.
My heate and warmth to toyling labourers,
My long dayes to bondmen, and prisoners,
My short nights to young married soules,
My drought and thirst to drunkards quenchlesse throates;
My fruites to Autumne, my adopted heire,
My murmuring springs, musicians of sweete sleepe,
To murmuring male-contents, whose well tun'd cares,
Channel'd in a sweete falling quaterzaine,
Do lull their eares asleepe, listning themselves.
And finally,—O words, now clense your course!—
Unto Eliza that most sacred Dame,
Whom none but Saints and Angels ought to name;
All my faire dayes remaining I bequeath
To wait upon her till she be returnd, &c.

Altogether *Summers Last Will* is the most interesting harvest entertainment in the English language and might well be revived.

It must have fascinated the children and have amused the older sort.

If Nash were not already convinced of the fact that he lacked rhythmic ability before he associated with Marlowe, by the time they had finished writing *Dido, Queen of Carthage* he could have had no further doubts.

The Tragedie of Dido, Queen of Carthage was played 'by the Children of Her Majesties Chapell' in 1592 or 1593, and was published in 1594. It also is a music drama, but of a new genre. There is nothing of Lyly in this play. It is a story told simply, yet poetically; and is designed so as to allow of much incidental and interpretative music. The grace and charm of the diction belong chiefly to Marlowe; the greater number of the compelling picturesque touches are from the hand of Nash.

There must have been strong intellectual sympathy between the youthful Nash and the more mature Marlowe. Marlowe's mind was larger, more speculative, more lyrical; he was a transcendental poet. Nash was more intense; his mind was analytical. Even as he intuitively sought out the intrinsic meaning of individual words, so he came to analyse and depict character. The soul of an individual as the soul of a word became his study, that which he endeavoured to express. In this he was Marlowe's superior. The interactions of these master minds can be well studied in this gem-like *Tragedie of Dido*. (For examples see Marlowe.)

During these early years Nash was slowly finding himself. Gradually he discovered that the flamboyant animation of Rabelais and Arentine was more akin to his genius than the euphuism of Lyly, the Italianate versification of Greene, or the lyricism of Marlowe. Various pamphlets in the vein of Arentine appeared from time to time during his career. They all evince a keen analysis of character and of life, and an ever-increasing command of words. English literature affords nothing which for sheer mastery of illuminating words can be compared with his *Lenten Stuffe* printed in 1599.

Greene died in 1592; Marlowe was killed on June 1, 1593; Peele, Lyly, and Nash remained as the leading dramatists of the moment. How greatly Nash had come to respect dramatic art is shown in his *Pierce Penilesse*:

> There is no immortalitie can be given a man on earth like unto plays. In playes . . . all cunning drifts overguilded with outward holinesse, all strategems of warre, all the canker-wormes that breede on the rust of peace, are most lively anatomized: They shew the ill success of treason, the fall of hasty climbers, the wretched ende of usurpers, the miserie of civil dissention, and how just God is evermore in punishing of murder.

During 1593-4 Nash wrote *The Unfortunate Traveller, or the Life of Jack Wilton*. This picaresque novel is filled with marvellous word-pictures. An abridged edition should be in every public and school library. Here is a scapegrace who has innumerable escapades, who remains irrepressible, overflowing with joyous life. Here is picture after picture of the high and low life of the time. Here are many figures drawn in detail, all of whom are made to yield continual instruction and amusement.

There is, however, running throughout the whole of this story, as there is through his pamphlets, and even in his new-coined words, a certain exaggeration, as if all were seen through a magnifying glass, an intensified truthfulness which makes for melodrama. There are as well such other concomitants of melodrama as rapid change of characters and scenes, slight connexion of episode with episode, lack of motive and underlying psychological cause. It might be objected that this is part of the picaresque novel. Quite true; and the picaresque novel put upon the stage becomes at once melodrama.

Among the characters whom Jack Wilton victimized was a certain purveyor of drink, a camp victualler, a tun-bellied coward, proud of his noble descent, who once was wont to drink on credit. He was fat, ruddy, open-mouthed, blear-eyed, and 'thought no scorn, Lord have mercy upon us, to have his great velvet breeches larded with the droppings of this dainty liquor' [cider],

&c. The thought at once suggests itself that this is Falstaffe grown old.

Given this clue it takes no great wit to discover that Prince Hal and Falstaffe of *Henry IV* are Jack Wilton's King and the old camp victualler. The study of Prince Hal, the picaresque hero who has wasted his youth in adventure, contains also an admixture of Jack Wilton himself. Falstaffe, as the victualler, is the butt of a whole series of picaresque escapades.

In *Henry IV* there will be found a long series of golden words such as only Nash could coin. Part I, which contains the greater part of the original play, was copyrighted in 1597 and published in 1598, without an author's name, while Nash was at Yarmouth. Shakespeare's enlarged version will be found in the Folio.

Examples of words:

> 'Revenge the fearing and disdain'd contempt of this proud King.' 'And now I will unclasp a secret booke and to your quick conceyving discontents Ile read you matter deepe and dangerous.' 'Why what a waspe-tongu'd and impatient foole art thou.' 'You have deceived your trust and made us doffe our easie Robes of Peace, to crush our old limbes in ungentle steele.' 'Will you againe unknitt this churlish knott of all-abhorred wars?'

And so a thousand others, the which no one but Nash could write.

Henry IV, Part I was once complete in itself. It depicted the life of Prince Hal (afterwards Henry V) during the later part of his father's reign and ended with the death of Henry IV and the coronation of Henry V. This complete play, in garbled form, still exists in the Deryng Manuscript. Presumably it was the play entered in Henslowe's Diary as new on November 28, 1595.

Henry V. While *Henry IV* was built on the first part of the old *Famous Victories of Henry V*, which was entered in the S. R. on May 14, 1594, by Thomas Creede, *Henry V* was worked up from the later part of the same play. This old play was referred to by Nash in *Pierce Penilesse* in 1593. *Henry V* continues the picaresque life of Prince Hal. It would seem as if the plan of this play were by Nash, but the diction, while his in parts, is as a whole more direct and simple than the remainder of his work. It contains the celebrated speech :

> O God of battles, steele my soldiers hearts,
> Take from them now the sense of reckoning, &c.

It also contains the equally famous :

> This day is called the day of Crispin.
> He that outlives this day, and sees old age,
> Shall stand a tiptoe when this day is named,
> And rouse him at the name of Crispin, &c.

These lines lack somewhat the Nash-like quality. They resemble those written by Chettle and the members of the realistic school. The probability therefore is that Nash planned this play and wrote it in conjunction with his friend Henry Chettle, even as he wrote earlier plays with Lyly, Greene, and Marlowe. Certainly Nash and Chettle were working together for the Strange-Chamberlain group; and presumably each assisted the other in all the plays produced for that group.

Richard II, as printed in 1597, is the precursor of *Henry IV*. It contains the struggle between Richard and Henry Bolingbroke, which resulted in the death of Richard and the coronation of Henry. It is so evidently the first part of the story of Henry IV, and connects so closely with it, that it was known both as *Richard II* and as *Henry IV*. Bacon states, 'That afternoon before the rebellion Merick had procured to be played before them the play of deposing King Richard the Second'. The report in *State Papers*, vol. vii, p. 60, reads: 'The Friday before Sir Gilly Merrick and some others of the earl's train having an humour to see a play, they must needs have the play of Henry IV.' As this story of Henry IV preceded historically the story of Prince Hal (Henry V), and as it was a Strange-Chamberlain play, it ought to appear in Henslowe's Diary. One month before Henslowe entered *Harey the V* as new he entered a new play called *Long-shanke* (August 29, 1595). Since Henry Bolingbroke is referred to as a tall man (Richard II calls him ' High Hereford ', and in *Henry IV* he is likened to a greyhound)

'Long-shanke' may have been the original title of 'Richard II, or the story of Henry IV'.

Richard II, Henry IV (Deryng), and *Henry V* belong together; all were owned by the Strange-Chamberlain company. Nash, their chief playwright, had a main finger in all three, and Chettle seems to have assisted him.

Richard's last soliloquy may be taken as an example of the diction of Nash in 1595:

> *Richard.* I have been studying how I may compare
> This prison where I live, unto the world:
> And for because the world is populous,
> And heere is not a creature but myselfe,
> I cannot do it: yet Ile hammer it oute:
> My braine Ile proove the female to my soule;
> My soule the father, and these two beget
> A generation of still-breeding thoughts;
> And these saime thoughts people this little world,
> In humours like the people of this world:
> For no thought is contented: The better sort,
> As thoughts of things divine, are intermixt
> With scruples, and do set the Word itselfe
> Against the Word, as thus:
> Come little ones, and then againe
> It is as hard to come as for a cammell
> To thread the small postern of a needles eye:
> Thoughts tending to ambition they doe plot
> Unlikely wonders: how these vain weake nailes
> May teare a passage throw the flinty ribs
> Of this hard world, my ragged prison walles:
> And for they cannot die in their own pride.
> Thoughts tending to Content, flatter themselves,
> That they are not the first of Fortunes slaves,
> Nor shall not be the last; like seely beggars
> Who sitting in the stocks, refuge their shame,
> That many have, and others must sit there,
> And in this thought they find a kind of ease,
> Bearing their owne misfortunes on the backe
> Of such as have before indurde the like.
> Thus play I in one person many people,
> And none contented, &c.

This is the congested cerebration of the speculative Nash. The ensuing by York is by the picture-painting Nash:

> *York.* Then (as I said) the duke, great Bullingbrooke,
> Mounted upon a hote and fiery steede,
> Which his aspiring rider seem'd to know
> With slow, but stately pace kept on his course,
> While all tongues cride, God save thee Bullingbrooke,
> You would have thought the very windowes spake:
> So many greedy lookes of young and old,
> Through casements darted their desiring eyes
> Upon his visage, and that all the walles,
> With painted imagery, had said at once,
> Jesu, preserve thee, welcome, Bullingbrooke,
> Whilst he from one side to the other turning
> Bareheaded, lower then his proud steeds necke,
> Bespake them thus, I thanke you, countrymen:
> And thus still doing, thus he past along.[1]

On May 7 and 23, 1595, there appeared at the Rose theatre the first and second parts of *Hercules*. In his *Lenten Stuffe* Nash seems to claim these plays as his own:

> That infortunate imperfit Embrion ... the Ile of Dogs ... breeding unto me such bitter throwes in the teaming as it did ... as if my braine had beene conceived of another *Hercules*, I was as terrified with my owne encrease (like a woman long travailing to be delivered of a monster) that it was no sooner borne but

[1] There were two further plays on Richard II; the first witnesses his coronation, the second his deposition and death. The first exists in Egerton Manuscript 1994, printed in 1870 as *A Tragedy of King Richard the Second*, reprinted in Germany in 1899. The second was witnessed by Dr. Simon Farman in 1611 at the Globe theatre. From an outline of it in his diary it seems to be a continuation of the Egerton play.

The Egerton play has borrowed hints from *Edward III, Richard II, Henry VI,* and *Richard III.* It is constructed on the alternate episode plan of *A Woman Killed with Kindness.* It is theatrical, and exhibits all the peculiarities of Thomas Heywood. It must have been written by him for the Queen's company before he joined the Strange-Chamberlain men at the Curtain in 1597. Presumably the play witnessed by Dr. Farman was a continuation of this play also by Heywood. Neither of these could be termed 'the story of Henry IV'. Both must have passed into the Globe repertoire in 1599.

I was glad to runne from it. Avoid or give ground I did . . . at
Great Yarmouth in Norfolke I arived in the later end of Autumne.

Doubtless this two-part drama was a picaresque play of the
gargantuan hero, exactly the sort of subject in which Nash
would have delighted. His connexion with *Hercules* is again
hinted at in *The Return from Parnassus*:

> *Thomas Nashdo.* I, here is a fellow (Judico) that carried the
> deadly stocke in his pen, whose muse was armed with a gag
> tooth, and his pen possest with *Hercules* furyes.

Nash began his dramatic career in association with Lyly. In
collaboration they wrote the Martin Marprelate tracts; and
against these same Martinists they wrote one or more plays
which were suppressed by the Revels Office in 1589.

At least two further plays seem to have been written by Nash
and Lyly in collaboration—*Much Ado about Nothing* and *Love's
Labour's Lost.* Both are in the main Lyly's, yet passages by
Nash can be found in each.

The 'Three Measures' by Beatrice without doubt belongs to
the author of 'the Seven Ages' and 'Eight kinds of Drunkenesse'.
It reads:

> If the Prince be too important [importunate], tell him here is
> measure in everything, & so daunce out the answere, for heare
> me Hero, wooing, wedding, and repenting, is as a Scotch jigge,
> a measure, and a cinquepace: the first suite is hot and hasty like
> a Scotch jigge (and full as fantasticall) the wedding manerly
> modest, (as a measure) full of state and aunchentry, and then
> comes repentance, and with his bad legs falls into the cinquepace
> faster and faster, till he sinkes into his grave.

Much Ado about Nothing may have been written before 1590,
but *Love's Labour's Lost* must belong to the period 1593–7, when
Lyly and Nash were quarrelling with Gabriel Harvey. Harvey
had been caricatured as a schoolmaster on the Oxford stage.
Lyly and Nash now proposed to stage him in London. This
they did in the guise of the pedantical parson Holofernes, who
extemporizes in hexameter verse, and in the play within the play
takes the part of Judas, and after announcing several times, 'Judas
I am . . .' is put 'out of countenance' and dismissed as an 'ass'.

Gabriel Harvey was the chief upholder of hexameter verse. Nash states:

> 'Gabriell Howlinglasse was the first inventer of English Hexameter verses.' 'Hexameter verse goes twitching & hopping in our language like a man running upon quagmires, up the hill in one Syllable, and down the dale in another.' (*Foure Letters Confuted.*)

Harvey had been staged in the name part of 'Pedantis' at Trinity College, Cambridge, 'as namely the concise and firking finicaldo fine schoolmaster . . . the just manner of his phrase . . . his nice gate on his pantoffles . . . the accent of his speech'. (*Saffron Walden.*) That Nash and Lyly were about to write a play on Harvey is disclosed in the two following statements from *Saffron Walden*:

> Comedie upon Comedie he [Harvey] shall have. . . . More than half of one of these I have done alreadie, and in Candlemas Tearme you shal see it acted, though better acted than hee hath been at Cambridge hee can never bee; where upon everie stage hee hath beene brought for a Sicophant and a sow-gelder.
>
> For Master Lillie (who is halves with me in this indignitie that is offred) I will not take the tale out of his mouth, for he is better able to defend himselfe than I am able to say he is able to defend himselfe, and in as much time as hee spends in taking tobacco one weeke, he can compile that which would make Gabriell repent himselfe all his life after. With a blacke sant he meanes shortly to bee at his chamber window.

The following verses are attributed to Harvey by Nash:

> O blessed health, blessed wealth & blessed abundance!
> O that I had these three for the losse of 30 commensments.

(To the Ewe-tree.)

> What may I call this tree, an Ewe tree, O bonny Ewe tree,
> Needes to thy boughs will [I] bow this knee, and vaile my bonnetto.

(To the Weather-cock.)

> O thou weathercocke that stands on the top of the church of Alhallowes,
> Come thy waies down if thou darst for thy crowne, and take the wall on us.

In one of his letters to Edmund Spenser, Harvey wrote: 'If I never deserve anye better remembrance, let mee rather be Epitaphed, The Inventour of English Hexameter; whom learned M. Standihurst imitated in his Virgill &c.' Among three verses sent to Spenser the following one appears:

> If so be goods encrease, then dayly encreaseth a goods friend.
> If so be goods decrease, then straite decreaseth a goods friend.
> Then God night goods friend, who seldome prooveth a good friend.
> Give me the goods, and give me the good friend, take ye the goods friend.
> Doovehouse, and Lovehouse, in writing differ a letter,
> In deede scarcely so much, so resembleth an other an other.
> Tyle me the Doovehouse trimly, and gallant, where the like storehouse?
> Fyle me the Doovehouse: leave it unhansome, where the like poorehouse?
> Looke to the Lovehouse: where the resort is, there is a gaye showe:
> Gynne port, and mony fayle: straight sports and Companie faileth.

Of the three verses sent to Spenser, Harvey wrote: 'Beleeve me, I am not to be charged with above one or two of the verses: and a foure or five wordes in the rest.' It would seem as if the above were the identical verse that was caricatured in *Love's Labour's Lost*.

Another of Harvey's verses which he thought worthy the attention of Spenser follows:

> Vertue sendeth a man Renowne, Fame lendeth Aboundaunce,
> Fame with Aboundaunce maketh a man thrise blessed and happie.
> So the Rewarde of Famous Vertue makes many wealthy,
> And the Regard of Wealthie Vertue makes many blessed:
> O blessed Vertue, blessed Fame, blessed Aboundaunce,
> O that I had you three, with the losse of thirtie Comencementes.
> Nowe farewell Mistresse, whom lately I loved above all,
> These be my three bonny lasses, these be my three bonny Ladyes,

Not the like Trinitie againe, save onely the Trinitie above all :
Worship and Honour, first to the one, and then to the other.
A thousand good leaves be for ever graunted Agrippa.
For squibbing and declayming against many fruitlesse
Artes, and Craftes, devisde by the Divls, and Sprites, for a
    torment,
And for a plague to the world : as both Pandora, Prometheus,
And that cursed good bad Tree, can testifie at all times.
Meere Gewegawes and Bables, in comparison of these.
Toyes to mock Apes, and Woodcockes, in comparison to these.
Jugling castes and knicknackes, in comparison of these.
Yet behinde there is one thing, worth a prayer at all tymes,
A good Tongue, in a man's Head, a good Tongue in a
    Wooman's.
And what so precious matter, and foode for a good Tongue,
As blessed Vertue, blessed Fame, blessed Aboundance.
                L'Envoy.
Marvell not, what I meane to send these Verses at Evensong :
On Neweyeeres Even, and Oldyeeres End, as a Memento :
Trust me, I know not a ritcher Jewell, newish or oldish,
Than blessed Vertue, blessed Fame, blessed Aboundaunce,
O that you had these three, with the losse of Fortie Valetes.

Harvey's aim in poetry, other than to write hexameters such
as the above, was ' to have nothing vulgare, but in some respecte
or other, and especially in lively Hyperbolicall Amplifications,
rare, queint, and odd in every pointe, and as a man woulde saye,
a degree or two at the leaste, above the reache, and compasse of
a common schollers capacitie'. Harvey and Holofernes seem to
have been cast in the same mould.

    Lines by Holofernes which were written in caricature of
Harvey's are :
The prayfull princesse pearst and prickt a prettie pleasing
    pricket;
Some say a sore ; but not a sore, till now made sore with
    shooting.
The dogges did yell ; put ell to sore, then sorell jumps from
    thicket :
Or pricket-sore, or else sorell ; the people fall a hooting.
If sore be sore, then ell to sore, makes fifty sores, O sore L !
Of one sore L and hundred make, by adding but one more L.

A bit of hexameter verse by Holofernes reads:
The Moone was a month old when Adam was no more,
And wrought not five-weekes, when he came to fivescore.
Still another set of hexameters by Holofernes, wrongly annexed to a prose passage by Nathaniel, who could not versify, is:
Such barren plants are set before us, that we thankful should be
(Which we of taste and feeling are)
For those parts that do fructify in us more than in he.
For as it would ill become me to be vaine, indiscreet, or a foole;
So were there a patch set on Learning, to see him in a schoole.
But *omne bene* say I, being of an old Father's minde,
Many can brooke the weather, that love not the winde.

Holofernes commends his verse-making in the manner of the Harveys: 'This is a gift I have, simple, simple; a foolish extravagant spirit, full of forms, figures, shapes.' (This hits at Harvey's mathematical similes, as 'apprehensions, motions, revolutions' hits at the astronomical activities of the Harvey brothers.) Holofernes concludes, 'these are begot in the ventricle of memory, nourished in the womb of pia mater, and deliver'd upon the mellowing of occasion: but the gift is good in those in whom it is acute, and I am thankful for it'. Such a statement at the period concerning such verse could have been made appropriately by no one but Gabriel Harvey, the father of hexameter verse.

The long word 'Honorificabilitudinitatibus' used by Nash in 'Physitions deafen our eares with the Honorificabilitudinitatibus of their heavenly Panachea, their soveraine Ginacum, their glisters', &c., appears also in *Love's Labour's Lost*, as do other peculiar words found only in this play and the prose writings of Nash.

In *Pierces Supererogation*, dated April 27, 1593, Harvey, after abusing Nash, states: 'Such an Antagonist hath Fortune allotted me, to purge melancholy, and to thrust me upon the Stage.' In another portion of the same tract, which portion was begun in 1589 and finished in 1593, Harvey writes of Nash and Lyly:
I am threatened with a Bable, and Martin menaced with a
Comedie: a fit motion for a Jester and a Player, to try what may

be done by employment of his facultie: Bables & Comedies are parlous fellowes to decipher, and discourage men, (that is the Point) with their wittie flowtes, and learned Jerkes: enough to lash any man out of countenance. Na, if you shake the painted scabbard at me, I have done: and all you, that tender the preservation of your good names, were best to please Pap-hatchet, and see Euphues [Lyly] betimes, for feare lesse he be mooved, or some One of his Apes hired, to make a Playe of you; and then is your credit quite undone for ever, and ever: Such is the publique reputation of their Playes. He must needes be discouraged, whom they decipher. Better, anger an hundred other, then two such; that have the Stage at commaundement, and can furnish-out Vices, and Divels at their pleasure. Gentlemen, beware of a chafing-penne, that sweateth-out whole realmes of Paper, and whole Theatres of Jestes: &c.

This places Lyly at the Theatre early in 1593.[1]

Nash was persuaded this same year to make peace with Harvey. He offered the olive branch in his introduction to *Christs Teares over Jerusalem*. Harvey continued his attacks in pamphlets and in private letters until he forced Nash to turn on him again in 1596, when he brought out *Have with you to Saffron Walden*. In this book Nash states:

His booke, or Magna Charta, which against M. Lilly & me he addrest, I having kept idle by me, in a by settle out of sight amongst old shooes and bootes almost this two yere.

He also states:

Comedie upon Comedie he shall have, a Morall, a Historie, a Tragedie, or what hee will. One shal bee called . . . the fifth and last A pleasant Enterlude of No Foole to the old Foole, with a Jigge at the latter ende in English Hexameters. . . . More than half of one of these I have alreadie, and in Candlemas Tearme you shal see it acted.'

This 'comedie' half written in 1596 and promised for 'Candlemas Tearme' early in 1597 was the play printed in 1598 as: 'A Pleasant Conceited Comedie called Loves Labours Lost, as

---

[1] From 1583 to 1597 Paris Garden, the Curtain, Rose, and other play-houses were not usually called theatres, that word being used to designate but one play-house, Burbage's 'Theatre'.

it was presented before her Highnes this last Christmas', which contains the ' old Foole' and the jigging 'English Hexameters'. It must therefore have been written during the later part of 1596. No copy of this original version has survived. There is no mention of a company in the title-page of the First Quarto. However, since it was revised by Shakespeare and published in 1598, it presumably was acted by the Queen's company at the Theatre under Lyly rather than by the Chamberlain company at the Curtain under Nash. In 1597 Nash went to Yarmouth; Lyly and the Revels Children opened at Blackfriars; and Shakespeare began rewriting the Queen's company's repertoire, his first acknowledged revision being this Lyly-Nash play of *Love's Labour's Lost*.

From 1593 until 1597 Nash was the dominating personality of the Strange-Chamberlain group of playwrights. In 1596 the company moved to the Curtain, where they became exceedingly popular. (See MARSTON, Satyre XI.) Thus far Nash had been Fortune's favourite; and so he continued until the Admiral's men botched up the ' embrion' of his *Ile of Dogs* in 1597, which suddenly, unexpectedly, brought disaster.

The *Ile of Dogs* was produced in the later part of July, 1597, and was promptly suppressed. The Admiral's men were restrained from producing further plays until August 11. Much has been written about this affair. Unfortunately Collier planted several forged entries in Henslowe's Diary concerning it. The only true entry is that of August 10, 1597, the latter part of which reads: ' beginning immediatly after this restraint is Recaled by the lordes of the counsell which restraynt is by meanes of playing the Ile of Dogs'. The restraint lasted at most not more than three weeks, not a very serious affair for the company. To Nash it brought banishment. As he wrote in *Lenten Stuffe*, he was 'glad to runne from it'.

Nash escaped from London, possibly by boat, and settled down at or near Great Yarmouth. Collier in his forged entries put him in prison and caused Henslowe to send him ten shillings. The fable that he was imprisoned arose from the Privy Council Acts of August 15, 1597, which, however, furnish proof quite to the contrary. The Acts mention: 'We caused some of the players to be apprehended and comytted to prison, whereof one of them was not only an actor but a maker of parte of the said plaie.' This does not include Nash, who had escaped, as is evident from: 'We praie you also to peruse such papers as were found in Nash his lodgings, which Ferrys, a messenger of the chamber, shall delyver unto you, and to certyfie us th' examynacions you take.' Had they captured Nash they would have examined him. In lieu of him they examined his papers.

Further 'proof' of the supposed imprisonment of Nash is found in various statements by his enemy Gabriel Harvey in *The Trimming of Thomas Nash*. Since Harvey admits, 1597, that Nash was then an unapprehended fugitive, and that he had never been in jail, his spiteful charges in the same book, that Nash was then in prison, and had been in every London prison, must be taken as hopes which were never realized. There is no proof that Nash was then or at any other time in any prison, save his own statement that he had once been in the Counter for debt.

Banishment, however, was as fatal to Nash as prison would have been. True, Meres in *Wits Treasury* (1598) endeavoured to cheer him in his exile with 'be not disconsolate . . . thine are paper dogges, neither is thy banishment like Ovids . . . comfort thyselfe sweete Tom with Cicero's glorious return to Rome', &c. But Nash never returned. For a while he remained cheerful with the hospitable people of Great Yarmouth, and in return for their kindness wrote his comical discourse on the *Red Herring*. But his exile told before long. He offered to return and stand trial; but his enemies preferred to keep him at a safe distance.

As his exile lengthened his bitterness grew. All the light wine of his life turned to vinegar, his happy sarcasm to bitter denunciation. A fishing village is a fitting place for long reflection and sorrowful introspection. Nash left London a joyous youth, full of patriotism, of artistic enthusiasm. Alone in Yarmouth or the country his youth soon ended; his mind became sombre;

his soul was tinged with tragedy. All paths seemed dulled to grey, the hope of a care-free life in a forest of Arden passed as a dream. His thoughts now found expression in more rugged rhythms, in great concentrated thought units, in stern characterization, in plots no longer filled with picaresque comedy, but throbbing with tragedy. To this period belong his *Macbeth*, *Timon of Athens*, and his *King Lear*.

Timon of Athens is the climax of the didactic dramas which Nash began with Lyly when they wrote against the Martinists. The same spirit is evident in all of his pamphlets, and in the *Ile of Dogs*. This strong didacticism continued throughout his career, impairing his dramatic abilities. It exiled him for the *Ile of Dogs*, embittered his life, and was part cause of his poverty and early death. He who scarifies the powerful rich should not expect their protection.

Timon of Athens is more pamphlet than play. It contains all Nash's disdain of gold and the vulgar rich. In no other work does he rise to greater heights of sarcastic eloquence than in *Timon*; in none does he more thoroughly expose the meanness of soul of money-grubbing humanity. The entire play centres on this theme.

That this play is by Nash no one, who thoroughly studies his pamphlets, his plays, or his life, can for a moment doubt. The apostrophes on gold, on thievery, on man's ingratitude, the concentrated figures of speech, and the characters all evince his hand and mind. Timon is akin to Lear as well as to melancholy Jacques. Timon, who gave his all to the Athens he loved and was exiled in poverty, is but Nash himself, once Court poet, flattered and loved by all, now banished.

This play must date some little time after 1597. Hope must have sustained Nash for a year or more. *Timon* is in the stern and terrible method of his later creations, when suffering had intensified into bitterness. It is perhaps later than *Macbeth*, yet is surely earlier than *King Lear*.

Although printed in the Folio *Timon* was never claimed by Shakespeare, but was attributed to him only by the Folio editors.

It bears no trace of Shakespearian additions. The only extant version is badly punctuated, and here and there fails to make sense. Examples:

Timon to the thieves:

> Take wealth, and lives together,
> Do villaine do, since you protest to, doo 't
> Like workemen. I'll example you with theevery:
> The sunnes a theefe, and with his great attraction
> Robbes the vaste sea. The moones an arrant theefe,
> And her pale fire, she snatches from the sunne.
> The seas a theefe, whose liquid surge, resolves
> The Moone into salt teares, &c.

Alcibiades to the Senators:

> Till now you have gone on, and fill'd the time
> With all licentious measure, making your willes
> The scope of Justice. Till now, myselfe and such
> As slept within the shadow of your power
> Have wander'd with our traverst Armes, and breath'd
> Our sufferance vainly: Now the time is flush,
> When crouching Marrow in the bearer strong
> Cries (of it selfe) no more: Now breathlesse wrong,
> Shall sit and pant in your great chaires of ease,
> And pursie Insolence shall breake his winde
> With feare and horrid flight.

Macbeth. On April 17, 1602, Henslowe bought of C. Massaye, one of the Admiral's men, a play-book of 'Malcolm, King of Scots'. Presumably this was the original version of *Macbeth*, sent from Yarmouth or the country by Nash to his old friend the actor Massaye.

Unfortunately no early copy of *Macbeth* has been found. The Folio version is a garbled revision by Shakespeare, or Middleton, or both. Nevertheless the whole base and undercurrent of the play as it exists to-day is by Nash. The wonderfully coined phrases are alone sufficient to identify it as his work.

Examples:

> That thrusted home
> Might yet enkindle you unto the crowne.

> This supernatural solliciting.

This castle hath a pleasant seat,
The ayre nimbly and sweetly recommends itselfe
Unto our gentle senses.

This Guest of Summer,
The Temple-haunting Barlet, doth approve
By his loved mansonry, that the Heavens breath
Smells wooingly here : No Jutty, frieze,
Buttrice, nor coign of vantage, but this bird
Hath made his pendant bed, and procreant cradle.

No one but a master artist with a deep understanding of meaningful words could have written such passages. Almost every word to be found in *Macbeth* can be found in the prose writings of Nash; many of them can be found nowhere else in literature. This fact alone should have opened the eyes of those who took the trouble to make a list of words used by this greatest of word-masters.

However, it is not in words that interest centres in *Macbeth*. It introduces a new Nash. Stern, powerful thought now dominates the rhythm; it masses itself into large figures of speech, into bold, impassioned apostrophes. The plot, though still on picaresque lines, presses onward as if directed by Nemesis. Verily Fate in the form of the three Witches controls all movement more inexorably, more horribly, than in the greatest Greek tragedies. The characters are terrifying in their intense grimness. The irresponsible picaresque hero is now driven of demons.

While the new Nash is thus manifest in *Macbeth*, despite the muddling Shakespearian additions, it is to *King Lear* that one must turn if he would find Nash in the final stage of his development.

King Lear was evidently left in manuscript. It was not quite finished. It is like a great work by Michael Angelo, rough-hewn with mighty blows, then left, the chisel marks all showing. Shakespeare, attempting to complete the work, has niggled here and elaborated there, weakening all, often obliterating the creator's intention, adding nothing but confusion.

The original manuscript found its way into the hands of a printer in 1608. The task of that printer was not an enviable one. To set up a play by Nash when perfectly polished, the punctuation all in place, the words carefully spelled, were difficult enough; but to edit his greatest play from a rough-cast copy was too difficult a task. The printer as best he could set all the words in order; the punctuation he often let care for itself. He even tore down and corrected pages of his impression after it had gone to press, so that there is considerable variety in the copies of this 1608 edition. Blessed be that printer; he did his best. His name was Nathaniel Butter.

He who would to-day understand *King Lear* must obtain one or more versions of this old Quarto of 1608, must concentrate his thinking powers to the utmost, and disregard the punctuation marks. He may then gather the greater part of the meaning. From the Folio version he may occasionally obtain a different reading of a single word; otherwise it is useless.

A single example must serve to illustrate the state and quality of this Quarto copy of *King Lear*. The Bastard replies to Edgar's challenge:

> In wisedome I should aske thy name,
> But since thy out-side lookes so faire and warlike,
> And that thy being some say of breeding breathes,
> By right of knight-hood I disdaine and spurne,
> With the hell hatedly ore-turn'd thy heart,
> Which for they yet glance by, and scarsely bruise,
> This sword of mine shall give them instant way.
> Where they shall rest for ever, trumpets speake.

Shakespeare revised the speech as follows:

> In wisedome I should aske thy name,
> And since thy out-side lookes so faire and warlike,
> And that thy tongue (some say) of breeding breathes,
> What safe, and nicely I might well delay,
> By rule of knight-hood, I disdaine and spurne;
> Backe do I tosse these Treasons to thy head,
> With the hell-hated lye, ore-whelme thy heart,
> Which for they yet glance by, and scarsely bruise,
> This sword of mine shall give them instant way,
> Where they shall rest for ever. Trumpets speake.

This makes no better sense than the printer's rendering. Shakespeare also mistook ' say ' (essay or taste) to mean speech. Evidently the original trouble lies in the punctuation and in ' hell hatedly ore-turned ' or ' hell-hated lye, ore-whelme '. The obvious rendering should have been :

> In wisdom I should aske thy name ; but,
> Since thy out-side looks so faire and warlike,
> And that thy being some say of breeding breathes,
> My right of knighthood I disdain; and spurne,
> With thee, hell-hated lies, return'd thy heart,
> Which for they yet glance by and scarsely bruise,
> This sword of mine shall give them instant way,
> Where they shall rest for ever. Trumpets speak!

The meaning of this, though concentrated, is clear, ' return'd thy heart ' being equivalent to ' I return thy hell-hated lies to thy heart '.

There are a few passages in the Quarto *King Lear* which are more complicated than the above ; some of which Shakespeare circumvented by omission. Those he revised and corrected he almost invariably made more obscure, so that Lear, as Hamlet, inadvertently became more mad.

Nash wrote *King Lear* about 1603. It was founded on the old play *King Leir and his Three Daughters*, which was last acted by the Queen's company in 1594. It is a true picaresque story, the characters being urged onward by a relentless fate. The scene changes continually, incident following incident in true picaresque manner. Lear and the Fool take the place of the regulation hero and his butt, only now the sad hero is the butt of fortune, the Fool serving as an intensifier.

The doggerel of the Fool in *King Lear* is the same as that found in *Summers Last Will*. Edgar's ' Fye, fo, and fum, I smell the blood of a British man ' had been used in one of the early pamphlets. The Fool's lines are full of meaning; but both rhythm and rhyme are erratic. These are characteristic traits of doggerel by Nash wherever found.

Nash was barely thirty years old when he wrote *King Lear*. He died soon afterwards. It was his swan-song.

Although the early plays by Nash were in interlude form, those dating after 1594, after he had written *Jack Wilton*, were fashioned in the picaresque manner. Picaresque form has many of the advantages of an interlude as it is developed through a series of episodes. It has the disadvantage that the hero tends to remain a static character. In such novels and plays leading characters, such as Jack Wilton and Don Quixote, do not change. They are fixed beings who in each new episode are subjected to new adventures.

A series of picaresque episodes can be unified in an historical play simply by depicting through them some one important event. In *Henry V* Prince Hal remains static; and unity is gained by confining the episodes to a narration of the French campaign. This means of obtaining unity is evidently very restricted and unsatisfactory. Interest in any play should be in the characters rather than in historical narrative.

In plays other than histories, if the hero is to remain static, unity must be gained through the action of some outside force. Such a force in *Henry V* is hinted at in those lines in *Henry IV* where the dying king confesses to Hal that in order to quell internal dissension he had had a purpose to 'lead out many to the Holy Land' and advises Hal: 'Be it thy course to busy giddy minds with foreign quarrels.' However, *Henry V* is held together by the simple story of a single French campaign. Had the impelling force of internal dissension been indicated and well exploited this play would have had greater power, due to a greater unity.

The external force which works upon Macbeth is the demon of evil symbolized in the three witches. In *King Lear* it is the demon of madness; and Timon and Alcibiades are pursued by the mean ingratitude of a debased democracy.

While the characters of these later plays are not as truly picaresque as Falstaffe or Prince Hal, they belong to the same category in that they do not shape their own destinies, but are moulded by external forces and events. There is an outside force in *Hamlet*, the Ghost; but this Ghost does not shape Hamlet's career. It is used simply as a means of disclosing a crime. Destiny more or less controls events in *Romeo and Juliet*, but never influences Romeo directly. He remains throughout a free agent. Hamlet and Romeo are not static characters; they develop from immature youths to ripe men. On the other hand, the picaresque characters of Nash remain at the end of the play even as they were at the beginning: mad Lear, credulous, brave Macbeth, heedless, reckless Timon. In this respect they differ little from the gluttonous coward Falstaffe or the cruelly ambitious Richard III, from Sancho Panza, or from those more modern picaresque heroes the 'Three Musketeers'.[1]

When Nash died is at present unknown. An epitaph places his death in 1601; but Dekker, who was his friend, places it shortly before that of Chettle, c. 1606. 'For Nash inveyed bitterly (as he was wont to do) against dry-fisted patrons, accusing them of his untimely death, because if they had given his muse that cherishment which shee most worthily deserved, hee had fed to his dying day on fat capons, burnt sack and sugar, and not so desperately have ventured his life and shortened his dayes by keeping company with pickle herrings.' 'He [Nash] had no sooner spoken this, but in comes Chettle,' &c. (*Newes from Hell.*)

[1] In a 'new Letter' of September 16, 1593, Gabriel Harvey presents a single hint as to the personal appearance of Nash : 'methinkes the raunging Eyes under the long haire', &c.

IX

GREENE AND NASH

(PATRIOTIC HISTORIES)

IN 1588 Greene went to Oxford to study the drama, and there took his second M.A. It must have been shortly after his return to London that he undertook, with Nash, a long series of patriotic historical dramas. Early in 1589 appeared his *Spanish Masquerado*, in 1590 *Orpharion* and other patriotic pamphlets. It was probably Dr. Gager, the famous head of the Oxford dramatic school, who changed Greene from a romantic into a patriotic author.

About 1589 Greene began a series of plays dealing with the 'Wars of the Roses'. These plays, as Lodge's *The Wounds of Civil War*, were written with the obvious intention of enforcing the belief that only through civil war could England's greatness be destroyed.

The 'Wars of the Roses' series consisted of: I, *Henry VI, Part I*, the loss of France due to civil contention in England, the heroism of Talbot, the beginning of the struggle between the houses of York and Lancaster; II, *Henry VI, Part II*, the fall of the Protector Duke Humphrey, the contention between the two houses of York and Lancaster; III, *Henry VI, Part III*, the death of York and of Henry VI; IV, *Richard III*, the rise and fall of Richard, the union of the two houses, York and Lancaster, under Richmond. These four plays make a complete unit, and were designed by the same hand.

All critics agree in giving Greene a large share in I, II, and III, though not in IV. All agree in assigning a collaborator in II and III, Peele, Marlowe, or Shakespeare. That Shakespeare had no share in the first creation of any of these plays is evident from Greene's accusation, also in that *Henry VI, Parts II* and *III*, and *Richard III*, were Strange-Chamberlain plays before Shakespeare joined that company.

Peele and Marlowe have been assigned shares in these plays because various critics, having decided against Shakespeare as a collaborator, could find no suitable substitute, save Peele or Marlowe. While run-over lines do occasionally occur in all four plays, there is nothing resembling the perfect free rhythm used by those masters. Whenever the rhythm flows freely it is in Greene's characteristic manner, often in verse form, and usually end-stopped. When the rhythm is uneven, the thought is usually vigorous. The author of these later lines was certainly not Marlowe or Peele, but 'Young Juvenal', Thomas Nash. Talbot is one of Nash's heroes; and Richard III is as truly his creation as is Prince Hal, Macbeth, or King Lear. Falstaffe, who first appears in this series, reappears in his *Henry IV* and *Henry V*.

While there is no evidence that Greene at any time wrote with Marlowe or Peele, there is Greene's statement that ' Young Juvenal' ' with me' 'writ a comedie', and there is the even more definite statement by Nash that they collaborated in other plays to be found in *Have with you to Saffron Walden* (1596).

> None that ever had but one eye, with a pearle in it, but could discern the difference betwixt him [Greene] & me; while he liv'd (as some Stationers can witnes with me) he subscribing to me in anie thing but plotting of Plaies, wherein he was his crafts master.

All critics seem to have overlooked this statement.

Henry VI, Part I, was not printed until 1623 in the 'Shakespeare' Folio. No one now attributes it to Shakespeare, but to Greene and a collaborator. That the co-worker was Nash is evident from such lines as:

> Hark! Hark! the Dauphin's drum, a warning bell,
> Sings heavy music to thy timorous soul.

> How are we park'd and bounded in a pale,—
> A little herd of England's timorous deer,
> Maz'd with a yelping kennel of French curs!
> And pale destruction meets thee in the face.

> Lean famine, quartering steel, and climbing fire,
> Who, in a moment, even with the earth,
> Shall lay your stately and air-braving towers.

As no early edition of this play is extant it is uncertain how much of it was rewritten and enlarged by Drayton and his associates.

Henry VI, Parts II and *III.* A garbled version of *Henry VI, Part II,* was printed in 1594 for Thomas Millington, author and company not recorded. (Presumably it was written by Shakespeare for the Pembroke company.) This version seems to be the same as that printed in 1660 as *Duke Humphrey's Tragedy,* by William Shakespeare. Unfortunately the only known copy of this edition was burned by Warburton's infamous servant. Part III of *Henry VI* was garbled into *The True Tragedy of Richard Duke of Yorke* by William Shakespeare for the Pembroke company and published in 1593, also for Millington, as if it were the original second part of *The Contention between the two houses of Yorke* and *Lancaster.*

The original versions of these two plays belonged to the Strange-Chamberlain company, and for them were enlarged by Drayton, *c.* 1600, into the present Folio versions of *Henry VI, Parts II* and *III.*

While many long passages of *Henry VI, Parts II* and *III,* of which no trace appears in the earlier Quartos, can be attributed to no one save Drayton, other passages, found therein, garbled versions of which appear in the earlier Quartos, must have belonged to the original versions. Among such passages are many which were evidently written by Greene and Nash.

Greene's participation in these plays has been established by external evidence and through his reference to them in his *Groatsworth of Wit.* External evidence of Nash's share therein contained in Chettle's introduction to his *Kind-hartes Dreame,* in which he states that the authorship of *Groatsworth of Wit,* and especially of that part which refers to *Henry VI, Part III,* was wrongfully charged against Nash. Nash would not have been thus charged had he not had a hand in the play referred to.

That both parts of the original 'Contention' plays, *Henry VI, Parts II* and *III,* were by the same authors is evident in that

Part III is a direct continuation of Part II, written in the same manner.

The following passages are in Greene's manner:

Iden [in his garden]. Lord, who would live turmoyled in the Court,
And may enjoy such quiet walkes as these?
This small inheritance my father left me,
Contenteth me and ['s] worth a Monarchy.
I seeke not to waxe great by others waning,
Or gather wealth I care not with what envy:
Sufficeth, that I have maintaines my state,
And sends the poore well pleased from my gate.
Henry VI, Part II.

Yorke. See, ruthelesse Queene, a haplesse Fathers teares:
This cloth thou dipd'st in blood of my sweet boy;
And I, with teares, doe wash the blood away.
Keepe thou the Napkin, and goe boast of this,
And, if thou tell'st the heavie storie right,
Upon my soule, the hearers will shed teares:
Yea, even my foes will shed fast-falling teares,
And say, Alas, it was a pittious deed.—*Henry VI, Part III.*

This last is in verse form and contains a refrain.

Greene's rhythmic repetition is well illustrated in the scene wherein a son mourns over his father whom he has unwittingly killed and a father in like manner mourns over his son, the King acting as chorus to their alternating laments.

Though written chiefly by Greene, many passages being in his characteristic verse form, the handiwork of Nash is continually made manifest throughout both plays by the forceful words and ideas which punctuate the more even flow of Greene's diction. A combination of the two will be found in the following examples:

Richard. I, Edward will use women honourably:
Would he were wasted, Marrow, bones and all,
That from his loynes no hopefull branch may spring,
To crosse me from the golden time I looke for:
And yet, betweene my soules desire, and me,
The lustfull Edwards title buryed,

Is Clarence, Henry, and his sonne, young Edward,
And all the unlook'd-for issue of their bodies,
To take their roomes, ere I can place my selfe :
A cold premeditation for my purpose. . . .

  .   .   .   .

What other pleasure can the world affoord ?
Ile make my Heaven in a ladies lappe,
And decke my body in gay ornaments,
And 'witch sweet ladies with my words and lookes :
Oh miserable thought ! And more unlikely,
Then to accomplish twentie golden Crownes.
Why Love forswore me in my mothers wombe :
And for I should not deale in her soft lawes,
Shee did corrupt frayle Nature with some bribe,
To shrinke mine arme up like a wither'd shrub,
To make an envious mountaine on my back,
Where sits Deformitie to mocke my body, &c.

Further signs of Nash appear in :

Let pale-fac't fear keepe with meane-borne man,
And finde no harbour in a royall heart.

  Warwick. But that the guilt of Murther bucklers thee,
And I should rob the Deaths-man of his fee,
Quitting thee thereby of ten thousand shames,
And that my Soveraignes presence makes me milde,
I would, false murd'rous coward, on thy knee,
Make thee begge pardon for thy passed speech,
And say, it was thy Mother that thou meant'st,
That thou thyselfe wast borne in bastardie ;
And after all this fearefull homage done,
Give thee thy hyre, and send thy soule to Hell,
Pernicious blood-sucker of sleeping men.

Compare this with the Bastard's challenge in *King Lear*. (See
NASH.)

Hitherto the critics have claimed these two *Henry VI* plays,
in their more perfect form, for Shakespeare, assigning to Greene,
however, a share in the garbled early Pembroke Quartos already
considered in the chapter on ' William Shakespeare, Reviser '.
They thus foist upon Greene considerable passages of the poorest
' boched ' doggerel to be found in all Elizabethan drama. That

Greene at any period wrote such stuff is inconceivable. The critics were faced by the uncomfortable dilemma: this botched doggerel was written either by Greene or by Shakespeare. Thoughtlessly they concluded that it was written by one of the greatest masters of verse form during his best period rather than by the illiterate Shakespeare at the commencement of his career.

Drayton, when revising these two *Henry VI* plays, added various lines which he had already used in *Edward II* and *The Massacre at Paris*, which plays have usually been assigned to Marlowe. Thus Marlowe came to be looked upon as a part author of these plays.

Richard III. A play on this subject was written in Latin by Dr. Legge of Oxford; and *The True Tragedy of Richard III* was printed as a Queen's company play in 1594. The extant First Quarto of *Richard III* was registered on October 20, 1597, and was published that same year by Andrew Wise, authorship unrecorded, 'as it hath beene lately acted by the Right honorable the Lord Chamberlaine his servants'. This precludes the possibility of Shakespeare having been its author, as he had not then joined the Chamberlain forces.

The second edition of 1598 bears Shakespeare's name, but it was not until 1602 that 'newly augmented' appeared on the title-page. Seemingly Shakespeare's additions were not made until that year, and were made on the text of the 1602 edition. These additions can be found in the Folio.

Since *Richard III* was 'lately acted' in 1597 it probably was completed by Nash some time after Greene's death. Having been written or rewritten several years after the other plays in the *Henry VI* series it is but natural to expect to find the work of Nash more mature therein. From the opening lines to the close his strains bear a richer burden.

> Now is the winter of our discontent,
> Made glorious summer by this son of Yorke:
> And all the cloudes that lowr'd upon our house
> In the deepe bosome of the Ocean buried, &c.

The groundwork of this play remains Greene's; but the forceful imaginative figures were coined by Nash. Under his hand Richard becomes a picaresque villain, comparable only to his other picaresque heroes. On every page expressions abound such as were coined by no one save Nash: *lascivious pleasing of a lute, an amorous looking-glasse, a wanton ambling nymph, This weake piping time of peace,* &c.

Richard III presumably passed from the Strange-Chamberlain company to Edward Alleyn and the Admiral's men, as Henslowe mentions a 'Richard Crockbacke' on June 24, 1602.

Robert Greene died in 1592, and although other of his historical plays can be discovered, these four will serve to illustrate his later method. Nash called him the master of all in the plotting of plays. This series amply justifies that commentary, for the plotting is masterly and is thoroughly carried out.

Throughout this series Greene's methods remain the same as in his early plays. He still writes interludes, historic in place of romantic; he still expresses himself freely in smooth-flowing verse, usually end-stopped; and the characteristic which most unmistakably marked his romantic work, verse form with a refrain, still marks these later plays. At times he reverts to end rhymes with telling effect, as in the climax to *Henry VI, Part I*, where he sings the death of Talbot and his son, and in such manner as to 'bring tears to the eyes of ten thousand spectators':

> *Servant.* O my deare lorde ; loe, where your sonne is borne!
> *Talbot.* Thou antique death, which laugh'st us here to scorn,
> Anon from thy insulting tyrannie,
> Coupled in bonds of perpetuitie,
> Two Talbots, wingèd through the lither skie,
> In thy despight, shall 'scape mortalitie.
> O thou whose wounds become hard-favoured death,
> Speake to thy father, ere thou yeeld thy breath! &c.

Passages cast in stanza form will be found in all of these plays. In *Henry VI, Part III,* Yorke censures the Queen in Italianate verse:

> Tis beautie that doth oft make Women prowd,
> But God he knowes, thy share thereof is small.

Tis Vertue, that doth make them most admir'd,
The contrary, doth make thee wondred at.
Tis Government that makes them seeme Divine,
The want thereof, makes thee abhominable.
Thou art as opposite to every good,
As the Antipodes are unto us,
Or as the South to the Septentrion.
Oh Tygres Heart, wrapt in a Womans Hide,
How could'st thou drayne the Life-blood of the Child,
To bid the Father wipe his eyes withall,
And yet be seene to beare a Womans face? &c.

This speech flows into periods like the chanting of a noble
chorus. The refrain is used in Yorke's ensuing speech:

See, ruthlesse Queene, a haplesse Fathers teares, &c.,

which has been quoted above.

Few if any critics have credited Greene with a share in
Richard III, yet his hymn-like stanzas can be found in every
scene.

Richmond. O thou whose Captaine I account myselfe,
Looke on my forces with a gracious eie;
Put in their hands thy brusing Irons of wrath,
That they may crush downe with a heavie fall,
The usurping helmets of our adversaries,
Make us thy ministers of chastisement,
That we may praise thee in thy victorie,
To thee I do commend my watchfull soule,
Eere I let fall the windowes of mine eies,
Sleeping and waking, oh, defend me still.

Earlier in this play the King laments the death of his brother
Clarence:

Have I a tongue to doome my brothers death,
And shall the same give pardon to a slave;
My brother slew no man, his fault was thought,
And yet his punishment was cruell death.
Who sued to me for him? Who in my rage,
Kneeld at my feete and bad me be advisde?
Who spake of brotherhood? Who of love?
Who told me how the poore soule did forsake

The mighty Warwicke, and did fight for me?
Who told me in the field of Teuxbury,
When Oxford had me downe, he rescued me,
And said ' Deare brother, live and be a King?' &c.

At times Nash breaks into this swelling music and destroys its
rhythm. Yet, when the passages are pure, Greene's rhythm rises
ever to ennobling song.

In no play has the refrain been more powerfully used than
in the night-scene, before the battle. While to Richmond ghost
after ghost enters and chants ' live and flourish ', to Richard they
cry 'dispaire and die! ' Let me sit heavie in thy soule tomorrow;
dispaire and die!'

1. Thinke upon Grey, and let thy soule dispaire.
2. Thinke upon Vaughan, and with guiltie feare,
   Let fall thy launce, dispaire and die.
3. Dreame on thy Cousins smoothered in the Tower,
   Let us be lead within thy bosome, Richard,
   And weigh thee downe to ruine, shame and death;
   Thy nephewes soules bid thee dispaire and die, &c.

Seemingly Nash somewhat disarranged the harmony of these
speeches, yet their force remains, solely through the increasing
effect of a dominant refrain.

The refrain is usable only when there is at least a similitude
of stanza form; and as Greene alone, and throughout all of his
work, clung fast to stanza form, so he alone and always made
effective use of the refrain.

Those who have lightly condemned Greene for the follies of
his life should in all humility remember that the English nation
will for ever owe him a debt of gratitude for the patriotism
engendered by his histories.

X

MICHAEL DRAYTON

(FORMAL POET)

MICHAEL DRAYTON was born at Hartshill, in the extreme north of Warwickshire, in 1563. He passed his youth as a page in the family of Sir Henry Goodere. There is no evidence that he attended either university; but he was well grounded in the classics and languages by a private tutor in the Goodere family. He went to London before 1591, and there became a dependant of various noblemen, among them Sir John Harrington, the celebrated poet and translator.

Drayton's first publication was ' The Harmonie of the Church. Containing The Spiritual Songs and Holy Hymnes, of godly men, Patriarckes and Prophets . . . reduced into sundrie kinds of English meter', &c. (1591). This publication was suppressed by the ecclesiastical authorities. It marks the beginning of Drayton's association with the anti-papal, anti-ecclesiastical movement of his day. Unlike Marlowe, who sought freedom in a larger hedonism, the unimaginative Drayton turned to the narrower field of Protestantism as taught by Wyclif. Orthodox he was and remained, but his orthodoxy was that of the new sect of the Scotch heir-apparent.

In *Wits Miserie* (1596) Lodge characterized Drayton as ' diligent and formall '; and Meres (1598) wrote of him:

> As Aulius Persius Flaccus is reported among al writers to be of an honest life and upright conversation; so Michael Drayton (quem toties honoris & amoris causa nomino) among schollers, soldiers, poets and all sorts of people is helde for a man of virtuous disposition, honest conversation and wel governed cariage, which is almost miraculous among good wits in these declining and corrupt times, &c.

In *The Return from Parnassus* (1600) Drayton is again praised for his Puritanism : ' he wants one true note of a poet of our time, and it is this: he cannot swagger it well at a tavern, or domineer at a pot-house '. Fuller later wrote of him: 'He was a pious poet, his conscience having always the command of his fancy, very temperate in his life, slow of speech, and inoffensive in company.'

In 1604 Drayton published his *Moyses a map of his Miracles*, in 1607 *The Legend of the Great Cromwel*, in 1630 *Noah's Flood*, and *David and Goliah*. While these are strictly religious productions the same spirit is to be found in almost everything he wrote. The *Life and Death of Sir John Oldcastle*, the one play with which he is at present credited, in part, is a panegyric on the celebrated Protestant Lord Cobham, familiarly known as Sir John Oldcastle.

Unfortunately Drayton has been judged almost solely by his later poetic work. Those who have come to know him chiefly through his grandiose but ponderous *Polyolbion* have judged him to be a heavy-handed, pompous, and monotonous Poet Laureate; nor could they conceive why his early contemporaries wrote of him as ' Golden-mouthed, for the purity and pretiousnesse of his stile and phrase', as of one 'by whom the English tongue is mightily enriched'.

That the author of *Polyolbion* was a popular playwright now seems to be an improbability. Had Henslowe's Diary not been found Drayton's activities as a dramatist might never have been suspected. Although Meres wrote, ' As Accius, M. Attilius and Milithus were called Tragoediographi because they writ Tragedies: so may wee truly term Michael Drayton Tragoediographus, &c.'; and although an unknown author in *Poems of Divers Humours* (1599) mentions Drayton's ' well written tragedies', both of these references were supposed to refer to his tragical poems. His share in *Sir John Oldcastle* was attributed to Shakespeare until Henslowe's Diary revealed the truth.

Like all of the greater dramatists of the period, Drayton never allowed his name to be attached to any published play. While proud of his poetry, which he continually corrected and reprinted under his own name, he concealed as far as was possible his connexion with the theatres. Play-making was to him a means of livelihood, as is journalism to many a present-day author.

Henslowe records Drayton's activities from December, 1597, until January, 1600, and partially from August, 1601, until June, 1602. During 1600 and 1601 he wrote exclusively for the Chamberlain's men, for whom he continued writing until after 1603. During 1598 and 1599 he wrote or helped to write some nineteen plays, more than nine each year. As he wrote plays from *c*. 1590 until 1604 or later he probably shared in the creation of some eighty dramas. Of these but one, and of the one a part only, has been hitherto universally placed to his credit. Some few commentators have granted him a share in the second and third parts of *Henry VI*, which earlier historians had assigned to Shakespeare.

The strong Protestant bias which is to be found in Drayton's later works may also be looked for in his plays. Other marked characteristics can be discovered in his known poetry. Not only was he a formalist in religion, but in his versification. In his first published work, the *Hymnes*, he notes that they are 'reduced into sundrie kinds of English meeter'; and for many years he expended much time and thought experimenting with 'meeter', greatly concerned with poetical technique, especially in verse form.

Whatsoever form Drayton decided upon for a production he invariably forced each line and stanza into it. Was the measure one of ten syllables, as in *Idea*, he applied the rule to each line and made it fit exactly. He wrote *Mortimeriades* in stanzas of seven lines and rewrote it in 'Ariosta's stanza' of eight lines because the latter 'hath majesty, perfection and solidity'. Throughout all of his work this characteristic worship of form dominates. His verse never flows freely, but is always checked by a fixed measure; the result being that most of his lines stop at the end of the measure, the stop being marked by a comma, semicolon, or a full stop. The preponderance of these end-stopped lines in all of his work is excessive. Another result of his method appears in the constant use of small words which serve only to fill up precisely each foot in each measure. End-stopped lines usually carry an accent upon the last foot. In early blank verse drama this produced the rhymed couplet; and in almost all folk-poetry it resulted in various sorts of rhymed verse. End-stopped verse is therefore usually associated with rhyme; and when rhyme is absent the verse seems incomplete. Whenever Drayton in his blank verse eschews rhyme this lack is felt. The mind of the reader, constantly halted at the end of each measure, seeks a resting-place in rhyme; and when rhyme is not present the mind feels cheated and bewildered. At times Drayton, despite himself, furnishes a rhyme, which then renders even more unsatisfactory those lines which are not rhymed. At times he frankly makes use of rhymed couplets; then and only then does his end-stopped verse seem satisfactory.

Although his end-stopped verse insistently called for rhyme Drayton had no real tonal sensitiveness. At times his rhymes are legitimate; at times they are bastard. Some of these bastard rhymes are of the eye; others he attempts to legitimize by fantastically assuming a contorted pronunciation (*majesty* is made to rhyme with both *me* and *die*); still others are unjustifiably illegitimate.

Having a dull ear, assonance, the balancing of sound against sound within a rhythm, or the building of internal rhythms, was impossible to Drayton. Free verse was beyond him. What colour or music appears in his work is accidental, or obtained through imitation of some such master as Spenser or Marlowe. His poetry remains formal. Carefully measured, it lacks freedom and movement.

Although Drayton lacked a sense of both colour and music he possessed a strong unflagging intellect. Seemingly he never tired, never ceased writing. *Polyolbion* would have exhausted the energies of an ordinary man of letters. It is but a small part of his output. Most writers would have tired of this self-imposed task after having written the allegorical history of Cornwall,

Devon, Dorset, and Hampshire. Drayton continued steadfastly onward until he had personified all the hills and streams and historical landmarks of every county in England. No furrow was so long but he ploughed to its end. Nor was his ploughing of meagre depth. Usually he turned up virgin soil. His lines are full of new metaphors, of interesting conceits, and of considered reflections. He planned broadly and logically, and completed intellectually and formally that which he had planned.

Drayton's poetry can be found in most public libraries. His plays were never acknowledged.

Sir John Oldcastle was written in the summer of 1599 by Munday, Drayton, Wilson, and Hathway. Henslowe's payments suggest that the greater part of the play was written by Drayton, and the internal evidence confirms the suggestion. It is a Protestant play centred about the figure of the reformer ' the good Lord Cobham '. Part I is very long, but it is solidly constructed. While the comic and less serious parts of this drama must be assigned to Hathway, Wilson, and Munday (' Fie, fie, paltry, to and fro ' of Murley being Munday's), the serious portions belong to Drayton.

Drayton's part of *Sir John Oldcastle* is in blank verse; it is end-stopped and precisely measured. Occasional rhymes appear in it, some of which are illegitimate. When arrested Lord Cobham consoles his wife in five-foot lines as follows :

> Come hither, lady—nay, sweet wife, forbeare
> To heape one sorrow on anothers necke :
> Tis griefe enough falsely to be accusde,
> And not permitted to acquite my selfe ;
> Do not thou with thy kind respective teares,
> Torment thy husbands heart that bleedes for thee,
> But be of comfort. God hath help in store
> For those that put assured trust in him, &c.

The worthy Protestant concludes :

> One solace find I setled in my soule,
> That 1 am free from treasons very thought :
> Only my conscience, for the Gospels sake,
> Is cause of all the trouble I sustaine.

This last line is deprived of the rhyme which should have brought it to a proper close.

Lord Cobham escapes from prison and, with his wife, seeks concealment in a wood, where they converse in carefully measured end-stopped lines:

> *Cobham.* My drowsie eies waxe heavy: Earely rising,
> Together with the travell we have had,
> Make me that I could gladly take a nap,
> Were I perswaded we might be secure.
> *Lady.* Let that depend on me: Whilst you do sleepe,
> Ile watch that no misfortune happen us.
> Lay then your head upon my lap, sweete Lord,
> And boldly take your rest.
> *Cobham.* I shall, deare wife,
> Be too much trouble to thee.
> *Lady.* Urge not that,
> My duty binds me, and your love commands.
> I would I had the skil with tunèd voyce
> To draw on sleep with some sweet melodie,
> But imperfection, and unaptnesse too,
> Are both repugnant, &c.

By careful contriving the lines have been exactly filled. Only an assiduous and conscientious formalist could have written, not these few lines, but hundreds of similar ones, in play after play, poem after poem.

The following bastard rhymes will be found in *Oldcastle*: *Wise–lives, prophane–again, loyaltie–clemencie–they, belong–over-flowne–gone,* &c. Of this play there was a second part which has been lost.

Sir John Oldcastle contains a line of descent of the Plantagenets which is a virtual duplicate of the same line as it appears in *Henry VI, Part III.* Yet it differs greatly from the same line as found in *The True Tragedy of Richard Duke of Yorke*, and in Holinshed. Starting with this clue Fleay first recognized Drayton's hand in the *Henry VI* series.

Such parts of *Henry VI, Parts II* and *III*, as were not used
by Shakespeare in his garbled Quartos of 1594 and 1595 were
presumably added at some period after 1598, before 1602. The
date of these additions is fixed by an entry in the Stationers'
Register of April 19, 1602, wherein first mention is made of the
first and second parts of *Henry VI*. The greater number of these
additions, as well as the conception of labelling the three plays
as *Henry VI, Parts I, II*, and *III*, must be attributed to Drayton,
who so loved serial dramas.

Peculiarly Draytonian is the 'sun-dial' passage in Part III. No
trace of this passage appears in Shakespeare's version. Yet had
it existed in the original manuscript he certainly would have
obtained at least parts of it for his *True Tragedy*. It was inserted
into King Henry's monologue during the battle.

> Oh God! me thinkes it were a happy life,
> To be no better then a homely Swaine,
> To sit upon a hill, as I do now,
> To carve out Dialls queintly, point by point,
> Thereby to see the Minutes how they runne: .
> How many makes the Houre full compleate,
> How many Houres brings about the Day,
> How many Dayes will finish up the Yeare,
> How many Yeares, a Mortall man may live.
> When this is knowne, then to divide the Times:
> So many Houres, must I tend my Flocke;
> So many Houres, must I take my Rest:
> So many Houres, must I Contemplate:
> So many Houres, must I Sport my selfe:
> So many Dayes, my Ewes have bene with yong:
> So many weekes, ere the poore Fooles will Eane:
> So many yeares, ere I shall sheere the Fleece:
> So Minutes, Houres, Dayes, Monthes, and Yeares,
> Past over to the end they were created,
> Would bring white haires, unto a Quiet grave.

Greene and the university poets invented rhythmic repetition. It is a poetic rather than a dramatic device. Drayton
merely imitated Greene when he began using it in drama.
Greene's repetitions are full of grace and harmony; Drayton's

are mechanical and intellectual. The one was an artist, the other an artificer.

In no instance does Henslowe record a play as solely by Drayton. Presumably his function was that of poet, one who put into well-measured verse the ideas or plots of his co-workers. As Dekker he was 'a gracer of tragedies'. Therefore in the ensuing remarks it will be assumed that while Drayton poetized the plays assigned to him he had assistance in both characterization and plot. For plot he evidently relied greatly upon Antony Munday.

Edward II. Among the plays which hitherto have not been attributed to Drayton the earliest and only one which can be safely assigned to him on both external and internal evidence is *Edward II,* which has almost universally been foisted on Marlowe.

Edward II was printed in 1594, as a Pembroke play. It was written before *A Looking-glass for London,* as Radogen therein is a caricature of Gaveston. The *Looking-glass* was produced by the Henslowe forces in March, 1592, therefore *Edward II* must date somewhat earlier. In 1598 Meres refers to Drayton's *Barons' Wars,* which contain the story of Gaveston and Edward, as 'The Civil Wars of Edward the second and the Barons', and compares Drayton to Lucan. But in another paragraph, where he treats of Drayton as a dramatist, comparing him to Accius (a writer of tragedies), he calls Drayton Tragoediographus, 'for his passionate penning the downfals of valiant Robert of Normandy, chast Matilda, and great Gaveston'. Two of these plays have disappeared; but Drayton's tragedy on 'great Gaveston' is preserved in *Edward II.* In still another paragraph Meres compares Drayton to Sophocles, remarking, 'Drayton is termed Golden-mouthed, for the purity and pretiousnesse of his stile and phrase'. Certainly this refers to the 'stile and phrase' of his tragedies, which remotely resemble those of the austere Sophocles.

The external evidence is strong; but the internal evidence is certain. Among the dramatists who in 1592 were capable of writing *Edward II* Drayton alone could have so pertinaciously applied the foot-rule to every line of a play as did the author of this tragedy. Nor could any other dramatist have made so many bastard rhymes.

Despite an earnest endeavour to preserve true blank verse form without rhyme, many rhymed couplets have crept into this tragedy. Among them appear the following bastards: *attends–laments, head–perished, is–bliss, knit–favorite, rejects–steps, be–felicity, out–killingworth, eyes–surprised, king–again, die–enmity–lie, niece–deceased, question–gone, droop–look, die–majesty, hell–exile, throne–crown, gone–fawn, affection–question, astray–embrodery, avail–repeal, fly–mercury, true–so–do, sun–companion, break–weak,* &c.

Although Drayton wrote *Edward II* with a five-foot rule in his hand he did not always succeed in fitting his phrases into the predetermined measure. His strict formalism was acquired only by dint of long and continued exertion.

Copies of *Edward II* can be found in almost all libraries. A few excerpts will serve to illustrate Drayton's method *c.* 1592.

The youthful King speaks to Mortimer:

> Thinke not that I am frighted with thy words,
> My father's murdered through thy treacherie;
> And thou shalt die, and on his mournefull hearse,
> Thy hatefull and accursèd head shall lie,
> To witnesse to the world, that by thy meanes,
> His kingly body was too soone interrde.
>   *Queen Mother.* Weepe not sweete sonne
>   *King Ed. III.* Forbid me not to weepe, he was my father,
> And had you lov'de him halfe so well as I,
> You could not beare his death thus patiently,
> But you I feare, conspirde with Mortimer, &c.
>   *Mortimer.* But hath your grace no other proofe then this?
>   *Ed. III.* Yes, if this be the hand of Mortimer.
>   [*He shows a paper.*]
>   *Mortimer.* Tis my hand, what gather you by this.
>   *Ed. III.* That thither thou didst send a murtherer.
>   *Mortimer.* What murtherer? bring foorth the man I sent.

Ed. III. A Mortimer, thou knowest that he is slaine,
And so shalt thou be too: Why staies he heere?
Bring him unto a hurdle, drag him foorth,
Hang him I say, and set his quarters up,
But bring his head back presently to me.
    Queen Mother. For my sake sweete sonne pittie Mortimer.
    Mortimer. Madam, intreat not, I will rather die,
Then sue for life unto a paltrie boy.
    Ed. III. Hence with the traitor, with the murderer.
    Mortimer. Base fortune, now I see, that in thy wheele
There is a point, to which when men aspire,
They tumble hedlong downe: that point I touchte
And seeing there was no place to mount up higher,
Why should I greeve at my declining fall, &c.

Earlier in the play Edward II, when giving up his crown,
laments:

Call me not lorde, away, out of my sight,
Ah pardon me; greefe makes me lunatick.
Let not that Mortimer protect my sonne,
More safetie is there in a tiger's jawes
Then his imbrasements. Bear this to the Queene,
                           [*Giving a handkerchief*]
Wet with my teares, and dried againe with sighes,
If with the sight thereof she is not mooved,
Returne it backe and dip it in my bloud.
Commend me to my sonne and bid him rule
Better than I, yet how have I transgrest,
Unless it be with too much clemencie?
    Trus. And thus, most humbly, do we take our leave.
    Ed. II. Farewell, I know the next newes that they bring,
Will be my death, and welcome shall it be.
To wretched men death is felicitie.
    Leicester. Another poast, what newes bringes he?
    Ed. II. Such newes as I expect: Come Bartley, come,
And tell thy message to my naked brest, &c.

In *Edward II* as in *Sir John Oldcastle* the thought often
changes suddenly from one object to another in the middle of a
speech or line. The mechanical rhythm continues nevertheless
jogging along uninterruptedly. This produces the strange feeling

of antagonism between thought and rhythm which is common to all of Drayton's dramatic verse, which in turn makes all of his characters seem more or less automata.

Edward III was entered in the Stationers' Register by C. Burby on December 1, 1595, and was printed by him in 1596. The verse is mechanically measured and is almost entirely end-stopped. There are many bastard rhymes: *eye–oratorie, lie–tapestrie, boast–cost, death–feast,* &c. The first part of the play deals with the maudlin love of Edward III for the Countess of Salisbury, even as the first part of *Edward II* treats of his father's love for Gaveston. The 'pretiousness and grace' of the earlier play are present; but with them appears a larger sincerity and a bolder conception. Formalism prevails, and the characters seem made of wood, despite rich and delicate imagery.

The Prince's speech after his first battle will serve to show the progress made by Drayton since he wrote *Edward II*.

> *Prince.* First having donne my duety as beseemed,
> Lords, I regreet you all with harty thanks.
> And now, behold, after my winters toile,
> My painefull voyage on the boistrous sea
> Of warres devouring gulphes and steely rocks,
> I bring my fraught unto the wishèd port,
> My Summers hope, my travels sweet reward :
> And heere, with humble duety, I present
> This sacrifice, the first fruit of my sword,
> Cropt and cut downe even at the gate of death,
> The king of Boheme, father, whome I slue ;
> Whose thousands had intrencht me round about,
> And laye as thicke upon my battered crest,
> As on an Anvell, with their ponderous glaves, &c.

The little scene between the wounded Audley and his Squire is one of the best in the play. It is mechanical, and ends in a bastard rhyme ; yet it is superior to any of Drayton's earlier work.

> *Esquire.* How fares my Lord ?
> *Audley.*　　　　　　Even as a man may do,
> That dines at such a bloodie feast as this.

Esquire. I hope, my Lord, that is no mortall scarre.
Audley. No matter, if it be; the count is cast,
And, in the worst, ends but a mortall man.
Good friends, convey me to the princely Edward,
That in the crimson braverie of my bloud
I may become him with saluting him.
Ile smile, and tell him, that this open scarre
Doth end the harvest of his Audleys warre.

This is a fine and brave idea, but it only calls attention to the angles, corners, and edges of its containing form.

Edward I, originally written by Peele while he was at Oxford *c.* 1583, was revised by an ardent anti-papist some time before 1593, when the extant edition was published. The episodes of this version are not only out of all sequence, but are so mangled that it is impossible to judge of it even as a revision. However, one fact is proved by the title as well as by internal evidence. Peele's play was revised by a Protestant in order to besmirch the lovely and Catholic Queen, Eleanor of Spain.

On March 5, 1593, a play was entered in the Stationers' Register by John Danter as 'The Pleasant history of Edward Lord of Lancaster, Knight of the holy crosse, with his adventures', &c. This was probably Peele's original play. The present revision was published the same year by Abell Jeffes as 'The Famous Chronicle of King Edward the first, sirnamed Edward Longshankes, with his returne from the holy land. Also the life of LLevellen rebell in Wales. Lastly, the sinking of Queene Elinor, who sunck at Charing-crosse, and rose againe at Pottershith, now named Queene hith.' The 'sirnamed Longshankes' calls to mind Drayton's 'Robert, Duke of Normandy, sirnamed Short-thigh '.

There is no external evidence that Drayton wrote the revised portions of *Edward I*; yet there is much in the revision resembling his work both in style and subject-matter. It is also the first of the King Edward series. And if Drayton once started on a series he never stopped until he had finished.

The Massacre at Paris: with the Death of the Duke of Guise first appears in Henslowe's Diary as a new play on January 30, 1593. It was revived in November, 1598. The extant version is ascribed to Marlowe and is of uncertain date: however, it shows no signs of the 1598 revision. Parts of this version were once among the Alleyn papers at Dulwich, and were used by Collier. It may have been written from or suggested by a ' Guise ' play by Marlowe.

The verse parts of *The Massacre* are unmistakably Drayton's. He measured it, and end-stopped it, and decorated it with bastard rhymes. It is utterly unlike anything written by Marlowe. The prose comedy scenes are by a second hand. The play was written to glorify the French Huguenots, even as *Sir John Oldcastle* was composed in praise of the English Protestants. The ideas running through both plays are similar, as is the treatment.

Being an earlier play and seemingly written in haste, *The Massacre* lacks the power and polish of Drayton's later work. He used various lines and ideas from his other plays (*Edward II*, &c.), and worked over an older play. The following grimly comic scene by his collaborator is worthy of Dekker:

> *Enter two men with the Admiral's body.*
>
> *1st Man.* Now sirrah, what shall we do with the Admiral ?
>
> *2nd Man.* Why, let us burne him for an heretick.
>
> *1st Man.* Oh no, his body will infect the fire, and the fire the aire, and so we shall be poisoned with him.
>
> *2nd Man.* What shall we doe then?
>
> *1st Man.* Let's throw him into the river.
>
> *2nd Man.* Oh twill corrupt the water, and the water the fish, and by the fish ourselves when we eate them.
>
> *1st Man.* Then throw him into the ditch.
>
> *2nd Man.* No, no, to decide all doubts, be ruled by me, let's hang him heere upon this tree.
>
> *1st Man.* Agreede.
>
> *They hang him.*

This may well be compared with the murder-scene in *Richard III*, First Quarto edition.

Other plays wholly or partly by Drayton are to be found. However, from the material already indicated a just estimate of his abilities can be formed. His peculiarities of style are obvious. His characterization suffers from lack of sympathy and enforced stiltedness. Of character interaction, cause and effect due to character, there is almost none. His plots, or rather the plots of such plays as he decorated with his verse, usually consist of a series of historically related episodes; there is thus no introduction, no climax, no resolution. Yet the stories are so closely knit historically that they have a certain unity. The episodes are literary, are filled with rhetoric, after the manner of the Pembroke school, rather than pantomimic action; the appeal is to the ear rather than to the eye.

Drayton was fond of serial dramas, having written, usually with others, *Edward, Parts I, II*, and *III; Earl Goodwin, Parts I* and *II; Civil Wars of France, Parts I, II*, and *III*, with Dekker, Part I of which still exists in *Trial of Chivalry; Black Bateman, Parts I* and *II; Oldcastle, Parts I* and *II*, and *Fair Constance of Rome, Parts I* and *II*, as well as the revision of all three parts of *Henry VI*.

On the whole Drayton was an upright, plodding puritanical formalist who could be depended upon to turn out average verse in regular instalments. He might well be likened in his life, but especially in his verse, to a motor-car with a single cylinder engine and a large fly-wheel which, once well started, plods regularly onward, never increasing its impetus no matter how steep the hill, never losing its impetus howsoever often the engine misses fire, a useful but scarce a pleasure-giving mechanism.

Drayton began writing for the Pembroke company. From 1597 until 1600 he wrote for Henslowe's companies. Thereafter, except for a short interval in the autumn of 1601, he wrote for the Chamberlain company at the Globe. He assisted Shakespeare in the revision of *Hamlet* in 1603.

XI

REVISION AND COLLABORATION

THE Plague of 1592 marks the end of the first period of Elizabethan drama. When the theatres reopened in 1593 a new era began. Greene, Marlowe, and Kyd were dead. The Pembroke company was bankrupt. The Queen's company was also in dire straits. The Sussex company was disbanded. Only the Admiral's company and Lord Strange's comparatively new company, both backed by Henslowe and Alleyn, passed through the hard times successfully. Some of the members of these two companies went abroad for a time, others toured the provinces. When the Plague had passed they returned to the Rose theatre and soon became the most important companies of the period. For some time they were the only companies having sufficient means to buy and produce new plays.

Great changes had also taken place in the minds of those who patronized plays. The Spanish Armada, followed by the Plague, engendered a new civic and national communism which ill sorted with medieval romances and artificial euphuism. Hence arose a demand for true tragedies, historical and domestic, and for realistic comedies full of human interest.

In order to express itself realism demanded ever more and more stage machinery. The wardrobe of the producing companies became extensive; scenic effects multiplied. Soon the leading companies had large sums invested in properties. As they became wealthy they became powerful. In 1592 Greene wrote of the actors as ' burres ' who ' sought to cleave ' to the dramatists. Ten years later the actor companies ruled supreme, the dramatists had become hirelings.

In order to understand the treatment to which plays were subjected during the ten years immediately after the Plague, it must be remembered that once a play was sold to a theatrical company it became the absolute property of that company. The companies looked upon plays as a present-day builder looks upon a house. If they needed altering the original designer, or any likely dramatist, was called in to do the work.

Old plays were thus patched and repatched until they would no longer serve. If new plays were constructed, at times one man undertook the whole work, but as often one man outlined the plot, another wrote the songs, a third the dialogue, a fourth the low comedy, &c. They were mason, carpenter, plasterer, steel-worker, plumber in the building of the house.

It is true that there had been revision and co-operation before 1593, but it was then the exception; it now became the rule; and individual creation became the rare exception. Unlike their great predecessors the younger dramatists became specialists, specialization being one of the concomitants of realism.

This system of revision and co-operation tended to destroy all sanctity of authorship. Little by little the dramatists were reduced to the status of hireling hacks absolutely dependent upon the whim of the actor companies. Rarely did an audience know who had created the parts it loved. Judging from Henslowe's Diary Henslowe himself often had no idea who had written some of the plays he purchased.

Such plays as were published were often printed surreptitiously, the author's name or names being omitted or wrongly given. Piracy flourished. The companies stole plays from one another, and the printers stole from the companies.

Never had authors laboured under more distressful conditions. It is not to be wondered that they were usually poor and often in the Counter for debt. Yet during this period (1593-1604) some of the best English dramas were written by these unfortunate starvelings.

Every specialist is marked, not alone by his subject-matter, but also by his mode of expression: the more limited the one the more marked the other. While it is very difficult to discover piece by piece the parts of a whole, constructed by several workmen, be it house or play, the task of assigning at large definite parts to each craftsman is simple once the speciality of each is known. In order to understand the work of the various members of the new school it is therefore necessary to examine each as to his speciality.

XII
ELIZABETHAN COMEDY

ALTHOUGH comedy had always been a part of Elizabethan drama it was especially after the Plague that comedy became an almost inseparable adjunct of drama. Various playwrights specialized in comedy, and scarce a play was written which did not contain comic relief.

It has been common usage to assert that comedy is based on a sense of superiority felt by the observer. Were this true great egoists would indulge in much laughter, and the appreciation of comedy would increase in direct ratio to the growth of self-esteem, which is almost the reverse of truth.

Comedy is based on the realization that the person at whom we laugh normally does or says something which, normal to him, seems abnormal, hence often amusing, to us. In order to realize that he is acting normally it is necessary for us first to understand his mentality or character. All true comedy is therefore based on the comprehension of the character of the person who affords us amusement. Its complexity varies according to the complexity of the character concerned.

In its simplest form comedy appears in the sayings or doings of innocents, children, animals, clowns, fools, rustics, servants, &c., the one necessary element being that the innocent shall be more or less simple-minded. The fact that he is simple-minded gives to his sayings or doings an orientation differing from the normal, and therefore they are likely to seem comical. The comedy of all clowns is thus based on a foreknowledge of their simple-mindedness, on the fact that they thus differ from the normal. Were we, the observers, as simple as clowns there could be no simple-minded, ' naïve ' comedy.

The naïve sayings and doings of children may at times seem comical to their elders; they do not seem comical to their child companions. Naïve comedy is therefore built on a comprehension of character. It is the simplest form of true comedy, only because it is based on the simplest of all characters—an innocent.

As characters become more complex the comedy caused by them tends to become more complex, and the need for careful character delineation becomes more imperative. The intensity of the comic effect depends almost entirely upon how thoroughly the audience has already grasped the character of the comedian.

The next development was a whole series of fairly simple comedy characters, each one of which exemplified a type; such were : the pedagogue, the French doctor, the overdressed fop, the self-conceited lover, the braggart, the shrew, the cuckold husband, all foreigners—Dutch, French, Welsh, &c., and many others. These were easily exploited types, familiar to the general audience, known at once by some such simple sign as costume or attitude. Few writers of comedy have passed beyond the use of these types. To this same category belong personified peculiarities.

After types come individualized characters. Such need careful preliminary exposition, otherwise they cannot be understood, cannot be used for the purposes of comedy. Very few playwrights have been able to conceive and introduce such characters.

Innocents, types or characters, may be used as static beings in a changing environment, as beings to whom things happen, on whom jokes are played, thus creating the comedy of situation; or they may themselves react against a static or changing environment. This later gives rise to pure comedy. In its simpler form it consists in the clown's observations on, or actions over, objects. It is more complex when a character reacts against a changing environment, usually against another character. (As when the clown through his own clever stupidity meets with the identical person from whom he is endeavouring to escape, or as when one character freshly observed from the point of view of another is made to seem ridiculous. Falstaffe is thus made comic by Prince Hal.)

The most refined comedy is produced when a character reacts

comically against himself: i.e. when a character, suddenly realizing that his mood or action is ridiculous, changes his point of view and draws attention to his past folly. Thus, his character having changed, his immediate past becomes environment against which he now reacts. This form of comedy is usually termed humour.

Comedy and Wit.

Although some wit is found in almost all comedies it is not a necessary concomitant. In fact it is an inferior ingredient and is often an indication of poor comedy. For wit is not founded on character; it is a purely intellectual product, the source of its origin being of no consequence. Whenever character is brought into a witty story it thereby gains an element of true comedy, it then ceases to be merely witty. Wit is produced by forcing upon an accepted idea or concept a new orientation which makes it seem bizarre or comical. In other words, wit is the Lilliputian comedy of concepts. If concepts are substituted for characters its laws are similar to those governing true comedy.

Comedy may be divided into two classes, incidental and contributory. In the early miracle plays and interludes comical episodes, having no relation whatsoever to the main theme of the play, were introduced in order to give the audience a respite. Such comedy is incidental. A few of these incidental episodes appear in the work of later dramatists. In Act 1 of *A Woman killed with Kindness* Heywood introduces a servants' hall episode which ends in a dance. It is purely incidental. Later in the same play some of the same servants are introduced into the main action; however, their actions remain entirely incidental. This marks the second stage of incidental comedy, when comedy characters are introduced into the story yet do not contribute to its development. The first phase is used when at a circus the clown and equestrian alternate, the second when both appear simultaneously in the same ring.

While incidental comic episodes are no longer used, incidental comic individuals still survive. This is in part due to the fact that a good comedian can please a part of the public however incidental his part may be.

Incidental wit is composed of irrelevant locution by characters more or less essential to the play. Much of Day's smart talk in *Humour out of Breath* is of this genre. It is found in intellectual passages only. (See also Ben Jonson's comedies.) All incidental comedy, or wit of whatsoever genre, is dramatically illegitimate.

Contributory comedy is from its very nature legitimate in that it assists in telling the story, in developing the plot or in elucidating character. In interludes and picaresque dramas comic episodes easily find a place. In dramas of intrigue, such as *A Woman will have her Will*, almost all the situations can be comical. Such comedy depends on external accidents and events. The sport lies in the action, in what happens to the characters.

While comedy varies in nature and degree according to the amplitude and distinctness with which the characters are originally presented, it is most effective when the change of point of view is extreme and is suddenly produced. So also wit depends on the sudden extreme change of point of view as well as upon the amplitude and distinctness of the original concepts.

Of legitimate contributory wit and comedy there are many varieties. Lyly introduced witty comedies of smart talk in which there was little character work and a slight plot. The comedy of plot and counter-plot, containing also much wit and somewhat more story, followed. Such comedies appealed to a limited intellectual audience. The general public rather favoured comedies having less wit but more pantomimic action, knock-about comedy and the comedy of situation. These were based also on plot and counter-plot, the greater number centred about the activities of rival lovers. Such are Haughton's *A Woman will have her Will*, in which one lover is suspended in mid-air in a basket while others lose themselves in the dark, and Day's *Humour out of Breath*, in which an old lover is ridiculed when blindfolded while his rival steals away with Lady Florimel.

More strictly humorous were various plays by Chapman and

Jonson. These were usually didactical and satirical, the people being personified eccentricities, types, not characters.

True comedy, based on character, came in with humanism. It was probably introduced by Peele, and was carried forward by Lyly, Dekker, and Chettle. To depict a character with sympathetic understanding, and then, still loving him, to cause him to be an object of mirth, can be done only by true humanists who at the same time are more or less philosophers.

XIII

THOMAS DEKKER AND HENRY CHETTLE

DEKKER and Chettle are the two great figures of the realistic movement. Both had been friends of Greene, Marlowe, Peele, and Nash; and though both looked upon these men as great masters, they developed new methods, a new drama. The plague of 1592 curtailed the exuberance of romanticism and engendered humanism; the drama in consequence became realistic.

Earlier writers had worked much realistic low comedy into their later plays; Dekker and Chettle perfected realism as the medium of humanism.[1] Through their efforts, not clowns alone, but kings and queens, lords and ladies, elves and witches were so intimately rendered that each seemed not only real but human. No longer were they obscure figures seen through the amber haze of romance, but human beings who revealed their inmost thoughts and feelings. It was an intimate age, an age of puritan democracy, when every one endeavoured to pry into his neighbour's business, his home, his religious belief, his soul.

It cannot be said of Dekker and Chettle that they ever became repellent in their realism. They never hunted the cesspools of life, nor depicted canker spots in the manner of the nineteenth-century realists. Their joy in the realities of life was the joy of a child who has discovered a bright pebble, an unknown flower, a winning smile on the face of a new friend. Among the hundreds of people they put upon the stage, beggars, liars, thieves, prostitutes, usurers, there is not one that is not for-givable, few that are not lovable, so well did they comprehend and enjoy human idiosyncrasies. No one has understood man-kind better, no one has depicted character more truthfully, more charitably.

Dekker and Chettle worked together from 1597 until 1603. To trace the share of each in their united efforts it is necessary first to consider each separately.

[1] Humanism is herein used to designate interest in and kindness towards all created beings, not the study of Latin literature.

XIV

THOMAS DEKKER

(Play-dresser)

THOMAS DEKKER was born *c.* 1570 and died *c.* 1641. Very little is known of his life, and that little is to be gathered almost entirely from his prose works and Henslowe's Diary. Jonson derides him in *Satiromastix* as one Demetrius Fannius, 'a play-dresser', but tells nothing new of his life or character.

Some critics suppose that Greene in *Menaphon*, published in 1589, depicts Dekker in ' Doron '. If Doron is meant for Dekker this would indicate that he was known as a literary man as early as 1588, at which date Fleay (*Chronicle of English Drama*) places him with the Admiral's company.

The earliest recorded mention of Dekker by name is in Henslowe's Diary: 'Lent unto thomas dowton the 8 of Janewary 1597 twenty shillinges to buy a booke of mr dickers lent.' As Henslowe did not begin his year until the May quarter the true date was January 8, 1598. In the next entry but one Henslowe records, 'lent unto the company the 15 of Janeway 1597 to bye a booke of Mr dicker called fayeton fower pownde.' This evidently completed the transaction. These entries show that in 1598 Dekker was a well-known and respected playwright. They mark the recorded beginning of his long connexion with the various companies which came under Henslowe's management.

The next entry in the diary is the ' ominous ' entry of the critics which ' marks the coming of disaster upon him '. The entry reads: 'Lent unto the company the 4 febreary 1598 to dise charge Mr dickers out of the counter in the powltrey the some of fortie shillinges.' This records a bit of spite on the part of a rival company. The same thing happened to Chettle and to William Byrde. In Byrde's case the prosecutor is mentioned: Thomas Pope of the Chamberlain company. Doubtless it was the Chamberlain (old Strange) company that brought suit against both Dekker and Chettle. The small sums were paid and the matter, for the moment, ended. However, the Chamberlain company was not content. In January, 1599, they again brought suit against Dekker. This time it took three pounds ten shillings to settle the case.

These slight persecutions had no effect on Dekker's industry. He continued working, more assiduously than any of his colleagues, except Chettle, for so long as Henslowe kept his diary.

With the ending of Henslowe's Diary in 1603 all authentic records of Dekker's life end, save two letters written by him to Edward Alleyn. The first is dated September 12, 1616. The second is undated, but belongs to the same period. Both were written from the debtors' prison, the King's Bench. The first is a friendly letter to Alleyn congratulating him on the completion of Dulwich College. The second was written to recommend a youth as a personal servant. In the first Dekker wrote: 'And it best becomes me to sing anything in praise of Charity, because albeit I have felt few hands warm through that complexion, yet imprisonment may make me long for them. I live amongst the Goths and Vandalls, where Barbarousness is predominant.' In the second he wrote: 'I give you thanks for the last remembrance of your love. I write now not poeticall,' &c. These statements include everything authentic that in any way indicates the time or length of Dekker's internment.

From the first letter it would seem as if he had then been but newly interned and had never been in such a prison before; otherwise why describe it to his old friend as a novelty? How long he remained is not indicated. It may have been months; it may have been years: no one knows. There is no evidence that he was ever again in prison; yet the critics hint that Dekker was a sad improvident who passed a great part of his life in jail.

It is only fair to state that almost every one who at that period followed the precarious career of letters was at one time or another in prison for debt.

Although contemporary documents bring to light so little of Dekker's life, his character is revealed in his works. Unlike many of his friends he began his career as a playwright and finished it as a pamphleteer. That he had a kindly disposition is evinced by the portraits of his friends. In *A Knight's Conjuring* (1607) he depicts Spenser, Watson, Kyd, Marlowe, Greene, Peele, Nash, and Chettle; nor is a mean or envious word written of any one of them. All is honest admiration. In the celebrated *Untrussing* of Ben Jonson, whom Dekker might well have handled roughly, all is written without bitterness, even with such kindness that Jonson was absolutely disarmed. The letters to the great founder of Dulwich College also disclose wholehearted sympathy and admiration.

But it is in the innumerable character studies found in his plays that Dekker shows his great sympathetic soul. Ever he depicts the good, never the evil side of life. Unremittingly he hopes for the best; optimism is the key-note of his existence. Far from being a reprobate, Dekker was a moralist. Had he written a few years earlier he would have produced moralities. Many of his plays lean strongly in that direction.

About 1605, when Chettle was dead and Alleyn had retired, Dekker ceased writing plays, and during the rest of his long life wrote little other than pageants and ethical pamphlets. That such a man was allowed to suffer poverty, was thrown into prison for debt, shows how little the world appreciates genius, how much pounds and pence outvalue human souls.

As literature Dekker's plays have been well reviewed by Lamb, Hazlitt, Swinburne, &c. Lamb wrote: 'He had poetry enough for anything.' Hazlitt's enthusiasm was even greater; of Dekker's methods he wrote:

> The execution is, throughout, as exact as the conception is new and masterly. There is the least colour possible used; the

pencil drags; the canvas is almost seen through: but then, what precision of outline, what truth and purity of tone, what firmness of hand, what marking of character! The words and answers all along are so true and pertinent, that we seem to see the gestures, and to hear the tone with which they are accompanied. . . . We find the simplicity of prose with the graces of poetry. The stalk grows out of the ground; but the flowers spread their flaunting leaves in the air.

Swinburne's praise is mixed with much condemnation, the whole burden of which is: 'Dekker was a Bohemian, a profligate, often in prison; his style is slovenly.' Over and over again he insists on Dekker's 'slovenliness'. Swinburne never understood the difference between literature and drama. It is true that Dekker's lines do not all flow in the same measured rhythm; many are broken, many incomplete; many rhythms limp; but they are thus rendered dramatic. The more dramatic Dekker's dialogue the more broken is his rhythm. It is this very unevenness which gives certain speeches their intimate tender emotionalism. The verse is not ornate; but it is intensely pathetic, dramatic.

The effect of broken rhythm can best be noted in symphonic music. While the great emotional movements grow increasingly rhythmical the dramatic and pathetic moments are always depicted in broken or hesitant rhythms. This is a universal law which Dekker evidently felt and observed.

As drama Dekker's work has never been satisfactorily treated, neither historically nor artistically. Whether or no he wrote plays as early as 1589 may never be known; yet his facile use of rhymed couplets, which were in great vogue about that time, supports such a theory. However, there are various plays, dating 1594 and 1595, which doubtless were his creations. These were written for the Strange and Admiral companies.

When the Strange company left the Rose in 1596 for the Curtain, Dekker seems to have gone with them, deserting them for the Admiral's and Pembroke companies in 1598, when the Strange forces united with the Queen's men. The few plays universally accredited to Dekker were written for the Admiral's men during this later period, 1598–1604.

While the Strange and Admiral's men were at the Rose the following plays with which Dekker had some connexion were produced: *Tasso's Melancholy*, *The Venetian Comedy*, *The French Doctor*, *Dioclesian*, *The Set at Maw*, *The Mack*, *Long Meg of Westminster*, *Fortunatus*, and *Troy*.

The Venetian Comedy and *The French Doctor* supposedly supplied the material for an old German play called *The Jew of Venice*, the source of which was English. That a play centring on a Jew was in existence as early as 1579 is evident from a statement in Gosson's *The School of Abuse*:

> And as some of the Players are farre from abuse: so some of their Playes are without rebuke: which are as easily remembered as quickly reckoned. ... The *Jew* and *Ptolme*, showne at the Bull, the one representing the greedinesse of worldly chusers, and bloody mindes of Usurers: The other, &c.

This may have been *The Venetian Comedy*.

In the Stationers' Register, September 9, 1653, there was entered 'The Jew of Venice by Thomas Dekker', and on July 22, 1598, James Roberts had entered 'The Marchant of Venice, or otherwise called The Jew of Venice'. This definitely identifies *The Jew of Venice* with *The Merchant of Venice*. Evidently Dekker rewrote some old play, as *The Venetian Comedy* or *The French Doctor*, into *The Jew of Venice* some time between 1596 and 1598, while the Strange-Chamberlain men were at the Curtain. Shakespeare 'corrected and enlarged' Dekker's play before 1600 into *The Merchant of Venice*. This is a stupid title, because the play is not about the merchant Antonio. It centres about Portia, the French Doctor, and Shylock the Jew.

The internal evidence also points conclusively to Dekker as the author of this play. No other writer could have so easily endowed Portia with her appealing humanism, could have sketched in either Jessica or Nerissa. In uneven and broken rhythm, so eminently characteristic of Dekker, this play abounds, despite the 'revisions and corrections' of Shakespeare. There is internal evidence also that this play is a revision of a Court play. It probably was originally an old play by Peele. Unfortunately no copy of Dekker's *The Jew of Venice*, printed in 1653, has been found. However, Shakespeare's part in this play must be small. He found a complete copy of it in the Strange-Chamberlain repertoire and probably altered it but slightly.

Dioclesian is, according to Fleay, the Dekker play which was rewritten by Massinger as *The Virgin Martyr* and printed in 1622. *The Set at Maw* was probably the original of *Match Me in London*, published in 1631 as by Dekker. *Fortunatus* was the basis of *The Whole History of Fortunatus*, written by Dekker in November–December of 1599 and printed in 1600. *Long Meg of Westminster*, entered in the Stationers' Register by Chettle's partner Danter on March 14, 1595, was certainly the original of *The Roaring Girl*, published as by Middleton and Dekker in 1611. *The Mack* was rewritten by Day as *Come see a Wonder*, which revision was published in 1636 under the title *The Wonder of a Kingdom* as by Dekker. *Troy* was rewritten by Dekker and Chettle in 1599 into two plays, *Troylus and Cressida* and *Agamemnon*. This exhausts the list of plays with which Dekker can be associated, on external evidence alone, during this first period. That he went to the Curtain with the Strange men seems clear. It may have been while there that he began his association with Chettle which continued until Chettle's death.

January, 1598, marks Dekker's return to the Rose. Henslowe furnishes a list of some forty-five plays spread over four years in the writing of which Dekker had a large or small share, an average of eleven each year. Nor does this include all of his work. Certainly he was no idler. Omitting the plays of which no trace can be found to-day, the list is as follows: *Phaeton*, January 8, 1598, rewritten by Ford as *The Sun's Darling, c.* 1612; *Civil Wars of France*, with Drayton, printed as *The Trial of Chivalry*, 1605; *Troylus and Cressida*, with Chettle, April 16, 1599. This play can be found complete in the First Quarto edition of 1609; 'Shakespeare's' revised version appears in the Folio. *The Shoemaker's Holiday*, July, 1599, printed in 1600; *Patient Grissill*, with Chettle and Haughton, October, 1599; *Fortunatus*, November–December, 1599; *Truth's Supplication to Candlelight*, January, 1600, rewritten as *The Whore of Babylon* by Middleton, *c.* 1607.

The Spanish Moor's Tragedy was written with Day and Haughton in February 1600. This play was wrongly identified by Collier and Fleay as *Lust's Dominion*; later critics have followed their lead. It is true that there is in *Lust's Dominion* a Moor; but the tragedy is not in the least like anything ever written by Dekker, or Day, or Haughton. The expression 'Spanish Moor' was used to distinguish a Moor from a Spaniard, even as 'French Canadian' is now used to designate a Frenchman from Canada. Othello was a Moor from Spain, hence a Spanish Moor. The best version of *The Spanish Moor's Tragedy* is the First Quarto of *Othello*, published in 1622. 'Shakespeare's' revision appears in the Folio.[1]

Psyche and Cupid was written by Dekker, Day, and Chettle in May, 1600. Parts of this play can be found in the revision by Heywood, who renamed it *Love's Mistress. A Medecine for a Curst Wife* (July, 1602) was written for the Admiral's men; but it was transferred to the Worcester company, of which Kempe was then leading comedy man. This may have been Dekker's revision of *The Taming of A Shrew*. Dekker received £6 for this play. The extant version, as found in the Folio, *The Taming of the Shrew*, bears many traces of garbling by the Chamberlain forces.[2] *The Patient Man and the Honest Whore* was written in March, 1602, by Dekker and Middleton, and printed in 1635 as by Dekker. *Lady Jane, or The Overthrow of the Rebels,*

---

[1] *Lust's Dominion*, built upon a tract 'A brief and true relation', &c., entered in the Stationers' Register, January 9, 1599, was originally assigned to Marlowe. This, however, left open the possibility that the Dekker-Day-Haughton play was *Othello*. *Lust's Dominion* was therefore assigned to Dekker, Day, and Haughton. A brief comparison of this play and *The Revenger's Tragedy* will enable any one to realize that the author of *Lust's Dominion* was Cyril Tourneur.

[2] For further consideration of this play see Appendix to this chapter.

Parts I and II, with Chettle, Heywood, Smith, and Webster, was
written in October, 1602, and printed in condensed form as *Sir
Thomas Wyatt* in 1607. *The Roaring Girl, or Moll Cut-Purse*,
published in 1611 as by Dekker and Middleton, was probably a
revision by Middleton of *Long Meg of Westminster*. *If This is
not a Good Play the Devill is in it* was printed in 1612 as by
Dekker. This is a morality in his earliest manner; presumably it
is a revised version of one of his youthful plays. This ends the
Henslowe list.

When the Paules Boys resumed acting in 1599 Dekker and
Marston among others began writing for them. One of the first
plays presented by this company was *The Wisdom of Doctor
Dodypoll*, printed in 1600 as having been 'sundrie times acted
by the children of Powles'. Dodypoll is an enlarged study of
the French doctor who was introduced as Doctor Caius in *The
Merry Wives of Windsor*. The two characters are identical, and
their language is the same.

> By garr you be a brave merry man; De fine proper man; de
> very fine, brave, little propta sweet Jack man. By garr me loov'a
> you, me honour you, me kisse-a your foote.
>
> Ho Zaccharee, bid Ursula brushe my two, tree, fine Damaske
> gowne. Spread de rishe coverlet on de faire bed, vashe de fine
> plate, &c.
>
> Vell dere be a ting metinke, by gars blur me know. Me be
> revenge, &c.
>
> Chok-a de selfe foule churle, fowle horrible, terrible pigge,
> pye cod.

Thus speaks Doctor Dodypoll.

> I begar is dat all? John Rugby give a ma pen an Inck: tarche
> un pettit, tarche [tarry] a little.
>
> Vat be al you, van, to, tree com for-a? Begar de Preest be
> a coward Jack knave, &c.

Thus speaks Doctor Caius.

Doctor Dodypoll was the product of several hands. Little other
than the fun seems to be Dekker's. As at this period he was
working with Chettle, Day, and Haughton, and because the

play greatly resembles *Patient Grissill*, it is safe to conclude that it was written by members of the same group, the basis of the play being originally by Lyly.

The meaning of the word 'dodypoll' is evident when taken in the sense used by Edward Alleyn in a letter to his wife of May 2, 1593, which ends: 'Farwell mecho mousin & mouse & farwell bess dodipoll.' Thus used affectionately it corresponds with the present-day 'stupid' or 'dotty-pate'.

Dekker continued writing for Paules Boys for some time. In 1602, with Marston, he wrote *Satiromastix* for them, and in 1604 *Westward Ho* and *Northward Ho* in conjunction with Webster.

Besides writing for Paules Boys both Dekker and Marston wrote for the Chapel Children. Parts of plays written for this company have been recently discovered, so he claims, by C. W. Wallace.[1]

Satiromastix, or The Untrussing of the Humorous Poet, was acted privately by Paules Boys and publicly by the Chamberlain company. It is full of clever character sketches. Jonson was so well caricatured as 'Horace' that for a time he gave up writing his 'humorous' plays. This was a triumph for Dekker.

In a Cambridge play which was written almost immediately after *Satiromastix*, and which appeared during the Christmas season of 1601–2, called *The Return from Parnassus*, there are several lines which clearly refer to *Satiromastix*. Kempe in character remarks therein:

> Few of the University men pen plaies well, they smell too much of that writer Ovid, and that writer Metamorphosis, and talke too much of Proserpina and Jupiter. Why heres our fellow Shakespeare puts them all downe, I, and Ben Jonson too. O Ben Jonson is a pestilent fellow, he brought up Horace giving the Poets a pill, but our fellow Shakespeare hath given him a purge that made him beray his credit.

Much time has been spent on speculation as to which of 'Shakespeare's' plays served as a purge to Jonson. The facts are that the Cambridge authors, knowing not the real author, sup-

---

[1] See *The Children of the Chapel*, 1908.

posed that Shakespeare wrote *Satiromastix* because it was played by the Chamberlain company at the Globe. As is evident from the Epilogue to Jonson's *Poetaster*, addressed to 'the reader', it was *Satiormastix* which caused him to 'beray his credit'.

This is a striking example of how the Globe plays came to be credited to Shakespeare. Had *Satiromastix* been published anonymously all the critics would have proclaimed it most positively as by Shakespeare. That the various actors, including Shakespeare, should have turned to Dekker as their paladin reveals at once the relative merit of these two men, even in the eyes of Shakespeare's own company.

From the evidence above it would seem that Dekker wrote little for the stage after 1605. He began writing pamphlets in 1606, and, except for pageants, wrote little else during the rest of his life. The retirement of Alleyn and the death of Chettle turned him from the stage.

Despite the fact that so many of Dekker's plays were rewritten by minor men there is sufficient material from which to gain a perfect idea of his aims and methods. There is no excess of vulgarity in any of his own work. What coarseness appears in the later revisions by Middleton, Ford, &c., is due entirely to them. The man who wrote *The Shoemaker's Holiday*, *Fortunatus*, *The Jew of Venice*, who created or re-created Friscobaldo, Portia, Desdemona, Candido, and good old Simon Eyre, had a pure mind as well as a warm heart.

A bit of purely Dekkerian work from *The Spanish Moor's Tragedy* [*Othello*] is Othello's relation of how he wooed Desdemona:
                              I did consent,
And often did beguile her of her teares,
When I did speake of some distressed stroake
That my youth suffered: my story being done;
She gave me for my paines a world of sighs;
She swore ifaith twas strange, twas passing strange;
Twas pittifull, twas wondrous pittifull;
She wisht she had not heard it, yet she wisht
That Heaven had made her such a man, &c.

Shakespeare changed 'sighs' to 'kisses'. No one but Dekker ever conceived a character like Desdemona. This old Quarto lacks a few lines, left out by the printer, which can be found, *sans* Shakespeare, in the Quarto of 1635.

Portia's 'quality of mercy' speech in *The Jew* [*Merchant*] *of Venice*, though built on thoughts by Chettle, is truly Dekkerian. It is cast in the same vein as Candido's speech on Patience in *The Honest Whore*.

> *Portia.* The quality of mercy is not strain'd,
> It droppeth as the gentle raine from heaven
> Upon the place beneath: It is twice blest,
> It blesseth him that gives, and him that takes,
> Tis mightest in the mightest, it becomes
> The throned monarch better then his crowne.
> .   .   .   .   .   .
> It is enthroned in the hearts of kings,
> It is an attribute to God himselfe;
> And earthly power doth then shew likest Gods,
> When mercy seasons justice, &c.

> *Candido.* Patience, my Lord! Why, tis the soul of peace;
> Of all the virtues, 'tis nearest kin to Heaven.
> It makes men look like gods. The best of men
> That e'er wore earth about him was a sufferer,
> A soft, meek, patient, humble, tranquil spirit,
> The first true gentleman that ever breathed.
> .   .   .   .   .   .
> Tis the perpetual prisoner's liberty,
> His walks and orchards. Tis the bond-slave's freedom,
> And makes him seem proud of each iron chain,
> As though he wore it more for state than pain:
> It is the beggar's music, and thus sings;
> Although their bodies beg, their souls are kings.
> O my dread Liege, it is the sap of bliss
> Rears us aloft, makes men and angels kiss;
> And last of all, to end a household strife,
> It is the honey 'gainst a waspish wife.

Other such passages can be found scattered throughout Dekker's known plays.

Dekker moralizes upon his text rather than philosophizes over related ideas. His rhythm is smooth, and his ideas simple, direct, almost obvious, his figures being derived from the main idea. They usually add a quality, seldom introduce a new concept.

In all these plays Dekker uses the same uneven, expressive rhythm, for which he was twitted in *The Poetaster*; at less serious moments he uses rhymed couplets in a peculiarly happy manner; at times he indulges in rare songs, rare beyond words. However, that for which Dekker stands alone is sympathetic character delineation. This especially holds of his women. His broken, hesitating rhythm is peculiarly adapted to the expression of their emotion. It in itself is pathetic, compassionate, exactly suited to his temperament. Had Dekker not been the staunchest of optimists his work might have become maudlin; as it was his robust courage and cheerful gaiety were but softened to an added grace, a feminine charm.

Dekker's Comedy.

Dekker's comedy resembles Lyly's in being almost entirely conversational. His characters, however, are not only courtiers and pages, but honest tradesmen, their wives, apprentices, and servants as well. The fun arises almost entirely from what they say, rarely from what they do.

Dekker's workaday people are a rollicking, exuberant, mad, merry crew, abounding in piquant phrases and comparisons, quaint paragrams, and trenchant observations on life and their fellows, full of rational common sense, ever pricking the bubble of pretentiousness, destroying shams, unveiling vices. A great part of the laughter is caused by the unexpected incongruous terms applied to ordinary qualities and objects or events in such manner as to create a species of caricature. For example, when Simon Eyre in *The Shoemaker's Holiday* is elected shrieve:

(Firk enters running.)

Firk: O Hodge, O mistress! Hodge, heave up thine ears; mistress, smug up your looks; on with your best apparel; my master is chosen, my master is called, nay, condemned by the cry of the county to be sheriff of the city for this famous year now to come. And time now being, a great many men in black gowns were asked for their voices and their hands, and my master had all their fists about his ears presently, and they cried 'Ay, ay, ay, ay!' and so I came away.

In his Court comedies Dekker passes into another realm, and although his method remains the same he assumes a different manner. The one world is realistic, materialistic; the other poetic, romantic. They express the two sides of his lovable nature, even as he expressed the two sides of the Elizabethan era—the one practical, materialistic; the other romantic and idealistic. The English race is still possessed of these two sides to its nature. At times one, at times the other, side dominates; rarely are the two found in balanced conjunction as in Queen Elizabeth and Thomas Dekker.

Dekker's historians have taken but slight notice of his Court comedies; yet to them he devoted a considerable part of his energies, and they contain some of his finest thoughts. The following example is from *Fortunatus*, played at Court during the Christmas season of 1599–1600:

> *Orleans*: But is't not a miserable tyranny, to see a lady triumph in the passions of a soul languishing through her cruelty?
> *Cyprus*: Methinks it is.
> *Galloway*: Methinks 'tis more than tyranny.
> *Princess Agripyne*: So think not I; for as there is no reason to hate any that love us, so it were madness to love all that do not hate us. Women are created beautiful only because men should woo them; for 'twere miserable tyranny to enjoin poor women to woo men: I would not hear of a woman in love, for my father's Kingdom.
> *Cyprus*: I never heard of any woman that hated love.
> *Agripyne*: Nor I. But we had all rather die than confess we love. Our glory is to hear men sigh whilst we smile, to kill them with a frown, to strike them dead with a sharp eye, to make you this day wear a feather and tomorrow a sick nightcap. O, why this is rare! There's a certain deity in this, when a lady by the magic of her looks can turn a man into twenty shapes.

Orleans: Sweet friend, she speaks this but to torture me.

Galloway: Ile teach thee how to plague her: love her not.

Agripyne: Poor Orleans.... I pray thee, sweet prisoner, entreat Lord Longaville to come to me presently.

Orleans: I will, and esteem myself more than happy that you will employ me.

.   .   .   .   .   .

Agripyne: Ah, how glad is he to obey! And how proud am I to command in this empire of affection. . . . Is't not a gallant victory for me to subdue my father's enemy with a look? Prince of Cyprus, you were best take heed, how you encounter an English lady.

Cyprus: God bless me from loving any of you, if all be so cruel.

Agripyne: God bless me from suffering you to love me, if you be not so formable.

Cyprus: Will you command me any service, as you have done Orleans?

Agripyne: No other service but this, that as Orleans you love me, for no other reason, but that I may torment you.

Cyprus: I will—conditionally—that in all company I may call you my tormentor.

Agripyne: You may—conditionally—that you never beg for mercy. Come, my Lord Galloway.

Galloway: Come, sweet madam.   [*The two depart.*]

This is sprightly and wondrously mellow.

Julia in *Patient Grissill* is another such English maiden, almost identical in character. Dekker took Greene's place as the Homer of women. Among all dramatists he stands supreme as the delineator of the ways of piquant and charming women.

Julia: Oh, for a drum to summon all my lovers, my suiters, my servants together!

Farneze: I appeare, sweet mistresse without summons.

Onophrio: So does Onophrio.

Urcenze: So does Urcenze.

.   .   .   .

Farneze: Well, mistress, wee appeare without drumming. What's your parley? And yet not so; your eyes are the drums that summons us.

Urcenze: And your beauty the colours we fight under.

Onophrio: And the touch of your soft hand armes us at all

pointes with devotion to serve you, desire to obey you, and vowes to love you.

Julia: Nay then, in faith, make me all souldier: mine eyes a drum, my beautie your colours, and my hand your armour. What becomes of the rest?

Far.: It becomes us to rest, before we come to the rest. Yet for a neede we could turne you into an armourie, as for example: your lips, let me see. . . . Oh yes; if you charge them to shoote out unkinde language to us that stand at your mercie, they are two culverins to destroy us.

Julia: That Ile try: my tongue shall give fire to my words presently.

All: Oh, be more mercifull, faire Julia!

Julia: Not I. Would you have mee pitie you and punish my selfe? Would you wish me to love? when love is so full of hate? How unlovely is love! How bitter, how full of blemishes!

. . . .

Julia: I charge you neither to sigh for love, nor speake of love, nor frowne for hate. If you sigh Ile mocke you; if you speake Ile stop mine eares; if you frowne Ile bend my fist.

Far.: Then you'le turne warrior in deede, &c.

Dekker as a Play-builder.

Dekker's comedy characters are as a rule well individualized. They are amusing, but they do not create comic action. Comic action, based upon the peculiarities of character, or arising from the interactions of the peculiarities of several characters, was beyond his unassisted power. This is well evinced in *The Honest Whore*. Therein Roger is laughter-provoking, but the transparent jokes practised upon Candid, the honest man, are neither dramatic nor comical.

Given a character as Horace in *The Untrussing of the Humorous Poet* Dekker could make him absurd, incongruous, mirth-provoking. However, the comic situations in which Horace is placed were certainly created by Marston. This also holds true of all the plays which Dekker either dressed or rewrote.

Plays still extant which Dekker may have plotted himself are *The Sun's Darling* [*Phaeton*], *The Shoemaker's Holiday*,

Fortunatus [a revision], *Truth's Supplication to Candlelight* [*The Whore of Babylon*], and *If This is not a Good Play the Devill is in it*. All of these except the *Shoemaker's Holiday* and *Phaeton* are moral interludes built in the simplest fashion. *Phaeton* is an allegorical interlude with a strong moral bias. Its plot is also simple, consisting of the courtship of the Sun's Darling by the four seasons. *The Shoemaker's Holiday* shapes better than the interludes. It contains at least the simple story of the temptation of Jane while her husband is away in the French wars. Dekker's plots are as transparent as his verse. While as a poet, a dresser of plays, a sympathetic delineator of female character, he far outranks his immediate associates, his place as a play-builder is almost at the bottom of the list. Some critics have condemned him because his plays were loosely constructed. It is not given to one man to be great in all things.

APPENDIX

The Taming of the Shrew.

A garbled version of *The Taming of A Shrew* was entered in the Stationers' Register on May 2, 1594, and was printed by Peter Short that same year, and again in 1596 'as it was sundrie times acted by the Right honorable the Earle of Pembroke his men'.

Henslowe records one performance of 'The Tamyng of A Shrowe' by the Strange (or Admiral's) men as an old play on June 11, 1594. As Short had already entered the garbled Pembroke version, and as he never included the Strange (or Admiral) company in either of his title-pages, it must be presumed that his version was not the one used by the Strange (or Admiral's) men.

Hitherto it has been assumed by the historians that *A Shrew* belonged to the Pembroke company and that Henslowe bought it from them for the single performance of June 11, the Pembroke company having in the meantime sold it a second time to Peter Short.

Since the Pembroke version, as printed, is a garbled version, it may be taken for granted that *A Shrew* originally belonged to either the Admiral's or Lord Strange's company, and that, as many another play, it was stolen from the owners by the Pembroke men some time before 1594, probably before the two companies went on tour early in 1593.

Evidences of garbled revision appear throughout the entire length of the Pembroke edition of *A Shrew*. The most noticeable mistakes arose from the Shakespearian method of connecting together two episodes containing similar material. The first of these rearrangements contains: the suggestion to Fernando [Petruchio] that he should marry Kate: his plan for wooing her: his proposal to her father: the father's consent: and then, without pause, the wooing of Kate. This forced the episode wherein she breaks her lute over the head of the music-master into a later scene. This episode thus lost all of its dramatic value. While these episodes are correctly arranged in *The Taming of the Shrew*, other episodes are wrongly placed in both versions.

The Shrew.

Some time after 1594 the correct version of *A Shrew*, owned by the Strange (or Admiral's) men, was rewritten into a new and longer play. This new play in turn was in part stolen, and, with the aid of parts of the Pembroke version of *A Shrew*, was compiled into the play now known as *The Taming of the Shrew*.

While the compiler of *The Shrew* made but slight use of the first part of the Pembroke version of *A Shrew*, he followed the latter part of it closely. In doing so he copied one of the false combinations of *A Shrew*.

In the correct, lost version of *The Shrew* the episodes in question must have been arranged as follows:

Episode 1.

Katherine is welcomed home by Petruchio. She gets no supper, is allowed no sleep. (She is untamed.)

Episode 2.

Hortensio forswears Bianca and departs to visit Petruchio. Tranio employs the Pedant to act the part of Lucentio's father, &c.

Episode 3.

The tailor episode. The gown is rejected, &c. Petruchio refuses to set out for the house of his father-in-law. He passes off stage. (Katherine is still untamed.)

Episode 4.

Katherine begs the servant for food. Petruchio and Hortensio enter with food. He demands thanks. Hortensio offers to eat with her. She thanks her husband and eats. The Tailor is recalled with the finery. They will go to her father's house. Hortensio departs in advance. (She is tamed.) The scene ends with:

> *Petruchio:* And now my honie Love,
> Will we returne unto thy Father's house,
> And revell it as bravely as the best,
> With silken coats and caps, and golden Rings,
> With Ruffes and Cuffes and Fardingales, and things:
> With Scarfes, and Fannes, and double change of brav'ry,
> With Amber Bracelets, Beades, and all this knav'ry.
> What hast thou din'd? The Tailor staies thy leasure,
> To decke thy bodie with his ruffling treasure.
>
> *(Enter Tailor.)*

Episode 5.

Lucentio is married, the Pedant having served as his father. Hortensio, having returned, decides to marry a widow and tame her as Petruchio has tamed Katherine.

Episode 6.

Petruchio and Katherine (tamed) are about to set out on the return journey. To them Lucentio's father. All set forth together.

It is evident that the tailor episode (3) should thus appear between the two food episodes, for in neither the first food episode (1) nor in the tailor episode (3) is Katherine tamed. It is as evident that the second food episode (4) should be the last of these three, as in it she is finally tamed, and Petruchio, pleased with her submission, then states 'The Tailor staies' (he had not gone far), and that they will go to her father's house in all finery, which plan, despite the text, is carried out in both *A Shrew* and *The Shrew*.

While in both of these plays the second food episode is made to precede the tailor episode, in *A Shrew* the two episodes are separated by the engagement of Lucentio and Bianca. In *The Shrew* the second food episode is followed immediately by the tailor episode. The last two lines of the second food episode— 'The Tailor staies'—were so suggestive that the compiler of *The Shrew* at once introduced the tailor episode.

Since Hortensio was present during the second food episode (4) it is evident that it belongs after the scene in which it is stated that he has gone to visit Petruchio. So also Hortensio's return and his decision to wed and tame the widow belong after Katherine has been tamed, and before she and Petruchio set forth on their return.

In both *A Shrew* and *The Shrew* these various episodes are badly disarranged. The false arrangement of many of these episodes in *The Shrew* arose mainly through a slavish copying of the sequence of events as found in the printed version of *A Shrew*.

Authorship.

The Pembroke edition of *A Shrew* is a garbled version of the lost play which belonged to either the Strange or Admiral company. It was compiled while Shakespeare was with the Pembroke company. The Folio edition of *The Shrew* is a second garbled version of a lost play which must have belonged to either Lord Worcester's or the Admiral's men, the only rival companies. It was compiled for the Chamberlain company while Shakespeare was one of its shareholders. Presumably Shakespeare compiled both of these extant plays.

The author of the lost Strange (or Admiral) version of *A Shrew* may remain for ever unknown. The light of his genius is but obscurely reflected in Shakespeare's compilation. Possibly it was Robert Greene. But he who rewrote that version into the lost version of *The Shrew* can be easily ascertained. External evidence appears in that Henslowe records the payment of £6 (from July 19 to September 22, 1602) in behalf of Lord Worcester's men (many of whom were originally Lord Strange's men) to Thomas Dekker for a play called *Medecine for a Curst Wife*. Internal evidence of Dekker's hand in *The Shrew* abounds on almost every page, despite the garbling.

Various writers have pointed out many Dekkerian words and phrases in *The Shrew*, but no one seems to have noted that the clever conversation of *The Shrew* is exactly that of Agripine and her suitors in Dekker's *Fortunatus*, and of the courtiers and Julia in his share of *Patient Grissill*.

The Pembroke version of *A Shrew* must have been written about 1593, after Shakespeare had written his version of *The True Tragedy . . . of Henry VI*, which, as *A Shrew*, was played by Lord Pembroke's men, and was also printed by Peter Short. In workmanship it greatly resembles Shakespeare's *True Tragedy*. *The Shrew* was written after Dekker had recast the original story in July–September, 1602. It must therefore be dated 1602 or later. In workmanship it greatly resembles Shakespeare's share of the revised *Hamlet*.

XV

HENRY CHETTLE

(Master Constructionist)

HENRY CHETTLE, born *c.* 1562, 'sonne of Robert Chettell late of London, Dier, Deceased', put himself apprentice to 'Thomas Easte citizen and Stationer . . . for vii years beginning Michalmas last paste', on September 29, 1577. On October 6, 1584, Chettle was admitted a freeman of the Stationers' Company, and in 1589 was sent to Cambridge by the company 'aboute the companyes affaires' (S. R.). He entered into partnership with J. Hoskins and John Danter in 1591, and signed himself 'Henry Chettle of London, Stationer' in Henslowe's Diary on October 22, 1598. Seemingly he kept up his connexion with the company until his death *c.* 1605.

Chettle's work as an actual printer must have ceased about 1596, when as a favour to Nash he 'squared and set . . . out in pages' *Have with you to Saffron Walden*. This appears from his letter written in defence of Nash, whom Gabriel Harvey had charged with abusing Marlowe, Greene, and Chettle. This very modest letter reads:

> I hold it no good manners (M. Nashe), beeing but an Artificer, to give D. Harvey the ly, though he have deserv'd it by publishing in Print,—you have done mee wrong, which privately I never found. Yet to confirme by my Art in deed, what his calling [i.e. Parson] forbids me to affirme in word, your booke being readie for the Presse, lle square & set it out in Pages, that shall page and lackey his infamie after him, at least while he lives if no longer.
>
> Your old compositer, Henry Chettle.

In a good printing-house the squaring and paging of a book is done by some one blessed with a keen sense of form, usually the head compositor. Chettle's promise to square and page Nash's book therefore hints that he was skilled in this ' Art '. His sense of artistic form may be gathered from the spacing of the print of *Have with you to Saffron Walden* (1596).

T. East, to whom Chettle was apprenticed, and Danter, with whom he formed a partnership, were among the most important publishers of the period. From their presses came many of the choice books of the Elizabethan age. So that while Chettle never attended either University he enjoyed that next best advantage, the association with all that was of worth in literature. At the same time he came into personal touch with all the great contemporary authors.

Chettle married early; there was at least one child, Mary, who died aged twelve on September 22, 1595. Dekker pictures Chettle's entry into the company of Marlowe, Peele, Greene, and Nash, after his death, as follows : ' In comes Chettle sweating and blowing by reason of his fatnes ; to welcome whom, because hee was of old acquaintance, all rose up,' &c. Among the quarrelling authors he was the peacemaker ; and was known as ' kind-hart ', which name he sometimes assumed in his writings. There must have been something of sterling worth about Henry Chettle, that, obscure printer's devil though he had been, he should have been taken up by this group of brilliant University men. When Greene and Marlowe had passed away Nash turned to Chettle and made of him a fast friend and boon companion. (See also NASH.)

By 1592 Chettle (aged 30) had risen to a place of consequence, not only in the publishing world, but in the world of letters. This same year he edited and printed Greene's *Groatsworth of Wit*, and wrote his pamphlet *Kind-hartes Dreame*, the introduction to which contains the well-known ' apology to Shakespeare '. It also contains the following lines, which illuminate his own career and methods : ' How I have, all the time of my conversing in printing, hindered the bitter inveying aginst schollers, it hath been very well known.' Farther on he states that he wrote this introduction ' as well to purge Master Nash of that he did not, as to justify what I did, and withal to confirm what Mr. Greene did '. He concludes: 'Had not the former reasons been, it [*Kind-hartes Dreame*] had come out without a father.'

Taken together these statements prove that in 1592 Chettle was a well-known author, although he wrote anonymously. They also force the inference that he continued writing anonymously. This inference is fully borne out in his *England's Mourning Garment*, published soon after the death of Queen Elizabeth in 1603, wherein a note to the reader states: 'I love as little as any man to come into print.' It is worthy of note that among all the authors of the period Chettle was almost the only one that lamented the death of England's greatest queen, and that did not hasten to flatter the new king.

But for Henslowe's Diary Chettle would have been unknown, save for the two pamphlets already mentioned and his short novel, *Piers Plainnes Seaven Yeres Prentiship*. This extreme reticence was due to innate modesty, and a dislike of controversy and enmity.

Piers Plainnes Seaven Yeres Prentiship was published by Chettle's partner, John Danter, in 1595. Seemingly no one has examined this little romance except Jusserand, who read at least some part of it, inserting a short quotation into his estimable volume on the English novel. It is printed in small, close, black-letter type which is not easily decipherable; perchance this explains why it has remained unread, unknown. The sole extant copy is in the Bodleian at Oxford.

Jusserand lightly dismisses *Piers Plainnes* as of little value. Had he puzzled out the entire text he might have arrived at a different conclusion. It is Chettle's only known novel; but through it he discovered that his true bent lay, not in the novel, but in drama.

The construction of *Piers Plainnes* is that of the drama. It is divided into three almost equal parts: (I) an introduction, (II) a central section devoted to the action which builds to a climax, and (III) a resolution.

In the introduction Piers appears as a shepherd from whom

Menalcas, his master, and Corydon, a neighbouring 'plough-swaine', demand his story. Piers consents. The story he relates is the drama of Hylenus, King of Thrace, the fortunes of his three children, and of Aeliana, Queen of Crete. Hylenus has two sons, the licentious Celinus and the virtuous Aemilius, and a daughter, Rhodope.

Celinus, having been disinherited, is persuaded by Admiral Celydon to depose his father and rule the kingdom. Hylenus, Aemilius, and Rhodope are seized and deported. Celinus becomes king and Celydon prime minister. The deported King, Prince, and Princess are landed severally in Crete, where the virgin Queen Aeliana rules, her uncle Rhegius being her protector. This young uncle is enamoured of his charge and endeavours to seduce her while hunting. She is rescued by Prince Aemilius and with him repairs to her palace. King Hylenus meanwhile has been discovered and is given a lodge 'at the forest edge', where he lives as a hermit. Rhodope was sold to some fisher-folk, who dwell by the sea at the far side of this same forest. Here ends the introduction.

The whole is treated as realistically as possible, following the motto found on the title-page, *Nuda Veritas*, for Chettle is the first of the realists. In order to give vraisemblance to this story Piers Plainnes recounts between episodes his personal history. He was apprenticed to Thrasilio, a Court jester, one dependent on the courtier Flavius, who took part in the uprising against King Hylenus. The jester sold 'Piers his yeres' to Flavius. Thus Piers was enabled to observe the rebellion and the ensuing exploits of the usurpers.

The introduction over, Piers and his companions refresh themselves preparatory to the second part of his story.

Part II, the action, opens in Thrace. Celinus as King leads a riotous life. Flavius, urged on by his 'baylie' Petrusio, also spends lavishly until he is bankrupt and forced to sell Piers to the broker Ulpian. In Crete Aeliana becomes enamoured of Aemilius; but the wicked uncle persists in his designs. King Hylenus remains in his cell. Rhodope lives as a fisher maiden. Admiral Celydon leads Celinus into excesses and plans to seize the throne. Each action is ready for its resolution: Part II ends. Piers and his companions then eat their midday meal.

Part III, the resolution, opens with Piers and the usurer, whose daughter, Ursula, accuses him of clipping gold. He is executed; his wealth is seized by Celinus. Piers is sold to the 'baylie' and with him eventually departs to a seaport, of which the 'baylie' has been appointed customs officer. Celinus and Admiral Celydon quarrel for Ulpian's gold. Celinus is overthrown and escapes to the seaport, where the 'baylie' endeavours to betray him. He kills the ' baylie' and with Piers escapes in an open boat. They are wrecked and cast ashore in Crete. Piers is rescued by the fisher-folk and Rhodope. Celinus, battered and torn, at the forest's edge, overhears a new plot by Rhegius against Aeliana. He is rescued by his hermit father and discloses the plot.

The leading characters now assemble at Aeliana's Court, where the resolution is completed. Piers, having found Court life too exciting, retires to a shepherd's life.

The resolution ended, Piers and Menalcas accept Corydon's invitation home to the evening meal. The sheep are folded and all depart.

Of each of his masters Piers sketches the character and environ-ment, clever little pictures, similar to those found in Dekker's pamphlets. Naturally these parts are much more real than those dealing with unknown Courts and kings.

Every character in the story is well motived and logically expanded through character interaction. The resolution takes place only when discordant characters have either annihilated one another or become harmonized. The plot is built and developed exactly as are Chettle's later creations, his plays. So exactly does this tale resemble his dramatic work in form that it might well have been one of his plays rewritten in novelette form. While it has much of Greene's romanticism and some of Nash's picaresqueness it is the first realistic story consistently built upon character and developed through character inter-action to be found in English literature.

Chettle sketches in the rich miser Ulpian and his spendthrift daughter as follows:

I was now made slave unto a mistres and a master, as farre different in nature as in yeares, he so miserable, that he could scarcely affoorde himselfe a meales meate: shee on the other side so delicate, that her curious taste could with no common diet be contented: small birds, in precious gellies concocted, were her ordinarie fare. Partridge was too grose, marie of a Pheasant (if intreated) shee would sometimes feed. . . .

For as in the Court were two Kings, so had we two commaunders: videlicet Ulpian my miserable master, and Ursula my lascivious mistres. Wonder not to heare, that riot should keepe house with wretchednes: for such is the pleasure of the heavens, that one iniquitie should consume another, commonly ill-getting fathers having loose spending children, verifying the olde approved proverbe ' Male a part male dilabuntur '. . . .

O miserable condition of covetous parents, and desperate resolution of riotous children: the first wearying out it selfe unmoderately to get: the last tiring out it selfe with insatiate desire to spend. . . .

Ulpian my master (whose sparing life not Niggardize herselfe can well expresse) albeit he used Ursula his daughter as a propertie to inthrall young Gentlemen, as hee had earst done Flavius: yet would grudge at anie money he parted with to maintaine her in fit estate, either for diet or apparell to entertain such, as in hope to bee heires to Ulpians treasure, dailye repaired to their destruction. She on the other side, I must needes say, (as such kinde creatures be) was kind harted inough, and when she could have met with his coffers, she was no lesse lavish of his bags, than loose of her behavior. For her part, shee was a right Anabaptist, all things were with her, and shee with everie one in common.

When first she thus attempted by pilfrie to breake into his ill purchase, and hee espied the decrease of his beloved crownes: Furie it selfe was not so furious. . . . marrie restitution could she not otherwise make, but with promise to cousen for him as manie Gentlemen as she might. For want of other securitie, he was glad to take her word for a bond, and for a month or two the case was wonderously altred, for while her woundes were healing, wee kept a long Lent. To describe our diet, were inough to fill all the Countrie with a dearth, &c.

Chettle was so dominated by his feeling for form that he could

scarce put pen to paper before he began grouping his ideas into com-
plementary sections. Even his prose tracts, *Kind-hartes Dreame*
and *England's Mourning Garment*, are arranged in sections.

Kind-hartes Dreame is divided into five parts: I is a message
from Antony Now-now to ballad singers; II is from Doctor
Burcot to quack-salvers; III is from Robert Greene to his enemies
and to his friend Thomas Nash; IV is from Tarleton to the
Puritans, who would do away with all plays and pleasures; V is
from William Cuckoe to all ' close Juglers '.

England's Mourning Garment opens with a shepherd's song,
followed by a brief history of Queen Elizabeth's ancestors.
Chettle then recounts the virtues of the dead queen, which he
divides into divine and moral. Of divine he treats of three:
Faith, Hope, and Charity. His sense of form forced upon him
the section ' Hope ', in which he had nothing to register. Of
moral virtues he includes five: Wisdom, Justice, Mercy, Temper-
ance, and Fortitude. His close is a funeral song by shepherds
which balances the opening song. The subject-matter of this
tract could have been exploited with greater ease and happier
results had it not been divided into set sections, none of which
permitted the inclusion of many ideas which might very well
have appeared in a funeral elegy on the great queen.

Chettle evinces his love of form in a minor way by constantly
making word-patterns, both in his verse and in his prose. Balanced
sentences, antithesis, alliteration, consonance, assonance, &c., were
in common use even before Lyly wrote *Euphues*. While many
authors regarded euphuistic paragraphs, full of cadenced repetition, as a new form of literary art, comparable to the sonnet,
Chettle used the various pattern-making devices merely as a
means to a larger end. Examples from his prose works follow.

From *Kind-hartes Dreame*.

> 'Faults there are in the professors as other men, this the greatest,
> —that divers of them beeing publike in everie ones eye, and talkt
> of in every vulgar mans mouth, see not how they are seene into,
> especially for their contempt, which makes them among most men
> contemptible.'

'So no purity of their impure profession can be equalled in imperfection, so impure is all, so vile, so daungerous.'

From *England's Mourning Garment* :

'For, saith he, the faults of Rulers (if any be faultie) are to be reprehended by them that can amend them.'

'Expert in nothing but ignorance.'

'Faith aboundantly shone in her, then yong, and lost not her brightnesse in her age.'

'And as she was ever constant in cherishing that faith wherein shee was from her infancie nourisht, so was shee faithful in her word with her people.'

'Men of much wealth and little conscience.'

Chettle's Known Plays.

When Chettle first began writing plays is not known. That it was some time before 1598 is proved by the fact that in that year Meres mentions him as one of the 'best for comedy'. This is the year in which Henslowe began recording payments to authors, giving usually the name of each play in which each author was concerned. The first Chettle record dates February 25, 1598; the play was *Robin Hood*, Part II, written in collaboration with Antony Munday.

Munday had sold Part I of *Robin Hood* to Henslowe in the beginning of February, for the 'mending' of which Chettle was paid ten shillings in November. It is evident from these entries that Chettle was already a master playwright, otherwise he would not have been employed to mend a play written by one whom Meres designated as 'our best plotter'.

From February, 1598, to May, 1603, according to Henslowe's record, Chettle had a hand in writing fifty-two plays, thus proving himself to have been the most prolific dramatist of the period. Nor does this include the whole of his activity, as part of Henslowe's record is missing, and there are periods during these seven years—one of six months—when Chettle did not write for Henslowe. That Henslowe looked upon Chettle as the leading dramatist of his group is evident, not only as he so often

employed him to recast and mend the work of the other dramatists, but because Chettle was the only dramatist to whom a re-
taining fee was paid.

Of all the plays in which Chettle had a hand historians have
discovered but four: the two plays on *Robin Hood* (1598),
Patient Grissill (1599), and *Hoffman* (1602). For ' mending
Robin Hood I' he received ten shillings. Five pounds was paid
for *Robin Hood*, Part II, one pound of which went directly to
Chettle, ten and later five shillings to Munday; how the remaining three pounds were divided is not recorded. For *Patient
Grissill* Chettle had one pound ' in earnest', when he planned
the play on October 16, 1599. The remaining nine pounds were
paid to Chettle, Dekker, and Haughton in December. Seemingly
this was a Chettle play with Dekker and Haughton additions.
For *Hoffman* Chettle received five shillings ' in earnest', and
probably part of two pounds ten shillings paid to Chettle and
Heywood for an unnamed play.

This ends the list of accredited Chettle plays; and were this
all that could be assigned to him it would somewhat justify the
comment: ' His career resolves itself into little more than a list
of titles and dates.' Having concluded that no idea of Chettle's
abilities could be gained from ' titles and dates', all save a few
biographers have passed him by in silence; and those few have
judged him from the one play *Hoffman*, which for some obscure
reason they assign to him in its entirety.

To these four accredited plays it is possible, to add one page
of manuscript to be found in *Sir Thomas More*, and, thanks to
Henslowe's Diary, *The Blind Beggar of Bednal Green*, written
by Chettle and Day late in May, 1600, and printed as by Day
in 1659.

Sir Thomas More is an old manuscript play originally written
by Antony Munday, preserved at the British Museum, reproduced in facsimile by John S. Farmer. As preserved it contains
a number of folio pages of alterations, additions, and revisions,
which are also in manuscript. Among these page 6 can be identi-

fied as in the handwriting of Henry Chettle (compare his hand-writing in Henslowe's Diary). This page was designed to take the place of two speeches which still appear in Munday's original.[1]

The Blind Beggar of Bednal Green was written between the 10th and the 26th of May, 1600, by Chettle and Day. Two further plays dealing with some of the characters of *The Blind Beggar* were written by Day and Haughton. They were the second part of the *Blind Beggar*, afterwards called *The Second Part of Tom Strowd* (January, 1601), and *The Third Part of Tom Strowd* (July, 1601). From Henslowe's record it seems that Chettle may have had a small share in Part III.

Neither of the 'Tom Strowd' plays could have included the 'Blind Beggar' himself, as his history was ended in Part I, which is the only one of the three parts that has survived. Unfortunately the extant copy of *The Blind Beggar* is badly garbled. Some of its episodes have been cut, some expanded, many displaced, while other episodes, which must have belonged originally to Part II and Part III of *Tom Strowd*, have been added. Despite the confusion almost all of those passages which tell the Blind Beggar's story can be accepted as parts of the original play. These therefore belong, some to Day, some to Chettle.

The Tragedy of Hoffman, or A Revenge for a Father, was printed in 1631 'as it hath bin divers times acted with great applause at the Phoenix in Drury-lane'. The Phoenix was from 1625 to 1637 the home of Lady Elizabeth's men, who were known as Queen Anne's men from 1603 until 1622, and as Lord Worcester's men before that period.

On the 29th of December, 1602, Chettle received '5 shillings' in part payment for a tragedy called 'Hawghman', this

---

[1] Other additions to this play are in the handwriting of Thomas Dekker. Still others (pages 8 *a*, 8 *b*, and *9*) have been assigned to Shakespeare. In all likelihood they are by Thomas Nash. If these assignments are correct the play must have been revised for the Strange company while it was at the Curtain, 1595-7.

' 5 shillings ' being charged against the Admiral's men ; yet the play later appears as a Worcester play. On the 17th of January following Henslowe paid to Chettle and Heywood, again for the Admiral's men, ' 20 shillings ' for an unnamed play. This account he then transferred to the debit of Lord Worcester's men. Probably this marks the cession of the play *Hoffman* to that company. This seems the more likely as traces of both Chettle and Heywood can be found in the extant version of *Hoffman*. The small sum of twenty-five shillings paid indicates that the payment was for a revision. The price of new plays had then risen to about eight pounds.

That *Hoffman* is a revision is indicated also in that throughout the later part of Act III and the beginning of Act IV Hoffman, when pretending to be Prince Otho, is called Prince Charles. His lines all bear the prefix Sarl, a misprint for Carl. Many of these ' Sarl ' lines display all of Antony Munday's peculiarities.[1] It would therefore seem that *Hoffman* was originally written by Munday and was rewritten into the extant version by Chettle and Heywood in 1602.

That Heywood had a share in the revision of *Hoffman* may be discovered by comparing various passages of it with *A Woman Killed with Kindness*, which he wrote two months after the revision of *Hoffman*.

Although no complete play by Chettle is to be found in this list it is possible, especially since the mannerisms of his collaborators can be discovered, to find various characteristics common to all the above plays which, strange to his associates, must be conceded as belonging to Henry Chettle.

---

[1] After having concluded that Munday was the original author of *Hoffman*, and having noted that the printer continually set up Sarl in place of Carl, I wondered if Munday's C might have resembled an S. Turning to the manuscript of his *Sir Thomas More* I discovered that he usually wrote capital C exactly as a script capital S : *cＳcＳ cＳcＳcＳ*. So far as I have been able to discover he is the only author of the period who wrote C in this peculiar manner.

Chettle's Collaborators.

JOHN DAY.

When John Day eventually found himself in such plays as *Humour out of Breath* and *The Parliament of Bees* his ability consisted in a dainty, witty handling of exceedingly animated figures for whom he contrived ever-changing entanglements and amusing escapades. As a medium he generally used rhymed couplets, rhymed so daintily, so easily, that the rhymes sound like happy accents marking the tempo of a joyous measure. There is no place in his plays for character work, for action of character upon character, for the development of plot through character, for anything serious or deep whatsoever.

Having become acquainted with Day in his later works it is not difficult to locate his share in *The Blind Beggar.* And having discovered his share therein at least a part of what remains must be assigned to Chettle. Care must be exercised not to include as Chettle's share various inserted 'Tom Strowd' episodes, such as the one containing the contest between Momford and Old Strowd in dropping angels, an evident addition. These additions were probably written by Haughton.

Day's share in this play, like a babbling brook, hurries and trips along, occasionally hesitating to form a swirl, never achieving a deep pool, always transparent. The scene between Old Momford (disguised as the Blind Beggar), his daughter Bess, and Young Playnsey, the villain of the piece, well displays Day's ability.

The Blind Beggar is in the garden; Bess enters in fright pursued by Playnsey:

> *Bess.* Father, dear father, succour me from shame, &c.

Playnsey enters:

> *Bess.* He comes!
> *B. Beggar.* Let him. Sit down, sit down I say.
> *Bess.* O how shall I escape reproach this day?
> *B. B.* Peace, heaven may give my byzon'd eyes their light,
> Stretching these crooked limbs straight and upright.
> *Playn.* Art thou fled hither? Thinkest thou his weak strength
> Can free thee? &c.

The Blind Beggar interposes :

> *B. B.* Oh, I am feeble, pray ye hurt me not,
> If it be true, as I have heard it told
> You married lately with Sir Robert's daughter.
>   *Play.* Father, I hate her, and she scorneth me,
> She pules, she sighs, she pines, she leaves her meat,
> She flies my bridal-bed, she bans, she raves
> That ere her father forc'd her to be mine.
>   *Bess.* Good sir, comfort her.
>   *Playn.* Comfort thou me, and I will comfort her.
>   *Bess.* I will not yield consent to such a sin.
> I scorn to be a Princes concubine.
>   *Playn.* Wilt thou be then my wife?
>   *Bess.*   No, I have sworn
> To dye as pure a maid as I was born.
>   *B. B.* How can she be your wife?
>   *Playn.*   My wife will die.
>   *B. B.* Tarry that time.
>   *Playn.*   All lingering I defie, &c.

The Blind Beggar must now depart to change his disguise into that of an old soldier :

>   *B. B.* Sir, I commit my daughter to your hands,
> But I beseech you woo her with fair words,
> She may without compulsion yield at last.
> I'll in and weep, for what can I do more?
> You're rich and strong, and I am week and poor, &c.
>   *Bess.* Oh me, do you forsake me!
>   *B. B.*   I a while I do.
> But Playnsey I'll anon be even with you. [*aside*]   [*Exit.*]
>   *Playn.* Now prettie Virgin how are you resolv'd?
>   *Bess.* I yield, yet though I yield I bend my knees,
> And ere my spotless Virgin shape I leese
> Let me delate the many miseries, &c.

The Blind Beggar in his second disguise rescues her. He also allows Playnsey to go free, in order that other adventures may follow.

THOMAS DEKKER. (See the foregoing chapter.)

WILLIAM HAUGHTON.

For his play *A Woman will have her Will* Henslowe paid Haughton in the spring of 1598. Although this was one year before *Patient Grissill* was written, his methods must have been similar to those used when he was writing his share in *Patient Grissill.*

A Woman will have her Will is full of intriguing action. It contains little poetic feeling. The thoughts are commonplace. Although the verse rhymes but seldom it is almost always end-stopped; lacking rhythm it has the feeling of rough-and-ready prose. The comedy is supplied by three foreigners and a native clown. The foreigners—Dutch, French, and Italian—speak each a different variety of broken English. Haughton seems to have made a special study of dialectical comedy. He uses explanatory monologues and asides. His strength lies in action, cause and effect being both sacrificed. The characters are set types; the three maids and their three English lovers are but slightly differentiated. The three foreigners differ only in that each speaks a different sort of broken English. There is nevertheless a certain unity in the play gained by the interaction, not of character, but of plot and counterplot. As a whole the play is solid, even heavy.

Example : Pisaro invites the three foreigners to dinner, that they may meet and court his daughters:

> *Pisaro.* A thousand welcomes friends: Monsieur Delion,
> Ten thousand Ben-venues unto your selfe,
> Signior Alvaro, Maister Vandalle:
> Proud am I that my roofe contains such Friends.
> Why Mall, Larentia, Math: Where be these Girls?
> *Enter the three sisters.*
> Lively, my Girles, and bid these strangers welcome;
> They are my friends, your friends, and our wel-wishers:
> You cannot tell what good you may have of them.
> Gods mee, why stirre you not? Harke in your eare,
> These be the men the choice of many millions
> That I your carefull Father have provided
> To be your Husbands: therefore bid them welcome.

Math. Nay by my troth, tis not the guise of maydes,
To give a slavering salute to men :
If these sweete youths have not the witte to doe it,
We have the honestie to let them stand.

The Dutchman. Gods sekerlin, dats un fra meskin, Monsieur
Delion dare de grote freister, dare wode ic zene, tis un fra
Daughter, dare hed ic so long lovde, dare heb my desire so
long gewest.

The Italian. Ah Venice, Roma, Italia, Francia, Angleterra,
not all dis orbe can shew so much belliza, veremanti de secunda
Madona, de hranda bewtie.

The Frenchman. Certes me dincke de mine, de peteta, de
little Angloise, de me Matresse Pisaro is un nette, un becues,
un fra, et un tendra Damosella.

An example of Haughton's prose comedy :

Anthony [a servant]. Why how now, Frisco; why laughest
thou so hartily ?

Frisco [the clown]. Laugh, M. Mouse : Laugh; ha, ha, ha !

Anthony. Laugh, why should I laugh ? or why art thou so
merry ?

Frisco. Oh maister Mouse, maister Mouse; it would make
any Mouse, Ratte, Catte, or Dogge laugh, to thinke what
sport we shall have at our house sone at night; . . . Now who
would thinke my Maister had such a monstrous plaguie witte.
Hee was glad as could be; out of all scotch and notch glad,
out of all count glad ! And so, sirra, he bid the three Uplandish
men come in their [the lovers'] steades and woe my young
Mistresses. Now it made mee so laugh to thinke how they will
be cosend, that I could not follow my Maister. But Ile follow
him; I know he is gone to the Taverne in his merry humor.
Now if you will keepe this as secret as I have hitherto, wee
shall have the bravest sport soone as can be. I must be gone;
say nothing.

THOMAS HEYWOOD.

Heywood's work in *A Woman killed with Kindness* is
theatrical rather than dramatic. Events therein happen suddenly
one after another, unmotived, melodramatic. Like many another
actor Heywood looked upon a drama as a thing, not of cause,
action, and effect, but of action and effect only. He therefore

was forced into using many asides in order to explain imminent action. Asides are the refuge of all dramatists who sacrifice, or who cannot indicate, cause. So also his characters suddenly change from one mood to another. They also are theatrical. An example of this is the electrical conversion of Sir Francis Acton, in *A Woman killed with Kindness*, from a hating villain to a loving saint when he essays to seduce Susan Mountford, the sister of his enemy. The passage reads:

> *Sir F.* Ha, ha! Now will I flout her poverty,
> Deride her fortunes, scoff her base estate;
> My very soul the name of Mountford hates.

(He is smitten by the maiden's eyes and starts back, exclaiming:)

> But stay, my heart! Oh what a look did fly
> To strike my soul through with thy piercing eye!

(Then follows a semi-aside in explanation.)

> I am enchanted; all my spirits are fled,
> And with one glance my envious spleen struck dead.
> *Susan.* Acton, that seeks our blood! [*She runs away.*]

A few of the best lines are :

> *Wendoll* [*aside, endeavouring to resist temptation*].
> I will not speak to wrong a gentleman
> Of that good estimation, my kind friend:
> I will not; Zounds! I will not. I may choose,
> And I will choose. Shall I be so misled,
> Or shall I purchase to my father's crest
> The motto of a villain? If I say
> I will not do it, what thing can enforce me?
> What can compel me? What sad destiny
> Hath such command upon my yielding thoughts?
> I will not—ha!

(Here the theatrical, sudden change of mood appears.)

> Some fury pricks me on.
> The swift fates drag me at their chariot wheel,
> And hurry me to mischief. Speak I must:
> Injure myself, wrong her, deceive my trust.

The lady quite reasonably asks him: ' Are you not well, sir?'
She then yields her virtue to him as suddenly and unreasonably
as he gives in to his theatrical passion.

This same sudden, unmotived theatricality appears in the
first scene of *Hoffman*. Prince Otho and his retainer Lorrique
have been cast ashore near the cell of Hoffman. Lorrique first
encounters Hoffman.

> *Hoffman.* Say didst thou serve the duke of Luningberge.
> *Lorrique.* His sonne Otho sir, I'me a poore follower of his;
> And my master is ayring of himselfe at your cell.

(How this servant knew the cell belonged to Hoffman is not
related.)

> *Hoffman.* Is he that scapt the wracke young Luningberg?
> *Lorrique.* I sir, the same sir, you are in the right sir.

After Hoffman has demanded, provided one had killed his
father would Lorrique be revenged, and Lorrique has answered
' Yes on the murtherer ', Hoffman rants on.

> *Hoffman.* On him, or anie man that is affied
> Has but one ounce of blood, of which hees part!
> He was my father. My hart still bleeds.
> Nor can my wounds be stopt till an incision
> I've made to bury my dead father in.

Here the sudden staginess begins:

> Therefore without protraction, sighing or excuses
> Sweare to be true, to ayd, assist me, not to stirre
> Or contradict me in any enterprise
> I shall now undertake, [now] or heareafter.

Without qualms or hesitation Lorrique assents, changing
masters from a prince to a madman. Thus a tool is gained with
little effort. Presumably in Munday's version Lorrique was told
who Hoffman's father had been. Heywood omitted all cause for
the clown's decision and hastened on to action. Lorrique swears,
and a few minutes afterwards is busy placing a ' burning crown '
upon the head of his late friend and patron.

This is but one of many passages rewritten by Heywood, all
of which are permeated with theatricality. Since *Hoffman* was

originally written by Munday and the revisions are chiefly by Heywood, Chettle could have had but a small share in this tragedy.

Although Heywood claims to have had 'a finger in two hundred plays', *A Woman killed with Kindness* is the only play which can unhesitatingly be ascribed to him. The other 'Heywood' plays were in all likelihood revisions. (See *Psyche and Cupid* and *Hercules*.)

ANTONY MUNDAY.

A part of Act I, scene i, of the first part of *Robin Hood* will serve as an illustration of Munday's style. Robin Hood confronts his enemies at his betrothal banquet.

> *Robin.* Sit downe faire Queen (the Prologues part is play'd;
> Marian hath told ye, what I bad her tell)
> Sit down Lord Sentloe, cousin Lacy sit:
> Sir Gilbert Broughton, yea, and Warman sit :
> Though you my steward be, yet for your gathering wit,
> I give you place: sit down, sit down, I say :
> Gods pity, sit. It must, it must be so,
> For you will sit, when I shall stand, I know.
>
> .   .   .   .   .   .
>
> Smile you, Queen Elinor? Laughst thou, Lord Sentloe?
> Lacy, lookst thou so blithe at my lament?
> Broughton, a smooth brow graceth your stern face ;
> And are you merry, Warman, at my moan?
> The Queen except, I do you all defy!
> You are a sort of fawning sycophants,
> That while the sun-shine of my greatness dur'd,
> Revelled out all my day for your delights ;
> And now ye see the black night of my woe
> O'ershade the beauty of my smiling good,
> You to my grief add grief; and are agreed
> With that false Prior, to reprieve my joys
> From execution of all happiness.
>
> .   .   .   .   .   .
>
>   Fell traitors, as you be,
> Avoid, or I will execute ye all,
> Ere any execution come to me! [*They run away.*]

Queen Elinor. No words to me, Earl Robert, ere you go?
Robin. Oh, to your highness? Yes; adieu, proud Queen;
Had not you been, thus poor I had not been.
Queen Elinor. Thou wrongst me Robert, Earl of Huntingdon.
And were it not for pity of this maid,
I would revenge the words that thou hast said.
             [*Exit Robin. Manet Queen Elinor and Maid Marian.*]
Marian. Add not, faire Queen, distress unto distress,
But, if you can, for pity make his less.
Queen Elinor. I can and will forget deserving hate,
And give him comfort in this woeful state.
Marian, I know Earl Robert's whole desire
Is to have thee with him from hence away;
And though I lov'd him dearly to this day,
Yet, since I see he dearlier loveth thee,
Thou shalt have all the furtherance I may.
Tell me, faire girl, and see thou truely tell,
Whether this night, to morrow, or next day,
There is no 'pointment for to meet thy love?
Marian. There is, this night there is; I will not lie,
And be it disappointed I shall die.
Queen Elinor. Alas, poore soul! My son, Prince John my
   son,
With several troops hath circuited the court,
This house, the city, that thou canst not scape.
Marian. I will away with death, though he be grim,
If they deny me to go hence with him, &c.

This is in Munday's best vein. It is a jigging vein, never rising
to any heights of serious emotion. In truth the more emotional
a passage becomes the more inconsequential Munday makes it.

Munday uses a few explanatory monologues, despite the fact
that he surpassed Day, Heywood, or Haughton, not in the plotting
of plays, but in the planning of interludes; for his dramas are
simple story-telling interludes. He also uses asides, a few of which
are legitimate, although the majority are explanatory. As he
merely tells a story in a series of episodes character work is non-
essential. His people are more or less real, usually historic per-
sonages, but their interactions are due, not to the effect of character acting on character, but to the fact that they happen to

participate in the same series of events. His lines are filled to measure, often with fiddle-faddle and froth, and are usually end-stopped. Good old 'Antony Balladino'! ('Tis Jonson's epithet.)

Chettle's share in the Foregoing Plays.

By sifting out those parts of each play which can be fixed upon as the work of his collaborators it is possible to obtain an approximate return which might be assigned to Henry Chettle. However, such a result, arrived at by separation, lacks positiveness. Positive evidence may be found first in Chettle's revision of a part of Munday's *Sir Thomas More.*

Munday's original version of the passages rewritten by Chettle is given in the foot-note.[1] Chettle used only the general idea con-

[1] Munday's original version. First speech :

Moore. Close them not then with teares, for that ostent,
gives a wett signall of your discontent.
If you will share my fortunes, comfort then.
an hundred smiles for one sighe : what, we are men.
Resigne wett passion to these weaker eyes,
which prooves their sexe, but grauntes nere more wise.
Lets now survaye our state : Heere sits my wife,
and deare esteemed issue, yonder stand
my looving Servaunts, now the difference
twixt those and these. Now you shall heare me speake,
like Moore in melanchollie. / I conceive, that Nature
hath sundrie mettalles, out of which she frames
us mortalles, eche in valuation
out prizing other. Of the finest stuffe,
the finest features come, the rest of earth,
receive base fortune even before their birthe.
Hence slaves have their creation and I thinke,
Nature provides content for the base minde,
under the whip, the burden and the toyle,
their lowe wrought bodies drudge in pacience.
As for the Prince, in all his sweet gorgde mawe,
and his ranck fleshe that sinfully renewes
the noones excesse in the nights daungerous surfeits,
what meanes or miserie from our birth dooth flowe,
Nature entitles to us, that we owe.
But we beeing subject to the rack of hate,
falling from happie life to bondage state

tained in Sir Thomas More's first speech, as well as the idea
contained in three lines near the end of the second speech. This
latter idea he finally rejected. His substitute for Munday's original
reads:

> *Moore.* Now will I speake like [a] man in melancholy
> For if greefes power could with her sharpest darts
> pierce my firme bosome ; heres sufficient cause
> to take my farewell of mirths hurtles lawes.
> Poore humbled Lady, thou that wert of late
> placde with the noblest women of the land
> Invited to their angell companies
> seeming a bright Starre in the Courtly Sphere,
> why shouldst thou like a widow sit thus low
> and all thy faire consorts moove from the clowds
> that overdreep thy beautie and thy worth
> Ile tell thee the true cause, the Court like heaven
> examines not the anger of the Prince
> and being more fraile composde of guilded earth
> shines upon them on whom the king doth shine
> smiles if he smile, declines if he decline
> Yet seeing both are mortall Court and king
> shed not one teare for any earthly thing
> For so God pardon me in my saddest hower
> thou hast no more occasion to lament,
> nor these, nor those, my exile from the court

having seene better dayes, now know the lack
of glorie, that once rearde eche high fed back.
But (you) that in your age did nere viewe better,
challendge not Fortune for your thriftlesse debter.

Latter part of Moore's second speech:

Pro haeris generosis servis gloriosum mori.
deare Gough, thou art my learned Secretarie,
you Mr. Catesbie Steward of my house,
the rest (like you) have had fayre time to growe
in Sun-shine of my fortunes. But I must tell ye,
Corruption is fled hence with eche mans office.
Bribes that make open traffick twixt the soule,
and netherland of Hell, deliver up
their guiltie homage to their second Lordes
then living thus untainted, you are well :
Trueth is no Pilot for the land of hell.

no nor this bodyes tortur werte imposde
as commonly disgraces of great men
are the forewarnings of a hastie death
than to behold me after many a toyle
honord with endlesse rest. Perchance the king
seeing the Court is full of vanitie
has pittie least our soules should be misled
and sends us to a life contemplative.
O happy banishment from worldly pride
when soules by private life are sanctifide
    Wife. O but I feare some plot against your life
    Moore. Why then tis thus; the king of his high grace
seeing my faithfull service to his state
intends to send me to the king of heaven
for a rich present: where my soule shall prove
a true remembrer of his majestie.
Come pre thee mourne not: the worst chance is death
and that brings endlesse joy for fickle breath./
    Wife. Ah but your children.
    Moore. Tush let them alone,
say they be stript from this poore painted cloth,
this outside of the earth; left houselesse, bare
they have mindes instructed how to gather more
there's no man thats ingenuous can be poore.
And therefore doo not weep my little ones
though you loose all the earth; keep your soules eeven
and you shall finde inheritance in heaven.
But for my servants theres my cheefest care
Come hether faithfull steward be not greevde
that in thy person I discharge both thee
and all thy other Fellow Officers
For my Great Master hath discharged mee.*

* A cancelled passage follows here:

    If thou by serving me hast suffred losse
    then benefit thy selfe by leaving mee.
    I hope thou hast not: for such times as theese
    bring gaine to Officers who ever leese
    Great Lords have onely name; but in the fall
    Lord Spend-alls Stuart's master gathers all
    But I suspect not thee admit thou hast
    Its good the servants save when Masters wast./

But you poore Gentlemen that had no place
t'inrich your selves but by loathd briberie
which I abhord, and never found you lovde
thinke when an oake fals underwood shrinkes downe
and yet may live though brusd, I pray ye strive
to shun my ruin for the ax is set
even at my root to fell me to the ground.
the best I can doo to prefer you all
with my meane store expect, for heaven can tell
that Moore loves all his followers more than well./

From the number of changes and corrections in the manuscript of this speech it is evident that Chettle wrote it without pause. Line 8 he first wrote 'seeming a bright Starre in the heaven of', &c.; he changed his conception, scratched 'heaven of', and wrote 'Courtly Sphere'. Line 22 he began 'no nor my mortall d', changed his conception, and wrote 'no nor this bodyes', &c. In line 36 he wrote 'if soules' and changed it into 'my soule'. In line 3 of More's third speech he wrote 'this outside of the earth; what have they', scratched 'what have they', and wrote 'left house-lesse, bare they have mindes', &c. He began line 10 of this speech with 'In you I', which he cancelled; and after line 13 wrote nine lines, all of which he crossed out. Various other minor changes were made. Evidently he wrote as he thought and changed his lines as his conceptions changed. Thus this passage furnishes an example of Chettle in the very act of creation.

There are various expressions in this revised page of *Sir Thomas More* which exhibit a mode of thought and construction peculiar to all of Chettle's work, by which his writings can be distinguished from those of almost all of his contemporaries. Such expressions are: ' mirths hurtles lawes '; ' The Court ... composde of guilded earth'; ' honord with endlesse rest'; 'this poore painted cloth, this outside of the earth'; ' loathd briberie.' These figures, tropes single and metaleptic, and synecdochical nouns or adjectives, are more concentrated than the ordinary similes and metaphors common to the generality of poets.

Day, Haughton, and Heywood, during the period in question,

seldom used any figures of speech ; Munday and Dekker both used them. Dekker's rare figures are as transparent as his verse and cannot easily be confused with Chettle's. Munday's figures are usually consciously conceived ; they also appear but rarely. A few of his best are : Of tears, ' Come breed not female children in your eyes.' Of the council table, ' Oh, serious square ! ' Ordinarily his figures are more obvious, as : ' France . . . having recovered the pale blood which Warre sluic'd forth,' 'Nor does the wanton tongue here screw itself into the ear that like a vise drinks up the iron instrument.' Leicester, speaking to Queen Elinor concerning her son John, remarks :

> Are you a mother ? Were you England's Queen ?
> Were Henry, Richard, Geoffrey your sons ?
> All sons but Richard, sun of all those sons ?
> And can you let this little meteor,
> This ignis fatuus, this same wandering fire,
> This goblin of the night, this brand, this spark,
> Seem, through a lanthorn, greater than he is ?
> By heaven, you do not well, by earth you do not !
> Chester, nor you, nor you Earl Salisbury ;
> Ye do not, no, ye do not what ye should.—*Robin Hood*, Part I.

Such figures, especially when they appear in Munday's bouncing verse, need not be mistaken for Chettle's.

While Chettle indulged in every known figure of speech, especially, as in the passages quoted above, in personification and parabolic philosophy, it is through the felicitous use of that most difficult though most concentrated of all figures of speech, the trope—the use of words in a sense different from that which they normally possess—that his share in any play can be most easily detected. Presumably it was through Nash that Chettle learned the value of forceful figures of speech. The two men differ in that the thoughts of Nash in their headlong, turbulent flight found expression in clever similes and metaphors, while those of Chettle converged and amalgamated into sententious tropes. Concentration is the soul of drama.

Chettle's Verse Form.

By applying both the positive and the negative methods to the dramas mentioned above it is not difficult to locate in each play various passages which certainly were written or strengthened by Henry Chettle.

Examples from *Patient Grissill*:
The Marquis opens the play with:

> Looke you so strang, my hearts, to see our limbes
> Thus suited in a hunter's livery?
> Oh, tis a lovely habite, when greene youth,
> Like to the flowry blossome of the Spring,
> Conformes his outward habite to his minde.
> Looke how yon one eyed wagoner of heaven, &c.
> .   .   .   Who gets a wife
> Must, like a huntsman, beate untrodden pathes
> To gaine the flying presence of his love.
> Looke how the yelping beagles spend their mouthes,
> So lovers doe their sighes; and as the deare
> Outstrips the active hound and oft turnes backe
> To note the angrie visage of her foe,
> Who, greedy to possesse so sweet a pray,
> Never gives over till he ceaze on her,
> So fares it with coy dames, who great with scorne
> [Shun] the care-pined hearts that sue to them;
> Yet on that feined flight, love conquering them,
> They cast an eye of longing backe againe,
> As who would say, 'be not dismaid with frownes,' &c.

The speech ends with:

> Lets ring a hunters peale, and in the eares
> Of our swift forest cittizens proclaime
> Defiance of their lightnes. Our sport done,
> The venson that we kill shall feast our bride.
> If she prove bad, Ile cast all blame on you;
> But if sweet peace succeede this amorous strife,
> Ile say my wit was best to choose a wife.

This is Chettle in one of his lighter moods. Grissill is somewhat more serious. When the Marquis is seemingly angry with her she beseeches:

> May I presume
> To touch the vaine of that sad discontent,
> Which swels upon my deare lord's angrie browe?

Again:

> Oh chide me not away.
> Your handmaid Grissill, with unvexed thoughts,
> And with an unrepining soule, will beare
> The burden of all sorrowes, of all woe,
> Before the smallest griefe should wound you so.

He complains of her eyes, 'they murder me', and she answers:

> Suffer me to part hence; Ile teare them out,
> Because they work such treason to my love.

He complains of her past poverty, of her present array:

> See, woman, heere hangs up thine auncestrie,
> The monuments of thy nobilitie.
> This is thy russet gentrie, coate and crest;
> Thy earthen honours I will never hide,
> Because this bridle shall pull in thy pride.

She replies:

> Poore Grissill is not proud of these attires;
> They are to me but as your liverie;
> And from your humble servant, when you please,
> You may take all this outside, which indeede
> Is none of Grissills: her best wealth is neede.
> Ile cast this gaynesse of, and be content
> To weare this russet braverie of my owne,
> For thats more warme than this. I shall looke olde
> No sooner in coarse freeze then cloth of golde.

The Marquis exclaims:

> O my Grissill,
> How dearely should I love thee;
> Yea, die to doe thee good, but that my subjects
> Upbraid me with thy birth, and call it base,
> And grieve to see thy father and thy brother
> Heav'de up to dignities.

Grissill answers:

> Oh, cast them downe,
> And send poore Grissill poorely home againe.
> High cedars fall, when lowe shrubs safe remaine.

This last idea appears in Chettle's part of *Sir Thomas More*, ' when an oake fals underwood shrinkes downe and yet may live '.

Father Janiculo is a patient philosopher:

> Come, Grissill, worke, sweete girle. Heere the warme sunne
> Will shine on us; and when his fires begin
> We'll coole our sweating browes in yonder shade.

Grissill would go inside to avoid men's eyes. He argues:

> Indeed, my childe, men's eyes do now-a-daies
> Quickly take fire at the least sparke of beauty;
> And if those flames be quencht by chaste Disdaine,
> Then their invenom'd tongues, alacke, doe strike
> To wound her fame whose beauty they did like.
>   *Grissill.* I will avoide their darts, and worke within.
>   *Janiculo.* Thou needst not: In a painted coate goes sin,
> And loves those that love Pride. None lookes on thee:
> Then keepe me companie. How much unlike
> Are thy desires to manie of thy sex!
> How manie wantons in Salivia
> Frowne like the sullen night, when their faire faces
> Are hid within doores; but, got once abroad,
> Like the proud sun they spread their staring beames:
> They shine out to be seene; their loose eyes tell
> That in their bosoms wantonnes doth dwell.

In another place he reproves his son, who has been railing because they were sent home from the Court:

> Peace, my sonne.
> I thought by learning thou hadst been made wise;
> But I perceive it puffeth up thy soule:
> Thou tak'st a pleasure to be counted just,
> And kicke against the faults of mighty men.
> Oh, tis in vaine! The earth may even as well
> Challenge the potter to be partiall
> For forming it to sundry offices.

Alas, the errour of ambitious fooles!
How fraile are all their thoughts, how faint, how weake!
Those that doe strive to justle with the great
Are certaine to be bruz'd, or soone to breake.
Come, come; mell with our osiers. Heere let 's rest;
This is olde homely home, and that 's still best.

While some of the above passages resemble Dekker's work, when Dekker is endeavouring to concentrate, they are cast in a different mould. None of them resembles Haughton's blank verse.

Further examples of Chettle's blank verse follow.

From *Hoffman*:

I doe not weare these sable ornaments
For Isabella's death, though she were deare,
Nor are my eyelids overflowne with teares
For Otho of Luningberg, wrackt in the Sound,
Though he were all my hope: but here's my care—
A witlesse foole must needs be Prussia's heire.

The scene between Lucibell and Lodowick seems to have been almost entirely written or rewritten by Chettle.

Lucibell. Noe; the cleare moone strowes silver in our path;
And with her moist eyes weepes a gentle dew
Upon the spotted pavement of the earth,
Which softens every flowre whereon I tread.
Besides, all travel in your company
Seemes but a walke made in a goodly bowre,
Where Loves faire mother strips her paramoure.
Lodowick. This is the chappell, and behold a banke
Cover'd with sleeping flowers that misse the Sunne.
Shall wee repose us till Mathias come?
Lucibell. The Hermit will soone bring him. Let 's sit downe.
Nature, or art, hath taught these boughs to spred
In manner of an arbour o're the bank.
Lodowick. No, they bow downe as vailes to shadow you:
And the fresh flowers, beguilèd by the light
Of your celestiall eyes, open their leaves
As when they entertaine the lord of day.
You bring them comfort like the Sunne in May, &c.

Lodowick. O breath-sweet touch! With what a heavenly
   charme
Doe your soft fingers my war-thoughts disarme, &c.
Pardon, chaste Queene of beauty; make me proude
To rest my toil'd head on your tender knee.
My chin with sleepe is to my bosome bow'd;
Faire, if you please, a little rest with mee, &c.

                                       [*He sleeps.*]

   Lucibell. By my troth, I am sleepy too. I cannot sing;
My heart is troubled with some heavy thing.
Rest on these violets, whilst I prepare
In thy soft slumbers to receive a share.
Blush not, chast Moone, to see a virgin lie
So neere a Prince; tis noe immodestie;
For when the thoughts are pure, noe time, noe place
Hath power to worke faire chastities disgrace.

Near the beginning of *The Blind Beggar of Bednal Green*
Duke Bedford accuses Momford of treachery:

Here's a large promise of ten thousand marks,
Your prise for Friday's work in yielding Guynes.
Know you this hand? Oh that on silver hairs,
After much honour won in flowring youth,
Should sit so huge a shame as on thine doth, &c.
These letters and the accidents succeeding
Condemn thee; and thou know'st by law of armes
Thou merit'st death with more than common torture;
But thy exceeding vallour, often tride,
Sets open Mercies gate, whose gentle hand
Leads thee from death, but leaves thee banishèd
From England, and the realms and provinces
Under protection of the English King, &c.
   Momford. Oh, miserable, miserable man!
Dishonour's abject, base reproache's scorn!
Why was mine age to this disaster born? &c.

Momford thus addressed one of his soldiers:

Wherefore stayest thou, my friend? Oh I know thee now.
Thou art not impudent; thou canst not begg;
Thou art a souldier, and thy wound-plow'd face
Hath every furrow fill'd with falling tears

That arms and honour should be thus disdain'd.
I have no gold to give thee but this chain;
I pray thee take it, friend; thou griev'st at me;
And I am griev'd thy want and wounds to see.

Old Strowd reproves his son for his prodigal attire:

Nay, Gentlemen, thus much I'll say for him:
Hee's a right Norfolk-man, mettle, all steel:
But I'll not have him use (t)his bravery.
The time has been when as a Norfolk yeoman
That might dispend 500 marks a year
Would wear such cloth as this sheeps russets gray;
And for my son shall be no president
To break those orders—Come off with this trash,
Your bought Gentility, that sits on thee
Like Peacock's feathers cock't upon a Raven.
Let true born Gentlemen wear gentries robes,
And Yeomen country seeming liveries, &c.
The sons discent's no better than her fathers.
Why should their cloathes be richer? I am as proud,
And think my self as gallant in this gray,
Having my table furnish't with good beef,
Norfolk temes bread, and country home bred drink,
As he that goeth in ratling taffity.
Let Gentlemen go gallant, what care I?
I was a Yeoman born, and so I'll dye.

Father Strowd must be related to Grissill. Certainly he was not created by John Day.

It is somewhat difficult to pick out passages by Chettle from *Robin Hood*. However, all passages of force or great seriousness may be denied Munday and attributed to Chettle. Such are:

Though muddy slaves, whose balladizing rhimes
With words unpolished shew their brutish thoughts,
Naming their maukins in each lustful line,
Let no celestial beauty look awry
When well-writ poems, couching her rich praise,
Are offer'd to her unstain'd virtuous eye:
For poetry's high-sprighted sons will rise
True beauty to all-wish'd eternity, &c.

When all these fields were walks for Rage and Fear;
(This howling like a head of hungry wolves,
That scudding like a herd of frighted deer);
When dust, arising like a coal-black fog,
From friend divided friend, joined foe to foe,
Yet neither those nor these could either know,
Till here and there, through large wide-mouthed wounds,
Proud Life, even in the glory of his heat,
Losing possession, belch'd forth streams of blood,
Whose spouts in falling made ten thousand drops
And with that purple shower the dust alaid:
At such a time, met I a trembling maid,
Seeming a dove from all her fellows parted.
Seen, known, and taken, unseen and unknown
To any other that did know us both,
At her entreats I sent her safely guided
To Dunmow abbey; and the guide, return'd,
Assures me she was gladfully receiv'd,
Pitied, and in his sight did take her oath.

Further forceful lines are those spoken by young Bruce, especially those delivered when he exposes the bodies of his mother and little brother in Act v :

Learn of thy love the Morning : She hath wept,
Shower upon shower of silver-dewy tears;
High trees, low plants, and pretty little flowers
Witness her woe. On them Her grief appears.
And as She drips on them, they do not let,
By drop and drop, their mother earth to wet.
See these hard stones, how fast small rivulets
Issue from them, though they seem issueless;
And wet-eyed woe on every thing is view'd
Save in thy face, that smil'st at my distress.
Oh, do not drink these tears thus greedily;
Yet let the morning's mourning-garment dwell
Upon the sad earth. Wilt thou not, thou churl?
Then surfeit with thy exhalations speedily;
For all Earth's venomous infecting worms
Have belch'd their several poisons on the fields,
Mixing their simples in thy compound draught, &c.

Rhymes appear here and there throughout almost all of Chettle's blank verse. His facility in the use of rhyme is well displayed in the shepherd's lament for the death of Queen Elizabeth, found near the beginning of *England's Mourning Garment* (1603):

Thenot. Collin, thou look'st as lagging as the day
 When the Sun setting toward his westerne bed,
 Shews, that like him, all glory must decay,
 And frolicke life, with murkie clowds ore-spred,
 Shall leave all earthly beautie mongst the dead;
 Such is the habite of thy new aray:
 Why art thou not preparde to welcome Maie,
 In whose cleere Moone thy younglings shall be fed
 With nights sweetes dewes, and open flowers of day?

Colin. I answere thee with ‘ woe and welaway ’.
 I am in sable clad
 Sith she cannot be had
 That me and mine did glad;
 There's all I'le say.

Thenot. Well-spoken Swaine, let me thy sorrowe ken.
 Rich soule, though wrong'd by idle Antike men,
 And driven by falshood to a clowdy den,
 Tell me thy griefe.

Colin. O it is past reliefe;
 And which is worst of worst,
 Bayards and beasts accurst,
 With grosest flattery nurst,
 Have sung her sacred name,
 And prais'd her to their shame,
 Who was our last and first.

Thenot. Deere Collin, doe not checke the humblest song.
 The will is ever maister of the worke.
 Those that can sing have done all Shepherds wrong,
 Like lozels in their cotages to lurke:
 The aire's the aire, though it be thicke and murke:
 If they to whom true Pastoralls belong,
 In needful layes,
 Use neither pipe nor tong,
 Shall none the vertuous raise?

Colin. Yes, those that merit Bayes,
Though teares restraine their layes,
Some weeping houres or dayes
Will find a time
To honor Honor still,
Not with a rural quil,
But with the soule of skil
To bless their rime.
Aye me! Why should I dote
On rimes, on songs, or note?
Confusion can best quote
Sacred Elizaes losse,
Whose praise doth grace al verse
That shal the same reherse.
No gold neede decke her herse;
To her al gold is drosse.

Chettle's verse is normally so well freighted with thought that at times it seems a trifle heavy. It has dignity, distinction, is serious, earnest, resolute, yet never becomes pompous, dull, or monotonous; it continually calls to mind the work of another thoughtful poet—Robert Browning. Though melodious, Chettle's verse differs from Dekker's, for it is seldom emotionally indicative. Yet, as Dekker's, it must be classed as free rhythm.

Chettle as Play Builder.

Another of Chettle's characteristics may be deduced from a comparison of the two parts of *Robin Hood.*[1] Part I is almost entirely by Munday. It is an enjoyable, old-fashioned interlude, written in rhymed couplets. Each episode was originally complete in itself; each was written around Robin Hood. A dozen more such episodes could have been added, or a number could have been taken away without damage, so slight is the plot. The characters are lay figures. There is no dramatic movement.

Robin Hood, Part II, begins as an interlude. Gradually a feeling of force contending against force creeps into the story; episode

[1] The *Robin Hood* plays were printed as: I. The Downfall of Robert, Earl of Huntington; II. The Death of Robert, Earl of Huntington.

fuses unconsciously into episode; the atmosphere and construction of the play changes; tragedy appears. The last half of Part II, after the death of Robin Hood, becomes a new play, which might well be entitled ' Maid Marion, her Tragedy '.

The two parts of *Robin Hood* epitomize the evolution of Elizabethan drama from romantic interlude to realistic tragedy. In Part II the conventional figures, introduced in Part I, gradually come to life; they grow, develop, and enact their tragedy.

With the characters the technique also changes. The old rhymed couplets of Part I diminish in number ; the stilted, well-measured rhythm gives way to a new species of dramatic speech-rhythm ; the episodes become fused in dramatic unity ; every line, speech, action, and scene becomes correlated; all is made mutually assistant and dependent. Thus to transform an old-fashioned interlude into a realistic drama was no light task ; to accomplish the feat successfully evinces true genius.

Patient Grissill, based upon an old moral interlude, also called *Patient Grissell,* by John Phillip (*1565*), was planned in October, 1599, when twenty shillings were paid 'in earneste'. Chettle then put it aside for other work until December 19th, after which date it was soon completed with the assistance of Dekker and Haughton.

When Chettle undertook to rewrite Phillip's old morality into a logical play, based on character, his first difficulty was to discover some reason for the Marquis's peculiar conduct. In the morality Politic Persuasion suggests that Grissell should be tried, after the manner of all godly persons, in order to prove whether or no she were truly submissive, meek, and patient. She was tried by her husband, even as Christians were daily tried by their Master.

Although Chettle accepted in part the premisses of Phillip, that Grissill's patience be tried, he nevertheless endeavoured to find a human basis for her husband's action :

' My bosom [is] burnt up with desires to try my Grissils patience.'

' Men, men, trie your wives ;
Love that abides sharpe tempests sweetly thrives.'

This latter denotes a longing for security, doubts of which naturally arise from such an ill-sorted marriage. The jealousy of his Court and subjects furnishes another basis. To his courtiers he remarks:

> 'I grieve to see you grieve that I have wrong'd my state by loving one whose baseness,' &c. A courtier replies: 'Your subjects doe repine at nothing more, then to beholde Janiculo, her father, and her base brother lifted up so high.'

The Marquis was also influenced by carping tongues. After the courtiers have departed he says:

> Begone then. Oh these times, these impious times!
> How swift is mischiefe! With what nimble feete
> Doth envy gallop to doe injury!
> They both confesse my Grissills innocence;
> They both admire her wondrous patience;
> Yet, in their malice, and to flatter me,
> Headlong they run to this impiety.
> Oh, whats this world but a confusèd throng
> Of fooles and mad men, crowding in a thrust
> To shoulder out the wise, trip downe the just!
> But I will try by selfe experience,
> And shun the vulgar sentence of the base.
> If I finde Grissill strong in patience
> These flatterers shall be wounded with disgrace, &c.

Had he not had absolute faith in Grissill, in his own judgement of her worth, he would never have risked the trial. The trial then is to confirm himself and to 'wound with disgrace' those who have opposed his choice.

As the trial progresses his pride in Grissill increases. Contrary to all seeming sense he thus derives pleasure from her pain. This he could not have done were it not that he knows she will reap her reward.

To humanize Grissill was an even more difficult problem. Yet this was accomplished by the simple process of making her closely akin to nature, and insisting that she is the property of her lord and master, that his word is law to her, that even her children belong solely and entirely to him. Once this point of view is accepted Grissill's conduct becomes logical.

The leading characters of Phillip's morality are Grissell, her father (Janicle), her mother, an uncle (Indigent Poverty), &c., and various personified abstractions: Fidence, Reason, Sobriety, Diligence (Chettle's Furio), Constancy, &c. Chettle dispensed with the mother, and in place of the uncle created a brother (Laureo) and a rustic (Babulo). These both serve to lighten the episodes in which Grissill appears at the home of her father.

There is no contrasting story in Phillip's morality. This Chettle corrected by introducing a shrewish woman and her fussy husband, and Julia and her suitors. Presumably he merely outlined their general place in the play, as Haughton supplied the contrasting Welsh couple, his specialty being dialect, while Dekker wrote the parts dealing with Julia and her suitors. The virile conception and consummate unity of the play belong to Chettle.

In this play he again brought automata to life; again discovered a motive for each action; and made each action so to influence each character as to cause further action. The people of this play are real, their actions, so far as the story will permit, natural; and all are interdependent. Ultimately they evolve a true drama. Chettle's hand may be discovered in the scenes which deal with the Marquis, Grissill, Furio, Mario, Lepido, and Grissill's home circle—Janiculo, Babulo, and Brother Laureo. Almost every passage by these characters bears Chettle's hall-mark—a concentrated figure of speech.

The Blind Beggar of Bednal Green tells the story of Lord Momford. When the play opens Momford is commander of the Pas de Calais in France while his daughter Elizabeth, affianced to Young Playnsey, has been left in the care of Robert Westford, her uncle. Westford plots with Young Playnsey to ruin Momford, seize his lands and goods, and marry Young Playnsey to his daughter Kate. Old Strowd, father of Tom, has a mortgage upon part of Momford's property. Of this Westford hopes and expects to cozen him. Through a forged letter Momford is disgraced in France, is proclaimed an exile from England, but is allowed to keep his lands and revenue. Here ends the introduction.

The action opens with Momford's return to England disguised, at first as an old soldier. He meets Young Playnsey and his father near Westford's home and follows them to the door. Scene ii opens with Westford urging his daughter Kate to agree to supplant her cousin Elizabeth as Playnsey's bride. Playnsey, his father, Momford, and Old Strowd enter to them. Playnsey refuses Bess Momford and agrees to marry Kate. Kate weeps and with Playnsey enters the house. Westford then turns on Bess, who has given her disguised father alms, and turns her from his door. Strowd [intervenes, quarrels with Westford, and agrees to fight their quarrel out privately on Bednal Green. In scene iii Young Strowd, Tom, is introduced with his servant, Swash. Tom is robbed of his fine cloak, when his father enters searching for him. Old Strowd is aghast at his son's remaining finery and exclaims, 'Is't possible my lands should maintain this attire! You Prodigal!' &c. He despoils Tom of his remaining finery, and when Tom is once more in honest 'sheeps russets gray' takes him away with him to Bednal Green. Several extraneous Tom Strowd episodes appear in the play, as printed, before this episode. They evidently do not belong in the story. Scene iv is on Bednal Green. Bess Momford, outcast, there meets her father, now disguised as a Blind Beggar. She leads him to a cottage on the edge of the Green. Westford and his nephew, Captain Westford, enter, to them the Strowds. Strowd and Old Westford dispatch their friends, then fight. Strowd runs Westford through and leaves him on the Green for dead. The Blind Beggar finds Westford and hides him in his cottage during his recovery. Strowd is arrested for murder. He orders Tom to 'work what means you can for my repreeve', while Swash is to hie to Chenford for one hundred pounds. During his recovery Westford confesses all his villainy to the Blind Beggar.

This is the impasse. The audience now knows well that all will be exposed in the end, hence can settle down to enjoy the comic mishaps during the unravelling of the plot. In serio-comic plays this turning-point, this assurance that all will be unravelled, should be as early in the action as is possible.

Swash is robbed on his return journey by the rascal Canbee and his associates, a moment before Tom arrives to help him. Canbee has also sold Tom a false reprieve. Tom hastens to return. Old Strowd is at the gallows. He is condemned, when Tom enters with the reprieve. It is found false, forged by Canbee. Strowd must hang. The Blind Beggar, Bess, and Westford enter. No murder has been committed. Strowd is saved. Tom swears to punish Canbee. Young Playnsey now falls in love with the Blind Beggar's daughter. Old Westford fears the Blind Beggar will disclose his villainy; together they plot the death of the Blind Beggar.

Tom and Swash discover Canbee and his fellows. They beat them, then pretend to turn rogues and join them. All are hired by Westford to kill the Blind Beggar. During the attempt Tom and Swash save the Beggar and his daughter. Old Playnsey, Old Strowd, and Captain Westford enter to stop the fighting. Tom discloses this new villainy. Momford, again disguised as a soldier, reveals Old Westford's confession. Challenges are given and accepted: Old Westford against Momford, Young Playnsey against Captain Westford, and Canbee against Tom Strowd. All appear before the King. They fight. Westford's side is beaten; he confesses. Momford discloses himself, and the King makes him Lord High Treasurer. Bess marries Captain Westford, who is made General ' of all our forces muster'd up 'gainst France '. The end.

While a comedy is somewhat less set in construction than a tragedy this play is a logical unit divided by a master's hand into introduction (cause), action, and effect (resolution). The characters are all well conceived and are consistently developed, and the action of the play is due to interaction of their idiosyncrasies. No character is superfluous; all assist in furthering the plot. The plotting of this play as well as the greater part of the character work is beyond the power of John Day. It therefore must be the work of Henry Chettle.

Since Dekker could delineate character, and Day and Haughton could fashion entangling intrigues full of animation and action, it is possible that the three working in conjunction might produce a play full of carefully delineated characters, a play in which discordant idiosyncrasies of character cause the action, and the elimination or harmonization of those discords brings about the resolution, a play of cause, action, and effect. Dekker could contribute some depth of thought, Day animated repartee, Haughton hullabaloo and action.

Fortunately one play written by these three exists in the First Quarto of *Othello*, originally called *The Spanish Moor's Tragedy*, written by Dekker, Day, and Haughton, for which they received £3 in part payment on February 13, 1600. As Chettle was at that time busy writing his *Damon and Pythias* it may be assumed that he did not assist his friends with this play.

The Spanish Moor's Tragedy [*Othello*] was founded on a tale contained in Cinthio's *Hecatommithi*. As the tale and the play run on almost parallel lines, the alterations made by Dekker, Day, and Haughton will demonstrate their abilities as play builders.

In Cinthio's story the villain is the Moor's Ensign. Having persuaded himself that any woman who could fall in love with a Moor might as easily become enamoured of an Ensign, he attempts to draw to himself the favour of Desdemona. He first becomes jealous of his Lieutenant, who is in the good graces of both the Moor and Desdemona, resolves to kill him, and then, if Desdemona still disdains him, to cause her ruin.

The most difficult problem to be solved when turning Cinthio's story into a play was how to dramatize the part of this villainous Ensign. He could have been treated, as in the old moralities, as the Devil's Advocate, who explains between each action his share therein; or he could be given an accomplice with whom he could plan his evil actions. The accomplice could have been one of Desdemona's kinsmen interested in freeing the family from possible heirs to the Moor, an enemy of the Moor who had been supplanted in command at Cyprus, or a villain introduced through a subsidiary plot.

When building the play Day and Haughton found that they needed some one to whom Iago could talk; and they took the most convenient object to hand, a gull with whose characteristics they were all familiar and who would serve as well the purposes of comedy. For the Ensign they created no new situations, but divided his original part between the gull (Roderigo) and the villain Iago. Roderigo is depicted as in love with Desdemona, while Iago plans the death of Cassio (the Lieutenant) and the ruin of Othello and his wife. Having given Roderigo the lover's portion a motive for Iago's villainies was lacking. This they supplied, somewhat lamely, by stating that Iago had hoped to be Othello's lieutenant and was supplanted by Cassio. This did not account for his desire to ruin Desdemona. A motive for this was not easily found. Iago hints once that he might take Othello's place in her affections; yet he plots her death. This was borrowed from Cinthio's tale. The only real reason for his action given by Day and Haughton is that Iago is so innately wicked that he plans Othello's discomfiture and Desdemona's death in order to satisfy his lust for crime. Having passed over Cinthio's cause and accepted his action, they perforce used a villain who committed crimes for no reasonable cause whatsoever.[1]

Although Roderigo is supposed to be in love with Desdemona he never once speaks to her. In fact, he comes into contact with no one throughout the entire play save Iago and Cassio. With Cassio he fights in the dark, and when he is dead Cassio states that he had never seen his face. He is a purely incidental figure, Iago's tool and foil. He is own cousin to Haughton's other gull, Emulo, in *Patient Grissill*.

In the story the Lieutenant is a typical military man of the time, unmarried, but having a home of his own, a frequenter of brothels. He is degraded by Othello, not for being drunk, &c., but for wounding a soldier who was on guard—a serious offence. He is wounded in the dark, not by Roderigo, but by the Ensign,

---

[1] Haughton uses the expression 'O mon Iago' in place of 'O the villain' several times in his part of *Patient Grissill*, written two months prior to *The Spanish Moor's Tragedy*.

who runs away and, returning with others, judges from the Lieutenant's wounds that he will die. In the play Cassio is made a bookish youth who knew only the theory of war. In Act 1 he is 'almost dambd in a faire wife'. This 'faire wife' then disappears, and the bookish Cassio is given a mistress and is made as well a frequenter of brothels. This 'mistress' in Cinthio's tale is a 'noted embroiderer' in the Lieutenant's household.

Desdemona and Othello remain as in the original story.

Certain other characters are introduced for stage purposes: Desdemona's father, the Duke, Senators, Officers, Montano (governor of Cyprus), Lodovico (cousin to Desdemona), and Gratiano, her uncle.

Once the play has opened the action follows Cinthio's story almost incident by incident until the arrival at Cyprus. In the story all shipped together. In the play they arrive in different ships. Desdemona arrives first, and while awaiting Othello indulges in some smart repartee, by Day, which is purely incidental. The ensuing drunken scene was substituted for the original episode in which the Lieutenant wounds the soldier on guard.

Again the play follows the story closely until the handkerchief is stolen. In the story Desdemona drops it in Iago's house when she picks up his child. He steals it, and later places it on the Lieutenant's bolster. The Lieutenant finds it, at once recognizes that it is Desdemona's, and goes to return it; but, as in the play, cannot gain access to her because Othello is in the way. He departs, and his 'embroiderer', seeing the handkerchief, wishes to copy its 'Moorish' design. While doing this she sits at an open window. The Ensign sees her with the handkerchief, and promptly brings Othello to witness that it is in the possession of the Lieutenant.

In the play Iago gets his wife to steal the handkerchief. This was done so that she might afterwards expose him. He leaves it in Cassio's chamber. Cassio fails to recognize it and gives it to his mistress Bianca, remarking, 'I like the worke well . . . I'de have it coppied'. Instead of being 'Moorish' it is now 'spotted with strawberries'. Bianca takes it and, escorted by Cassio, departs. Cassio returns, and while he is talking with Iago, over-watched by Othello, Bianca re-enters. Cassio exclaims :

> What doe you meane by this haunting of me ?
> *Bianca.* Let the Divel and his dam haunt you, what did you meane by that same handkercher you gave mee even now ? I was a fine foole to take it. I must take out the whole worke . . . there give it the hobby horse wheresoever you had it. Ile take out no worke on't.

Thus Othello is allowed to discover that the handkerchief is in the possession of Cassio. It is crudely managed, and is somewhat overdone for the sake of comic effect.

In order to cause his exit Cassio is made to run after his mistress, 'Shee'll raile i' the streete else'. The stage is thus cleared for Othello and Iago.

Once more the play follows the story until the finale. In the story the Ensign murders Desdemona in her bedchamber, the Moor looking on. They then tear down part of the house, which is old, and give out that the ceiling fell upon Desdemona while she was sleeping. The Moor then degrades the Ensign, who with Cassio returns to Venice, where he accuses the Moor of murdering his wife and attempting the life of the Lieutenant. The Moor refused to confess, was exiled, and later killed by Desdemona's kinsmen. The Ensign lived in wickedness and crime for some years, but eventually was punished. His wife then published the entire story.

Such an ending needed revision. In the play Othello kills Desdemona without thought of concealment. Naturally the first person to enter the bedroom discovers his guilt, and, being Iago's wife, exposes all the villainy. The denouement is therefore rather sudden.

Of the three parts of a properly constructed play—cause, action, and effect—this play consists almost entirely of action. The action builds to its impasse climax, when Othello kneels and swears to be revenged; it then begins over again as if no climax had been reached and builds to a new impasse climax, when Othello, having seen the handkerchief in Cassio's hand, exclaims:

'I will chop her into messes', and 'Get me some poison, Iago'.

This last climax is the impasse climax of the story. Until he has seen the handkerchief the Moor, though suspicious and jealous, is not convinced. The handkerchief episode convinces him. From that moment Desdemona's fate is sealed. The Moor no longer seeks for proof, though further proof is thrust upon him in Desdemona's sorrow for the Lieutenant's misfortune.

In the play, even after his second decision to kill Desdemona, Othello still seeks for proof. He questions Iago's wife, Emillia, then in a mad fit examines Desdemona. Emillia re-enters and defends her mistress. Othello departs. Iago enters and endeavours to calm them. This portion should have preceded Othello's resolution to kill Desdemona. It was probably designed to exhibit the Moor's 'melancholy', which in Cinthio's story took place before, not after, the Moor was convinced of his wife's guilt. Otherwise the denouement is well constructed.

From the above examination it appears that, given a good story, Dekker, Day, and Haughton, by following it closely, could obtain an interesting if not a well-constructed plot. As in the other plays by Day and Haughton the interest lies almost entirely in the action. It is a play of intrigue. The introduction is weak, the impasse climax indecisively indicated, and the resolution confused. In its large outlines the play is badly constructed and lacks form. The hand of Chettle was wanting.

If no other plays by Chettle existed, from those already mentioned a sufficiently clear idea of his work and methods could be gleaned. In them Chettle appears as the first dramatist to display action as the outcome of character, the first to create drama from the interaction of character. This is the important new element which he brought into Elizabethan drama. While Lear and Macbeth meet their ends, the one because he is old and foolish, the other because he is ambitious, both are manœuvred by outside forces; both are static characters impelled by fate. Interest in these plays, as in all the early plays of Lyly, Greene, Marlowe,

Peele, Lodge, Nash, and Kyd, centres in the external objective events of a varying fortune. Marlowe devoted two entire plays to Tamburlaine, yet his character remains undisclosed.

In all the plays of Chettle the interest lies in the internal struggles of humanity. Maid Marion, Grissill, and the Blind Beggar reveal their inmost thoughts and souls.

Character studies are but the basis of humanistic drama, the raw material. The dramatic action is due to the interaction of character upon character. Once the carefully studied characters are brought together the ensuing action should be a natural growth based upon the harmonies and discords of their individual idiosyncrasies. The end of each humanistic drama is a resolution, the discordant elements having been brought into harmony or annihilated. This is exactly the method followed by Chettle in the last part of *Robin Hood*, Part II, in *Patient Grissill*, and in *The Blind Beggar*; the same method is still used by all humanists.

The weakness of the majority of writers of this school is a lack of dramatic imagination. It is far easier to conceive characters than to imagine their possible and probable actions and inter-actions. To make realistically possible the sayings and doings of but a single character often proves too difficult a task for the imagination. It is this quality of structural imagination which differentiates Chettle from his associates and marks him a man of supreme genius. His people are perhaps not as happily lyrical as are those of Dekker, yet all words, thoughts, actions, and re-actions reciprocate harmoniously.

It is in the larger elements of drama that his inspiration particularly manifests itself—in the skilful introduction of the various characters, the dramatic counterbalancing of one against another, of group against group, the masterly building of the climax, and, when it has passed, the simple, sudden resolution and after-climax. In their large outlines *Patient Grissill* and *The Blind Beggar* are perfectly designed. If they are slightly disfigured by the decorations of a Haughton or a Day that was not the fault of the original designer.

Chettle's Comedy.

In 1598 Meres mentioned Chettle among 'the best Poets for Comedy'. As no plays by Chettle had been published he probably had little precise knowledge of Chettle's share in any particular play; however, he had heard that he wrote comedy. Before assigning to Chettle any of the comic episodes contained in the plays thus far under consideration it is well to summarize the abilities of his associates. Dekker's high-spirited wit and humour have been discussed in a previous chapter. Haughton's comedy contains much 'patter' and many comic situations. When he wrote *A Woman will have her Will* he still thought suggested nastiness was funny. Day also obtained his merriment greatly from situations. He was superior to Haughton in that he avoided nastiness, and, in place of coarse, heavy jests, used badinage and whimsical fancy. Heywood's comedy smacks of the theatre and is usually incidental. His characters are types who indulge in rather coarse wit. In *A Woman killed with Kindness* there is one of his incidental episodes by the servants, part of which reads:

Jack Slime. I come to dance not to quarrel. Come, what shall it be? 'Rogero'?

Nicholas Jenkins. 'Rogero', no; we will dance 'the beginning of the world'.

Sisly Milkpail. I love no dance so well as 'John come kiss me now'.

Nicholas. I that have ere now deserv'd a cushion call for the Cushion dance.

Roger Brickbat. For my part I like nothing so well as Tom Tyler.

Jenkin. No, we'll have 'the hunting of the Fox'.

Slime. The 'hay', the 'hay'! There's nothing like the 'hay'.

Nicholas. I have said, do say, and will say again——

Jenkin. Every man agree to have it as Nick says?

All. Content.

Nicholas. It hath been, it now is, and it shall be . . .

Sisly Milkpail. What Master Nicholas? What?

Nicholas. 'Put on your smock o' Monday', &c.

This is preliminary patter before the main business—a country-dance. Antony Munday's comedy consists mostly of enthusiastic buffoonery and burlesque. It lacks even droll situations, and, as the comedies of Day, Haughton, and Heywood, is not based on character.

Having already discovered Chettle's ability as a delineator of character, as one who makes action the outcome of character interaction, whose each plot is a natural growth based upon the discords and harmonies of individual idiosyncrasies, it may be presumed that his comic episodes will be, not incidental, but contributory, and will arise from the interacting idiosyncrasies of well-delineated characters. Such comedy was beyond the power of Haughton, Heywood, Day, Dekker, or Munday. If such comedy appears in any of the plays under consideration it must therefore be attributed to Henry Chettle.

In *Patient Grissill* there are several sorts of comedy. There is the boisterous quarrelling of Haughton's Welsh couple—rough-and-tumble action by types; there is the smart repartee of Julia and her courtly admirers, by Dekker, who also contributed some low comedy in which a group of rogues and beggars eat up the tarts, pasties, and meats of a banquet prepared for the Duke by Haughton's Welshman. Dekker has put character into Julia and the beggars; but the comical doings and sayings, the intrigue and repartee of the entire Dekker-Haughton group, remain almost entirely incidental to the central plot. Quite different is the comedy of that worthy individual Babulo. Neither Simon Eyre, Othello, Candid, Friscobaldo, nor any of Haughton's types, is so solidly constructed.

In all literature there is but one Babulo. Dekker's figures, although painted in charming colours, seem flat in comparison, for Babulo is not painted; he is as it were constructed. He is made of flesh and bone, has substantial legs and arms, and a moulded frame, a stiff neck, and a hard head; he is organic, individual. As neither Dekker nor Haughton has ever created such a figure, as he is not incidental but contributory to the plot, and as he appears only in the episodes written by Chettle, it must be presumed that he was formed and fashioned by Chettle's hand.

Tom Strowd in *The Blind Beggar of Bednal Green* is a second such cohesive comic character, organic, individual. He could not have been created by Day; therefore he also must be assigned to Henry Chettle. Unfortunately there are no further comedy characters by Chettle in the plays already mentioned; however, these two will serve to illustrate his manner and method.

It is impossible to give a complete idea of Babulo without quoting almost all of the main plot of *Patient Grissill*; yet some idea of his character may be gained from extracts. He first appears in Act I, scene ii:

> *Enter Janiculo, Grissil, and Babulo, with two baskets begun to be wrought.*
>
> *Babulo* [*to Janiculo*]. Olde master, heere's a morning able to make us worke tooth and naile (marrie, then we must have victualls): the sun hath plai'd boe peep in the element anie time these two houres, as I doe some mornings when you cal. 'What Babulo!' say you. 'Heere, Master', say I; and then this eye opens; yet don is the mouse—lie still. 'What Babulo!' sayes Grissil. 'Anone' say I; and then this eye lookes up; yet downe I snug againe. 'What Babulo!' say you againe, and then I start up, and see the Sunne, and then sneeze; and then shake mine eares; and then rise; and then get my breakfast; and then fal to worke, and then wash my hands; and by this time I am ready. Heer's your basket; and, Grissil, heer's yours.
>
> *Janiculo*. Fetch thine own, Babulo. Let's ply our busines.
>
> *Babulo*. God send me good lucke, master.
>
> *Grissill*. Why, Babulo, what's the matter?
>
> *Babulo*. God forgive mee; I think I shall not eate a peck of salt: I shall not live long, sure. I should be a rich man by right, for they never doe good deedes but when they see they must die; and I have now a monstrous stomache to worke, because [therefore] I think I shall not live long.

In a previous chapter it is stated that 'The most refined comedy is produced when a character reacts comically against himself', &c. This exactly applies to Babulo.

Babulo departs for firewood wherewith to fry fish for breakfast. While he is gone the Duke and his courtiers enter. Babulo returns hurriedly.

> *Babulo.* Master, I have made a good fire. Sirha Grissill, the fishe . . .
>
> *Janiculo.* Fall on thy knees, thou foole: see, heere's our Duke.
>
> *Babulo.* I have not offended him; therefore Ile not ducke and he were ten dukes. Ile kneel to none but God and my Prince.
>
> *Laureo.* This is thy Prince. Be silent, Babulo.
>
> *Babulo.* Silence is a virtue: marrie, 'tis a dumbe virtue. I love virtue that speaks, and has a long tongue like a bel-weather, to leade other vertues after. If he be a Prince, I hope hee is not Prince over my tongue. Snails! Wherefore come all these? Master, heere's not fish enough for us. Sirha Grissill, the fire burnes out.
>
> *Marquis.* Tell me, my love, what pleasant fellow is this?
>
> *Grissill.* My aged father's servant, my gracious lorde.
>
> *Babulo.* How, ' my love'! Master, a worde to the wise, *scillicet* me, ' my love'.
>
> . . . .
>
> *Marquis.* Babulo, Grissill, thy mistresse, now shall be my wife.
>
> *Babulo.* I think, sir, I am a fitter husband for her.
>
> *Marquis.* Why shouldst thou think? 1 wil make her rich.
>
> *Babulo.* That's al one, sir. Beggars are fit for beggars, gentle-folkes for gentlefolkes. I am afraid that this wonder of the rich loving the poor wil last but nine daies. . . . Are not you he that came speaking so to Grissill heere? Doe you remember how I knock't you once, for offering to have a licke at her lips?
>
> *Marquis.* I doe remember it, and for thy paines a golden recompence Ile give thee.
>
> *Babulo.* Why doe, and Ile knock you as often as you list.

When Grissill's father, Laureo, and Babulo are sent home from Court Babulo remarks:

> Great was the wisdome of that taylor that stitch't me in motley, for hee's a foole that leaves basket-making to turne courtier. I see my destiny dogs me: at first I was a foole, for I was born an innocent; then I was a traveller, and then a basket-maker, and then a courtier; and now I must turne basket-maker and foole againe: the one I am sworne to, but the foole I bestowe upon the world, for *stultorum plena sunt omnia,* adue, adue.

When in turn Grissill and her babes are sent home Babulo finds her:

Enter Babulo with a bundle of osiers in one arme and a childe in another ; Grissill after him with another childe.

Babulo. Hush, hush, hush, hush; and I daunce mine own childe, and I dance mine owne childe, &c. Ha, ha; Whoop, olde master; so ho, ho, looke heere! And I dance mine own childe, &c. Heere's sixteene pence a weeke and sixteene pence a weeke, eight groates, sope and candle. I met her in Osier Grove, crying 'hush, hush, hush, hush'. I thought it had been some beggar woman, because of her pitcher, for you know they beare such household stuffe to put drinke and porrage together. And I dance mine, &c.

. . . .

Janiculo. How now, my childe, are these thy pretty babes?
Babulo. And I dance myne owne child. Art thou there; art thou there?
Janiculo. Why art thou thus come home? Who sent thee hyther?
Grissill. It is the pleasure of my princely lord,
Who taking some offence to me unknowne,
Hath banish't me from care to quietnes.
Babulo. A fig for care! Olde master, but now olde graundsire, take this little Pope Innocent. Wee'll give over basket-making and turne nurses. She has unckled Laureo. It's no matter ; you shall goe make a fire. Grandsire, you shall dandle them. Grissill shall goe make pap; and Ile licke the skillet; but first Ile fetch a cradle. It's a signe 'tis not a deare yeare when they come by two at once. 'Heer's a couple', quoth Jacke dawe. Art thou there? Sing grandsire.

Soon he re-enters with a cradle.

Babulo. Come, where be the infidels? Heere's the cradle of security, and my pillow of idlenes for them, and their grandsire's cloake, not of hypocrisie, but honesty to cover them.
Janiculo. Lay them both softly downe. . . . Ile charme their eyes to take a sleepe by sweet tun'de lullabyes.
Golden slumbers kisse your eyes,
Smiles awake you when you rise.
Sleepe, pretty wantons; doe not cry, &c.

The picture would have been incomplete without the kindly cheer and philosophy of beloved, homeless Babulo. He is so much a part of Grissill's drama that without him her return home would have been unbearable, for her father is very old and her brother austere. When Furio enters and bears away her babes Babulo remains to mother her, watch over her, and lighten her sorrow with his shrewd observations and humane philosophy. For Babulo is a true philosopher; his entire life has been a living philosophy. The momentary accidents of his changing environment have neither warped nor puffed up his soul; he has always remained true to himself and has judged the world's trifles at their worth. When Furio orders them all to return to Court he is not angry, but tells Furio he is not playing the game:

> Good Furio, vanish: we have no appetite. Tell your master clownes are not for the court. We'll keepe court ourselves: for what doe courtiers but wee doe the like? You eate good cheere, and wee eate good bread and cheese; you drinke wine, and we strong beare; at night you are as hungry slaves as you were at noone—why, so are wee; you goe to bed; you can but sleepe—why, and so doe wee. In the morning you rise about eleven of the clocke—why, there we are your betters for wee are going before you; you weare silkes, and wee sheepeskinnes. Innocence carries it away in the world to come; and, therefore vanish, good Furio; torment us not, good my sweet Furio.

There is only one fault to be found in the treatment of Babulo: he does not appear in the final family reunion. Without Babulo this play would have failed, for of them all he best exemplifies 'patience' and 'sweet content'; yet in the finale he has been crowded out by the incidental Dekker-Haughton group.

The Blind Beggar of Bednal Green.

In the extant copy of *The Blind Beggar of Bednal Green* the comedy parts by Tom Strowd have been enlarged, amended, and garbled to such an extent that the original episodes are almost smothered. However, the episode wherein Swash is robbed by

Canbee of £100 seems to have escaped mutilation, although it is not entirely free from interpolation.

Enter Canbee disguised.

Canbee. This damb'd perpetual rogue Swash has kept me here in little ease of the bare ground, hungry, cold and comfortless, ever since two hours afore day. I am hungry for the hundred pound he brings, cold at my heart for fear he come without it, and comfortless least, if he have it, he comes with company; but *Lupus in fabula* here he comes; what, and alone! Excellent, the 100£ myne own then.

Enter Swash.

Swash. I discover none. The danger is past. I think I may with safety put up an honest weapon. [*He sheathes his sword.*] Thou terror to all theeves sleep there. My young Master promised to meet me. He stayes somewhat long; but he knows Swash is able to stand under the strokes of a dozen false slaves. Oh that I could meet with a theef now to try my valour.

Canbee. Stand, sirrah, and deliver!

Swash. O lord! Theeves, theeves; oh, oh!

Canbee. Peace, villain, or Ile cut out thy tongue and make a rasher of the coals on't. Deliver the mony.

Swash. Yes, good Mr. Theef, with all my heart. There 'tis; I am glad I had it for you.

Canbee. So am I too, sir. Come hold up; I must now bind you hand and foot for running after me.

Swash. I pray you do bind me hard. Do, good Mr. Theef; harder yet, sir.

Canbee. So; now farewell. Your mony goes with me, sir.

Swash. Farewell, kind Mr. Theef. [*Exit Canbee.*] O pox choke him for a slave. Theeves, theeves, theeves! Help, help, help!

Here there is an interpolation; then Tom enters.

Tom Strowd. Why, what's the matter, Swash? How came'st thou thus? Ha!

Swash. I am rob'd, master.

Tom. How rob'd? I hope not so, man!

Swash. Yes 'faith; there was six Theeves set upon me; I very manfully kill'd seven of the six and the rest carried away the mony, &c.

Canbee re-enters without disguise.

> *Canbee.* . . . What mr. Strowd and Swash. How comes this?
> *Tom.* Why Swash is rob'd, man.
> *Canbee.* Rob'd, I would I had been with thee, Swash.
> *Swash.* I, honest Mr. Canbee, and you had been with me I had scaped well enough then.

Canbee then gives Tom the forged reprieve.

Tom Strowd is a Norfolk man; and east-countrymen are supposed to be honest and shrewd if somewhat slow. Therefore when Tom catches Canbee and Canbee exclaims, ' Are you faln out with your father? Fall in with us helter skelter. You shall fare no worse than we do ', Tom hesitates: ' Man, what wouldst thou have me to turn Cony catcher?' Canbee answers: ' Oh sir, your only bravest life that can be.' Then Tom shrewdly considers that he may thus trap Canbee: ' I think it were not amiss: for I have seen wheat and barley grow amongst cockell and darnell and many an honest man keep knaves company.' He joins the thieves and by his honest shrewdness and courage brings them to justice.

Tom Strowd is an integral part of the plot. He is solidly built, and, although designedly inferior to Babulo in that he himself does not change his point of view, he belongs to the same general category.

It is to be noted that Chettle's comedy in the above two plays is never incidental as is that of Dekker, Day, and Haughton, nor does it contain Jonsonian patter. Sometimes it is the comedy of situation, but usually it is due to individual idiosyncrasies and is built upon character.[1]

---

[1] It has been noted in the chapter on ' Nash ' that when Chettle was forming his style he was in daily association with Thomas Nash. In his prose works, such as *The History of the Red Herring*, Nash constantly changes his point of view, thus creating comedy. In his plays this method is employed by melancholy Jacques of *As You Like It*.

Chettle's Philosophy.

The strong philosophical undercurrent which can be found in all of Chettle's plays often finds expression as well in his prose tracts. Examples:

From *Kind-hartes Dreame*:

'Everything hath in itself his virtue and his vice: from one selfe flower the bee and spider suck honny and poison.'

'Every simple hath his virtue, every disease his beginning: but the remedy resteth from the knowledge of the cause.'

From *England's Mourning Garment*:

'... for Humilitie is Charitie's sister. They are two twins borne at one time; and as they are borne together in any soul whatever, so doe they live and die together, the humble spirit being ever charitable and the charitable ever humble. For it is as impossible to have a proud man charitable as to reconcile fire and water.'

Of Queen Elizabeth:

'Shee came unto the crowne after her royall sister's death, like a fresh Spring even in the beginning of Winter, and brought us comfort as the cleare Sunne doth the storme-dressed marriners; shee left the crowne likewise in the Winter of her age and the beginning of our Spring, as if the Ruler of Heaven had ordained her coronation in our sharpest Winter to bring us happinesse and uncrowned her in our happiest Spring to leave us in more felicitie by her succeeder.'

From *Piers Plainnes*:

'But as in earth there is no perfection without some impediment, no beauty without her blemish, rust fretting the purest steel, canker the finest silver, so this nobleman,' &c. 'The gods of Fortune are as herself fickle. It is our virtues that in despite of Fortune will make us fortunate.' 'When Shame, companion of Sin, tainted his pale cheeks with vermilion colour.' 'Affection blindly judgeth, and will neither be by reason restrained nor by extremitie bridled.'

Whether philosophic calm induces fatness or fatness induces philosophic calm, certainly fat men, according to their ability, are usually philosophers. Chettle is a good example of this almost universal law. Philosophic calm almost always induces a wide outlook on life together with a strong sense of humour, another concomitant of fatness.

Catiline's Conspiracy.

During August, 1598, Robert Wilson and Chettle received '25 shillings in earnest' of a play called Catiline's Conspiracy. This was probably a revision of an older play on the same subject mentioned by Gosson. The Chettle-Wilson play was one of the anti-civil war plays which were so in vogue during the restless period of 1598-9, which culminated in the Essex conspiracy of February, 1600.

Ben Jonson was then collaborating with Chettle and others for the Admiral's men. In 1611 he brought out his Catiline his Conspiracy, in which passages by Chettle appear like patches of masonry in a Jonsonian fabrication of wattle and mud.

The Tragedy of Brutus: Julius Caesar.

In 1607 a play dealing with the life of Caesar called The Tragedie of Julius Caesar was printed as 'privately acted by the students of Trinity colledge in Oxford'. The title-page reads: The Tragedie of Caesar and Pompey or Caesar's Revenge. It was certainly originally written by Robert Greene about 1588, at which time he took his Oxford degree. This play tells the whole story of the struggle between Pompey and Caesar, of the murder of Caesar, and the death at Philippi of Cassius and Brutus.

On November 8, 1594, Henslowe records the first performance of a new play called Caesar and Pompey ('sesar & pompie'); and on June 18, 1595, he records another new play called 'The Second Part of Caesar' ('the 2 pte of sesore'). Seemingly this marks the revision of Greene's play into two parts, one dealing with Caesar and Pompey, the other with Caesar and the conspirators. While Part I was relatively successful Part II was a failure. It was staged but twice.

In September, 1598, Henslowe personally loaned Chettle
'34 shillings in earnest' of a play called 'Brute'. This was a
purely personal loan settled privately. The plot of this play
then lay incubating in Chettle's mind until October 12, when
Henslowe loaned 'the company' '10 shillings in earnest', later,
'£3 for the book,' and, finally, on October 22, '£2. 10s. in full':
total £6, which was given to Henry Chettle for his play called
'Brute', this being the then regular price for a new play. This
must have been a tragedy of *Brutus*. That it was the play now
known as *Julius Caesar* is evident from even a superficial
examination of the Folio text, which still contains lines showing
that it is a revision of the second part of the 'Caesar' play of
1595. In Act I, scene i, there is a reference to the first part
of *Caesar and Pompey*. Marcellus exclaims:

> O, you hard hearts, you cruell men of Rome,
> Knew you not Pompey? Many a time and oft
> Have you climb'd up to walles and battlements,
> To towres and windowes, yea, to chimney tops,
> Your infants in your armes, and there have sate
> The live-long day, with patient expectation,
> To see great Pompey passe the streets of Rome, &c.

He continues:

> And do you now put on your best attire?
> And do you now cull out a holiday?
> And do you now strew flowers in his way,
> That comes to triumph over Pompey's blood?

This passage, so suggestive of Drayton, is quite unnecessary
in the extant version of *Julius Caesar*; but it is so noticeable
a link connecting this play with the play on Pompey that the
conclusion must be drawn that it originally belonged to the
'Part II' which continued the story of Caesar and Pompey.

The Folio version of *Julius Caesar* exactly follows the history
of Brutus as found in Plutarch's *Lives*. There was no one of the
period, save Chettle, who could have conceived this play on
Brutus in its large outlines, who could have built such a consistent
structure about so mild a character.

There are many passages in *Julius Caesar* so suggestive of Drayton that the earlier failure of 1595 (*Caesar*, Part II) must be attributed in great part to him. In his *Barons' Wars* he made use of some of the ideas still to be found in Antony's last speech:

This was the noblest Roman of them all:

.   .   .   .   .

His life was gentle; and the elements
So mixed in him, that Nature might stand up
And say to all the world, This was a man!

This appears in Drayton's *Barons' Wars* as:

Such one he was (of him we boldly say)
In whose rich soul all sovereign powers did suit,
In whom in peace the elements all lay
So mixt, as none could sovereignty impute;
As all did govern, yet all did obey;
His lively temper was so absolute,
That' seemed, when heaven his model first began
In him it showed perfection in a man.

If Drayton's share in the 1595 Part II of *Caesar* were no better than this sample it should have failed. Drayton recast this passage in a later edition. It still remains poor in comparison with Chettle's celebrated encomium.

In his *Mirror of Martyrs*, 1601, Weever wrote:

The many-headed multitude were drawne
By Brutus' speech, that Caesar was ambitious;
When eloquent Mark Antonie had showne
His virtues, who but Brutus then was vicious?

This evidently refers to the extant *Julius Caesar*, showing that it was written before 1601.

On May 22, 1602, Henslowe paid Drayton, Munday, Webster, Middleton, and the rest, for a play called *Caesar's Fall* (or 'two shapes'). Nothing is known of this play. It may have treated of one of the later Caesars.

William Shakespeare also had something to do with a Julius

Caesar play. This is proved by Ben Jonson's comment in *Timber*:

> 'Many times he (Shakespeare) fell into those things, could not escape laughter, as when he said in person of Caesar, one speaking to him, "Caesar, thou dost me wrong." He replied, "Caesar did never wrong but with just cause."'

This passage does not occur in the Folio *Caesar*; but the line that gave it birth does there appear. It reads, 'Know, Caesar doth not wrong; nor without cause will he be satisfied.' Evidently the Folio version was the original which Shakespeare revised into a play now lost: having been lost, perchance in the Globe fire, the Folio editors substituted for it the original *Tragedy of Brutus* written by Chettle in September, 1598.

In this play of *Julius Caesar* Brutus will be at once recognized as the elder brother of the student Hamlet. The construction of the play is not up to Chettle's standard. Doubtless his share in the work consisted in Mark Antony's speech, the character of Brutus, and a general reconstruction of the plot. A great number of the less important speeches may be attributed to Drayton and his assistants. They are florid, and lack the dramatic intensity which is always to be found in Chettle's work.[1]

Chettle's play on Brutus has been confused with one called *Brute Greenshallde*, by Day. Henslowe had made the last payment to Day for his play before the end of July, 1598. As Chettle received his first payment in September of that year there can be no connexion between these two plays.

The Merry Wives of Windsor.

The Merry Wives of Windsor was based on an old play of *c.* 1592, presumably the *Jealous Comedy* or *The French Doctor* of Henslowe's Diary. This original contained all of the story except that part which deals with Falstaffe. The Falstaffe part was added before 1602, when the Folio version was written and

---

[1] Parts of *Julius Caesar* were shifted out of proper sequence by the Folio editors. For example, the Brutus-Messala episode of Act IV, scene ii, belongs at the beginning of the scene, not in the middle of it where it is now placed.

the First Quarto printed. Both of these versions are incomplete and are based on versions of the play which are lost.

On November 25, 1598, Henslowe records a new play by Chettle called *Tis no Deceit to deceive the Deceiver*. In the First Quarto of the *Merry Wives* this maxim is several times made use of. The title fits the play and it must have been the original of the Folio version. (For further discussion of this play see *Merry Wives of Windsor*, Part I, pp. 82–87.)

The construction of *The Merry Wives* is unmistakably Chettle's. Dame Quickly is a replica of the Nurse in *Romeo and Juliet*. Falstaffe is taken from *Henry V*, but he is here a new man. Chettle has developed the bare outline into a rich study of the egoistical glutton. Pistol, Bardolfe, and Nym are also introduced from *Henry V*.

In this connexion it must be noted that *Henry V*, in which Nym, Bardolfe, and Falstaffe appear, and which was rewritten from the old *Famous Victories of Henry the Fifth* for the Strange company in 1595, was in all likelihood a Nash-Chettle play. Nash was chief author for the Strange men at that time. Many lines of that play have the true ring of Chettle's verse, but the picaresque treatment of the subject is in the manner of Nash. It was afterwards rewritten. The original, somewhat garbled, exists in the Quarto of 1600. (See also NASH.)

Hamlet, Prince of Denmark.

The original tragedy of *Hamlet, Hamlet's Revenge*, by Kyd, belonged to, and was played by, the Pembroke company at the Theatre. In 1593–4 a copy of it was sold to the Strange-Chamberlain men, with whom it went to the Curtain in 1596. In all likelihood it was based on a Danish original and was brought from Denmark to England by William Kempe when he returned about 1588.[1]

[1] It is unlikely that Kyd could have worked up the play from the scant material to be found in Saxo Grammaticus or in the French translation thereof by Belleforest.

The first revision of Kyd's *Hamlet's Revenge,* i.e. the 'Corambis' *Hamlet,* must have been written some time between 1598 and 1600. The earliest references to this revision are:

Ben Jonson's *The Case is Altered* (late in 1599):

> *Angelo.* But first Ile play the ghost: Ile call him out.

The Wisdom of Dr. Dodypoll, played by Paules Boys either late in 1599 or early in 1600, printed in 1600:

> *Hamlet.* Let Wisdome answere: I aske what is a man?
> A pancake tost in Fortune's frying pan.
> *Doctor.* Vot flying pan? By garr I tink de foolish petit Jack is mad.

The reference is to Hamlet's last monologue, found only in the Second Quarto. This hit at *Hamlet* was probably in answer to the passage in the 'Corambis' *Hamlet* which refers to the Children companies. It also seems to hint that *Hamlet* was being played at the Fortune theatre.

As the company which acted the 'Corambis' *Hamlet* was travelling (see player's speech), and as it had presented the play in 'both Universities', it must have been on tour during the summer of 1599. Hence the first revision must be dated January–June, 1599.

While the 'Corambis' version of Hamlet's advice to the players is very caustic and seems aimed at Will Kempe, the later version is modified so as not to be offensively taken by him. Kempe belonged to the Shakespeare-Burbage company until 1599. Hence the 'Corambis' text must at that time have belonged to a rival company. Kempe left the Shakespeare-Burbage group and joined the Oxford-Worcester group, thenceforth called Lord Worcester's men, on or before March 10, 1602; and on July 7 of that year Chettle was paid 'xx shillings' in earnest 'of a tragedye called ... a danyshe tragedy'. Probably that was when the 'advise to players' was rewritten. Certainly the Globe playwrights had no reason to write the original censure of Kempe while he was still in their company or to rewrite it after he had deserted them.

At the commencement of the autumn season of 1602 the

Worcester company moved to the Rose theatre. Dekker, Chettle, and others had been writing for both the Admiral's men and the Worcester company, and now when Henslowe began financing both groups, he for a time mixed their accounts. On July 19 he recorded a payment to Dekker for *Medecine for a Curst Wife* for the Admiral's men, when, as is evident from later entries, the play was written for Worcester's men. On July 7 he records a payment 'in earnest' to Chettle for a 'danyshe tragedye'. No further mention is made of this work, although 'in earnest' usually indicated that more payments were to follow when the work was finished. He did not begin regularly recording payments made for the Worcester men until somewhat later, by which time the 'Danish Tragedy' must have been finished. Presumably, therefore, any further payments for this play were made before Henslowe began to book the Worcester accounts regularly. The only known Danish tragedy of this period is *Hamlet, Prince of Denmark*. Probably the above payment was in part for those additions to the 'Corambis' text which, obtained by a reporter late in 1602, were used by 'Shakespeare' for his greatly enlarged version, printed in 1604. That the greater part of the 'Corambis' *Hamlet* and much of the 'enlarged' version are by the same author cannot be disputed. The deduction seems to follow that the chief author of the 'Corambis' *Hamlet* and of parts of Shakespeare's enlarged version was Henry Chettle.

No author of the period, save Chettle, ever produced a plot so logically compact, in which the development depends so thoroughly upon character interaction. In this respect it surpasses *Romeo and Juliet*. No one save Chettle the master builder could have divided this play so dramatically into its three parts of introduction, action, and resolution. No one save he used such concentrated figures of speech. No other author indulged in similar speculative philosophy.[1]

[1] From the data in hand the history of the various Hamlet plays may be outlined as follows: Kyd's *Hamlet's Revenge* was written for Lord Pembroke's men before 1590. In 1593 when that company broke up it was sold to the Strange-Derby-Chamberlain company. For the younger members of this

Various writers have pointed out similarities between parts of *Hoffman* and *Hamlet*. These similarities occur only in Chettle's share of *Hoffman*, which contains echo after echo of the 'Corambis' *Hamlet*. Compare the mad speeches of Lucibella and Ofelia:

Enter Lucibella mad.

(to Roderick and Mathias)

> *Lucibella.* Oh, a sword! I pray you kill me not;
> For I am going to the rivers side
> To fetch white lillies and blew daffadils
> To sticke in Lodowicks bosome, where it bled,
> And in mine owne. My true love is not dead.
> Noe. Y'are deceiv'd in him. My father is;
> Reason he should [be], he made me run away;
> And Lodowick too, and you Mathias too.
> Alacke for woe, yet whata the remedy?
> We must run all awaye: yet all must dye.
> 'Tis soe, I wrought it in a sampler:
> 'Twas heart in hand, and true loves knots and words,
> All true stitch, by my troth: the posie thus:
> 'No flight, deare love, but death shall sever us.'
> Nor that did not neyther, &c.

One argues with another:

> Your selfe to kill your selfe were such a sinne
> As most divines hold deadly.

company, the Oxford-Worcester group, it was rewritten in 1598–9 by Henry Chettle, who therein made sport of Kempe's acting, Kempe being then a Chamberlain man. Additions and revisions were made by Chettle in July, 1602, Kempe having by then joined the Worcester company. Late that month James Roberts entered Kyd's play in S. R. (*The Revenge of Hamlet Prince of Denmarke*). Possibly he did not print it; no copy has survived. The Shakespeare-Chamberlain group then obtained a garbled version of the Worcester play. It was 'corrected, amended and enlarged' by Shakespeare and Drayton during 1602–3 and produced about July, 1603, when the Worcester group in revenge gave their 1599 version to the printer Nicholas Ling. Ling published it in 1603 as by William Shakespeare, thus pretending that it was the 'enlarged' Shakespeare version. Shakespeare then gave Roberts his 'enlarged' version. Roberts took it to Ling, who brought it out evidently with the understanding that the 1599 Worcester play should be suppressed. It was never reprinted.

and Lucibella catches at the word 'kill':

> *Lucibella.* I, but a knave may kill one by a tricke,
> Or lay a plot, or soe, or cog, or prate,
> Make strife, make a man's father hang him,
> Or his brother. How thinke you, goodly Prince,—
> God give you joy of your adoption,—
> May not trickes be used?

This last was addressed to Hoffman, who exclaims:

> Alas, poor lady.

Lucibella replies:

> I, that's true. I am poore, and yet 'have things;
> And gold rings, and amidst the leaves greene a . . .'
> Lord how doe? Well I thanke God. Why, that's well;
> And you, my Lord; and you too. Never a one weep!
> Must I shed all the teares? Well, he is gone;
> And he dwells here ye sayd. Ho, Ile dwell with him.
> Death, dastard, divell, robber of my life,
> Thou base adulterer that partst man and wife,
> Come, I defie thy darts, &c.

She breaks into song once in the above; and sings other snatches of song very like those sung by Ofelia:

> Loe, heere I come a woing my ding, ding,
> Loe, heere I come a suing my darling,
> Loe, heere I come a praying to bide a, bide a

(again she breaks off singing, in the manner of Ofelia)

> How doe you, Lady? Well, I thanke God. Will you buy a
> bargane I pray; its fine apparrell, &c.

Among the passages added to the old *Hamlet* by Chettle those which caught the public in 1599 and which have held it ever since are the two speculative monologues 'To be or not to be' and 'What is a man?' These two passages contain the essence of the new Hamlet, for in them he is exhibited not alone as the speculative philosopher, but as the first philosopher in Elizabethan drama who raises the question of the future life, of life after death. As has been remarked in 'The Revision of *Hamlet* and of *Romeo and Juliet*', this made of *Hamlet* a problem play. It also raised it above the level of all contemporary drama. This place it still holds. It is therefore interesting to search for indications of similar speculation among the works of the period. In his additions to *Sir Thomas More* Chettle registers two conventional beliefs. More will go from 'worldly pride' to 'a life contemplative'—'to the King of Heaven for a rich present'. He states: 'the worst chance is death and that brings endlesse joy for fickle breath'; also 'keep your soules even and you shall finde inheritance in Heaven'. This is about as far as any one went until *Hamlet* appeared. A conventional idea of the future life had been accepted without question. *Hamlet* raised the first doubt, began the never-to-be-ended questioning. Hitherto Elizabethans had disagreed with one another as to how souls should be saved, but, except for a few atheists, had universally agreed in accepting a future state of nebulous 'heavenly bliss'. *Hamlet* forced them to face the problem of the future in concrete terms.

If Kyd's *Hamlet* contained the germ of this 'to be' monologue it probably consisted in an atheistical denial of any future life whatsoever. Chettle accepts the future life, for he was anything but an atheist or a materialist; he merely questions the conditions of that life.

In April, 1600, Henslowe paid Chettle £1 in earnest of a play called *The Wooing of Death*. This was written shortly after the 'Corambis' *Hamlet* had been staged. Probably it also contained speculations on death. It was the immediate successor of *Cupid and Psyche*, which contains, or rather contained, a series of dialogues explaining the allegorical significance of the trials undergone by Psyche, the Soul. These were by Chettle. A part of one that remains reads:

> *Midas.* But why should Venus, being Queen of love,
> Wish her son Cupid to enamour her [Psyche]
> Of some base groom, misshapen and deform'd?
> *Apuleius.* By Venus here is meant Intemperate Lust.
> Lust woes her son Desire t'inflame the Soul
> With some base groom, that's to some ugly Sin.

Desire is good and ill. The evil swears
To obey his mother Venus and vex Psyche;
But Cupid, representing True Desire,
Doats on the Soul's sweet beauty, sends his servant
Zephyrus, in whom Celestial Pleasure's meant,
T' entice his love, the Soul, to his chaste bed,
Giving her Heaven for her lost maidenhead.
  Midas. Only one riddle more and I have done.
Why did the poor girl Psyche take such paine?
What scrambling shift she made to climb the mountain,
And crawl through brakes and briars to get a husband.
  Apuleius. This shews how many strong adversities,
Crosses, pricks, thorns and stings of conscience
Would throw the ambitious Soul, affecting Heaven,
Into dispair and fainting diffidence,
Which Psyche must pass through: the Soul must fly
Through thousand lets to seek eternity.

Unfortunately the portion interpreting the Soul's journey to and from Hell has been omitted from Heywood's revision.[1]

---

[1] A discussion of the three-part division, &c., of *Hamlet* will be found in 'The Revision of *Hamlet* and of *Romeo and Juliet*'. The 'enlarged' 1604 version of *Hamlet* was written by Shakespeare and Drayton.

XVI

DEKKER AND CHETTLE

IT is evident, from Henslowe's Diary, that Chettle was called upon time and again to furnish the framework of a play, or to reshape a formless play into some semblance of a drama. In this he had no noteworthy rival. Chettle was the great master builder; but it was the intimate touch of Thomas Dekker that changed the mansion into a home, especially if perchance he placed therein a few of his most lovable characters.

Troylus and Cressida.

Troylus and Cressida, written by Dekker and Chettle in April, 1599, and *Agamemnon*, written in May of the same year, were evidently derived from the old play *Troye*. A part of the 'plat' card of *Troye* is to be seen at the British Museum, and has been printed in the *Henslowe Papers*.

Chettle divided *Troye* into the comedy of *Troylus and Cressida* and the tragedy of *Agamemnon*. The tragedy was lost; but the comedy was twice published in quarto in 1609, by Bonian and Walley. In one edition there is a preface claiming: ' Heere [is] a new play, never stal'd with the stage, never clapper-clawd with the palmes of the vulgar,' &c. Having learned that their ' Shakespeare' discovery was not ' new' the editors in their second edition suppressed this vainglorious preface.

Shakespeare or his associates obtained a complete and correct copy of this play; the additions, to be found in the Folio, are therefore few. Here and there they rewrote a passage which seemed obscure, occasionally they added a line, once a long passage. A number of passages in the original do not appear in the Folio.

James Roberts registered a *Troylus and Cressida* on February 7, 1603, 'as it is acted by my Lo. Chamberlin's men', exactly as he registered *Hamlet* the previous year. The inference is that the Chamberlain company had by then obtained a copy of the Dekker-Chettle play.

Bits of the old *Troye* remain in this play, but Chettle has recast the plot and with Dekker's assistance has remade the characters. In Cressida they give an exquisite study of a fascinating maiden whose butterfly affections are attracted by each new male. Her love is constant; but the object of her love is ever changing. Only Dekker could depict such a creature, leaving all the bloom on her dainty wings. Such maidens often drive their serious-minded swains mad. Troylus was cured by the death of his beloved brother Hector. Cured? No, diverted. This play by its very differences continually recalls *Romeo and Juliet*. The one is the comedy, the other the tragedy, of the devoted lover.

As *Hoffman*, *Troylus and Cressida* contains many an echo of *Hamlet* and *The Merchant of Venice*. All were written about the same date and contain similar thoughts. Examples follow :

I. Nestor on the proposed combat between Hector and Achilles :

> . . . Though 't be a sportfull combat,
> Yet in the triall much opinion dwells;
> For here the Troyans tast our deerest repute
> With their finest pallat. And trust to me, Ulysses,
> Our imputation shal be odly poizde
> In this vilde action: For the successe,
> Although perticuler, shall give a scantling
> Of good or bad unto the generall.
> And in such indexes (although small pricks
> To their subsequent volumes) there is seene
> The baby figure of the gyant masse
> Of things to come at large.

II. Hector during a discussion as to whether or no Helen shall be returned to the Greeks :

> *Hector.* Brother, shee is not worth what shee doth cost the keeping.
> *Troylus.* What's aught but as 'tis valued?
> *Hector.* But valew dwells not in perticuler will.
> It holds his estimate and dignity
> As well wherein 'tis precious of itselfe
> As in the prizer. 'Tis madde idolatry

To make the service greater then the God :
And the will dotes that is attributive
To what infectiously it selfe affects,
Without some image of th'affected merit.

This recalls the 'Quality of Mercy' speech.

> *Troylus.* I take today a wife, and my election
> Is led on in the conduct of my will ;
> My will enkindled by mine eyes and eares
> (Two traded pilots twixt the dangerous shore[s]
> Of Will and Judgement). How may I avoyde,
> Although my Will distast what it elected,
> The wife I choose ? . . .
> . . . It was thought meete
> Paris should do some vengeance on the Greekes.
> Your breth with full consent bellied his sailes ;
> The seas and winds (old wranglers) tooke a truce
> And did him service ; hee toucht the ports desir'd,
> And for an old Aunt whom the Greeks held captive
> He brought a Grecian queene, whose youth & freshnesse
> Wrincles Apolloes and makes pale the morning.
> Is she worth keeping ? Why, shee is a pearle
> Whose price hath lansh't above a thousand ships
> And turn'd crown'd kings to merchants.

This seems to contain much of the old *Troye*.

The next passage is more in Chettle's usual vein :

> If youle avouch 'twas wisdome Paris went :
> As you must needs—for you all cried 'go, go'.
> If youle confess he brought home worthy prize :
> As you must needs—for you all clapt your hands
> And cri'd 'inestimable' ; why do you now
> The issue of your proper wisdomes rate,
> And do a deed that never Fortune did—
> Begger the estimation which you priz'd
> Richer then sea and land ? . . .

> And Jove forbid there should be done amongst us
> Such things as might offend the weakest spleene
> To fight for and maintaine.

Paris. Else might the world convince of levitie
As well my undertakings as your counsells;
But, I attest the Gods, your full consent
Gave wings to my propension, and cut off
All feares attending on so dire a project:
For what (alas) can these my single armes?
What propugnation is in one man's valour
To stand the push and enmitie of those
This quarrell would excite?

(Very like Hamlet this.)
                    Yet I protest
Were I alone to passe the difficulties,
And had as ample power as I have will,
Paris should nere retract what he hath done,
Nor faint in the pursuite.

Hector argues:
                    . . . thus to persist
In doing wrong extenuates not wrong,
But makes it much more heavie. Hector's opinion
Is this, in way of truth, &c.
        Troylus. . . . But, worthy Hector,
She is a theame of honour and renowne,
A spurre to valiant and magnanimous deeds,
Whose present courage may beate downe our foes,
And fame in time to come canonize us.
For I presume brave Hector would not loose
So rich advantage of a promis'd glory
As smiles upon the fore-head of this action
For the wide world's revenew.

These speeches, though intermixed with bits from *Troye*, contain much of Chettle's straightforward, concentrated philosophic thought.

The comedy of this play, by Pandarus and Thersites, is all contributory. Pandarus is the male counterpart of the Nurse in *Romeo and Juliet*. The construction is three-part: introduction, action, and resolution. The introduction, in which numerous characters are quickly introduced to the audience, is most cleverly managed. Each part opens with the Trojans in Troy.

Psyche and Cupid.

Psyche and Cupid, written before May 10, 1600, by Dekker, Chettle, and Day, was reworked into *Love's Mistress* by Heywood, and published in 1636. A long quotation from *Psyche and Cupid* can be found, assigned to Dekker, in *England's Parnassus* (No. 2232), the latter part of which Heywood inadvertently lost from *Love's Mistress.*

The sisters of Psyche have arrived at her new domicile :

> *Psyche.* Welcome deare sisters : With the breath of Love,
> Poore Psyche gives kind welcome to you both.
> O tell me then, by what auspitious guide,
> You came conducted to this sacred place?
> *Astioche.* Sister, you shall : When many a weary step
> Had brought us to the top of yonder mount
> Milde Zephirus embrac'd us in his armes,
> And in a cloud of sweete and rich perfumes,
> Cast us into the lap of that greene meade,

No.
2232
> Whose bosome stucke with purple violets,
> Halfe budded lillies, and yoong musk-rose trees,—
> About whose waste the amorous woodbine twines,
> Whilst they seeme maidens in a lover's armes,—
> There on the curled forehead of a banke,
> That sweld with Camomill, over whose bewtie
> A wanton hyacinth held down his head,
> And by the winds helpe oft stole many a kisse,
> He sate us downe, and thus we did arive.

> *Psyche.* And happily ariv'd : Nature and Art
> Have strove to make this dale their treasurie, &c.

Heywood changed 'mount' to 'rocke', and rewrote the line 'Cast us into the lap of that greene meade' so as to read 'Brought's unto the skirts of this greene meade'. He then omitted the rest of the speech by Astioche. That the nine beautiful lines belong as inserted above is evident from the way in which they connect with Psyche's ensuing lines.

Another bit of Dekker found also in *England's Parnassus*

(No. 1464) belongs in Psyche's prayer to Night and Silence. The invocation to 'Dumbe Silence' was omitted by Heywood.

> *Psyche.* Times eldest daughter, Night, mother of ease,
> Thou gentle nurse, that with sweet lullabies
> Care-waking hearts to gentle slumber charmst!
> Thou smooth-cheek'd negro, Night, the black-eyd queen
> That rid'st about the world on the soft backs
> Of downy raven's sleek and sable plumes,
> And from thy chariot silent darkness flings[t],
> In which man, beast, and bird envelop'd,
> Take their repose and rest:

No.
1464
> Dumbe Silence, sworne attendant on black Night,
> Thou that hast power to close up Murmures jawe,
> To stop the barking of the watchful hound,
> And charme the gagling of those watchful fowle
> That saved Joves Capitoll, milde Queen of rest.

> Psyche entreats thee
> Noe Jarre nor sound betray her bold attempt.

Heywood omitted the central portion of this invocation and connected the final two lines to the earlier part; thus the prayer to 'Dumbe Silence' was lost, which renders the entreaty that 'Noe Jarre nor sound betray her bold attempt' rather nonsensical.

For the Dekker-Chettle-Day work in *Love's Mistress* Heywood has received much praise:

> He did not deal skilfully with the invisible world, and yet he was not altogether unacquainted with the winged spirits of the air; . . . he introduces them gracefully into 'Love's Mistress', one of the most beautiful and purest masques founded upon classical mythology.

The original must have been even more spiritual than Heywood's garbled version.

This exhausts the list of Dekker-Chettle plays as found in Henslowe's Diary, which ends suddenly in May, 1603.

Merchant of Venice.

During the two years that the Strange-Chamberlain men were at the Curtain theatre Dekker and Chettle were two of their chief playwrights. When the Queen's men joined the Chamberlain forces both writers went to Henslowe at the Rose. Such plays as they wrote while at the Curtain must in part be looked for among the Chamberlain repertoire, now contained in the ' Shakespeare ' Folio. One of these plays has been identified as *The Jew* [or *Merchant*] *of Venice.* It certainly was Chettle who pulled the love-story of Portia and Bassanio and some old play on a vengeful Jew into a compact, perfect drama. Many of the character studies are as evidently by Dekker. Another play belonging to this same period is *Romeo and Juliet.*

Romeo and Juliet.

The extant First Quarto of *Romeo and Juliet* is a revision of an old play. It was written between July, 1596, and April, 1597, for Lord Strange's men while they were at the Curtain. This version was augmented by its authors before 1598, when the Second Quarto appeared with Shakespeare's amendments.

The First Quarto can without hesitancy be ascribed to Dekker and Chettle. It is cast into the regular three-act form common to all Chettle's best work. Truly his is Romeo's description of daybreak when he and Juliet are about to part :

> *Romeo.* It was the Larke, the Herald of the Morne,
> And not the nightingale. See Love what envious strakes
> Doo lace the severing clowds in yonder East.
> Night's candles are burnt out, and jocund Day
> Stands tiptoes on the mystie mountaine tops.

Compare this with Chettle's opening lines on daybreak at the beginning of *Patient Grissill* :

> Look how yon one-ey'd wagoner of heaven
> Hath, by his horses' fiery-winged hoofes,
> Burst ope the melancholy jayle of Night,
> And with his gilt beames' cunning alchimy

Turn'd all these cloudes to gold, who (with the winds)
Upon their misty shoulders bring in Day.
Then sally not this morning with foule lookes;
But teach your jocund spirits to ply the chase:
For hunting is a sport for emperors.

Dekker's hand is also traceable throughout this First Quarto edition of *Romeo and Juliet*. One of his marks is his use of the poem by Richard Edwards containing 'music hath her silver sound' which he used in both *Fortunatus* and *Satiromastix*. But more truly Dekkerian is the invocation to Night which he added to this play after the First Quarto was written, and which appears in garbled form in the Second Quarto.

Of all English poets none seems to have been so enamoured of Night as Dekker. Chettle preferred the dawn. In the comments on *Romeo and Juliet*, in 'The Revision of *Hamlet* and of *Romeo and Juliet*', the appeals to Night by both Juliet and Psyche have been quoted. Both disclose Dekker's fondness for the 'smooth-cheeked Negro, Night', as does the following passage from *The Jew [Merchant] of Venice* :

(Portia and Nerissa are returning home at night.)

> *Portia.* That light we see is burning in my hall:
> How farre that little candell throwes his beames,
> So shines a good deede in a naughty world.
> *Nerissa.* When the moon shone we did not see the candell.

Another reference to the moon is to be found in *If This is not a Good Play, &c.* :

> Blest star of light, stucke there to illuminate
> This world darkened ore with sin: thou watchest late,
> To guide men's coming home . . .
> All hail to thee, now my best guide, be given!
> What needs earth's candle, having the lamp of heaven.

Another example may be found in *Satiromastix*:

> *Terril.* O Night, that dyes the Firmament in black,
> And like a cloth of cloudes doth stretch thy limbes
> Upon the windy tenters of the Ayre:
> O thou that hang'st upon the back of Day,

Like a long mourning gowne; thou that art made
Without an eye, because thou shouldst not see
A lover's revels, nor participate
The bridegroomes heaven, &c.

A last example may be taken from *Old Fortunatus*:

And three times [seen] frantic Cynthia naked ride
About the rusty highways of the skies
Stuck full of burning stars, which lent her light
To court her negro paramour grim Night.

The literary critics have universally condemned this old
version of *Romeo and Juliet*; yet as stage-drama it is far better
than Shakespeare's revision. Unfortunately no manager has ever
restaged it. It was printed by John Danter, Chettle's partner in
the house of Danter, Hoskins, and Chettle.

There were several periods when neither Dekker nor Chettle
wrote for Henslowe. Critics, unable to account for Dekker during
those periods, conveniently place him in prison, letting him out,
however, in time to write *Satiromastix* for Paules Boys in 1602.
Why do they not place Chettle, Day, Hathway, Drayton, and
Munday in prison with Dekker, as they all ceased writing for
Henslowe during these same periods?

The fact is that July, 1600, marks the separation of the
Pembroke and Admiral companies and the creation of the Derby-
Oxford-Worcester company. The Admiral's men moved to the
new Fortune. Dekker, Chettle, and various other writers must
have remained with Lord Worcester's men at the Boar's Head or
the Rose. Henslowe did not finance this new company until
August, 1602. The absence of Dekker and Chettle is thus ex-
plained. Far from being in prison they were busy writing plays
for the new Worcester company.

Heywood, ex-actor, following Shakespeare's example, now
undertook the role of playwright-in-chief to the Worcester men.
Kempe deserted him, so virtually did Dekker and Chettle, who
thenceforth wrote almost exclusively for the Admiral's men.

Many of the plays which Shakespeare and company revised

were obtained immediately after the reorganization of the Derby-Oxford-Worcester company in 1601–2.

Dekker's strange ability to depict the most disagreeable characters without making them abhorrent was shared by Chettle. Working together for many years their views on life, on art, their theories, grew alike; but their abilities never changed. Dekker never became a master plotter and Chettle, the greatest of all English play-builders, never acquired Dekker's sympathetic touch. No one save Dekker could have created a sympathetic Shylock. So that while Chettle may not make the disagreeable abhorrent, may make it interesting and humorous, he seldom makes it sympathetic. The one had a philosophic intellect, the other a heart overflowing with emotion. Together they wrote dramas than which none have ever been more perfect.

Historical plays had appeared in great numbers during the heroic romantic period. Realistic histories by the humanists were a later birth. In Plutarch's *Lives* the humanists found material half shaped to their hands. Yet to model the material into such plays as *Julius Caesar* and *Antony and Cleopatra* needed the hand of a super-plotter.

Antony and Cleopatra.

While in *Julius Caesar* Chettle was handicapped by the work of others, in *Antony and Cleopatra* he disregarded the work of various earlier authors and gave his genius free rein. Not only has he told the entire story of Antony and Cleopatra, but he has as a background thrown upon the canvas the whole Roman world with its mass of intrigue and ambition, its cruelty and hard barbarism, figure after figure, Pompey, Caesar, and Lepidus, each leading an army, cold Octavia, and the rest. And in contrast, still as background, he paints Egypt, its culture and its luxury. And all these elements are shown at war, on sea, and then again on land, battle after battle of minds as well as of arms, in which Egyptian culture is gradually overcome by Roman barbarism.

Standing out against this overwhelming movement Antony and Cleopatra, fated figures, enact their tragedy. In place of the gods, whose quarrels regulate and foredoom the mortals in Greek tragedies, Chettle uses as his *deus ex machina* the conflict of two civilizations; and it is to this conflict that Antony and Cleopatra owe their doom rather than to their various individual mistakes and misunderstandings. In this play humanism and realism find perfect expression, for not only Antony and Cleopatra, but the great massed movements of civilization are humanized.[1]

Antony and Cleopatra marks the zenith of Chettle's career. It is his supreme achievement. Every part of it synchronizes and harmonizes with every other part; all are necessary; all are perfectly knit into a great unity. To know Chettle it is only necessary to study this one play. Having done so, a glance backward at

[1] Like *Hamlet*, *Antony and Cleopatra* has been enlarged and corrupted by Shakespeare, Jonson, and company. The greater number of the original lines were retained and the additions, as in the other 'amended' plays, were inserted chiefly in the climax and the resolution. However, the grand outline of the structure still stands and many of the inserted passages can be eliminated: one such appears after Antony falls upon his sword. That for the moment he is supposed to be dead is evident not only from Plutarch, wherein he is said to have reposed upon his couch in order to bleed to death, but because in the play Diomedes questions: 'Lives he?' while Dercetas cries: 'Thy death and fortunes bid thy followers fly. This sword but shewn to Caesar with this tidings shall enter me with him.' Yet in the 'amended' version Antony having fallen in presumed death is revived by Shakespeare as follows:

How! not dead? not dead?
The guard! how! Oh, dispatch me.

Enter Guard, &c.

1 Guard. What's the noise?
Ant. I have done my work ill, friends;
Oh make an end of what I have begun.
2 Guard. The starre is fallen.
1 Guard. And time is at his period.
All. Alas, and woe!
Ant. Let him that loves me strike me dead.
1 Guard. Not I.
2 Guard. Nor I.
3 Guard. Nor any one.

This, as the other insertions, is based on hints from Plutarch. It is theatrical piffle and need not be mistaken by any one for Chettle's handiwork.

his earlier work, *Romeo and Juliet, Hamlet, The Merry Wives, Troylus and Cressida, Patient Grissill, The Blind Beggar,* &c., will discover the same constructive genius manifest in all. No other author of the period possessed this gift.

In each of Chettle's plays there is the same perfect introduction of characters, the relation of each to each being promptly given; there is then the gradual unfolding of the interaction, leading to the impasse or plot climax; there is the same logical resolution and the sudden ending in a slight after-climax. His episodes are short and shift as suddenly as those of a kinematograph drama. In *Antony and Cleopatra* the scene changes more than forty times, and the story, though continuous, is woven from three strands, all of which can be easily followed if the scenes are quickly changed.

Of the three unities Chettle preserved the unity of story, changed unity of time into continuity of time, and disregarded unity of place. While this method gained him an immense ever-shifting background it necessitated utmost concentration in each episode. This he achieved in each of his plays from *Romeo and Juliet* to *Antony and Cleopatra.*

Many of the characters in *Antony and Cleopatra*, notably the women, were filled in by Dekker. Not that Chettle lacked ability as a delineator of female character—far from it—but that Dekker, with few strokes, deftly made sympathetic everything he touched; and the portraits of Cleopatra, Charmian, Iras, and others have precisely this quality of provoking sympathy which was bestowed upon characters by Dekker alone.

Dekker began his artistic career with simple portraits such as those of Portia, Nerissa, and Long Meg of Westminster and her lower-class companions, all of whom present but one side of their natures. Gradually his portraiture grew more complex in Simon Eyre, Desdemona, Katherine, Julia, and finally in that most cleverly sketched-in portrait of Cressida. His later plays are crowded with figures drawn in with the sudden, true strokes of a great master; yet each stands separate, distinct, sympathetic.

In *Antony and Cleopatra*, the characters, though so numerous, are even more complex; many belong entirely to Chettle; yet those evincing Dekker's touch are delineated with utmost skill and distinctness. Created by the two in combination they are more perfect than any they could have created unassisted. Antony sums up what to Dekker and Chettle seemed the noblest qualities of man. Cleopatra discloses all they had learned of the seductive spell, the elusive mystery of woman.

Dekker supplied many other dramatists with portraits, and Chettle supplied others with plots; but their happiest efforts were when working together. *The Honest Whore* and *Othello* lack Chettle's directing hand, and *Robin Hood*, Part II, *The Blind Beggar*, and *Julius Caesar* want Dekker's sympathetic portraiture.[1]

Henry Chettle was neither a courtier nor a university man, but an honest, solid, philosophical bourgeois. Neither his wit nor his language had been artificially polished, but his brain had been developed by his association with men and books. There is nothing intellectually clever about his work, no useless ornamentation on his structures, for he never played tricks with his medium. Though fat and full of humour he was always serious, for he never wasted energy. There is nothing exuberantly Dekkerian even in his comedy. It is dry but full of salt. For this reason those plays which he wrote alone lack the charm and grace found in those ' dressed up ' by Dekker. His ability to concentrate, combined with his sense of form, enabled him to present in each play either a vast world of implied action, as in

[1] *Coriolanus* is usually associated with *Julius Caesar* and *Antony and Cleopatra*. Malone has shown that it was written in 1606. It belongs chiefly to Ben Jonson, and in part fills the present gap in his writings between *Volpone* (1605) and *The Silent Woman* (1609), being more closely related to the latter. Unlike Chettle's plays it is not constructed. It remains a simple, historical narrative, following step by step Plutarch's life of Coriolanus. It thus includes two dramas : I. The struggle between the people led by Junius Brutus and the patricians led by Coriolanus, resulting in a victory for the people and the banishment of Coriolanus. II. The relinquished revenge and self-sacrifice of Coriolanus. While these two parts are related historically, dramatically each stands alone. Alone either would have sufficed for the framework of a perfect play.

Antony and Cleopatra, or, were the theme simpler, a mass of philosophical observations, as in *Troylus and Cressida* and *Hamlet*, or a well-developed secondary story, as in *Patient Grissill* and *Psyche and Cupid*, or a double story, as in *The Merry Wives of Windsor* and his novelette *Piers Plainnes*. So well packed are his plays that in comparison most others seem but paltry. Yet his plays are not what might be termed action plays. They are not spectacular, for the action is always psychological rather than physical. The interest centres neither in bodily contortions nor in mental gymnastics, but in the troubled emotions of the soul. It is perchance this trait which most thoroughly differentiates his work from that of all the great playwrights of the Elizabethan period. For this alone he can be placed, as he was right worthily placed by Dekker, in Elysium with those his fellow men of genius—Marlowe, Peele, Greene, and Thomas Nash.

This completes the list of great Elizabethan dramatists. The university men were all dead by the end of Queen Elizabeth's reign. Dekker and Chettle, supreme exponents of humanism, ceased writing soon after her death. With them Elizabethan drama ended. Jonson, Chapman, Marston, and the rest, with the assistance of the architect Inigo Jones, carried on under King James. Times and customs had changed, great plays were no longer appreciated, and drama soon died under the baneful blight of Puritanism.

XVII
CONCLUSION

THAT which is new in the present work is first a deduction : since Shakespeare, together with Burbage and Kempe, received the Court payment on March 15, 1594; since the Burbages owned the Theatre and acted there from 1576 until 1597; since neither Shakespeare, Kempe, nor Burbage appear in Henslowe's Diary from 1592 to 1597; since from 1593 to 1599 Shakespeare always associated with Kempe and Burbage, the deduction follows that Shakespeare must have been with Kempe and Burbage at the Theatre from 1593 to 1597.

From the above it follows that Shakespeare was not one of Lord Strange's men from 1592 to 1594, while they played at the Rose, nor of the Lord Chamberlain's men who acted at the Rose and the Curtain from 1594 to 1597: hence it follows that none of the Strange nor Chamberlain plays written from 1592 to 1597 were written by Shakespeare.

The above leads to a second deduction: since the Burbage-Shakespeare group joined the Chamberlain's men at the Curtain in 1597; since various Chamberlain plays were revised, corrected, or enlarged and printed after 1597 as by William Shakespeare, it follows that Shakespeare's share in these plays must be limited to the corrections and additions appearing in the revised versions of old Strange-Chamberlain plays. Part I, including the chapter on ' William Shakespeare—Reviser ', is based almost entirely on these two deductions.

Part II is based on the conception that plays should be examined and judged as drama, not as literature. By utilizing this conception some of the individual characteristics of each dramatist are ascertained and various plays are assigned to their evident creators. The old literary method of valuing a play according to its literary excellence and of assigning a play to an author because words or phrases found therein appear more or less frequently in his accepted works has proved inadequate. The application of dramatic rather than literary tests at once established the dramatic value of the ' Corambis ' *Hamlet* and of the first version of *Romeo and Juliet,* and laid bare the dramatic methods, the craftsmanship, of each playwright. It exposed each author's weakness and his strength. Some such result might have been foreseen considering that during the Elizabethan era each dramatist, except Ben Jonson, built his plays unregulated by rules, each after his own fashion.

Dramatic craftsmanship is but little known even among professional dramatists. A few of the secrets of the craft have been necessarily, though reluctantly, disclosed. Necessarily, because in order to understand how a play is built some knowledge of the craft is necessary. How great is this need can be judged from the fact that hitherto it has been the tendency for literary workers to assign to one man, be it Bacon, Shakespeare, Raleigh, or Lord Oxford, all the more literary plays written from 1593 to 1603 simply because all possess a similar literary flavour. Any one having even a fair understanding of dramatic craftsmanship could not possibly assign to one man plays as dissimilar in structure as *Antony and Cleopatra, King Lear,* and *The Tempest.* Yet any one having no knowledge of the craft might reasonably suppose all came from the same workshop.

A literary artist holds to a dramatic craftsman about the same relation that an interior decorator holds to an architect. Spenser wrote poems, while Chettle constructed plays. Painters have decorated the walls of buildings which were planned and constructed by architects. These mural decorators knew as little of architecture as Spenser knew of drama. Santa Sophia, the Sistine Chapel, Notre Dame, and the Pantheon should be judged as architecture, not as decorations, even as Chettle's plays should be judged as drama, not as literature.

The gradual evolution of architectural construction has been traced by many historians; the development of dramatic construction has never been written. No one has realized what innumerable experiments, what quarrels, discussions, what heartbreaking failures, joy-giving successes, attended the gradual evolution of even a single dramatic element such as free rhythm. How triumphantly Marlowe sang when he discovered heroic blank verse! And how Peele must have rejoiced when, having experimented with one rhythm after another, he finally rediscovered the lyrical free rhythm of his master Euripides! To these discoveries Greene contributed the haunting suggestiveness of the refrain which he brought from the songs of trouvère and troubadour. Marlowe brought power, Peele facility, Greene preserved rhyme and the refrain. Between them they worked out the new dramatic medium free rhythm, at times measured and majestic, at times intertwining rhythm within rhythm, at times emphasizing a meaning with rhyme or refrain.

Speech rhythm is but one of the new elements of drama. It might well be termed the new building material of the Elizabethan age. With it plays were built first on French, Latin, Italian, or Spanish models. Gradually a new design came into being. This arose chiefly through the inherent English love of character. The presentation of individualized characters was introduced by Peele, Marlowe, Greene, Nash, &c., who also began using the action of one character upon another as an element of drama. Character interaction led to character consequences; hence arose cause, action, and effect, built upon character. The perfectly balanced three-part drama of character introduction, character interaction, and the resolution of character interaction, was a new creation, purely English, purely Elizabethan. In it the machinations of the gods of Greek drama and the accidental circumstances of Latin drama found no place. This was the supreme product of Elizabethan drama: a carefully schemed, carefully balanced structure best exemplified in the 'Corambis' *Hamlet* and in *Antony and Cleopatra*. While very few of the plays of the period attained to the structural perfection of these two plays, even as very few Elizabethan houses attained to the perfection of Burghley House or Hatfield, yet these must stand as supreme examples of Elizabethan dramatic architecture, examples which all the builders of the age strove to copy, imitate, or excel.

Each age has produced only a few men who could construct great dramas. In this respect the Elizabethan age is no exception. Greene and Kyd must be ranked as second-grade constructors. When they were dead Peele, Nash, Lyly, and Chettle remained, together with a number of third-rate builders, such as Marston, Jonson, Haughton, and Heywood. Dekker and Drayton must be regarded as play decorators rather than as play builders. The master architect of the period was of course Henry Chettle. Nor did Chettle always produce a perfect design. His work consisted chiefly in hurriedly remodelling the badly conceived and confused plans of other men.

Although Henry Chettle, printer's apprentice and publisher, became the greatest of play builders, the elements of dramatic form were discovered almost entirely by his various friends, that brilliant group of university men—Marlowe, Peele, Lyly, Greene, and Nash. They were all cultured; and in all likelihood it was their university training, their love of refinement in speech, their literary tastes, which caused them to look upon drama, not as a separate art or craft, but as a peculiar form of literature. Yet each discovered one or more elements foreign to literature, but essential to drama. They also fought and won the battle against the moral interlude and stilted, unnatural dialogue. They discovered not only the new building material, free speech rhythm, but carried out every sort of experiment in structural design. It only remained for Chettle to select from their experiments those elements which proved useful and essential. The secret of his greatness is that he realized what was essential and adopted it.

It cannot be asserted that Chettle handled all the dramatic elements bequeathed to him as skilfully as they had been individually handled by his brilliant confreres. Certainly he never wrote free rhythm like Peele's, heroic verse like Marlowe's, never arranged stage pictures as exquisitely as did Greene. His university friends were greater artists; but Chettle surpassed them as an architect. They embellished everything they touched; Chettle made all things seem real. *Nuda veritas* was his motto, and utility the aim of each of his dramatic lines.

When Dekker placed Marlowe, Greene, and Peele together in Elysium, and to them joined Nash and Chettle, he grouped together all the greater Elizabethan dramatists, except himself and Lyly. When they joined the group the seven summed up the greatness of the age. Of these all were university men except Chettle and Dekker. Of the university men all were courtiers except Robert Greene, who belonged originally among the clericals. Oxford was the cradle of Elizabethan dramatists.

While each of these dramatists succeeded in certain lines, no one by himself was able to write a faultless play. Each was limited in his abilities. A few almost perfect plays were written in collaboration. Lyly and Peele, Greene and Nash, Lyly and Nash, Chettle and Dekker, Nash and Chettle, produced plays beyond the abilities of either. The creation of a perfect play seems to require the efforts of more than one great craftsman.

For many years closet students have endeavoured to persuade a reluctant world that one William Shakespeare wrote all the great dramas of his age. Certainly they knew little of dramatic craftsmanship. But what sort of a peculiar mixture of imbecile and superman do they suppose this imaginary Shakespeare to have been? He who wrote *A Midsommer Nights Dreame*, full of poetry and courtly dialogue, and then so forgot his literary craftsmanship that he wrote the rugged verse of *King Lear* and the unpolished verse of much of *Othello*? Who so carefully planned *Romeo and Juliet* and *Hamlet* and then lost all sense of design in his *Henry IV, Parts I* and *II*? Who so wondrously staged the Roman-Egyptian tragedy and then

assembled passages from Plutarch into *Coriolanus*? Unable to
distinguish one sort of drama from another, these critics assign
to this mutable 'superman' melodramas of blood by Kyd, music
dramas by Peele, picaresque plays by Nash, and humanistic
plays by Dekker and Chettle. Nonchalantly they explain everything away by saying, 'Though uneducated Shakespeare was a
" genius " '.

This is an age of logic. Every one now realizes there is no
effect without its proper cause. Therefore sophists, endeavouring to account for the 'genius' of Shakespeare, presume
'inspired'. Having thus postulated a cause for his genius they
rest content. What, then, is the cause of 'inspiration'? Some
would say the Universal Spirit, or First Cause. In other words,
when the Universal Spirit wishes to manifest itself it does so
by inspiring a genius. But the Universal Spirit is omnipresent.
Therefore all things are at all times more or less inspired, and
every thought and every flower, every expression, is due to the
inspiration of the Universal Spirit; and the medium of that
expression is more or less a genius.

All manifestations of the Universal Spirit follow exact laws.
The wild rose always manifests through its briar, the blackberry
through its bramble, the lark's song comes from the throat of the
lark. Great thoughts come from cultured minds; and great men
are great not because they are inspired, but they are greatly inspired because they are already great men. A genius is a great
man greatly inspired. The adjective 'inspired' therefore adds
nothing to the word 'genius'. To state that Shakespeare was a
great dramatist because he was an inspired genius is merely
stating that he was inspired greatly because he was already a
great man, which proves nothing, provides no cause.

Genius is based on culture, and culture is the co-ordination of
innumerable impulses into a synthetic organism. It is a growth.
The man who cannot co-ordinate his impressions will lack culture, as will he who has few impressions to co-ordinate. The
children of big cities often fall into the first class, the children

of isolated places are often found in the second class. The advantage of a university training lies not in that it provides impressions, but in that it inculcates co-ordination. The habit of co-ordination is not acquired by all university men, nor is it confined to them alone; and the impulses and impressions which assist in the growth of culture are more numerous and intense in the outside world than in scholastic circles.

The quality and peculiarities of each man's culture growth depend almost entirely on his environment. One man assimilates from nature, another from machinery, a third from music, a fourth from other people, a fifth from all these sources combined. The culture of each will be broad or narrow according as he co-ordinates broadly from all sources or narrowly from only a few. Lyly's culture was derived from the art, literature, music, and the political and Court life of his time, mingled with youthful impressions derived from his ecclesiastical father and his grammarian grandfather. On the other hand, Chettle's sources of culture were books, his university friends, and London life.

Since genius is based on culture and culture is the co-ordinated summation of a man's conscious and unconscious impressions, the expression of genius in any art or craft must in the end be an expression of his culture. Given the entire product of genius the culture from which it sprang can be postulated.

The co-ordination of a number of impressions into a new creation produces a sensation of elevation. If the creation is sudden and intense and the culture mass is small it produces a terrific sensation. The mind seems flooded with light and its owner feels intensely inspired, becomes an enthusiast of one idea. If the culture mass is large its owner enjoys a pleasant sensation, soon forgotten in the quest of greater co-ordinations. This sensation of elevation, of inspiration, accompanies the birth of each new thought, each new creation. Often the creator knows not all the elements which his mind has co-ordinated into his new work, for many of them are subconscious, but all at one time or another had been received into his culture mass; the sudden co-ordination may have been due to general excitation or to the introduction of one or more new elements.

It follows, therefore, that great creations can come only from men of great culture, and that each man's creations are strictly governed by his culture mass.

All of the university dramatists were possessed of a broad culture, but no one of them, nor any one individual of the age, possessed a culture mass ample enough to serve as the basic source of all the varied plays of the Globe repertoire. William Shakespeare passed almost every day of his life from c. 1589 until after 1604 as an actor of repertoire plays in a stock company; his culture mass must have been slight indeed, as slight as that of 'Shakespeare the Reviser'.

Many writers have been unable to accept William Shakespeare, howsoever inspired, as the author of the Globe repertoire. Some few, endeavouring to find a substitute, have settled on Lord Francis Bacon, he being, they consider, the most learned man of the period. Bacon came of a family of lawyers; he grew to manhood and passed all of his life among lawyers and politicians. For relaxation he took up science as a hobby. His known culture mass would therefore have hindered rather than have helped him in the writing of plays. Had he written plays they would have been as cold and intellectual as his scientific essays and his political discourses.

There exists in England and in America a large army of amateur playwrights who, knowing little of the difficulties, and having a small culture growth, nevertheless think they are able to write astounding dramas. Great dramatists are more rare than great doctors, lawyers, architects, or engineers. They require a broader culture growth. It is easier to accomplish lasting results in almost any other profession. But so long as the idea persists that any unskilled, uncultured penman can co-ordinate the events of life and the actions of character into great plays, so long will mediocre penmen write worthless plays. And so long as the

Shakespeare legend remains, that an unskilled, uncultured 'genius' was the creator of England's best dramas, so long will all endeavour seem useless, the attainment of a broad culture a waste of energy. Once this legend is destroyed an aspirant may hope by dint of hard work and earnest striving to learn the elements of the craft, to acquire a broad culture, and to express his culture in plays perchance as well constructed as those by Chettle, as vigorous as those by Nash, as witty as those by Lyly, or as refined and musical as those by Peele, or he may assist another in creating works of even greater merit.

For many years Elizabethan drama provided entertainment for none save the cultured few of the Court circle. It was supported by the Queen and various wealthy lords. The actors were retainers of that lord under whose name and licence they performed. Soon these actors, in order to augment their slight fees, began acting publicly in tavern yards. Finally in 1576 two theatres were built, and some four of the companies began a semi-independent career. They were still controlled, each by some one lord, and were still subsidized in one way or another. The Queen reserved to herself the various groups of choristers who performed plays accompanied by music and singing. In order to lighten her expenses she permitted these boys to sing and act at weddings and receptions. From 1583 until 1589 they also acted in public. They were then inhibited and reorganized into one private company, called 'The Children of Her Majesty's Revels'.

From 1589 until 1597 this company was the only private company in London; and it was the only one which presented music drama. The public companies provided both Court and commons with ordinary secular plays. The Children provided the Court circle with Court comedies and music dramas. They were the Grand Opera Company of the period. This company was managed by Hunnis, and their plays were written by Peele, Marlow, Lyly, and other university men. In 1597 they resumed public acting. Hunnis and Peele had died and the company was managed by Nathaniel Gyles and Lyly. The company then ceased presenting music drama and became the rival of the regular public performers.

It has often been remarked that English music flourished during this period and died away soon afterwards. The explanation seems obvious. It rose and fell with music drama, with the grand opera of the period.

Popular drama gradually extended its activities until from the cultured few of the Court circle it appealed to the entire populace of London. As it became more popular it became less cultured. Its early tradition of educational uplift turned into a striving to amuse the vulgar. The passing of Queen Elizabeth marks also the passing of Elizabethan drama. It is obvious that the quality of Elizabethan drama was due to the quality of the audience; as the culture of the audience declined so did the quality of the plays.

Elizabethan drama developed suddenly, and almost independently of foreign influence. Until the arrival of Peele and Marlowe the best examples were the quaint plays of John Heywood and Robert Wilson. Seven years thereafter many of the best plays of all history had been written and precedents established for all succeeding work. This sudden development was due partly to the genius of the men concerned, but greatly to the fact that these men were in daily communication with one another. Naturally they quarrelled; but in the love of their art they soon forgot their quarrels and laboured each to advance the movement. Lyly, Peele, and Greene ridiculed Marlowe's mighty lines, yet all loved 'kindly Kit Marlowe'; and Marlowe promptly modified his lines. Without these friends he might have always written bombastically. So each influenced each and all influenced the succeeding group—Nash, Chettle, Dekker, Drayton, and the rest. One and all collaborated, at one time or another, with almost every other member of his period. The sudden development and sustained excellence of Elizabethan drama was therefore due in part to the enthusiastic unselfish collaboration of all concerned. Ben Jonson set the fashion of single selfish aloofness. His egoism and his printing of his own plays ended for the time the old spirit of common self-abnegation.

The elements which made for the greatness of Elizabethan drama may be summed up as:
A select, permanent, cultured audience.
Cultured dramatists.
Co-operation among dramatists.
A trained company of repertoire actors; and for music drama trained actors, singers, and musicians.
A suitable theatre.
These elements in part appeared again during the Restoration period, the second-best era in English dramatic history. The chief lack during this period was that of co-operation among the dramatists. Since then dramatic history records little that is not mediocre until the Gilbert and Sullivan combination was formed. Here again almost all of the elements are found; but the combination of creators was a slight one, and the culture of the audience left much to be desired. English music and drama will again rise to eminence when the necessary elements are once again united into one active unit. The elements are available; but the union has not taken place, except in a minor way in Ireland and various provincial towns. As a prelude to this union the universities should once again take their place as cradles of prospective dramatists.

Such a union will never occur in an endowed theatre controlled by Government officials, catering for the mob, nor in a 'Shakespeare' theatre, nor in a County Council theatre. Such are for the uncultured—efficient as a means of education, but useless as a source of great drama. The source of great drama will ever remain a cultured audience catered to by a group of cultured craftsmen.

Author's Final Note.

Having studied the plays of the Elizabethan period during the last several years, as I look back over them I find there is something lacking from all of them, something to be found in the least page by Euripides. Each and all lack depth, not depth of intellect, nor occasionally of emotion, but of soul. They are physiological rather than psychological. Lyly upheld courtly conduct, while Marlowe expressed the revolt against littleness and outworn dogmas, and Chettle and Dekker sympathized with every sort of character; but none of their play-people were in any way related to the greater universe other than physically or historically, nor is it hinted in any play, save obliquely in *Hamlet*, that any character had a soul which was linked with the Universal Soul, called God.

England had become successful in trade, finance, war; and success, while it breeds admiration for power, for the strong man, never inculcates a feeling of man's relation to, or dependence upon, the Universal Spirit; in truth it produces a thorough belief in man's independence and self-sufficiency, which was the dominant characteristic of the Elizabethan age, which still exists in many a self-made man.

Elizabethan plays therefore lack those finer elements which have made the dramas of Euripides universal and transcendental. The Elizabethans had lost consciousness of God. Religious belief had changed into questioning agnosticism, into unquestioning belief in the power of material things, or into sectarian quarrels and Puritanical fanaticism. Even Hamlet's monologue on the hereafter is a questioning as to expediency which harks back to the metaphysics of Aristotle, but not to the transcendentalism of Plato. Had Elizabethan England, as the Athenian Republic, met with disaster when at the height of her success a searching of soul might have resulted, giving rise to doubts as to man's self-sufficiency, doubts as to the value of the entire intellectual Renaissance movement, resulting in transcendental tragedies as great or greater than those of ancient Greece.

F   I   N   I   S

APPENDIX

ELIZABETHAN PLAYS

AMONG the various editors and printers of Elizabethan plays first place must be given to John S. Farmer, who brought out collotype reproductions of one hundred and fifty-two volumes of plays. William Griggs printed photographic facsimiles of forty-three volumes, chiefly 'Shakespeare' quartos; and Methuen published in facsimile the four 'Shakespeare' folios. The First Folio has been reproduced in facsimile also by H. Staunton, S. Lee, J. O. Halliwell-Phillips, L. Booth, &c.

Of printed plays useful editions are: Malone's Variorum 'Shakespeare', Grosart's 'Greene' and 'Nash', Brooke's 'Marlowe', Bond's 'Lyly', Boas's 'Kyd', &c., Farmer's individual plays, other than those in his collotype series, Steevens's *Twenty Plays of Shakespeare*, the *Old and New Shakespeare*, and the Malone Society reprints, Dodsley's *Old Plays*, with Collier's two added volumes, S. Low's Parallel Text editions.

As printed plays are more or less unreliable it is to be hoped that eventually all the old plays will be reproduced in facsimile.

BIBLIOGRAPHY

Aberon's Vision. Shaks. Soc., 1843.
Ashmolean MSS., Nos. 1125–33, Bodl. Lib.
Aubrey, John. *Brief Lives.* MS. in Ashmolean Museum.
Bandello's Novels. J. C. Nimmo, 1895.
Chettle, Henry. *Piers Plainnes.* Bodl. Lib.
Cohn, A. *Shakespeare in Germany.* 1865.
Collections. Malone Soc., 1907–8–9–11–13–23.
Daniel, Samuel. *Works.* Grosart edition.
Dekker, Thomas. *Non-dramatic Works.* Grosart, 1884-6.
Dodsley's *Old Plays.* 1825.
Egerton Papers. British Museum.
Feis, Jacob. *Shakespeare and Montaigne.* 1884.
Feuillerat, A. *John Lyly.*
Fleay, F. G. *A Biographical Chronicle of the English Drama.* 1891.

390   BIBLIOGRAPHY

Fleetwood Report. British Museum.
Gosson. *St. Paul Records.*
Greene, Robert. *Complete Works.* Grosart edition, 1881.
Halliwell, J. O. *Outlines of Life of Shakespeare.*
Henslowe's Diary. W. W. Greg, 1908.
Henslowe's Papers. W. W. Greg, 1908.
Jusserand, J. J. *The English Novel of Shakespeare's Time.* 1908.
Kenilworth Festivities. Laneham's letter.
Lyly, John. *Works.* R. W. Bond edition, 1902.
Malone, E. *Plays and Poems of Wm. Shakespeare.* 1790.
Meres, Francis. *Palladis Tamia or Wits Treasury.* 1598.
Montaigne. Florio's translation.
Pipe Rolls.
Plutarch's *Lives.*
Remembrancia. W. H. and H. C. Overall, 1878. Also Malone Soc.
     Collections, i. 1907.
Revels, Extracts from. P. Cunningham; also A. Feuillerat.
Shakespeare Jahrbuch. 1889.
Stationers' Register. Arber's transcript.
Stotsenburg, J. H. *An Impartial Study of the Shakespeare Title.* 1904.
Sykes, H. O. *Sidelights on Shakespeare.* 1919.
Twine, L. *The Patterne of Painfull Adventures.* 1576, 1607.
Two Elizabethan Stage Abridgements. W. W. Greg, 1923.
Wallace, C. W. *The Children of Blackfriars.* 1908.
—— *Shakespeare and his London Associates.* 1910.
—— *The First London Theatre.* 1913.
Wood, Anthony à. *Athenae Oxonienses.*
Young, William. *The History of Dulwich College.* 1889.

These are the more important of the many books bearing on the subject of Elizabethan drama.